BARRON'S

Pass Key to the

ACT®

NINTI

George Ehrenhaft, Ed.D.

Robert L. Lehrman, M.A.

Fred Obrecht, M.A.

Allan Mundsack, M.A.

© Copyright 2012, 2010, 2008, 2006, 2004, 2001, 1998, 1995, 1993
by Barron's Educational Series, Inc.

All inquiries should be addressed to:
Barron's Educational Series, Inc.
250 Wireless Boulevard
Hauppauge, New York 11788
www.barronseduc.com

ISBN: 978-1-4380-0115-9

ISSN 1942–7263

Printed in the United States of America
9 8 7 6 5 4 3 2 1

10%
POST-CONSUMER
WASTE
Paper contains a minimum
of 10% post-consumer
waste (PCW). Paper used
in this book was derived
from certified, sustainable
forestlands.

Contents

Preface

If you plan to go to college, you may take the ACT. This book is designed to help you understand the sections that make up the ACT and prepare you for excelling on each one.

Specifically, this book contains:
— a complete introduction to the ACT test
— a description of the different types of questions you will find on the test
— review and practice of the subject matter in each of the test areas (English, mathematics, reading, science reasoning, and the optional writing section)
— basic tips on how to deal with the different types of questions
— two full-length simulated practice tests modeled on the actual ACT (complete with answer explanations)

Because of the convenient size of this book, you can easily carry it with you to use for impromptu study sessions—while waiting for an appointment, riding on a bus or train, or during study hall.

If, after studying the review sections and taking the two practice tests, you believe that you are prepared for the test, then take it with confidence. If you think you need more practice, pick up *Barron's ACT*, which has been helping students like you prepare for the ACT for 40 years. It contains many more practice exercises and additional practice tests, with thorough answer explanations.

Acknowledgments

Page 153, Passage: William Sims Bainbridge, *Sociology*, Barron's Educational Series, Inc., 1997, pp. 26–27.

Page 161, Passage: "Groundwater: A Community Action Guide," Concern, Inc., Washington, D.C., June 1984.

Pages 168–170, Passage: Paulette W. Campbell, "Ancestral Bones: Reinterpreting the Past of the Omaha," *Humanities*, November/December 2002, National Endowment of the Humanities.

Pages 175–176, Passage: Mark Twain, *Life on the Mississippi* (1883) "The River and Its History," reprinted in *The Family Mark Twain*, Harper and Bros., 1935, pp. 5–6.

Pages 299–300, Passage: Joseph Conrad, "Gaspar Ruiz: A Romantic Tale," *The Complete Short Fiction of Joseph Conrad*, Volume I, The Ecco Press (NY, 1991), pp. 239–242.

Pages 309–310, Passage: "The Health Effects of Caffeine." Printed with permission of American Council on Science and Health, *www.acsh.org*.

Pages 404–405, Passage: "Characteristics of the Abusive Situation," *Guide to Legal Relief*, Governor's Commission on Domestic Violence, New York, October, 1984.

Pages 407–408, Passage: William Sims Bainbridge, "1940: The Invasion from Mars," *Sociology*, Barron's Educational Series, Inc., 1997, pp. 156–158.

Test-Taker's Checklist for the ACT

BASIC STRATEGIES

✔ *Budget your time.* Work swiftly: don't linger over difficult questions.

✔ *Don't leave any question blank.* There is no penalty for guessing, so it pays to answer every question.

✔ *Read each question carefully.* Answer the question asked, not the one you may have expected.

✔ *Save the hardest questions for last.* Build momentum and confidence by answering the easy questions, then go back and answer ones that initially stumped you.

✔ *Mark answers cleanly and accurately.* Check the numbering of your answer sheet often. Erase completely; leave no stray marks.

✔ *Change answers if you have a reason for doing so.* However, it's usually best not to change based on a hunch or a whim.

Preparing for the ACT

1

THE ACT

The ACT is required for admission to many colleges. It takes just under 3 hours to complete and consists of multiple-choice questions in English, math, reading, and science. In addition, for students applying to colleges that require or recommend it, the ACT offers an optional writing test consisting of an essay to be written in 30 minutes.

Subject	Number of Questions	Time
English	75	45 minutes
Mathematics	60	60 minutes
Reading	40	35 minutes
Science Reasoning	40	35 minutes
Writing (optional)	1 essay	30 minutes

Before registering for the Writing Test, check the admissions requirements of colleges to which you plan to apply. Or consult the ACT web site (*www.act.org*) for the names of institutions that expect applicants to take this test. If you don't yet know where you'll apply, sign up for the test anyway. Later, if you decide not to take this test, you can cancel your registration any time before test day by calling the ACT at (319) 337-1270.

Since policies and procedures change from time to time, it's best to verify registration and test requirements on the official ACT web site to avoid unpleasant surprises.

Primary Focus of the ACT

Although ACT questions focus on subjects studied in high school, **the test emphasizes thinking skills.** To answer most of the questions, you must solve problems, draw conclusions, make inferences, and think analytically. Colleges prefer students who can figure out answers rather those whose main strength is simply the ability to memorize and recall information.

Parts of the ACT

1. **The English Test** measures your mastery of the skills needed to write well. In particular, it tests:

Usage and Mechanics		
Punctuation		10 questions
Grammar and Usage		12 questions
Sentence Structure		18 questions
	Total	40
Rhetorical Skills		
Writing Strategy		12 questions
Organization		11 questions
Style		12 questions
	Total	35

Satisfactory performance on the English Test tells a college that you know the conventions of standard grammatical English and that you can punctuate and write complete, carefully structured sentences. The test further assesses your understanding of rhetoric, that is, whether you can tell when a piece of writing is unified, well organized, and consistent in style.

On the English Test you are given five prose passages, each about 325 words. Portions of the passage are underlined and numbered. Most of the questions ask you to decide whether the underlined sections are correct, and, if not, which of four alternative choices is the most appropriate substitute. An item may contain an error in punctuation, sentence structure, or some other aspect of grammar and usage. If all the underlined sections are correct, the choice "NO CHANGE" is the right answer. The remaining questions on the English Test, which ask you to judge the quality of expression, unity, clarity, or overall effectiveness of the writing, refer to passages in their entirety or to selected portions of the text.

If you take the Writing Test, you'll receive an additional score that combines the results of both the English and Writing Tests. This combined English/Writing Test score is a separate number that has no effect on your scores on either the English or Writing Test. Colleges are likely to consider all these scores in their admissions process. Then, they'll use them again to place you in an appropriate English course during your freshman year.

2. **The Mathematics Test** measures knowledge and understanding of mathematics, in particular:

Pre-Algebra	14 questions
Elementary Algebra	10 questions
Intermediate Algebra	9 questions
Coordinate Geometry	9 questions
Plane Geometry	14 questions
Trigonometry	4 questions

Each of the 60 items presents a mathematical problem that you must solve by using algebra, geometry, or trigonometry. This is not a test of your ability to memorize elaborate formulas or perform extensive computations. Accuracy and knowledge of basic formulas are important, but your mathematical reasoning skills count the most.

For each problem, you must pick one of five alternative solutions, one of which may be "None of the above." About half the items on the test are application items that require you to perform a sequence of operations. Another eight items require you to analyze the sequence of operations and conditions of the problem. The remaining problems test your basic mathematical proficiency.

Certain kinds of calculators may be used on the test, but if you bring a calculator, be sure you know how to use it. Install fresh batteries just before the exam. For more details, refer to the "ACT's calculator policy" on the ACT web site.

3. **The Reading Test** measures your ability to understand materials similar to those read in college courses. The test consists of four passages, each about 750 words, drawn from four different areas of knowledge:

Prose Fiction: novels and short stories	10 questions
Social Studies: anthropology, archaeology, business, economics, education, geography, history, political science, psychology, and sociology	10 questions
Humanities: architecture, art, dance, ethics, film, language, literary criticism, music, philosophy, radio, television, and theater	10 questions
Natural Science: anatomy, astronomy, biology, botany, chemistry, ecology, geology, medicine, meteorology, microbiology, natural history, physiology, physics, technology, and zoology	10 questions

Passages are excerpts from books, articles, periodicals, and other publications. Because each passage contains whatever information you need for answering the questions, no additional background or knowledge is required.

4. **The Science Reasoning Test** assesses your ability to think like a scientist. On the test you must answer questions about seven sets of scientific information presented in three formats:

Data Representation: graphs, tables, other schematics	15 questions
Research Summaries: several related experiments	18 questions
Conflicting Viewpoints: alternative interpretations of several related hypotheses or views that are inconsistent with each other	7 questions

The sets of information come from biology, chemistry, physics, and the physical sciences, including earth science, meteorology, astronomy, and space science. Three of the seven groups of questions are presented as graphs, charts, tables, or scientific drawings similar to those found in science journals and texts.

5. **The Writing Test** is meant to test your ability to plan and compose a clear, concise, and persuasive essay in a relatively short time—30 minutes, to be precise.

In addition, it provides colleges with useful information about how well you can 1) think, 2) organize ideas, 3) express yourself, and 4) use standard English.

BEFORE TAKING THE ACT

Choosing a Test Date

Most students take the ACT during the spring of the junior year or at the beginning of the senior year. The date you choose works neither for nor against you in the eyes of college admissions officials.

IF YOU TAKE THE ACT AS A:	
Junior	**Senior**
1. You will get a clearer picture of your prospects for admission to the colleges you may be considering. As a result, you can make more realistic college plans.	1. You are likely to earn higher scores, because you will have had more courses and more experience.
2. You will have more opportunities to retake the ACT. Hoping to improve scores, students often use the time between exams to prepare themselves more thoroughly.*	2. You will have the opportunity to retake the ACT but with less preparation time between examination dates.
3. You'll have one less thing to worry about during the hectic college application season early in your senior year.	3. You will easily meet most early-decision and regular college application deadlines, which usually fall sometime between mid-October and March for fall admissions.

*By taking the April, June, or December exam, you can apply for Test Information Release (TIR). For a fee, ACT will send you a complete copy of the test you took along with your answers and an answer key. Your TIR will show you the questions you missed—useful information if you decide to retake the ACT.

If you took the Writing Test, you'll also receive a copy of the essay question, a scoring rubric, and the scores assigned by two readers. A photocopy of your actual essay will be added to your TIR for an additional fee.

Registering for the ACT

The ACT is given several times a year. The exact dates, times, and testing sites are listed on the ACT web site and in the college counseling or guidance offices of most high schools. You can also request information by phone.

Due to increased test security measures being instituted in the 2012–2013 test year, be sure to check the official ACT web site for the most up-to-date information on what you need to register for the ACT as well as what to bring with you on test day.

The registration deadline is approximately one month before the exam. Late registration is available any time until about two weeks prior to the test date.

Evaluating Your Performance

After taking the model tests at the end of this book, use the following four steps—or five steps if you took the Writing Test—to evaluate your performance:

1. **Check your answers.** Use the answer key provided after each exam. Return to each question you missed and try it again. Chances are good that you'll get it right the second time around. To be fair, however, don't count it as a correct answer when you calculate your test score.

2. **Read all the answer explanations.** Don't skip explanations for questions you got right. They often contain helpful insights into shorter or different methods of answering questions. For each question you got wrong, be sure you understand why you made an error. That will help you avoid making a similar mistake in the future.

3. **Calculate your overall test score.** Following each exam you'll find instructions for figuring out your test score. The process will yield several different kinds of scores including raw scores, scale scores, and the composite score—all explained later in this chapter. *Note:* For the Writing Test, you'll get a separate score, not included in your overall ACT score.

4. **Rate your performance.** Use the chart below, which shows ranges of raw scores—that is, the number of correct answers on each of the four tests.

RATE YOUR PERFORMANCE				
Rating	**English**	**Mathematics**	**Reading**	**Science Reasoning**
Excellent	66–75	54–60	35–40	36–40
Very good	54–65	44–53	29–34	29–35
Above average	45–53	30–43	24–28	20–28
Below average	36–44	21–29	19–23	14–19
Weak	25–35	14–20	14–18	9–13
Poor	0–24	0–13	0–13	0–8

If you get more than 88 to 90 percent of the questions right, your ACT performance rating will be "excellent." Right answers on roughly 71 to 87 percent of the questions yields a "very good" rating. And you'll earn an "above average" rating for correctly answering 60–70 percent of the questions in English, reading, and science, and 50–70 percent of the questions in math.

To boost your score in any area, refer to the table of contents in this book to find the appropriate sections to study.

5. Evaluate your essay. The Writing Test can be scored by using the self-evaluation chart found at the end of each exam. Scores on the essay range from 1 (low) to 6 (high).

Getting Ready for Test Day

Since the ACT concentrates on four subjects found in all schools, most students are well prepared for the examination by the time they reach eleventh or twelfth grade. If you haven't taken a math course recently, however, or if you don't remember your basic English usage, reviewing the appropriate sections of this book will help. However, studying specifically for the Reading Test or the Science Reasoning Test may not be very fruitful. In fact, it's hard to know exactly what material would be worth studying. It would be smart, however, to devote considerable time to taking the practice tests in this book.

Overall familiarity with the ACT not only reduces test anxiety but enhances performance. Self-assurance, the feeling that you will do well, helps too, but be wary of overconfidence. Regardless of how ready you think you are, remember that it's impossible to be too well prepared for the ACT.

On Test Day

On the day of the test, bring:

- Your ACT ticket of admission.
- Three or more sharpened #2 pencils with erasers—a few more if you're taking the Writing Test.
- Proper identification. In light of new test security procedures, be sure to check the official ACT web site before you head for the testing venue to ensure that you have the right documentation to gain admission. Otherwise, you may be turned away.
- Calculators (optional). You may use a calculator on the Math Test, but only one that is authorized by the ACT.
- Candy or gum, if you feel the need. (Eating snacks or anything more substantial is not permitted during the examination.)

Leave at home:

- Books, notebooks, dictionaries, scrap paper.
- iPods, cell phones, and all other electronic communication devices.
- Noisy jewelry, including watches that beep.

Throughout the exam, listen attentively to the proctors' announcements. Proctors will distribute test materials, instruct you in test procedures, show you how to fill out the answer sheet, and answer administrative questions.

If you need assistance during the exam, raise your hand to summon a proctor. Don't talk to anyone else, and don't leave your seat without a proctor's permission.

Answering the Questions

Regardless of how quickly you like to work, read every word of every question. Don't read the first few words of the question and presume that the rest follows a familiar pattern.

For each question on the English, Reading, and Science Reasoning Tests, you are given four possible answers, and your task is to choose the best one. Sometimes a choice is partly true. For example, one answer to a reading question may be valid for only part of the reading passage. A better choice would be the answer that pertains to the whole passage. Therefore, it is very important to read all the choices before making your decision. Experts in testing say that the most obvious choice on a difficult question is usually wrong. Consequently, you should *look* for the answer that is most obvious, but you should not discount it as a possibility.

Each problem on the Mathematics Test offers five possible answers. You are to choose the only correct one. Before making a choice, try to predict the approximate answer. Then scan the choices to see which one comes closest to your prediction. The best choice may be the one you predict. Nevertheless, you should work out the solution to the problem in the space provided in the test booklet. If your solution fails to correspond with any of the choices, pick "None of these" as your answer. But double-check your calculations as well as the question itself, especially if your answer differs radically from any of the choices. If you plan to use a calculator, make sure it's working properly and is set in the correct mode.

Answer every question on every test, even if you have to guess. You don't lose credit for a wrong answer, and you may make a lucky guess. Before you resort to guessing, though, try to eliminate any obviously wrong choices. By discarding one choice that you know is way off the mark, the chances of hitting the jackpot are improved. By eliminating two wrong answers, they jump to fifty-fifty—pretty decent odds in any circumstances.

To complete an item, fill in the oval on your answer sheet that corresponds with the answer you've chosen. If you change your mind later, be sure to erase your original answer completely. Because the scoring machine can't distinguish between your intended answer and the one you changed, press hard on your eraser. Incidentally, studies have shown that it's faster to blacken the ovals on the answer sheet from the center outward than from the perimeter to the center. Try it. You could save a minute or two during the course of the exam—a minute that might be used more productively in finding correct answers.

While working on any of the tests, you may write in the exam booklet. Since there are no restrictions, you may underline, cross out, make any marks you wish. Be mindful, however, that extensive writing takes time. If possible, develop a shorthand system of notations.

Using Time Effectively

Each test on the ACT lasts a prescribed length of time. Once a test is over, you may not return to it. And you are not permitted to work on a test that has not yet officially begun. After the first two tests, you'll have a 10- to 15-minute break.

To do your best on the ACT, it's useful to know approximately how much time you have to work on each problem or question. With practice, you will soon begin to sense whether you are working at a rate that will allow you to finish each test within its time limit. The following analysis indicates the time allowed for each test.

The periods of time allowed for each test are sufficient for almost every student to finish. To answer all the questions, however, you must work deliberately. If you finish a test before the time is up, check your answers, especially those that you're unsure about. Make sure that you've blackened only one oval for each question. If time is about to be called and you haven't finished the test, fill in answers at random on your answer sheet. A lucky guess or two will raise your score.

Just before test day, reread these pages. Knowing just what to expect and how to make the best use of the allotted time will work to your advantage during the exam.

Test	Content	Length of Time Per Question	Comments
English 75 questions	5 passages, 15 questions each	30 seconds	Easy questions should take only a few seconds.
Mathematics 60 questions	Questions generally increase in difficulty from beginning to end.	Less than 60 seconds except for the hard ones	Spend as little time as possible on the early questions to allow more time for the harder ones.
Reading 40 questions	4 passages, 10 questions each	3–4 minutes per passage, 4 minutes for 10 questions or about 25 seconds per question.	Some passages may take more or less time to completely master.
Science Reasoning 40 questions	7 sets of questions with 5–7 questions per set; questions within a set often increase in difficulty	2 minutes per passage; 30 seconds for each question	Try to spend less than 5 minutes on the easier questions, allowing more time for the harder ones.
Essay	1 essay question	30 minutes	5–6 minutes planning time; 15–20 minutes writing; 3–5 minutes proofreading and editing

TEST SCORES

About two and a half weeks after the test, scores are posted online. Writing Test scores are mailed about two weeks after that along with a printout of scores for all the multiple-choice questions. (Your scores will also be sent to your high school and to the colleges you designated on your ACT registration.) If you have questions, go to "Ask a Question" on the ACT web site.

To calculate test scores, the ACT uses the following procedure:

1. First, the ACT counts the number of questions you got right on each of the four multiple-choice tests. These are called *raw scores*. (No points are deducted for incorrect answers or unanswered questions—the reason that guessing is encouraged.)

2. The four raw scores are then converted to *scale scores* ranging from 1 (low) to 36 (high). Scale scores are averaged and rounded to the nearest whole number to give you a *composite score*—the score that you're most likely to recite when asked, "Hey, what did you get on the ACT?"

   Scale scores also provide evidence of your readiness for college work. The ACT has correlated certain minimum scale scores—called the *benchmark* scores—with grades earned by college freshmen in selected courses.

   For example, a scale score of 22 on the ACT math test is the benchmark for a 50 percent chance of your earning a B or higher in a college algebra course. It's also the benchmark for a 75 percent chance of a C or higher. The same odds apply to the benchmark scores on other ACT tests:

Test	Benchmark Score	College Course
English	18	College Composition
Reading	21	Social Sciences/Humanities
Science	24	Biology

   In 2011 only 25 percent of ACT test-takers met or exceeded all four benchmark scores. On individual tests, 66 percent met or surpassed the English benchmark score. On the reading test 52 percent met or exceeded the benchmark score; on the math test, 45 percent, and in science, 30 percent.

3. In addition to a composite score and a scale score for each of the four tests, you'll receive *subscores* in English, math, and reading—12 subscores in all. No direct arithmetical relationship exists between subscores and individual test scores. In other words, the test scores in each subject are *not* the sum of

the subscores. At best, subscores will give you a general idea of your strengths and weaknesses in each academic area. A high subscore in algebra and a poor one in geometry, for instance, indicates that you ought to immerse yourself for a while in the geometry section of this book.

4. If you took the ACT Writing Test, you'll get two additional scores: a Writing Test subscore reported on a scale of 2 (low) to 12 (high) and a combined English/Writing score reported on a scale of 1 to 36. The combined English/Writing score is calculated using weighted numbers. That is, the English test counts as two-thirds of the total, and the essay counts one-third. (Note: Your score on the multiple-choice English test will remain the same whether or not you took the Writing Test.)

Along with these numerical results you'll also find a comment or two about your essay from the ACT readers. For a fee you can also arrange for a copy of the essay itself to be made available to your high school and to the colleges you listed on your ACT registration form.

COMPOSITE SCORES AND COLLEGE ENROLLMENT

Although ACT will shower you with scores of many kinds, the one score that seems to matter most is the composite score, the number that presumably indicates whether you'll qualify for admission to certain colleges or universities—or by implication, tells you that you have what it takes to do the work there. The ACT, however, advises you not to jump to any conclusions based on your composite score. In other words, don't overinterpret your composite score because no single test can measure your skills and the state of your knowledge with absolute precision.

Indeed, neither a very high nor very low ACT score will make or break an application for admission. While important, the score is just one of several criteria that admissions officials consider when making decisions about an applicant. Many college web sites list the average ACT scores of students in the freshman class. Based on that information, you may want to aim for more competitive or for less competitive colleges. Or you may decide to retake the ACT with the hope of improving your score.

Theoretically, you can take the ACT as often as you like, up to seven times—if you have the stomach for it. However, years of experience show that over half the students (about 57 percent) who've taken the ACT more than once raised their scores, but 22 percent did worse, and the scores of 21 percent stayed about the same.

How Colleges Use ACT Scores

Although ACT scores are used primarily for admissions, they are sometimes used to place freshmen in remedial, regular, or advanced courses. A college advisor may also use ACT scores to help you choose a major, schedule a realistic course load, pick extracurricular activities, define educational and career goals, and avoid a variety of potential academic problems. Based on the scores, you may also be eligible for certain scholarships or part-time campus jobs.

Some Perspective

For better or worse, ACT scores affect you and your college plans. Like so many other matters that need your attention during junior and senior year, taking the ACT is one of the rites of passage between childhood and adulthood. To become familiar with the ins and outs of the ACT takes lots of effort and many hours of your time. Maybe you're already suffering from information overload—and we're only in the first chapter of this book. What's more, you should check out the ACT web site (*www.act.org*), which, because it contains many more details about every aspect of the ACT, will probably address every one of your concerns and questions.

It's normal to feel stressed, perhaps even overwhelmed, by the challenges of applying to college, keeping up your grades, and maintaining some sort of balance between work and play. Remember, though, that millions of students before you have met these challenges successfully. You can, too, particularly if you don't allow the experience to get you down.

Good luck.

2

Preparing for the English Test

DESCRIPTION OF THE ENGLISH TEST

The English Test consists of 75 multiple-choice questions based on five prose passages with portions of their text underlined and numbered. Next to each numbered part are four responses corresponding to the test item. Sometimes the question will test your understanding of usage and mechanics. You will have to decide whether to leave the underlined text as it is or substitute one of the choices. Other questions will test your understanding of rhetorical skills, such as the order of items within a passage, the organization of a passage, or the appropriateness or consistency of the language. Questions measuring rhetorical skills may ask you to select how a general statement might be better supported or whether a different arrangement of the passage's parts might be more meaningful. You have 45 minutes to complete the 75 items.

Here is a sneak peek. Read the passage and answer the questions. Do not refer to the correct answers until you have tried to answer the questions yourself. (On the actual ACT, questions appear to the right of the underlined words and boxes. Here, however, questions follow the passage.)

Sample Passage

All creatures in the animal kingdom have the instincts of curiosity and fear. Man alone was endowed with <u>imagination, which</u> was bound to
<u></u>
₁
complicate matters for him. Whereas a fox, let us say, was able to shrug off the mysteries of the heavens and such whims of nature as lightning and earthquakes, man <u>had demanded</u> an explanation. And so began the myths,
₂
the ancient creeds, witchcraft, astrology, <u>they told fantastic tales</u> of
₃
wanderings into the unknown reaches of space and time, the distortions of the mental and physical capabilities of man himself. Evidently, these "explanations" were not enough: Man developed a thirst for something *beyond* the ever-growing knowledge brought to him by empirical scientific research. The French call this *le culte de merveilleux*. We call it science fiction. ☐ 4

1. **A.** NO CHANGE
   B. imagination; which
   C. imagination, a fact that
   D. imagination, on which

2. **F.** NO CHANGE
   G. had been demanding
   H. demanded
   J. demands

3. **A.** NO CHANGE
   B. fantastic tales
   C. They were told fantastic tales
   D. fireside stories

4. If the writer wanted to include more information about the early history of science fiction, which of the following would be most effective for the passage as a whole?

   F. A listing of current science fiction writers
   G. A discussion of recent science fiction movies
   H. A discussion of the "fantastic tales" that made up the origins of science fiction
   J. A discussion of witchcraft

   (CORRECT ANSWERS: 1. C 2. H 3. B 4. H)

The Usage/Mechanics questions test your understanding of punctuation, grammar, and sentence structure.

✔ *Punctuation:* 13%. These questions concern the use of punctuation marks (apostrophes, colons, commas, dashes, exclamation points, hyphens, parentheses, question marks, quotation marks, and semicolons) and, in particular, their function in clarifying the *meaning of the prose selection*.

✔ *Basic grammar and usage:* 16%. Items in this category test your knowledge and understanding of verbs, adverbs, and adjectives; subject-verb agreement, and agreement of pronoun and antecedent; and the proper use of connectives.

✔ *Sentence structure:* 24%. These items deal with the makeup of the sentence, including the relationship of clauses, the correct use and placement of modifiers, parallelism, and consistency in point-of-view and tense.

The Rhetorical Skills questions are almost equally distributed among three categories: strategy, organization, and style.

✔ *Strategy:* 16%. Questions involve examining some of the options the author has decided upon, particularly the author's choice of supporting material. Is it effective, appropriate, and sufficient in amount and quality? Another is the choice of writing vehicle—for example, the descriptive essay, the persuasive essay, the biography, or the comparison-contrast model. You will be asked to judge the writer's handling of these options.

✔ *Organization:* 15%. Questions on organization will most often involve re-arrangement of sentences in a paragraph or paragraphs within a passage. You may also be asked to spot extraneous material that has little or nothing to do with the main idea, and to indicate places where additional material might strengthen the paragraph.

✔ *Style:* 16%. In these questions, you may be asked to choose an adjective that best describes the style of the prose passage, to select the best phrase of several that have the same words but in a different order, or to choose alternative words. You will be asked to select text that matches the style and tone of the passage, and to choose words or phrases that most concisely express an idea.

LONG-RANGE STRATEGY

As a student planning to take the ACT test, you are already engaged in what is probably the most important of the long-term strategies, that is, learning as much as you can about the test and about the questions you are expected to answer.

More suggestions:

- If you have enough time before you take the actual test, improve your prose "ear" by reading good, informative prose under relaxed conditions, perhaps even on a daily, limited basis.
- Be sure you understand the format of the English Test, the time limitations, the number and types of questions, and the form of the answer sheet.
- Discuss the test frankly with your English teacher. Ask about your strengths and weaknesses in the skills to be tested. Does your teacher see anything in your habits or work that suggests problems you may have with the test? If so, how can you deal with those problems?
- Search out all avenues of help. Perhaps your school counselor has practice tests or other materials on test taking. Also, if there are ACT study groups in your school or community, join one, by all means. The additional practice will give you confidence, and you will find that sharing problems with other prospective test-takers is another good way to build confidence. Consult the on-line help at the *www.act.org* web site.

- Talk with your friends and family about the test and any fears you might have. Keep in mind that the ACT is only one of several means by which you will be evaluated and your admission to a college or university determined. Do not magnify its importance to the degree that you cannot prepare or perform effectively.

Anxiety affects your perception and use of language. Before you take the ACT test, you should come to terms in your own mind that you will do your best and that nobody, including yourself, has a right to ask more of you than that.

Now look over the Test-taking Tips that follow, and practice the habits and skills that will help you do your best.

TEST-TAKING TIPS

Concentrate. On the morning of the test, reduce as many of your distractions, obligations, and plans as possible. Have no social events planned—either before or after the test—so that your full attention is on your answers. Leave adequate time to arrive at the test center. It is better to be a little early.

Work carefully. Before you arrive, be familiar with the test directions. When the test begins, listen carefully to any directions read to you by a proctor or played on a tape. In marking the answer sheet, be sure to put each answer in the right space. If you skip a question because it is taking too much time, be careful to skip the corresponding space on the answer sheet. Focus only on the test; block out any distractions.

Pace yourself. You have 45 minutes to answer 75 questions, or roughly nine minutes for each passage and its questions.

Read with purpose. Before you begin to answer the questions, quickly skim the passage. Then, answer each question in light of its context.

Carefully examine the underlined parts. Think about the principles of usage involved in each question and focus on the one that applies. Many of the questions concern more than one aspect of usage, especially in the answer options. Be sure that the answer you choose does not introduce another error while correcting the first!

Decide on the best answer. As you approach each question, it is probably best to think how the underlined portion would be expressed in standard written English.

Eliminate choices by substituting each of the answers for the underlined portion of the test.

Have a positive mental attitude!

USAGE/MECHANICS

Comma

Among its many functions, the comma is used to set off independent clauses, items in a series, coordinate adjectives, parenthetical expressions, and nonrestrictive phrases or clauses.

Use a comma to separate independent clauses joined by a coordinating conjunction (*and, but, for, or, nor, yet,* or *so*).

EXAMPLES

He wanted to be a salesman, but no jobs were available.

The people refused to send their children to school, and the school building stood empty the entire year.

Be sure you understand that this rule applies to the joining of *independent clauses*, that is, complete sentences. The use of the coordinating conjunction to join compound subjects (*Bush* and *Gore* debated three times), pairs of phrases (The food at that restaurant is prepared *without care* and *without taste*), compound verbs (Phil *ran* the office and *acted* as athletic director), or the like does not require the comma.

Use commas to separate items in a series.

EXAMPLES

Friendly, small, and innovative are adjectives that accurately characterize this college.

He went to the basement, set the trap, and returned to the kitchen to wait.

Use a comma to separate coordinate adjectives modifying the same noun.

EXAMPLES

He washed his new, black, shiny pickup.

Himalayan cats have long, silky, heavy fur.

To test whether adjectives are coordinate, reverse their order or insert *and* between them. If the phrase still makes sense, they are coordinate adjectives and require a comma.

Use commas to set off nonrestrictive (amplifying or explanatory) phrases and clauses from the rest of the sentence.

PARTICIPIAL PHRASE

Having spent his last penny, Luster tried to borrow a quarter from his boss.

PREPOSITIONAL PHRASE

At the beginning of each game, a noted singer gives his rendition of "The Star-Spangled Banner."

ADVERBIAL CLAUSE

When the composer was finished with the prelude, she began work on the first movement.

Use a comma to set off contrasting and nonessential phrases and clauses.

EXAMPLES

Mary Jennings, who was my best friend, dropped the class.

The first offer on the Blake house, which had been on the market for almost a month, was very disappointing.

Be sure to distinguish between these *nonrestrictive* interrupters and the *restrictive modifiers*, which are not set off by commas. Nonrestrictive modifiers add information but do not limit or change the meaning of the sentence. Note how the meaning changes when the clause is restrictive.

RESTRICTIVE

The young woman who was my best student dropped the class.

The young woman is now identified as the best student. Here is another example of a nonrestrictive clause:

EXAMPLE

Cardiac patients who have artificial valve implants are required to take anticoagulants for the rest of their lives.

Use a comma to set off nonrestrictive phrases and clauses that follow the main clause.

EXAMPLES

Jessica wanted to see the ice show, not the circus.

Few fans thought the reigning heavyweight champion could win, although he was superior to the challenger in every category.

Use commas to set off an appositive. An appositive is a noun or noun phrase that renames or explains the noun it follows.

EXAMPLE

The novel, a mystery about a secret island off the Washington coast, was an instant bestseller.

Use commas to set off words in direct address. Words in direct address identify the one being spoken to.

EXAMPLE

Excuse me, Beth, but aren't you late for your tennis lesson?

Semicolon

The semicolon is generally used to separate coordinate elements in a sentence, that is, items of the same grammatical nature. Most often, it is used between related ideas that require punctuation weaker than a period, but stronger than a comma. In addition, the semicolon divides three or more items in a series when the items themselves contain commas.

Use a semicolon between related independent clauses not joined by a coordinating conjunction.

EXAMPLES

A mature male gorilla may be six feet tall and weigh 400 pounds or more; his enormous arms can span eight feet.

New York has twelve major stadiums; Los Angeles has fifteen.

Use a semicolon between independent clauses joined by a transitional word (conjunctive adverb).

Frequently, two independent clauses are joined, not by a coordinating conjunction, but by a transitional word (conjunctive adverb) introducing the second clause. A semicolon must be used between the clauses, because these transitional words (*accordingly, also, consequently, finally, furthermore, however, indeed, meanwhile, nevertheless, similarly, still, therefore, thus,* and the like) are *not* connecting words.

EXAMPLE

A female coyote will not bear pups if her diet consists of fewer than fifty rodents a week; thus, Mother Nature achieves a population balance.

Use a semicolon to separate coordinate clauses if the clauses themselves have commas.

EXAMPLE

The warranty on the car covered extensive repairs to the electrical system, front end, transmission, fuel injection system, and valves; but the amount of time and inconvenience involved in returning each time to the dealer cannot be ignored.

Use a semicolon to separate items in a series when the items themselves contain internal punctuation.

Normally, three or more items in a series are set off by commas; however, when they are made more complex by commas and other punctuation, they are separated by semicolons.

EXAMPLE

> The trio was composed of a cellist named Grosz, who had been a European virtuoso for many years; a pianist who had won a major music festival in 1954, 1955, and 1958; and a violinist who had studied in Budapest, Vienna, and Munich.

Colon

The colon is a signal that something is to follow: a rephrased statement, a list or series, or a formal quotation. Use a colon in a sentence if you can logically insert *namely* after it.

Use a colon at the end of a complete statement to show anticipation—that is, to show that amplifying details follow, such as a list, a series of items, a formal quotation, or an explanation.

EXAMPLES

> Of all the gauges in an airplane cockpit, three are crucial: the altimeter, the gas gauge, and the crash-warning indicator.
>
> After five minutes of silence, the actor uttered those famous words: "To be or not to be; that is the question."
>
> A popover has four common ingredients: flour, milk, salt, and butter.

Problems that occur in the use of the colon usually result from the following lapses:

1. A complete statement (independent clause) does not precede the colon.

   incorrect: Tasks that I must complete today: mow the lawn, read two chapters of history, and tidy my room.

   correct: I must complete several tasks today: mow the lawn, read two chapters of history, and tidy my room.

2. A colon incorrectly separates essential parts of a sentence.

   incorrect: In updating my computer, I added: a hard disk, a laser printer, and a fine-resolution monitor. (The colon separates the verb from its direct objects.)

   correct: In updating my computer, I added some new components: a hard disk, a laser printer, and a fine-resolution monitor.

also correct: In updating my computer, I added a hard disk, a laser printer, and a fine-resolution monitor.

3. There is more than one colon in a sentence.

incorrect: The success of the action depended upon three variables: that the weather would hold out, that the supplies would arrive on time, and that the enemy would be short on three things: planes, ammunition, and food.

correct: The success of the action depended upon three variables: that the weather would hold out, that the supplies would arrive on time, and that the enemy would be short on planes, ammunition, and food.

Hyphen

The hyphen has two main uses: to divide syllables at the end of a line and to link words in certain combinations. It is also used in compound numbers from twenty-one to ninety-nine.

EXAMPLES

She wore a well-used raincoat.
BUT
Her raincoat was well used.

The past-due bill lay unnoticed behind the couch.

The bill, past due, lay unnoticed behind the couch.

Note

A compound adjective with an adverbial -*ly* modifier is never hyphenated: the *poorly designed* interchange.

Apostrophe

In addition to indicating possession, the apostrophe is used to take the place of omitted numbers (class of '02) and omitted letters or words in contractions (wasn't [was not], o'clock [of the clock]), and to indicate plurals that might otherwise be confusing (A's [not As]).

Use an apostrophe to show the possessive case of nouns and indefinite pronouns.

1. The possessive case of singular nouns (either common or proper) is indicated by adding an apostrophe and an *s*.

EXAMPLES

> George's speech, the senator's campaign, anyone's opinion, the boss's office, Charles's book.

2. The possessive case of plural nouns ending in *s* is formed by adding only the apostrophe.

EXAMPLES

> the girls' softball team, the waitresses' union, the Harrisons' antique cars.

> **Note**
>
> Irregular plurals, such as men or children, form the possessive by adding an apostrophe and an *s*: men's, children's.

A common error is to confuse possessive pronouns and contractions, particularly *its* and *it's* (meaning it is) *their* and *they're* (*they are*), and *whose* and *who's* (*who is*). Possessive pronouns have no apostrophe.

AVOID using an apostrophe with a plural noun:

(Don't add an apostrophe when possession isn't indicated.)

EXAMPLE

> FAULTY: The Perkins' and the Rists' were going fishing together.
> REVISED: The Perkins and the Rists were going fishing together.

AVOID using an apostrophe with a personal pronoun.

(*His, hers, its, ours, yours, theirs,* and *whose* are possessives, serving to provide possessive forms of the pronouns *he, she, it, we, you, they,* and *who*.)

EXAMPLE

> FAULTY: The hairbrush used by Nichol was clearly her's.
> REVISED: The hairbrush used by Nichol was clearly hers.

Dash

The main function of the dash, like parenthesis, is to enclose information within a sentence. Dashes are generally more forceful and therefore should be used sparingly, since they highlight the ideas and items they enclose.

Use dashes to indicate hesitation, or a sudden break in thought or sentence structure, or to set off appositives and other explanatory or parenthetical elements.

The dash adds emphasis to any part of a sentence that can be separated from the rest of the sentence.

EXAMPLE

The skydiver—in spite of his broken leg—set a new record for endurance.

Some specific uses of the dash are:

1. To interrupt continuity of prose

EXAMPLE

"I really can't tolerate—Well, never mind."

2. To emphasize appositives

EXAMPLE

The items she had asked for in the new car—CD player, navigation system, sunroof—were all included.

Question Mark

A question mark indicates the end of a direct question. A question mark in parentheses signals doubt or uncertainty about a fact such as a date or a number.

Use a question mark after a direct question.

EXAMPLES

When are we going to eat?

Ask yourself, what are the odds of winning?
(It is also correct to capitalize the word *what*.)

A question mark in parentheses may be used to express doubt.

EXAMPLE

> The Dean's notes, published in 1774 (?), are considered the novel's origin.

Note

The use of the question mark as a mark of irony or sarcasm is not usually considered proper: The superintendent's important (?) announcements took all morning.

Exclamation Point

An exclamation point is an indicator of strong *emotional* feelings, such as anger, joy, shock, surprise, or fear. It may also be used to express irony or emphasis. Like the dash, it should be used sparingly.

Use an exclamation point after a command, an interjection, an exclamation, or some other expression of strong emotion.

command: Stop!
interjection: Wow! Fire! Help!
emotional expression: Don't tell me you won again! How wonderful!

Quotation Marks

One of the main uses of quotation marks is to signal the exact words of a writer or speaker. Quotation marks are also used to enclose the titles of short literary or musical works (articles, short stories or poems, songs), as well as words used in a special way.

Enclose direct quotations in quotation marks.

EXAMPLE

> "We will wage war wherever it takes us," Winston Churchill pledged.

Quotation marks should enclose only the exact words of the person quoted.

EXAMPLE

> Winston Churchill pledged that "we will wage war wherever it takes us."
> (NOT ... pledged "that we will ...")

Use single quotation marks to enclose a quotation inside another quotation.

EXAMPLE

"My favorite saying, 'A day without a slice of apple pie is a day lost,'
"said Dr. Annaheim, "is causing me to be in trouble with health addicts."

Commas and periods *always* belong *inside* quotation marks; semicolons and colons, outside. Question marks and exclamation points are placed inside the quotation marks when they are part of the quotation; otherwise, they are placed outside.

EXAMPLES

What did he mean when he said, "I know the answer already"?

"The case is closed!" the attorney exclaimed.

Note

When a quoted sentence is interrupted by a phrase such as *he said* or *she replied*, two pairs of quotation marks must be used, one for each part of the quotation. The first word of the second part of the quoted material should not be capitalized unless it is a proper noun or the pronoun *I*.

EXAMPLE

"There are two sorts of contests between men," John Locke argued,
"one managed by law, the other by force."

AVOID using quotation marks:

When the quotation marks are used to set off a simple title. (Quotation marks are not used around titles unless they contain or are themselves direct quotations.)

EXAMPLES

FAULTY: "My Great Adventure Last Vacation"
REVISED: My Great Adventure Last Vacation

FAULTY: "Optimism in William Faulkner's The Bear."
REVISED: Optimism in William Faulkner's "The Bear."

When they use ordinary nicknames or esoteric terms that are not being explained.

<u>EXAMPLES</u>

> FAULTY: As Chairman of Microsoft, "Bill" Gates preferred his nickname.
> REVISED: As Chairman of Microsoft, Bill Gates preferred his nickname.
>
> FAULTY: Birds of the Alaskan "tundra" are Canada Geese and Golden Plovers.
> REVISED: Birds of the Alaskan tundra are Canada Geese and Golden Plovers.

When the quotation marks are used to justify or apologize for slang or trite phrases that are not appropriate for your writing. (If slang is effective, employ it without quotation marks.)

Parentheses

Parentheses, like dashes, are used to set off words of explanation and other secondary supporting details—figures, data, examples—that are not really part of the main sentence or paragraph. Parentheses are less emphatic than dashes and should be reserved for ideas that have no essential connection with the rest of the sentence.

Use parentheses to enclose an explanatory or parenthetical element that is not closely connected with the rest of the sentence.

<u>EXAMPLE</u>

> The speech that he gave on Sunday (under extremely difficult circumstances, it should be noted) was his best.

If the parenthetical item is an independent sentence that stands alone, capitalize the first word and place a period inside the end parenthesis. If it is a complete sentence within another complete sentence, do not begin it with a capital letter or end it with a period. A question mark or exclamation point that is part of the parenthetical element should be placed inside the parenthesis.

EXAMPLES

On Easter, I always think of the hot cross buns I used to buy for two cents apiece. (At the time, the year was 1939, and I was three years old.) Congressman Jones (he was the man who once proposed having no entrance standards for community college students) gave a speech decrying the lack of basic skills on campuses today.

The absurd placement of the child-care center (fifteen feet from a class-room building!) was amateur architecture at its worst.

MINI-QUIZ

The following sample questions represent ways in which the above skills might be tested on the ACT. (On the actual test, questions appear to the right of the underlined words and boxes. Here, however, questions follow the passage.)

What lies behind the creative genius of our greatest <u>authors</u> has been
₁
the subject of speculation over the past two centuries. There is little doubt
that many of the <u>worlds</u> creative geniuses experienced miserable <u>lives</u> most
₂   ₃
often, they suffered a personal and extreme brand of deprivation that
profoundly affected the quality of their daily lives. Almost <u>always</u>, the depth
₄
of their misery is related to the greatness of their genius. One who reads
both Emily Bronte's *Wuthering Heights* and the <u>best known</u> critical
₅   ₆
discussions about her work cannot escape the <u>conclusion,</u> that Emily was
₇
the product of a punitive and abusive <u>environment,</u> it is difficult to avoid
₈
the further conclusion that the strength and authenticity of her <u>novel</u> the
₉
vulnerabilities and palpable yearnings of its main characters—are
<u>related however, faintly</u> to her personal affliction.
₁₀

1. **A.** NO CHANGE
   B. authors'
   C. authors,
   D. author's

2. **F.** NO CHANGE
   G. world's
   H. worlds'
   J. world's,

3. **A.** NO CHANGE
   B. lives:
   C. lives;
   D. lives,

4. **F.** NO CHANGE
   G. always;
   H. always—
   J. always:

5. **A.** NO CHANGE
   B. "Wuthering Heights"
   C. Wuthering Heights
   D. Wuthering-Heights

6. **F.** NO CHANGE
   G. best, known
   H. best-known
   J. "best known"

7. **A.** NO CHANGE
   B. conclusion;
   C. conclusion—
   D. conclusion

8. **F.** NO CHANGE
   G. environment;
   H. environment—
   J. environment?

9. **A.** NO CHANGE
   B. novel;
   C. novel—
   D. novel:

10. **F.** NO CHANGE
    G. related; however faintly,
    H. related, however faintly,
    J. related (however faintly)

Answers and Explanations

1. **(A)**

The noun *authors* is a simple object in this sentence and requires no punctuation.

2. **(G)**

The plural *geniuses* are a possession of the world and require that it signal that possession with an apostrophe.

3. **(B)**

The words occurring after *lives* form an independent clause and so must be set off with a stronger mark of punctuation. The colon is the best choice in this context because the following statement gives specific focus to the general statement made in the sentence's introductory clause.

4. **(F)**

Set off introductory phrases with a comma.

5. **(A)**

Underline (set in italics) novels and other larger works of literature.

6. **(H)**

Hyphenate compound adjectives preceding the noun they modify.

7. **(D)**

The adjective clause following the noun *conclusion* is a restrictive modifier and so does not take separating punctuation.

8. **(G)**

The clause that follows necessitates a strong mark of punctuation. Since it is closely related in meaning to the previous independent clause, the most appropriate choice is the semicolon.

9. **(C)**

The dash at the end of this phrase requires a matching dash at the beginning. Dashes are appropriately used to give special emphasis to parenthetical phrases such as this one.

10. **(H)**

The phrase *however faintly* is parenthetical and must be set off by commas.

BASIC GRAMMAR AND USAGE

The following list of principal parts features verbs that sometimes cause trouble in speaking and writing.

Subject-Verb Agreement

Nouns, verbs, and pronouns often have special forms or endings that indicate *number*—that is, whether the word is singular or plural. A verb must agree in number with the noun or pronoun that is its subject.

A verb agrees in number with its subject.

A singular subject requires a singular verb; a plural subject, a plural verb.

SINGULAR	PLURAL
The *house has* three bathrooms.	Many *houses have* more than one bathroom.
UCLA is my choice.	*UCLA, Berkeley, and Stanford are* my favorites.
My *cat*, a Persian named Gus, *is* awake all night.	*Cats*, according to this article, *are* almost always nocturnal.
Mandy, together with the other girls, *wants* a pizza for lunch	*Mandy and the other girls want a* pizza for lunch.

Do not let **intervening words obscure the relationship between subject and verb.** Find the subject and make the verb agree with it.

EXAMPLES

> A column of wounded prisoners, townspeople, and exhausted soldiers *was spotted* struggling over the horizon. (*Was spotted* agrees with its subject, *column*, not with the intervening plural nouns.)

> She, her brother, and her friends from upstate *have* always *bought* tickets to the rock concert. (The verb agrees with the plural subject.)

Principal Parts of Verbs

All verbs have four principal parts: the *present* (NOW), the *past* (YESTERDAY), the *present participle* (the -ING form of the verb), and the *past participle* (the form of the verb with HAVE). To find the principal parts of a verb, just remember the clues NOW, YESTERDAY, -ING, and HAVE.

The following list features verbs that sometimes cause trouble in speaking and writing.

PRESENT	PAST	PAST PARTICIPLE
become	became	become
begin	began	begun
bid (offer)	bid	bid
bid (command)	bade	bidden
bite	bit	bit, bitten
blow	blew	blown
break	broke	broken
bring	brought	brought
burst	burst	burst
catch	caught	caught
choose	chose	chosen
come	came	come
dive	dived, dove	dived
do	did	done
drag	dragged	dragged
draw	drew	drawn
drink	drank	drunk
drive	drove	driven
eat	ate	eaten
fall	fell	fallen
fly	flew	flown
forget	forgot	forgot, forgotten
freeze	froze	frozen
get	got	got, gotten
give	gave	given
go	went	gone
grow	grew	grown
hang (suspend)	hung	hung
hang (execute)	hanged	hanged
know	knew	known
lay	laid	laid
lead	led	led
lend	lent	lent
lie (recline)	lay	lain

PRESENT	PAST	PAST PARTICIPLE
lie (speak falsely)	lied	lied
lose	lost	lost
pay	paid	paid
prove	proved	proved, proven
raise	raised	raised
ride	rode	ridden
ring	rang, rung	rung
rise	rose	risen
run	ran	run
see	saw	seen
shake	shook	shaken
shrink	shrank	shrunk
sing	sang, sung	sung
sink	sank, sunk	sunk
speak	spoke	spoken
spring	sprang	sprung
steal	stole	stolen
swim	swam	swum
swing	swung	swung
take	took	taken
tear	tore	torn
throw	threw	thrown
wear	wore	worn
weave	wove	woven
wring	wrung	wrung
write	wrote	written

VERB FORMS AND VERBALS

A high percentage of verb-related errors occurs because the reader confuses *verb forms*—that is, the different forms that an action word can assume—with entirely different structures known as *verbals*—words formed from verbs but not used as verbs in a sentence. Known as *participles*, *gerunds*, and *infinitives*, verbals form important phrases within the sentence.

Infinitives

An infinitive is ordinarily preceded by *to* and is used as a noun, an adjective, or an adverb.

noun: *To err* is human. (Subject)

adjective: The survivors had little to *celebrate*. (*To celebrate* modifies the noun *little*.)

adverb: To *please* his children, Jerry bought a new pool. (*To please* modifies the verb *bought*.)

Gerunds

A gerund always ends in *-ing* and functions as a noun.

subject: *Writing* is very rewarding.

subjective complement: My favorite occupation is *binding* books.

direct object: He now regrets *resigning*.

object of preposition: After *sealing* the letter, he went for a walk.

Participle

A participle acts as an adjective in the sentence.

EXAMPLES

> *Growling* threateningly, the gorilla intimidated the crowd. (*Growling* modifies *gorilla*.)

> The floor *invaded* by termites was made of oak. (*Invaded* modifies *floor*.)

PRONOUNS

Pronouns are most often employed as substitutes for nouns, but some can also be used as adjectives or conjunctions. To master pronouns and be able to spot errors in their use, you need to understand pronoun *case* (nominative, possessive, objective), pronoun *number* (singular or plural), and pronoun *class* (personal, demonstrative, interrogative, relative, indefinite).

Personal Pronouns

A personal pronoun indicates by its form the person or thing it takes the place of: the person speaking (first person), the person spoken to (second person), or the person or thing spoken about (third person).

Demonstrative Pronouns

Demonstrative pronouns (*this, that, these, those*) take the place of things being pointed out.

Interrogative Pronouns

Interrogative pronouns (*who, whom, whose, which,* and *what*) are used in questions. *Who, which,* and *what* are used as subjects and are in the nominative case. *Whose* is in the possessive case. *Whom* is in the objective case, and, like all objects, it is the receiver of action in the sentence.

The most common error involving interrogative pronouns is the tendency to use *who* instead of *whom*.

Relative Pronouns

Relative pronouns (*who, whom, whose, which, what,* and *that*) refer to people and things. When a relative pronoun is the subject of a subordinate clause, the clause becomes an adjective modifying a noun in the sentence.

Indefinite Pronouns

Indefinite pronouns (*all, another, any, both, each, either, everyone, many, neither, one, several, some,* and similar words) represent an indefinite number of persons or things. Many of these words also function as adjectives ("*several* men").

MINI-QUIZ

The following sample questions represent ways in which the above skills might be tested on the ACT. (On the actual test, questions appear to the right of the underlined words and boxes. Here, however, questions follow the passage.)

Operators and manufacturers of nuclear reactor power facilities are making increased use of robots to improve operations and maintenance, lower operating costs, increasing plant availability and equipment reliability,
1
enhanced workersafety, and reduce worker exposure to radiation. There is
2
no doubt in the field that advanced telerobotic systems can have made
3
more effective use of human operators, expert systems, and intelligent machines; in fact, few of the world's leading nuclear plant designers believe
4
that a facility without modern robotic and telerobotic systems

will have become obsolete in a very few years. The design of
  5
future nuclear plants and supporting facilities—particularly these involving
                                                          6
fuel recycling—should incorporate considerations for use of robotic

systems.

    A committee of scientists critical of the move toward robotics believe
                                                                    7
that existing methods for controlling and preprogramming the typical robot is
                                                                          8
appropriate for only a limited number of jobs in nuclear facilities, mainly

because it simply require too much supervision. In addition, existing robots
         9
are limited in their ability to sense their surroundings and interpreting sensor
                                                             10
data, a prerequisite for handling unexpected problems during the routine

executions of tasks.

1. A. NO CHANGE
   B. increases
   C. increase
   D. increased

2. F. NO CHANGE
   G. enhancing
   H. enhances
   J. enhance

3. A. NO CHANGE
   B. can make
   C. can be made
   D. can be making

4. F. NO CHANGE
   G. some
   H. one
   J. none

5. A. NO CHANGE
   B. would have become
   C. becomes
   D. will become

6. F. NO CHANGE
   G. they
   H. those
   J. that

7. **A.** NO CHANGE
   B. believes
   C. believed
   D. have believed

8. **F.** NO CHANGE
   G. were
   H. are
   J. will be

9. **A.** NO CHANGE
   B. it simply required
   C. they simply require
   D. it simply requires

10. **F.** NO CHANGE
    G. interpret
    H. interpreted
    J. has interpreted

Answers and Explanations

1. **(C)**

The verb *increase* needs to be an infinitive to be parallel with the series of infinitive phrases that comprise the end of the sentence.

2. **(J)**

The verb *enhance* needs to be an infinitive to be parallel with the series of infinitive phrases that comprise the end of the sentence.

3. **(B)**

The passage is written in the present tense and employs the present tense in generally true statements.

4. **(G)**

Some is the more logical choice of indefinite pronoun here; the use of *few* in the text renders the sentence meaningless.

5. **(D)**

The future tense is made necessary by the trailing phrase "in a very few years."

6. **(H)**

Demonstrative pronouns take the place of things *being pointed out.* In this case, the word *those* is more appropriate for the antecedent *facilities* because those facilities will be built in the future.

7. **(B)**

The subject of the verb is the singular noun *committee*.

8. **(H)**

The subject of the verb is the plural noun *methods*.

9. **(D)**

The subject of the verb is the singular personal pronoun *it*, the antecedent of which is the noun *robot*.

10. **(G)**

Interpret is one of a pair of parallel infinitives (*to sense* and *to interpret*) modifying the noun *ability*.

SENTENCE STRUCTURE

In addition to the NO CHANGE response, the questions on the ACT English Test that deal with sentence structure will offer three alternatives, each one a restructuring of the underlined part. Errors in sentence structure include such items as sentence fragments, run-on sentences, misplaced modifiers, and lack of parallelism. These topics are reviewed in this section.

Sentence Fragments

A sentence fragment is a part of a sentence that has been punctuated as if it were a complete sentence. It does not express a complete thought but depends upon a nearby independent clause for its full meaning. It should be made a part of that complete sentence.

incorrect:	I was not able to pick up my child at her school. *Having been caught in heavy traffic.* (Participial phrase)
revised:	Having been caught in heavy traffic, I was not able to pick up my child at her school.
	or
	I was not able to pick up my child at her school. I had been caught in heavy traffic.
incorrect:	The cat sat on the water heater. *Unable to get warm.* (Adjective phrase)
revised:	Unable to get warm, the cat sat on the water heater.

Run-on Sentences

Probably the most common error in writing occurs when two sentences are run together as one. There are two types of run-on sentences: the *fused* sentence, which has no punctuation mark between its two independent clauses, and the *comma splice*, which substitutes a comma where a stronger mark, either a period or a semicolon, is needed.

fused: Jean had no luck at the store they were out of raincoats.

comma splice: She surprised us all with her visit, she was on her way to New York.

To correct a run-on sentence, use a period, a semicolon, or a coordinating conjunction (*and, but, or, nor, for*) to separate independent clauses.

Note the following examples of run-on sentences and the suggested revisions.

fused: Eric is a bodybuilder he eats only large amounts of meat.

revised: Eric is a bodybuilder; he eats only large amounts of meat.

comma splice: He had never seen Alex so prepared, he even had backup copies of his study sheets!

revised: He had never seen Alex so prepared. He even had backup copies of his study sheets!

comma splice: His father was an artist, his mother was an accountant.

revised: His father was an artist, and his mother was an accountant.

Connectives

Connectives that join elements of equal rank are called coordinating conjunctions (*and, but, or, nor, so, for, yet*). Connectives that introduce a less important element are called subordinating conjunctions (*after, before, although, because, if, whenever, since, when, as, until,* and others).

Coordinating conjunctions link words, phrases, and clauses that are of equal importance.

EXAMPLES

The pilot *and* the crew boarded the plane.

The road ran through the valley *and* along the river.

Compound sentences are formed when coordinating conjunctions link two independent clauses.

You can sign the loan papers on Friday, *or* you can sign them on Monday.

Subordinating conjunctions are used in sentences to connect clauses that are not equal in rank—that is, in sentences in which one idea is made subordinate to another. There are many subordinating conjunctions. Some of the important ones are *after, as, because, before, if, in order that, once, since, unless, until, whenever,* and *wherever.*

We covered up the newly planted citrus trees *when* the temperature began to drop.

Until I saw her in person, I thought Cher was a tall woman.

Modifiers

Adjectives and Adverbs

The purpose of adjectives and adverbs is to describe, limit, color—in other words, to *modify* other words. Adjectives modify nouns or pronouns, and generally precede the words they modify. Adverbs describe verbs, adjectives or other adverbs. Some words can be used as either adjectives (He has an *early appointment*) or adverbs (*He arrived early*).

Adjectives

Problems that students face with adjectives frequently relate to the use of degrees of comparison. There are three degrees: the *positive*—the original form of the word (*straight*); the comparative—used to compare two persons or things (*straighter*); and the superlative—used to compare more than two persons or thins (*straightest*). If not understood, the spelling and form changes involved can sometimes confuse the unwary student.

Adverbs

Adverbs (either as words, phrases, or clauses) describe the words they modify by indicating *when, how, where, why, in what order,* or *how often.*

Probably the most persistent and frustrating errors in the English language involve either *incorrect modification* or else *inexact modification* that is difficult to pin down.

In most cases, if you can keep your eye on the *word or phrase being modified*, it is easier to avoid the following pitfalls.

Misplaced Modifiers

To avoid confusion or ambiguity, place the modifying words, phrases, or clauses near the words they modify.

Dangling Constructions

A dangling modifier literally hangs in the air; there is no logical word in the sentence for it to modify. Frequently it is placed close to the wrong noun or verb, causing the sentence to sound ridiculous:

EXAMPLE

Driving through the park, several chipmunks could be seen. (Were the chipmunks driving?)

CORRECTION: *Driving through the park, we saw several chipmunks.*

EXAMPLE

Constructed entirely of plastic, heart patients use a valve that weighs less than six ounces. (Are the patients constructed entirely of plastic?)

CORRECTION: *Heart patients use a valve constructed entirely of plastic that weighs less than six ounces.*

MINI-QUIZ

The following sample questions represent ways in which the above skills might be tested on the ACT. (On the actual test, questions appear to the right of the underlined words and boxes. Here, however, questions follow the passage.)

The life of famed watchmaker Abraham-Louis Breguet was, from beginning to end <u>(1747–1823). A</u> steady progression toward fame and
₁ fortune. Breguet soon revealed a lively interest that developed into a veritable passion for things mechanical <u>in his stepfather's shop.</u> He studied
₂ with the famed jeweler Abbot Marie for twelve <u>years, his vocation</u> was
₃ henceforth decided. <u>Living in the Swiss cantons</u> on the French border,
₄ watch-making had already been developed on a large scale by refugee

French families, <u>because</u> it was limited almost exclusively to inexpensive
₅
products. <u>Young Breguet, on the contrary, demonstrating very early a</u>
₆
<u>decided disgust for shoddy workmanship, as well as a genius for precision</u>
₆
<u>work, had an attitude he never lost.</u>
₆
   In 1802, <u>Breguet, receiving the gold medal at an exhibition of</u>
₇
<u>industrial products, sat at the table of the first consul.</u> Throughout his
₇
reign, Napoleon's interest in the works of the watch master, principally
those of high precision, never slackened. <u>The face studded with brilliant</u>
₈
<u>diamonds and rubies, Napoleon acquired Breguet's most ambitious</u>
₈
<u>creation the day after it was completed.</u>
₈
   The fall of the empire did not affect <u>either his fortunes adversely or</u>
₉
<u>his renown,</u> which had spread throughout Europe. The exhibition of 1819 in
₉
which Breguet presented a collection of his most important works was a
triumphant compendium of his life, <u>by then more than seventy years old.</u>
₁₀

1. **A.** NO CHANGE
   B. (1747–1823), a
   C. (1747–1823) a
   D. (1747–1823); a

2. **F.** NO CHANGE
   G. (Place at the beginning of the sentence.)
   H. (Place after the verb revealed.)
   J. (Delete altogether; the phrase is not related.)

3. **A.** NO CHANGE
   B. years his vocation
   C. years, then his vocation
   D. years, and his vocation

4. **F.** NO CHANGE
   G. (Place this phrase after border.)
   H. (Place this phrase after families.)
   J. (Delete altogether; the phrase is not related.)

5. **A.** NO CHANGE
   B. but
   C. even though
   D. however

6. **F.** NO CHANGE
   G. Young Breguet, on the contrary, demonstrating very early a decided disgust for shoddy workmanship, as well as a genius for precision work, an attitude he never lost.
   H. Young Breguet, on the contrary, demonstrated very early a decided disgust for shoddy workmanship, as well as a genius for precision work, an attitude he never lost.
   J. Young Breguet, on the contrary, demonstrated very early a decided disgust for shoddy workmanship, as well as a genius for precision work, and had an attitude he never lost.

7. **A.** NO CHANGE
   B. In 1802, Breguet, receiving the gold medal at an exhibition of industrial products, sitting at the table of the first consul.
   C. In 1802, Breguet received the gold medal at an exhibition of industrial products and sat at the table of the first consul.
   D. In 1802, Breguet sat at the table of the first consul, receiving the gold medal at an exhibition of industrial products.

8. **F.** NO CHANGE
   G. The face studded with brilliant diamonds and rubies, Breguet's most ambitious creation, the day after it was completed, was acquired by Napoleon.
   H. The face studded with brilliant diamonds and rubies the day after it was completed, Napoleon acquired Breguet's most ambitious creation.
   J. Napoleon acquired Breguet's most ambitious creation, the face studded with brilliant diamonds and rubies, the day after it was completed.

9. **A.** NO CHANGE
   B. The fall of the empire did not adversely affect either his fortunes or his renown, which had spread throughout Europe.
   C. Adversely, the fall of the empire did not affect either his fortunes or his renown, which had spread throughout Europe.
   D. The fall of the empire did not affect either his fortunes or his renown adversely, which had spread throughout Europe.

10. **F.** NO CHANGE
    G. (Place this phrase at the beginning of the sentence.)
    H. (Place this phrase, bracketed with commas, after the word Breguet.)
    J. (Delete this phrase; it is not relevant.)

Answers and Explanations

1. **(B)**

This sentence contains the parenthetical interruption "from beginning to end (1747–1823)," which must be set off by commas. Any stronger mark of punctuation after the parentheses results in two fragmented sentences.

2. **(G)**

The only logical position in this sentence for the prepositional phrase *in his stepfather's shop* is at the beginning of the sentence where it will correctly modify the noun *Breguet*.

3. **(D)**

A compound sentence is the most appropriate vehicle for these two ideas of equal importance. A comma is used before the coordinating conjunction that joins coordinate clauses.

4. **(H)**

The only logical position in this sentence for the participial phrase *Living in the Swiss cantons* is next to the noun it logically modifies, *families*.

5. **(B)**

Only a connective signaling contrast like but makes sense in this context, especially in the light of the next sentence.

6. **(H)**

This choice allows the main clause to emphasize the major characteristics of the subject, and correctly subordinates the parenthetical phrase, "an attitude he never lost."

7. **(C)**

The act of receiving the gold medal is logically as important as sitting with the first consul, and should not be subordinated in a participial phrase.

8. **(J)**

The phrase *the face studded with brilliant diamonds and rubies* modifies the noun *creation* and so must be placed next to it.

9. **(B)**

The adverb *adversely* logically modifies only the verb *affect* and should be placed near it.

10. **(H)**

The phrase *by then more than seventy years old* appropriately modifies the noun *Breguet* and should be placed next to it, set off by commas since it is a parenthetical addition.

CONSISTENCY AND TENSE

Verbs in Subordinate Clauses

Because *tense* indicates the time of the action and *voice* indicates whether the subject is the agent of the action (*active:* Tom *saw*) or the recipient of the action (*passive:* Tom *was seen*), both of these verb forms are central to the consistency of a sentence or passage.

The Present Infinitive

Always used the present infinitive (to run, to see), after a perfect tense (a tense that uses some form of the helping verb *have* or *had*).

The Subjunctive Mood

Verbs may be expressed in one of three moods: the *indicative*, used to declare a fact or ask a question; the *imperative*, used to express a command; and the *subjunctive*, generally used to indicate doubt or to express a wish or request or a condition contrary to fact.

Is When, Is Where, Is Because

The use of *is when, is where, is because* is always incorrect. The reason is simple: *when, where,* and *because* introduce adverbial clauses; and a noun subject followed by a form of the verb *to be* must be equated with a noun structure, not with an adverb clause.

PARALLELISM

Parallel ideas in a sentence should be expressed in the same grammatical form. If they are not, the sentence will be unbalanced.

A series of coordinated elements should be parallel in form.

incorrect: He *enjoys plays, exhibitions,* and *to walk* every morning. (An infinitive is paired with two nouns.)

correct: He enjoys *going* to plays, *visiting exhibitions,* and *walking* every morning.

> or

He enjoys *plays, exhibitions,* and morning *walks*.

incorrect: The union wanted *pay increases* and *that there would be shorter work-
              ing hours.* (A noun is paired with a noun clause.)

correct: The union wanted *pay increases* and shorter *working hours.*

**The constructions that follow correlative conjunctions (*both-and, either-or,
neither-nor, not only-but also, whether-or*) should be parallel in form.**

incorrect: He was *neither qualified* to lead this country *nor was he willing.*

correct: He was *neither qualified nor willing* to lead this country.

TRANSITIONAL WORDS AND PHRASES

Words of transition are clues that help the reader to follow the writer's flow of
ideas. Confusion can result, however, when an illogical or incorrect connective
is used. The following list includes more commonly used transitional words and
phrases, and the concepts they suggest.

Concept

Addition	also, furthermore, moreover, similarly, too
Cause and Effect	accordingly, as a result, consequently, hence, so, therefore, thus
Concession	granted that, it is true that, no doubt, to be sure
Conclusion	in short, that is, to conclude, to sum up
Contrast	although, but, however, nevertheless, on the contrary, on the other hand
Example	for example, for instance

MINI-QUIZ

The following sample questions represent ways in which the above skills
might be tested on the ACT. (On the actual test, questions appear to the
right of the underlined words and boxes. Here, however, questions follow
the passage.)

Crime and Punishment by Fyodor Dostoevsky is a topical novel

dealing with philosophical doctrines, <u>political,</u> and social issues widely
                                          1
discussed in Russia just after the 1861 reforms. <u>By most critical essays,</u>
                                                     2
treating Dostoevsky's work <u>has employed</u> psychological or biological
                              3

points of view. Because *Crime and Punishment* is a passionate, masterly portrayal of internal psychological conflict, a general assumption has evolved in the general critical world that the author wrote, at least in part, from personal experience. <u>Nevertheless,</u> Dostoevsky's biography has been
<u>4</u>
endlessly probed, explored, <u>and it was thoroughly analyzed.</u>
<u>5</u>

In 1849, Dostoevsky was convicted of consorting with known radical <u>factions; however, has was sentenced</u> to a four-year prison term. Many
<u>6</u>
critical commentaries on *Crime* and *Punishment* consider this experience formative and essential, certainly a major source of the creative impulses that eventually resulted in the execution of the novel. The epilogue of the novel <u>had been set</u> in Siberia, where he was imprisoned. When <u>talking</u> to
<u>7</u>   <u>8</u>
his fellow prisoners, he must have focused on crime and guilt and thought about the psychology of the criminal mind <u>granted that</u> he lived among
<u>9</u>
hardened convicts. One must ask, though, why he waited until 1865 to write *Crime and Punishment*. One possible answer <u>is because</u> he wrote the novel
<u>10</u>
in part to speak against foreign ideas adopted by the Russian radicals of the 1860s.

1. **A.** NO CHANGE
   B. politically
   C. politics
   D. that are political

2. **F.** NO CHANGE
   G. Because of most critical essays
   H. Most critical essays,
   J. Most critical essays

3. **A.** NO CHANGE
   B. have employed
   C. should employ
   D. employ

4. **F.** NO CHANGE
   G. Hence,
   H. On the contrary,
   J. Furthermore

5. **A.** NO CHANGE
   B. and being analyzed.
   C. and analyzed.
   D. subject to analysis.

6. **F.** NO CHANGE
   G. factions, yet, he was sentenced
   H. factions and was sentenced
   J. factions; moreover, he was sentenced

7. **A.** NO CHANGE
   B. is set
   C. was set
   D. has been set

8. **F.** NO CHANGE
   G. having talked
   H. he had talked
   J. having been talking

9. **A.** NO CHANGE
   B. as
   C. knowing that
   D. considering that

10. **F.** NO CHANGE
    G. is when
    H. is where
    J. is that

Answers and Explanations

1. **(C)**

A noun is necessary in this position to be parallel with the other noun objects in this series, *doctrines* and *issues*.

2. **(J)**

As it stands, this sentence contains an error in predication, beginning with one construction, *By most critical essays*, and continuing with a different one, *treating Dostoevsky's work has employed . . . points of view*. It is incorrect to separate a subject from its verb, as in choice H.

3. **(D)**

The verb must agree with its plural subject *essays* and maintain the established present tense.

4. **(G)**

The logic of the sentence requires a cause/effect transitional marker like *Hence,* not the contrast or addition markers suggested by the alternative choices.

5. **(C)**

The parallel series of past participles in this sentence requires this option: *has been probed, explored, and analyzed.*

6. **(H)**

The logic of this sentence requires a transitional word suggesting either *cause* or *addition.* Since the acts of *conviction* and *sentencing* seem to be of equal weight, the conjunction *and* is a sound choice.

7. **(B)**

Use the historical present tense when relating events that occur in fiction.

8. **(F)**

The present participle is used for an action going on at the same time as the main verb.

9. **(B)**

The use of the subordinating conjunction as is a sound choice in this position because it creates an adverb clause that modifies the verbs *focused* and *thought.* The other choices create modifiers of the subject to little effect.

10. **(J)**

Only the use of the words *is that* in this spot forms a noun structure that equates with the noun *answer.* The other choices form adverb clauses that cannot equate with the noun.

RHETORICAL SKILLS

KINDS OF QUESTIONS

Some questions on the English ACT will ask you to choose the most effective introductions and conclusions, both of paragraphs and essays. Others will ask you to select the most logical transitions between sentences or between paragraphs. You will most likely be asked if a passage is appropriate for a particular audience or what kind of supporting details should be added to strengthen a paragraph. You may also be asked whether a particular sentence or paragraph is relevant to the selection.

WORD CHOICE

Diction

Some of the questions on the English Test will require you to decide the appropriateness of a word in its context. A word is *appropriate* if it fits the reader, occasion, and purpose for which the writing is intended.

Wordiness

To avoid wordiness, eliminate language that either duplicates what has already been expressed or adds nothing to the sense of the statement.

Omissions

A common error in written English is the careless omission, especially the omission acceptable in speech but not in writing. Some of these are likely to pop up on the ACT.

MINI-QUIZ

The following sample questions represent ways in which the above skills might be tested on the ACT. (On the actual test, questions appear to the right of the underlined words and boxes. Here, however, questions follow the passage.)

(1)

Modern literary criticism is a literary specialty composed of many varying and inharmonious parts. There are, however, five major trends in contemporary criticism that take into account almost every significant critical essay written in the twentieth century. It is the critics' differing opinions on the purpose of literature that create the divisions or schools of modern criticism. These schools or approaches to literature are the moral, the psychological, the sociological, the formalistic, and the archetypal. 1

(2)

The oldest view, the moral approach, originated with Plato when he ordered Homer banished from his fictional utopian republic. "Poetry," said Plato, "by its very nature appeals to the emotions rather than to the intellect and is, therefore, potentially dangerous." Here is the first expression of concern over the effect of literature on life, and this concern becomes the primary concern of the moral critic, who gauges all literature by its ability to aid and comfort man, and convey a higher ideal of life. 2

(3)

As you can imagine, the psychologists got into the act and started linking
<u>3</u>
novels with Freud and Jung and that crowd and their theories that man is
<u>3</u>
a victim of society and his own biological drives. Psychological critics
<u>3</u>
argue that literature that advocates chastity, gentility, and other virtues
is frustrating to the normal drives of man and is therefore unhealthy.
The psychological school studies the author's life as a means of
<u>4</u>
understanding his writings, the characters and their motivation in the
<u>4</u>
literature itself, and the creative process as a psychological evolution.
<u>4</u>

(4)

Looking at what it is that makes folks tick when they get together in
<u>5</u>
towns and the like is what the sociological critic does. A literary work is
<u>5</u>
studied in order to discover the degree to which it acts as a mirror of society
through contemporary social theory and practice. $\boxed{6}$

(5)

Used as an isolated method, each approach to literary commentary
has serious drawbacks, leading to narrow and restrictive readings. Used
collectively, however, the five approaches can deal with every facet of a
work, enabling a balanced and complete interpretation of literature. $\boxed{7}$

(6)

The most influential method of contemporary criticism, however,
is the formalistic, or "new" criticism. Assuming that literature has intrinsic
meaning, the school advocates the close study of texts themselves, rather
than extrinsics such as society or the author's biography. The primary route
<u>8</u>
by which a formalistic critic reveals and expresses his views on a classic
<u>8</u>
work of literature is by means of a very ambitious and comprehensive
<u>8</u>
examination and scrutiny of the text of the novel itself.
<u>8</u>

(7)

The archetypal approach studies literature in its relation to all men,
assuming a "collective unconscious" that binds all men from all time. The
archetypal critic <u>eyeballs</u> a work in an attempt to disclose its reliance on
<u>9</u>
either a specific myth or a universal pattern of thought, both of which
might reveal a man's subconscious attempt to link himself with all
humanity, past and present. $\boxed{10}$

1. This entire passage was probably written for readers who are:

   A. college or college-bound literature students.
   B. poor readers who require supplemental material.
   C. interested in the scientific method.
   D. foreign students preparing for an English proficiency test.

2. Which of the following statements is best supported by the details supplied in paragraph number 2?

   F. The moral view is the most important by far.
   G. The moral approach is really a religious view.
   H. The moral approach is the oldest and most noble of the critical modes.
   J. The moral critical view requires rigid standards of behavior of its adherents.

3. Which of the suggested sentences below make the best introduction to paragraph 3 and the best transition from 2?

   A. NO CHANGE
   B. In contrast to this idea is the psychological approach to literature, a school that originated with Freud and his theory that man is a victim of both the repressive mores of society and his own biological compulsions.
   C. The psychological approach to literature is our next mode of criticism.
   D. Next, we have the psychological school of criticism, a hands-on way of looking at the nitty-gritty of an author's life.

4. Suppose at this point in the passage the author wanted to revise the third paragraph so that it is more appropriate for younger students? Which of the following revisions of this sentence would accomplish that purpose most effectively?

   F. NO CHANGE
   G. The Freudian and post-Jungian school focuses upon the subject's experiential past as a means of explicating his creative output, personality projections, and basic drives, as well as the genesis of the creative process.
   H. This way of talking about a book we have read lets us think about the author's life to see if it is related to the story, to think about the characters in the story and decide whether or not they make sense, and to ask why the author wrote the book.
   J. Psychological criticism tells us to look at the authors first, as if the author's life really always tells you that much. Anyway, you study the author's life and supposedly learn more about the book from an analytical, what-makes-us-tick point of view.

5. **A.** NO CHANGE
   B. As the boy's choir did in William Golding's novel *The Lord of the Flies*, man tends to organize his ruling bodies according to his inner drives.
   C. When people get together, whether they are savages or yuppies, they form social units. This process is what the sociological critic studies.
   D. The study of man's drives when he is organized into a state is the province of the sociological critic.

6. What kind of supporting details could strengthen this paragraph?

  F. A list of American states and major cities.
  G. A list of authors that have written "sociological novels."
  H. Examples of ways a novel can mirror contemporary society.
  J. A consistent way to gauge the quality of life.

7. This paragraph is organized according to which of the following schemes?

  A. A general statement followed by a number of specific examples.
  B. A narrative structure controlled by the events being described.
  C. A typical classification/division format where the topic is broken down into groups and labeled.
  D. A simple contrasting paragraph, with the point on the first sentence contrasting sharply with the next.

8. F. NO CHANGE
  G. A close, in-depth examination of a work's structure and language is the primary characteristic of this highly analytical mode of commentary.
  H. A close, in-depth examination in which scholars scrutinize very minutely the actual text of a work of literature is the main primary characteristic of this highly analytical mode of commentary.
  J. The main way a critic reports on a book is really by looking very closely at the words and sentences.

9. A. NO CHANGE
  B. peruses
  C. ponders
  D. studies

10. Choose the sequence of paragraph numbers that makes the structure of the passage most logical.

  F. 1, 3, 5, 6, 7, 4, 2.
  G. 1, 2, 4, 3, 7, 6, 5.
  H. 1, 2, 3, 4, 6, 7, 5.
  J. 1, 2, 7, 6, 5, 4, 3

Answers and Explanations

1. **(A)**

The subject and tone of the passage clearly addresses serious students of literature.

2. **(H)**

The details supplied in paragraph 2 bear out solely this statement.

3. **(B)**

This choice highlights the obvious contrast between the critical schools described in the two paragraphs, and effectively introduces the topic that is supported in the paragraph. The other choices either fall short of introducing the paragraph topic or depart markedly from the style and tone of the passage.

4. **(H)**

This choice is written for a younger reading level, yet roughly covers the main points of the original sentence. The other choices (G and J) either do not communicate the main points of the original sentence, or are not written for young readers.

5. **(D)**

Only this choice concludes the paragraph clearly and effectively, while maintaining the style of the passage.

6. **(H)**

The original paragraph *does* lack specific examples of literary works that mirror their contemporary society. The information conveyed in the other choices is off the topic of the paragraph.

7. **(D)**

The paragraph does, indeed, contain two sentences, one contrasting sharply with the other.

8. **(G)**

This choice is the only one that expresses the primary characteristics of the formalistic critic with economy of language and in a style consistent with that of the passage. The other choices are either wordy or lacking in content or compatible style.

9. **(D)**

The word *studies* is consistent with the tone of the passage. The other choices suggest activities that are other than scholarly.

10. **(H)**

The paragraphs in this passage are linked to each other by means of transitional statements, and by means of the controlling order established near the end of paragraph 1.

SAMPLE ENGLISH TEST

The ACT English Test consists of five prose passages and 75 questions, with a 45-minute time limit. The test is designed to measure your ability to discern and remedy errors and awkwardness in punctuation, grammar and usage, and sentence structure. You will also find questions about the prose—for whom the passage is intended, for example, or how the paragraph or sentence might be improved with reorganization or additional material.

The following two practice passages are intended to familiarize you with questions that approximate those on the ACT. Each passage is followed by 30 multiple-choice questions. These passages are approximately double the length of the ones on the actual test. If you want to time yourself, allow 18 minutes to read each passage and answer the questions.

> _Directions:_ The following test consists of 60 items. Some concern underlined words and phrases in context; others ask general questions about the passages. Most of the underlined sections contain errors or inappropriate expressions. You are asked to compare each with the four alternative answer choices. If you consider the original version best, choose letter A or F: NO CHANGE. For each question, select the alternative you think best. Read each passage through before answering the questions based on it. (On the actual test, questions appear to the right of the underlined words and boxes. Here, however, questions follow the passage.)

Note

Answers and explanations appear at the end of each passage.

Passage 1

A peaceful oasis in the midst of the bustling San Fernando Valley, San Fernando Mission has been declared a historic cultural monument by the City of Los Angeles, according to a bronze plaque at the entrance to the mission. In addition to being an active <u>religion</u> center, <u>many tourists come</u>
₁ <u>to the mission each year</u> to stroll through the well-tended grounds and
₂
<u>they admire</u> the unique architecture of the restored mission buildings.
₃
The entrance to the mission quadrangle opens <u>onto</u> the east garden, a
₄
large <u>grass covered</u> courtyard in the middle of which is a flower-shaped
₅

fountain modeled after one that stands in Cordova, Spain. Wind rustles through the branches of the trees, and water tinkles in the fountain, <u>also</u> the
6
sounds of traffic outside the walls only accentuate the tranquility of the setting. Strolling about the grounds, the smell of spring flowers scenting the air and the sunlight warm upon your back, <u>one can easily</u> imagine being
7
back two hundred years during the time of the founding of the mission. The present-day mission compound, however, with its air of serenity and unhurried repose, is nothing like the mission in its heyday, when it was the scene of bustling activity and <u>the labor was diligent</u> by hundreds of Indians
8
under the direction of a few Spanish Franciscan padres.

San Fernando Mission, founded in 1779 by Padre Fermin Lasuen and named for a saintly king of thirteenth-century Spain, <u>it was</u> the seventeenth
9
of California's twenty-one missions <u>stretching</u> in a chain from San Francisco
10
to San Diego. The purpose of the mission chain was to create centers of Christian civilization <u>who would want</u> to convert the California Indians and
11
prepare them for Spanish citizenship.

Mission San Francisco was established <u>centrally</u> between the missions
12
of San Buenaventura and San Gabriel, at a distance of one day's journey from each. The <u>site chosen</u> for the <u>mission—land</u> that had been used by
13   14
Don Francisco Reyes, first mayor of the Pueblo de Los Angeles, to graze cattle—was rich in water, in fertile, arable soil, and <u>it had an Indian</u>
15
<u>population</u>, all necessary elements for a successful mission.
15
The chapel—an exact replica of the original, which was built between 1804 and 1806 and destroyed by the 1971 earthquake—is long and narrow, with adobe walls decorated by frescoes of native designs. The overall effect of the frescoes, the colorful Spanish altar hangings, and the stations of the Cross <u>are</u>, as one writer put it, "a glorious, if barbaric spectacle!"
16
Although there <u>is a number of</u> windows on the south wall of the chapel,
17
there is only one window on the north wall. It is not known whether this architectural detail was meant to keep out cold winds from the nearby mountains or <u>as a defense against a potential attack by hostile Indians.</u>
18
Behind the chapel is a cemetery, where many of the natives and other early settlers attached to the mission were buried. Only a few wooden crosses and <u>there is one large gravestone</u> mark the final resting places
19

of approximately 2,000 persons buried there. Beyond the burial grounds is a <u>fountain: fed</u> by a small stream and surrounded <u>in</u> foliage and a flower garden.
₂₀ ₂₁

<u>Across the compound, stands</u> the "convento"—the largest original mission building in California—with its famous corridor of twenty-one Roman arches that today <u>front</u> San Fernando Mission Road. Two stories high, with four-foot-thick adobe <u>walls that keeps</u> the inside cool on even the hottest summer <u>day.</u> It served as living quarters for the missionaries and visitors in the early 1800's. <u>Tourists taking pictures inside the mission should bring high-speed color film.</u>
₂₂ ₂₃ ₂₄ ₂₅ ₂₆

Just inside the entrance hall <u>an atmosphere is able to be felt</u> of great age, perhaps due in part to the stillness that seems to echo within the brick-floored rooms. Then again, this feeling might be due to the <u>odor, emanating</u> from the nearby wine cellar, a musty smell that grows stronger as one moves slowly down the whitewashed <u>stairs—past</u> a deep tub cut from rock where grapes were once pressed underfoot. ☐30
₂₇ ₂₈ ₂₉

1. **A.** NO CHANGE
   B. religions
   C. religious
   D. more religious

2. **F.** NO CHANGE
   G. many tourists are invited to the Mission each year
   H. it is a place where many tourists come each year
   J. people come

3. **A.** NO CHANGE
   B. they were admiring
   C. admiring
   D. admire

4. **F.** NO CHANGE
   G. out into
   H. wide into
   J. for

5. A. NO CHANGE
   B. grass-covered
   C. grass covering
   D. grass, covered

6 F. NO CHANGE
   G. while
   H. moreover,
   J. furthermore,

7. A. NO CHANGE
   B. you can easily
   C. it seems easy to
   D. one easily

8. F. NO CHANGE
   G. diligent labor
   H. that labor was industrious
   J. labor that was diligent

9. A. NO CHANGE
   B. it had been
   C. it will be
   D. was

10. F. NO CHANGE
   G. and it stretched
   H. that was stretching
   J. widely stretched out

11. A. NO CHANGE
   B. which was hoping
   C. seeking
   D. needing

12. F. NO CHANGE
   G. in a great spot
   H. well within and
   J. OMIT the underlined phrase.

13. A. NO CHANGE
   B. cite chosen
   C. sight chose
   D. site choosed

14. **F.** NO CHANGE
    G. Mission: land
    H. Mission; land
    J. Mission. Land

15. **A.** NO CHANGE
    B. there also were Indians,
    C. it had Indians,
    D. in an Indian population,

16. **F.** NO CHANGE
    G. was
    H. is
    J. will have been

17. **A.** NO CHANGE
    B. were a number of
    C. are a number of
    D. should be a number of

18. **F.** NO CHANGE
    G. hostile Indians.
    H. defending against an Indian attack.
    J. an attack against hostile Indians.

19. **A.** NO CHANGE
    B. one large gravestone
    C. there might have been a gravestone
    D. there most likely is a gravestone

20. **F.** NO CHANGE
    G. fountain. Fed
    H. fountain; fed
    J. fountain fed

21. **A.** NO CHANGE
    B. overhead in the
    C. about with
    D. by

22. **F.** NO CHANGE
    G. Across the compound, stood
    H. Across the compound stands
    J. Across the compound, is standing

23. A. NO CHANGE
   B. fronts
   C. fronting
   D. fronted

24. F. NO CHANGE
   G. walls, that keep
   H. , walls that keep
   J. walls, that keeps

25. A. NO CHANGE
   B. day, it
   C. day—it
   D. day: it

26. F. NO CHANGE
   G. Retain the position of this sentence in the passage but place it in its own paragraph.
   H. Move this sentence to the beginning of the paragraph.
   J. OMIT the underlined sentence.

27. A. NO CHANGE
   B. may be feeling an atmosphere
   C. one feels an atmosphere
   D. an atmosphere can be felt

28. F. NO CHANGE
   G. odor; emanating
   H. odor. Emanating
   J. odor emanating

29. A. NO CHANGE
   B. stairs, passed
   C. stairs; passed
   D. stairs, past

30. Is the mention of the odor appropriate and effective at the end of this passage?
   F. No, because it introduces a new element at the end of the passage.
   G. Yes, because the musty odors of old buildings and old wine presses appropriately reflect the age of this historic mission.
   H. Yes, because the description of the odor is somewhat suspenseful, and mentioning it gives a mysterious quality to the passage.
   J. No, because an odor is generally perceived as offensive.

Answer Key

1. C	6. G	11. C	16. H	21. D	26. J
2. H	7. B	12. J	17. C	22. H	27. C
3. D	8. G	13. A	18. G	23. B	28. J
4. F	9. D	14. F	19. B	24. H	29. D
5. B	10. F	15. D	20. J	25. B	30. G

Answer Explanations

1. **(C)**

The underlined word is intended to modify the noun *center* and so must be an adjective.

2. **(H)**

The introductory phrase *In addition to being an active [religious] center* clearly refers to the mission, not the tourists. Therefore, the main clause must begin with the word *mission* or with the referent pronoun *it*.

3. **(D)**

The infinitive *to admire* is parallel in construction with *to stroll*, with which it is paired: *to stroll . . . and to admire.*

4. **(F)**

No other choice is idiomatically correct.

5. **(B)**

Hyphenate a compound adjective that precedes the noun it modifies.

6. **(G)**

Conjunctive adverbs (such as *also, moreover*, and *furthermore*) used to join clauses must be preceded by a semicolon. *While*, a subordinating conjunction used to introduce an adverb clause, is properly preceded by a comma.

7. **(B)**

Avoid a shift in point of view, from the second person *your* to the third person *one*. Choice C incorrectly makes *it* the word modified by the introductory participial phrase.

8. **(G)**

The prepositional phrase *of bustling activity* requires a parallel object, *diligent labor*. Choice J is wordy.

9. **(D)**

The sentence has two subjects: *San Fernando/it. It* is unnecessary.

10. **(F)**

The participial phrase *stretching in a chain* ... correctly modifies the noun *missions*. Choice G incorrectly uses *it* to refer to the plural word *missions*. H also incorrectly uses a singular form, *was*, which does not agree with *missions*, the antecedent of *that*. J is wordy.

11. **(C)**

The other options either carry meanings inappropriate to the sense of the passage or contain faulty grammar.

12. **(J)**

Centrally repeats the idea of *at a distance of one day's journey from each. In a great spot* is too colloquial for this passage. Choice H is wordy.

13. **(A)**

The correct word to use here is *site*, meaning location. The verb forms *chose* and *choosed* in choices C and D are incorrect.

14. **(F)**

A pair of dashes precedes and follows an interrupting parenthetical element.

15. **(D)**

Only this option is parallel with the other prepositional phrases: *in water, in ... soil, and in ... population.*

16. **(H)**

The singular subject *effect* requires the singular verb *is*. The predominant tense of the passage is the present.

17. **(C)**

The phrase *a number of* is plural in meaning and takes the plural verb *are*. Choice B is wrong, since the predominant tense of the passage is the present. D changes the meaning of the clause.

18. **(G)**

The infinitive phrase *to keep out* needs a parallel second object: *to keep out cold winds . . . or hostile Indians.*

19. **(B)**

A simple noun is needed to form the other half of the compound subject: *crosses and . . . gravestone.*

20. **(J)**

The participial phrase *fed by a small stream* is a restrictive modifier and should not be separated from the noun it modifies, *fountain*, by a punctuation mark. Choice G introduces a sentence fragment.

21. **(D)**

The correct idiom is *surrounded by*.

22. **(H)**

In an inverted sentence, do not use a comma to separate a short adverb construction from the verb it modifies.

23. **(B)**

The subject of the verb *front* is the relative pronoun *that*, which refers to the singular noun *corridor*, not the plural *arches*. Thus, the correct verb form is *fronts*. Choice C is a participle, not a verb form. D shifts to the past tense.

24. **(H)**

The subject of the verb *keep* is the relative pronoun *that*, which refers to the plural noun *walls*. Do not use a comma to separate a restrictive clause from the word it modifies (G and J).

25. **(B)**

A comma is used to separate the introductory phrase *two stories high . . . day* from the main clause of the sentence. Choice A creates a sentence fragment.

26. **(J)**

This sentence has no bearing on the topic of the passage.

27. **(C)**

As a rule, it is better to avoid the passive voice. The active voice is more direct and forceful.

28. **(J)**

The participial phrase *emanating from the nearby wine cellar* is a restrictive modifier and cannot be set off by commas. Choice H introduces a sentence fragment.

29. **(D)**

A comma is called for at this point for clarity. A dash is too great a mark of separation. Choices B and C incorrectly substitute the verb form *passed* for the preposition *past*.

30. **(G)**

This descriptive paragraph adds a meaningful sense impression to the passage.

Passage 2

Each of the paragraphs in this passage is numbered, but may not be in the most logical position. The last question asks you to select the correct number.

(1)

Sometime around the middle of January, after reading about standard organic gardening techniques, prospective home gardeners should make a list of the vegetables most enjoyed by their families. Sitting down with a few seed catalogs, preferably those from local companies such as Santa Rosa Gardening Co. or Burbank Farms—whose catalogs contain detailing
                              1   2
planting instructions for Southern California, including the proper planting dates for each of the distinct climatic regions—they should review the directions for growing vegetables, narrowing the choices to crops easy to grow. And although January is an ideal time here to plant such winter vegetables such as beets, broccoli, peas, lettuce, and swiss chard, novice
                         3
gardeners might do well to plan a spring garden as a first effort. For one thing, summer vegetables like tomatoes, zucchini, and beans are easy to grow, they require little in the way of additional care once they have been
     4

planted and are growing well. And for another, spring—traditionally a time of renewal—seems the right time of year to begin a gardening project.

(2)

These differences make it impossible <u>that gardeners</u> in Southern California
5
to follow <u>in an explicit way</u> the advice given in nationally circulated
6
magazines and books on organic gardening. Instead, these methods <u>must</u>
7
<u>be adopted</u> to the particular climate in this area. Some suggestions follow
7
that may be helpful to fellow gardeners in the San Fernando Valley region.

(3)

Just as organic gardening differs from gardening with the help of a
chemical <u>company. Gardening</u> in Southern California differs dramatically
8
from gardening in almost every other part of the country. For one thing,
crops <u>will be planted</u> here almost any time during the year, whereas spring
9
gardens are the rule in most other parts of the country. Diversity of weather
systems within the relatively small area that <u>encompassing</u> Southern
10
California is another distinction. For instance, coastal communities
experience cool, damp weather for much of the year, while the San
Fernando and San Gabriel valleys are blistering hot in summer and cold in
<u>winter—some</u> inland valleys even encounter frost and freezing
11
temperatures! Thus, although these areas <u>separate</u> by fewer than fifty
12
miles, the climates are disparate, necessitating the use of distinct
gardening techniques for each locale.

(4)

After deciding what vegetables to grow, <u>a rough draft is made</u> of the
13
garden, which should be located in an area of <u>flat well-drained</u> ground that
14
<u>has gotten</u> at least six full hours of sun daily. Taller-growing crops should
15
be put on the north side of the garden so that they do not shade any low-
growing <u>vegetables; except</u> those that cannot survive the intense summer
16
sun. The latter include lettuce and many other greens. The rows, or beds,
should be wide enough to accommodate the <u>particular kind of a</u> crop to be
17
grown. The wider the rows, of course, the more crops the garden <u>will have</u>
18

produced. This is known as "intensive gardening" and is ideal for small
<u> </u>   <u> </u>
18   19
backyard gardens. One suggestion is to make the beds three feet wide,

with enough space between them to allow easy access for cultivating,

weeding, and to harvest mature plants. However, two-foot beds are
<u>   </u>
20

also okay.
<u>   </u>
21

(5)

After the plan has been drawn up and the seeds will be ordered, the next
<u>   </u>
22
step is to prepare the soil properly, one of the most important procedures
<u>   </u>
23
in insuring a successful harvest. Testing the soil for deficiencies is a must;
<u>   </u>
24
soil-testing kits are available from most home improvement stores and
<u>   </u>
24
gardening centers. The organic gardening books and magazines

mentioned earlier go into heavy detail regarding soil composition, testing,
<u>   </u>
25
and preparation. Following their recommendations will contribute for the
<u>   </u>
26
success for the gardening project.
<u>   </u>
26

(6)

Once the condition of the soil is ascertained by the person doing the
<u>   </u>
27
gardening, deficient elements (such as phosphorus, potassium,
<u>   </u>
27
magnesium, or sulphur) can be added. In addition to these minerals;
<u>   </u>   <u>   </u>
27   28
however, enough fertilizer to get the seedlings off to a good start should be
<u>   </u>
28
incorporated into the soil. ☐29 ☐30

1. A. NO CHANGE
   B. Farms—who's
   C. Farms; whose
   D. Farms. Whose

2. F. NO CHANGE
   G. details of
   H. detailed
   J. in detailed

3. A. NO CHANGE
   B. like
   C. such as;
   D. as

4. **F.** NO CHANGE
   G. grow. Since these vegetables require
   H. grow. Requiring
   J. grow, requiring

5. **A.** NO CHANGE
   B. to be a gardener
   C. to go on being a gardener
   D. for gardeners

6. **F.** NO CHANGE
   G. explicitly
   H. in a more explicit way
   J. explicitly and definitely

7. **A.** NO CHANGE
   B. should be adopted
   C. must be adapted
   D. must adopt

8. **F.** NO CHANGE
   G. company; gardening
   H. company, gardening
   J. company: gardening

9. **A.** NO CHANGE
   B. can be planted
   C. have been planted
   D. ought to be planted

10. **F.** NO CHANGE
    G. encompassed
    H. has encompassed
    J. encompasses

11. **A.** NO CHANGE
    B. winter;—some
    C. winter—Some
    D. winter, some

12. **F.** NO CHANGE
    G. are separated
    H. must be separated
    J. were separated

13. A. NO CHANGE
   B. a rough draft should be made
   C. the gardener should make a rough draft
   D. it is necessary to make a rough draft

14. F. NO CHANGE
   G. flat, well-drained
   H. flat, well drained
   J. flat and well drained

15. A. NO CHANGE
   B. will have gotten
   C. got
   D. gets

16. F. NO CHANGE
   G. vegetables except
   H. vegetables: except
   J. vegetables. Except

17. A. NO CHANGE
   B. kind of a
   C. kinds of a
   D. OMIT the underlined words.

18. F. NO CHANGE
   G. would of produced.
   H. will produce.
   J. is producing.

19. A. NO CHANGE
   B. This close spacing
   C. Which
   D. This here

20. F. NO CHANGE
   G. harvesting
   H. to be harvesting
   J. so we can harvest the

21. A. NO CHANGE
   B. alright.
   C. all right.
   D. allright.

22. **F.** NO CHANGE
    G. should be ordered,
    H. were ordered,
    J. have been ordered,

23. **A.** NO CHANGE
    B. properly. One
    C. properly; one
    D. properly; it is one

24. **F.** NO CHANGE
    G. must, as soil-testing
    H. must, soil-testing
    J. must because soil-testing

25. **A.** NO CHANGE
    B. much detail
    C. exquisite detail
    D. alot of detail

26. **F.** NO CHANGE
    G. in the success
    H. to the success
    J. for the successfulness

27. **A.** NO CHANGE
    B. Once the condition of the soil is ascertained by the gardener, elements that are lacking in sufficient quantity (such as phosphorus, potassium, magnesium, or sulphur) can be added by the gardener.
    C. Once the gardener ascertains the condition of the soil, he or she can add deficient elements (such as phosphorus, potassium, magnesium, or sulphur).
    D. Once, the gardener ascertains the condition of the soil, deficient elements (such as: phosphorus, potassium, magnesium, or sulphur) can be added.

28. **F.** NO CHANGE
    G. minerals however,
    H. minerals, however—
    J. minerals, however,

29. This passage is most likely directed to readers who:

    A. are experts in gardening and need little advice.
    B. are residents of Southern California and have never had a garden.
    C. are residents of Freeport, Maine, and are just curious about gardening in a warmer state.
    D. have gardened so much that they hope never to see another bud.

30. Select the correct order of the numbered paragraphs so that the passage will read in logical sequence.

   F. NO CHANGE
   G. 3, 2, 1, 4, 5, 6
   H. 1, 2, 4, 5, 3, 6
   J. 4, 2, 3, 1, 5, 6

Answer Key

1. A	6. G	11. A	16. G	21. C	26. H
2. H	7. C	12. G	17. D	22. J	27. C
3. D	8. H	13. C	18. H	23. A	28. J
4. J	9. B	14. G	19. B	24. F	29. B
5. D	10. J	15. D	20. G	25. B	30. G

Answer Explanations

1. **(A)**

A pair of dashes is used to separate a parenthetical element from the rest of the sentence; a comma is not used with the dash. Choice B (who's) is a contraction of who is or who has, neither of which makes sense in this context. Choice D introduces a sentence fragment.

2. **(H)**

The correct choice is the past participle *detailed*, which acts as an adjective to modify the noun phrase *planting instructions*. The present participle *detailing* carries meaning that does not apply to this sentence. Choice J adds a word that does not make sense in the structure of the sentence.

3. **(D)**

The sentence already contains the word *such* (*such winter vegetables as*). Choice B offers an ungrammatical construction, *such . . . like*.

4. **(J)**

This is the only correct option. The other choices produce sentence fragments or a comma splice.

5. **(D)**

Idiomatic English requires the contruction *impossible for gardeners . . . to follow.*

6. **(G)**

The other choices are wordy or redundant.

7. **(C)**

The correct word here is *adapted,* meaning modified to suit. *Adopted* means taken as is.

8. **(H)**

Use a comma to separate an introductory adverb clause from the main clause.

9. **(B)**

The verb phrase *can be planted* also means *are planted* in the context of this sentence. The other options do not carry this essential additional meaning.

10. **(J)**

Use the present tense to express generally true statements.

11. **(A)**

A dash is used for emphasis to separate a parenthetical comment from the rest of the sentence. It is not used together with a semicolon. Choice C incorrectly capitalizes the word *some.* D introduces a comma splice.

12. **(G)**

The passive voice is required when the subject is acted upon. The present tense is consistent with the rest of the passage.

13. **(C)**

Without a logical noun to modify (*gardener,* for example), the introductory phrase would dangle.

14. **(G)**

Place a comma between coordinate adjectives. The compound adjective *well-drained* takes a hyphen when it precedes the noun it modifies.

15. **(D)**

The predominant tense in this passage is the present.

16. **(G)**

Do not use a punctuation mark to separate a restrictive phrase from the word it modifies. The phrase beginning *except those . . .* limits *low growing vegetables.* Choice J would create a sentence fragment.

17. **(D)**

The other choices are unnecessarily wordy and also introduce an error. (*Kind of a* is not idiomatic English.)

18. **(H)**

The simple future tense, showing expectation, is appropriate here because the passage is set in the present tense. *Would of* is incorrect grammatically.

19. **(B)**

The pronoun *This* needs a specific antecedent for clear reference. Since there is none, the meaning of *This* has to be clarified. Choice C introduces a sentence fragment. D is redundant, as *here* repeats the meaning of *This*.

20. **(G)**

The gerund *harvesting* is required, to be parallel with the other gerunds, *cultivating* and *weeding*.

21. **(C)**

Choice A is colloquial. B and D are misspellings.

22. **(J)**

The verb must agree in tense with *has been drawn*.

23. **(A)**

Set off a nonrestrictive appositive phrase with a comma. Choice B introduces a sentence fragment; D, a comma splice.

24. **(F)**

A semicolon is used to separate clauses that are closely related. The transitional words in Choices G and J change the meaning. H creates a comma-splice sentence.

25. **(B)**

The other options are either inappropriate or incorrect.

26. **(H)**

The correct idiom is *contribute to*.

27. **(C)**

The passive voice (*is ascertained* and *can be added*) is less forceful and usually results in more wordy sentences than the active voice. Choice D incorrectly places a comma after the conjunction *Once* and a colon after *such as*.

28. **(J)**

The word *however* is used here as an adverb, not as a conjunctive adverb introducing a clause, and so should be set off by commas as a simple parenthetical word.

29. **(B)**

The references to the southwestern climate, to aids for novice gardeners, and to gardening techniques indicate that this article is addressed primarily to first-time gardeners in Southern California.

30. **(G)**

Paragraph (3) is clearly the introduction to this passage; it makes general statements about the topic that are supported by data in subsequent paragraphs. The phrase *These differences* that begins paragraph (2) directly relates to the ending of paragraph (3). The step-by-step process begins with paragraph (1) and continues in order with paragraphs (4), (5), and (6).

Preparing for the Mathematics Test

3

DESCRIPTION OF THE MATHEMATICS TEST

The ACT test in mathematics is a 60-minute test designed to evaluate your mathematical achievement in courses commonly taught in high school. This test includes questions from the areas of pre-algebra, algebra, plane geometry, intermediate algebra, coordinate geometry, and trigonometry.

STRATEGY

The review in this chapter includes many examples of problems with detailed commentary on their solutions, as well as many practice exercises. The practice exercises also have complete solutions and explanations. The best plan is to work each practice problem on your own, and then check your solution with the one given in this book. If your answer is the same, you can be reasonably sure you did the problem correctly, even though your procedure may be different. Also, the chapter is intended to be review, not a textbook on mathematics. No attempt is made to prove most statements; they are merely presented as facts. If you want justification for a given statement or if you want more practice on a particular topic, consult a textbook that covers the material in a nonreview manner.

ARITHMETIC/PRE-ALGEBRA

Three Meanings of the Symbol "−"

Many students have problems with the symbol $-$. The reason is that the symbol actually has three distinct meanings. So make sure you have a clear understanding of them.

1. When this symbol appears between two numbers, it always means "subtract." Thus $7 - 4$ can be read either as "7 subtract 4" or "7 minus 4."
2. When the symbol appears to the left of a numeral, it is properly read as "negative." Thus, -8 is read as "negative 8." The word *negative* means that the number is located to the left of zero on the number line.

3. In any other position, however, the symbol "–" should be read as "opposite." In particular:

$-x$ means the opposite of x.

$-(-9)$ means the opposite of negative 9.

$-(a + b)$ means the opposite of the sum of a and b.

$-[-(-8)]$ means the opposite of the opposite of negative 8.

-5^2 means the opposite of 5 squared.

Absolute Value

The absolute value of any number is its distance from the origin on a number line. The symbol for this operation is $|x|$. An alternative (and more algebraic) definition of absolute value is

$$|x| = \begin{cases} x & \text{if } x \geq 0 \\ -x & \text{if } x < 0 \end{cases}$$

Addition

If the two numbers are either both positive or both negative, add the absolute values of the numbers and prefix the answer with the sign that is common to the original numbers.

$$(-2) + (-5) = -7 \quad 5 + 3 = 8 \quad -4 + (-6) = -10$$

If the two numbers have opposite signs, subtract the absolute values of the numbers (the smaller from the larger) and prefix the answer with the sign of the original number that has the larger absolute value.

$$-7 + 9 = 2 \quad 4 + (-3) = 1 \quad 5 + (-9) = -4$$

Subtraction

The definition of subtraction is

$$a - b = a + (-b)$$

This definition says, "a minus b equals a plus the opposite of b." In other words, to subtract, add the opposite of the number following the subtraction sign.

- $2 - 5$
  $= 2 + (-5)$
  $= -3$

  Change the operation to addition and replace the number following the subtraction sign by its opposite. Follow the rules for addition.

- $5 - (-3)$
  $= 5 + 3$
  $= 8$

  Change to addition, replace second number by its opposite. Add.

- $-7 - 8$ Change to addition, replace second number by its oppo-
  $= -7 + (-8)$ site. Add.
  $= -15$
- $-2 - (-4)$
  $= -2 + 4$
  $= 2$

Multiplication

To multiply two numbers, multiply their absolute values and prefix the answer with a sign determined by the following rule:

If the two numbers have the same sign, the product is positive, $+$. The sign of a positive number is always optional. If the two numbers have opposite signs, the product is negative, $-$.

$$(-3)(4)=-12 \qquad (-5)(-4)=20 \qquad 3(-7)=-21$$

Division

The rule for division is similar to the rule for multiplication. Divide the absolute values of the numbers, and prefix the answer with a sign determined by the following rule:

If the two numbers have the same sign, choose $+$. If the two numbers have opposite signs, choose $-$.

Of course, division by zero is undefined.

$$-15 \div 3 = -5$$
$$\frac{-28}{-7} = 4$$
$$\frac{0}{-8} = 0$$
$$\frac{28}{0} \text{ is undefined.}$$
$$\frac{0}{0} \text{ is undefined.}$$

Exponents for Whole Numbers, n, and Real Numbers, x

For whole numbers, n, and real numbers, x:

$$x^n = x \cdot x \cdot x \cdot \ldots \cdot x \qquad (n \text{ factors of the base } x)$$
$$x^1 = x$$
$$x^0 = 1, x \neq 0$$

It is important to remember that any exponent always refers only to the symbol immediately to its left. Thus:

$5^3 = 5 \cdot 5 \cdot 5 = 25 \cdot 5 = 125$

$-2^4 = -(2 \cdot 2 \cdot 2 \cdot 2) = -16$ (-2^4 is read as "the opposite of 2 to the fourth power.")

Order of Operation

So that everyone gets the same answer for an expression like

$$1 + 3 \cdot 4 \qquad \text{or} \qquad -2^2,$$

the order in which operations are to be performed must be defined.

ORDER OF OPERATION RULES

1. Perform all operations inside grouping symbols first. Grouping symbols include parentheses: ( ), brackets: [ ], braces: { }, and a bar: $\dfrac{2+3}{7}$ or $\sqrt{9+16}$

2. Do all roots and exponents in order from left to right.

3. Do all multiplications and divisions in order from left to right. (This rule does NOT say, "Do all multiplications and then do all divisions.")

4. Do all additions and subtractions (and opposites) in order from left to right.

PRACTICE EXERCISES

Perform the indicated operations.

1. $3 - 5 \cdot 7$
2. $-2(3 - 4)^3 - 2$
3. $5\{2[3(4 + 1) - 3] - 2\} - 7$
4. $\dfrac{3(-4)}{2} + (-2)^2(3) - (-3)(-3)^2 + \dfrac{-5}{-1}$
5. -5^2
6. $(-5)^2$

Solutions

1. $3 - 5 \cdot 7 = 3 - 35 = 3 + (-35) = -32$
2. $-2(3 - 4)^3 - 2 = -2[3 + (-4)]^3 - 2$
   $\qquad\qquad\qquad\quad = -2(-1)^3 - 2$
   $\qquad\qquad\qquad\quad = -2(-1) - 2 = 2 - 2$
   $\qquad\qquad\qquad\quad = 2 + (-2) = 0$

3. $5\{2[3(4 + 1) - 3] - 2\} - 7$

$\quad = 5\{2[3(5) -3] - 2\} - 7$

$\quad = 5\{2[15 - 3] - 2\} - 7$

$\quad = 5\{2[15 + (-3)] - 2\} - 7$

$\quad = 5\{2[12] - 2\} - 7$

$\quad = 5\{24 - 2\} - 7$

$\quad = 5\{24 + (-2)\} - 7$

$\quad = 5\{22\} - 7 = 110 - 7$

$\quad = 110 + (-7) = 103$

(These steps show extreme detail. Many steps may be omitted.)

4. $\dfrac{3(-4)}{2} + (-2)^2(3) - (-3)(-3)^2 + \dfrac{-5}{-1}$

$\quad = \dfrac{3(-4)}{2} + 4(3) - (-3)(9) + \dfrac{-5}{-1}$

$\quad = \dfrac{-12}{2} + 12 - (-27) + 5$

$\quad = -6 + 12 - (-27) + 5$

$\quad = -6 + 12 + 27 + 5$

$\quad = 6 + 27 + 5$

$\quad = 33 + 5 = 38$

(All multiplications and divisions are done before any additions or subtractions.)

5. -5^2 means "the opposite of five squared"

$\quad -5^2 = -(5 \cdot 5) = -25$

6. $(-5)^2$ means "negative five, squared"

$\quad (-5)^2 = (-5) \cdot (-5) = 25$

Prime and Composite Numbers

A whole number is *prime* if and only if it has exactly two factors.
A whole number greater than 1 is *composite* if and only if it is not prime.

PRACTICE EXERCISES

Determine whether each of the following numbers is prime or composite:

1. 143   **5.** 1

2. 151   **6.** 89

3. -5 **7.** 91

4. 79

Solutions

1. Composite   (The factors are 1, 11, 13, 143.)
2. Prime
3. Neither   (According to the definitions, both prime and composite numbers are whole numbers.)
4. Prime
5. Neither
6. Prime
7. Composite (The factors are 1, 7, 13, 91.)

Prime Factorization

You have to know how to express a whole number as a product of prime factors. For example, $12 = 2 \cdot 2 \cdot 3 = 2^2 \cdot 3$. There are two useful methods to accomplish this task.

Method 1: Factor tree. Find the prime factorization of 72. First name any two factors of 72 (not necessarily prime), say 8 and 9. Each of these numbers can be factored. Continue this until all factors are prime. It is convenient to arrange these numbers in a tree.

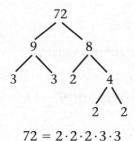

$$72 = 2 \cdot 2 \cdot 2 \cdot 3 \cdot 3$$

Method 2: Repeated division by primes. Determine the prime factorization of 120. First name any prime number that divides 120, and perform the division; then repeat the process with the quotient until the last quotient is also prime. The factorization consists of all the prime divisors and the last quotient.

$$
\begin{array}{r}
5 \\
3 \overline{\smash{)}15} \\
2 \overline{\smash{)}30} \\
2 \overline{\smash{)}60} \\
2 \overline{\smash{)}120}
\end{array}
$$

$$120 = 2 \cdot 2 \cdot 2 \cdot 3 \cdot 5$$

Therefore the prime factorization is $120 = 2 \cdot 2 \cdot 2 \cdot 3 \cdot 5 = 2^3 \cdot 3 \cdot 5$.

You may find that this is easy with a calculator.

PRACTICE EXERCISES

Determine the prime factorization of each of the following numbers:

1. 50   **2.** 300   **3.** 73   **4.** 1617   **5.** 243

Solutions

1. $50 = 2 \cdot 5^2$

2. $300 = 2^2 \cdot 3 \cdot 5^2$

3. 73 is prime, so there is no prime factorization. In particular, the answer is not $1 \cdot 73$.

4. $1617 = 3 \cdot 7^2 \cdot 11$

5. $243 = 3^5$

Fractions

The Fundamental Principle of Fractions states that any fraction is equivalent to a fraction obtained by multiplying the numerator and denominator by the same nonzero number:

$$\frac{a}{b} = \frac{ak}{bk}, \quad b, k \neq 0$$

This property is used to reduce fractions to lowest terms:

$$\frac{12}{18} = \frac{2 \cdot 6}{3 \cdot 6} = \frac{2}{3}$$

$$\frac{90}{108} = \frac{45}{54} \quad (k = 2)$$

(This reduction can be done in stages.)

$$= \frac{5}{6} \quad (k = 9)$$

This same property is used to rewrite a fraction so that it has a specific denominator:

$$\frac{5}{9} = \frac{?}{63} = \frac{35}{63} \quad (k = 7)$$

$$\frac{5}{8} = \frac{?}{120} = \frac{75}{120} \quad (k = 15)$$

PRACTICE EXERCISES

Reduce each fraction to lowest terms.

1. $\dfrac{20}{50}$

3. $\dfrac{60}{84}$

2. $\dfrac{18}{30}$

4. $\dfrac{108}{162}$

Rewrite each fraction so that it has the specified denominator.

5. $\dfrac{4}{5} = \dfrac{?}{70}$

7. $\dfrac{7}{12} = \dfrac{?}{180}$

6. $\dfrac{5}{8} = \dfrac{?}{96}$

Solutions

1. $\dfrac{2}{5}$ ($k = 10$)

5. $\dfrac{56}{70}$ ($k = 14$)

2. $\dfrac{3}{5}$ ($k = 6$)

6. $\dfrac{60}{96}$ ($k = 12$)

3. $\dfrac{5}{7}$ ($k = 12$)

7. $\dfrac{105}{180}$ ($k = 15$)

4. $\dfrac{2}{3}$ ($k = 54$)

Proper and Improper Fractions and Mixed Numbers

An improper fraction can be changed to a mixed number or a whole number. A mixed number is a special form that represents the sum of a whole number and a proper fraction:

$$\frac{7}{5} = 1 + \frac{2}{5} = 1\frac{2}{5}$$

To determine the mixed number that is equivalent to an improper fraction, divide the denominator into the numerator. The quotient becomes the whole number part of the mixed number, and the remainder becomes the numerator of the fraction part of the mixed number.

PRACTICE EXERCISES

Change each improper fraction to a corresponding mixed number.

1. $\dfrac{23}{5}$

3. $\dfrac{105}{7}$

2. $\dfrac{87}{13}$

4. $\dfrac{72}{16}$

Change each mixed number to a corresponding improper fraction.

5. $7\dfrac{3}{4}$

7. $5\dfrac{11}{12}$

6. $12\dfrac{3}{7}$

Solutions

1. $4\dfrac{3}{5}$

6. $\dfrac{87}{7}$

2. $6\dfrac{9}{13}$

7. $\dfrac{71}{12}$

3. 15 (not a mixed number)

4. $4\dfrac{1}{2}$ (Be sure to reduce the fraction to lowest terms.)

5. $7\dfrac{3}{4} = \dfrac{31}{4}$ (The numerator is 7(4) + 3 = 31.)

Addition and Subtraction

The rules for addition and subtraction of fractions are as follows:

$$\frac{a}{b} + \frac{c}{b} = \frac{a+c}{b} \text{ and } \frac{a}{b} - \frac{c}{b} = \frac{a-c}{b}$$

To add or subtract fractions with the same denominator, add or subtract the numerators and keep the same denominator. These rules are very easy to apply; however, difficulty with these operations comes in four areas:

1. If the fractions do not have the same denominators, they must first be changed so that there is a common denominator. For example:

• $\dfrac{5}{12} + \dfrac{7}{16} = \dfrac{20}{48} + \dfrac{21}{48} = \dfrac{41}{48}$ The lowest common multiple of 12 and 16 is 48.

2. If the numbers to be added or subtracted are given as mixed numbers, there are two methods of performing the operations. For example:

- $3\dfrac{2}{3} + 5\dfrac{1}{2} = 3\dfrac{4}{6} + 5\dfrac{3}{6}$ Add the fraction parts and whole number parts separately.

$\quad\quad = 8\dfrac{7}{6}$ Since the fraction part is an improper fraction, the answer must be expressed in simplest form.

$\quad\quad = 8 + 1\dfrac{1}{6} = 9\dfrac{1}{6}$

OR

- $3\dfrac{2}{3} + 5\dfrac{1}{2} = \dfrac{11}{3} + \dfrac{11}{2}$

$\quad\quad = \dfrac{22}{6} + \dfrac{33}{6}$ Write each mixed number as an improper fraction and then add according to the rule.

$\quad\quad = \dfrac{55}{6} = 9\dfrac{1}{6}$ Change the answer back to a mixed number.

3. The answers must normally be expressed in simplest form.

$\dfrac{1}{6} + \dfrac{1}{2} = \dfrac{1}{6} + \dfrac{3}{6} = \dfrac{4}{6} = \dfrac{2}{3}$ The answer has been reduced.

4. In subtraction of mixed numbers, borrowing or regrouping must be done carefully.

$5\dfrac{2}{3} - 1\dfrac{3}{4} = 5\dfrac{8}{12} - 1\dfrac{9}{12}$ Borrow 1 from the 5 and add it to the fraction part of the mixed number

$\quad\quad = 4\dfrac{20}{12} - 1\dfrac{9}{12}$ $\left(1 + \dfrac{8}{12} = \dfrac{20}{12}\right)$.

$\quad\quad = 3\dfrac{11}{12}$

Some calculators will perform operations with fractions.

PRACTICE EXERCISES

Add or subtract as indicated, and express the answer in simplest form.

1. $\dfrac{3}{7} - \dfrac{1}{9}$

2. $\dfrac{7}{20} + \dfrac{3}{16}$

3. $4\dfrac{1}{2} - 2\dfrac{1}{3}$

4. $8 - 5\dfrac{5}{8}$

5. $3\dfrac{2}{5} - 1\dfrac{3}{4}$

6. $\left(-2\dfrac{3}{5}\right) + 1\dfrac{1}{2}$

Solutions

1. $\dfrac{3}{7} - \dfrac{1}{9} = \dfrac{27}{63} - \dfrac{7}{63} = \dfrac{20}{63}$

2. $\dfrac{7}{20} + \dfrac{3}{16} = \dfrac{28}{80} + \dfrac{15}{80}$ LCM of 20 and 16 is 80.

$\qquad\qquad = \dfrac{43}{80}$

3. $4\dfrac{1}{2} - 2\dfrac{1}{3} = 4\dfrac{3}{6} - 2\dfrac{2}{6} = 2\dfrac{1}{6}$

4. $8 - 5\dfrac{5}{8} = 7\dfrac{8}{8} - 5\dfrac{5}{8}$ Borrow 1 from 8.

$\qquad\qquad = 2\dfrac{3}{8}$

5. $3\dfrac{2}{5} - 1\dfrac{3}{4} = 3\dfrac{8}{20} - 1\dfrac{15}{20}$ Borrow 1 from 3 and add to the fraction part.

$$= 2\dfrac{28}{20} - 1\dfrac{15}{20}$$

$$= 1\dfrac{13}{20}$$

6. $\left(-2\dfrac{3}{5}\right) + 1\dfrac{1}{2}$ All rules of signs that apply to positive and negative integers apply also to fractions.

$$= \left(-2\dfrac{6}{10}\right) + 1\dfrac{5}{10}$$

$$= -1\dfrac{1}{10}$$

Multiplication

The rule for multiplication of fractions is as follows:

$$\frac{a}{b} \cdot \frac{c}{d} = \frac{ac}{bd}, \quad b, d \neq 0$$

This rule states that, to multiply any two fractions, one must multiply the numerators and denominators separately.

Division

The rule for division is as follows:

$$\frac{a}{b} \div \frac{c}{d} = \frac{a}{b} \cdot \frac{d}{c}, \quad b, c, d \neq 0$$

This rule states that, to divide fractions, one must replace the divisor with its reciprocal and change the operation to multiplication.

- $2\frac{1}{2} \cdot 3\frac{5}{6} = \frac{5}{2} \cdot \frac{23}{6}$

$$= \frac{115}{12} = 9\frac{7}{12}$$

Mixed numbers must be changed to improper fractions before multiplying.

- $\left(-3\frac{4}{5}\right) \cdot \left(-6\frac{1}{3}\right) = \left(\frac{-19}{5}\right) \cdot \left(\frac{-19}{3}\right)$

$$= \frac{361}{15} = 24\frac{1}{15}$$

The same rules of signs apply.

- $7\frac{1}{4} \div \left(-2\frac{3}{5}\right) = \frac{29}{4} \div \left(\frac{-13}{5}\right)$

$$= \frac{29}{4} \cdot \left(\frac{-5}{13}\right)$$

$$= \frac{-145}{52} = -2\frac{41}{52}$$

Change to improper fractions.

Replace divisor by reciprocal, and change operation to multiplication.

PRACTICE EXERCISES

Perform the indicated operations, and express the answers in simplest form.

1. $-2\frac{4}{9} \cdot \left(4\frac{1}{2}\right)$

2. $3\frac{1}{3} \div 1\frac{3}{7}$

3. $12 \div 2\frac{2}{3}$

Solutions

1. $-2\frac{4}{9} \cdot 4\frac{1}{2} = \frac{-22}{9} \cdot \frac{9}{2}$

Cancel both 2 and 9.

$$= \frac{\overset{-11}{\cancel{-22}}}{\underset{1}{\cancel{9}}} \cdot \frac{\overset{1}{\cancel{9}}}{\underset{1}{\cancel{2}}} = -11$$

2. $3\dfrac{1}{3} \div 1\dfrac{3}{7} = \dfrac{10}{3} \div \dfrac{10}{7}$ Change to improper fractions.

$= \dfrac{10}{3} \cdot \dfrac{7}{10}$ Replace divisor.

$= \dfrac{\overset{1}{\cancel{10}}}{3} \cdot \dfrac{7}{\underset{1}{\cancel{10}}}$ Cancel.

$= \dfrac{7}{3} = 2\dfrac{1}{3}$

3. $12 \div 2\dfrac{2}{3} = \dfrac{12}{1} \div \dfrac{8}{3}$

$= \dfrac{12}{1} \cdot \dfrac{3}{8}$

$= \dfrac{3}{1} \cdot \dfrac{3}{2}$

$= \dfrac{9}{2}$

$= 4\dfrac{1}{2}$

Percents

The word *percent* literally means hundredths, so 25% means $\frac{25}{100}$, which reduces to $\frac{1}{4}$. Since "hundredths" could also be interpreted as divided by 100, and dividing by 100 can most efficiently be accomplished by moving the decimal point two places to the left, 25% is also 0.25. Therefore we have two rules:

RULES WORTH MEMORIZING

1. To change a percent to a fraction, omit the percent sign, divide by 100, and reduce the fraction.
2. To change a percent to a decimal, omit the percent sign and move the decimal point two places to the left.

To change either a fraction or a decimal to a percent, the rules above are reversed:

1. To change a fraction to a percent (do the division to get a decimal), multiply by 100 and attach a percent sign.
2. To change a decimal to a percent, move the decimal point two places to the right and attach a percent sign.

EXAMPLES

Change each percent to both a fraction and a decimal.

• 78%   Fraction: $\dfrac{78}{100} = \dfrac{39}{50}$ Decimal: 0.78

• 2.5%   Fraction: $\dfrac{2.5}{100} = \dfrac{25}{1000}$ (Multiply numerator and denominator by 10 and then reduce.)

$\qquad\qquad\qquad = \dfrac{1}{40}$

Decimal: 0.025

• $3\dfrac{1}{3}$%   Fraction: $\left(3\dfrac{1}{3}\right) \div 100 = \dfrac{10}{3} \div 100 = \dfrac{10}{3} \cdot \dfrac{1}{100}$

$\qquad\qquad\qquad = \dfrac{1}{3} \cdot \dfrac{1}{10} = \dfrac{1}{30}$

Decimal: $3\dfrac{1}{3}\% = 3.333...\% = 0.0\overline{3}$

Change each of the following to a percent.

• $\dfrac{4}{5}$ $\dfrac{4}{5}(100\%) = \dfrac{400}{5}\% = 80\%$

• 7 $7(100)\% = 700\%$

• $\dfrac{3}{8}$ $\dfrac{3}{8}(100\%) = \dfrac{3}{8}\left(\dfrac{100}{1}\right)\%$

$\qquad\qquad = \dfrac{3}{2}\left(\dfrac{25}{1}\right)\% = \dfrac{75}{2}\% = 37\dfrac{1}{2}\%$ or 37.5%

• 0.34 $0.34 = 0.34(100)\% = 34\%$

PRACTICE EXERCISES

Change each percent to both a fraction and a decimal.

1. 53%

2. 129%

3. $12\dfrac{1}{2}\%$

4. 0.1%

5. 200%

Change each number to a percent.

6. 0.8

7. $\dfrac{5}{8}$

8. $\dfrac{3}{5}$

9. 0.003

10. $\dfrac{3}{11}$

Solutions

1. Fraction: $\dfrac{53}{100}$

   Decimal: 0.53

2. Fraction: $\dfrac{129}{100} = 1\dfrac{29}{100}$

   Decimal: 1.29

3. Fraction: $12\dfrac{1}{2} \div 100 = \dfrac{25}{2} \cdot \dfrac{1}{100}$

   $$= \dfrac{1}{2} \cdot \dfrac{1}{4} = \dfrac{1}{8}$$

   Decimal: $0.12\dfrac{1}{2} = 0.125$

4. Fraction: $\dfrac{0.1}{100} = \dfrac{1}{1000}$

   Decimal: 0.001

5. Fraction: $\dfrac{200}{100} = 2$

   Decimal: 2

6. $0.8 = 0.8(100)\% = 80\%$

7. $\dfrac{5}{8} = \dfrac{5}{8}(100\%) = \dfrac{500}{8}\% = 62\dfrac{1}{2}\%$ or 62.5%

8. $\dfrac{3}{5} = \dfrac{3}{5}(100)\% = \dfrac{300}{5}\% = 60\%$

9. $0.003 = 0.003(100)\% = 0.3\%$

10. $\dfrac{3}{11} = \dfrac{3}{11}(100)\% = \dfrac{300}{11}\% = 27.\overline{27}\% = 27\dfrac{3}{11}\%$

Applications of Percent

Most percent applications are variations of this sentence:

$$A \text{ is } P \text{ percent of } B.$$

In this sentence, A is the amount (or percentage), P is the percent (or rate), and B is the base. The key to solving a percent problem is to translate the problem into the form of the sentence above. Consider the following example:

The enrollment in an algebra class dropped from 30 students to 27. What percent of the class dropped out?

In this problem we are asked to find the percent, P.

The base is always the quantity before any change, 30.

The number of students that dropped out is the amount (or percentage), 3. Hence the sentence is

$$3 \text{ is } P \text{ percent of } 30.$$

Once the problem has been written in the proper form, a proportion may be written:

$$\frac{P}{100} = \frac{A}{B}$$

To solve any proportion, $\dfrac{x}{y} = \dfrac{z}{w}$, first cross-multiply, and then divide by the coefficient of the unknown.

In the problem above, $\dfrac{P}{100} = \dfrac{3}{30}$, $30P = 300$ 10% of the
                                       $P = 10$ students
                                                  dropped.

EXAMPLES

- Find 12% of 350.
  A is unknown, $P = 12\%$, and $B = 350$. Substituting into the percent proportion gives

  $$\frac{12}{100} = \frac{A}{350}$$
  $100A = 4200$ Cross-multiply.
  $A = \underline{42}$ Divide by 100.

- What percent of 75 is 90?

    $A = 90$, P is unknown, and $B = 75$.

    $$\frac{P}{100} = \frac{90}{75}$$

    $$75P = 9000$$

    $$P = 120 \qquad \text{The answer is } \underline{120\%}.$$

- 35.1 is 78% of what number?

    $A = 35.1$, $P = 78\%$, and B is unknown.

    $$\frac{78}{100} = \frac{35.1}{B}$$

    $$35.1 = (0.78)B \qquad \text{Divide by 0.78.}$$

    $$B = \underline{45}$$

PRACTICE EXERCISES

Solve the following percent problems:

1. How much interest is earned in 1 year on an investment of $25,000 at 12% annual interest?

2. Last month Dale's paycheck was $840.00. If she is to receive a raise of 5% on this month's check, what should be the amount of this month's check?

Solutions

1. Interest is 12% of $25,000.

    A is unknown, $P = 12\%$, and $B = 25,000$.

    $$\frac{12}{100} = \frac{A}{25,000}$$

    $A = 0.12(25,000) = 3000$

    The interest is $3000.

2. This is a percent-increase type of problem.

    Dale's new salary is 105% (100% + 5%) of her old salary.

    The new salary is 105% of $840.

    A is unknown, $P = 105\%$, $B = 840$.

    $$\frac{105}{100} = \frac{A}{840}$$

    $A = 1.05(840) = 882$

    Dale's new salary is $882.

ALGEBRA AND COORDINATE GEOMETRY

Substitution

If $a = b$, then b may be substituted for a in any expression with no change in meaning.

EXAMPLES

Evaluate each expression if $a = 3$, $b = -2$, and $c = -5$. (The rules for order of operations given previously are important.)

1. $a + b - c$ $3 + (-2) - (-5) = 3 + (-2) + 5$
$$= 1 + 5 = 6$$

2. ab^2c $3(-2)^2(-5) = 3(4)(-5)$
$$= 12(-5) = -60$$

3. $ab + ac - bc$ $3(-2) + 3(-5) - (-2)(-5)$
$$= -6 + (-15) - 10$$
$$= -6 + (-15) + (-10)$$
$$= -21 + (-10) = -31$$

Any of these may be done using a calculator.

PRACTICE EXERCISES

If $x = -2$, $y = 4$, and $z = -3$, evaluate the following expressions:
1. $x - yz$
2. $xy + yz$
3. xyz^2

Solutions

1. $x - yz = -2 - 4(-3)$
$$= -2 - (-12)$$
$$= -2 + 12 = 10$$
2. $xy + yz = -2(4) + 4(-3)$
$$= -8 + (-12) = -20$$
3. $xyz^2 = -2(4)(-3)^2$
$$= -2(4)(9)$$
$$= -8(9) = -72$$

Equations

The set of numbers that makes an open equation true when substituted for the variable is called the *solution* set. The numbers themselves are called the *solution*. (The solution set of the equation $2x + 1 = 7$ is {3}.)

Equations that have the same solution set are called *equivalent* equations. There are two basic rules to use in order to solve equations. The application of either rule guarantees that an equivalent equation will result.

Addition Property of Equality

1. If $a = b$, then $a + c = b + c$ for any number c.

Multiplication Property of Equality

2. If $a = b$, then $ac = bc$ for any number $c \neq 0$.

The process of solving an equation is to produce a sequence of equivalent equations, the last one of which looks like

$$x = \text{constant}$$

from which the solution set can easily be found.

PRACTICE EXERCISES

Solve the following equations:

1. $5x - 6 = 2x + 9$
2. $3(m - 4) - (4m - 11) = -5$
3. $1.2(x + 5) = 3(2x - 8) + 23.28$
4. $\dfrac{2x + 1}{3} + \dfrac{1}{4} = \dfrac{2y - 1}{6}$
5. $\dfrac{3y - 1}{5} - \dfrac{2y + 1}{4} = 1$

Solutions

1. $5x - 6 = 2x + 9$ Add $-2x$ to both sides.
   $3x - 6 = 9$ Add 6 to both sides.
   $3x = 15$ Divide by 3.
   $x = 5$ Solution set is {5}.

2. $3(m - 4) - (4m - 11) = -5$
   $3m - 12 - 4m + 11 = -5$
   $-m - 1 = -5$
   $-m = -4$
   $m = 4$ Solution set is {4}.

3. $1.2(x + 5) = 3(2x - 8) + 23.28$ Multiply by 100.

$$120(x + 5) = 300(2x - 8) + 2328$$
$$120x + 600 = 600x - 2400 + 2328$$
$$120x + 600 = 600x - 72$$
$$600 = 480x - 72$$
$$672 = 480x$$
$$x = \frac{672}{480} = 1.4 \text{ Solution set is } \{1.4\}.$$

4. $\dfrac{2x + 1}{3} + \dfrac{1}{4} = \dfrac{2x - 1}{6}$ Multiply by 12.

$$4(2x + 1) + 3 = 2(2x - 1)$$
$$8x + 4 + 3 = 4x - 2$$
$$8x + 7 = 4x - 2$$
$$4x + 7 = -2$$
$$4x = -9$$
$$x = -\frac{9}{4} \quad \text{Solution set is } \left\{-\frac{9}{4}\right\}.$$

5. $\dfrac{3y - 1}{5} - \dfrac{2y + 1}{4} = 1$ Multiply by 20.

$$4(3y - 1) - 5(2y + 1) = 20$$
$$12y - 4 - 10y - 5 = 20$$
$$2y - 9 = 20$$
$$2y = 29$$
$$y = \frac{29}{2} \quad \text{Solution set is } \left\{\frac{29}{2}\right\}.$$

OPERATIONS ON POLYNOMIALS

Addition and Subtraction

To add or subtract polynomials, first use the distributive property as needed to get rid of parentheses and then combine similar terms. Usually the terms of a polynomial are arranged in the order of descending degree in a specified variable. For example:

$$(3x^2 + 5x - 4) + (2x^2 - 7x - 3)$$
$$= 3x^2 + 5x - 4 + 2x^2 - 7x - 3$$
$$= 5x^2 - 2x - 7$$

$$(2x^2 - 6xy + 3y^2) - (x^2 - xy + 2y^2)$$
$$= 2x^2 - 6xy + 3y^2 - x^2 + xy - 2y^2$$
$$= x^2 - 5xy + y^2$$

Multiplication

Multiplication of a monomial by a polynomial of several terms is merely an extension of the distributive property.

$$-2a(3a^2 - 5a + 8) = -6a^3 + 10a^2 - 16a$$

Multiplication of two polynomials of more than one term each is also an extension of the distributive property. It is easier, however, to follow the rule "Multiply each term of one polynomial by each term of the other polynomial and then simplify."

$$(a + b - c)(2a - b + c)$$
$$= a(2a - b + c) + b(2a - b + c) - c(2a - b + c)$$
$$= 2a^2 - ab + ac + 2ab - b^2 + bc - 2ac + bc - c^2$$
$$= 2a^2 + ab - ac - b^2 + 2bc - c^2$$

Multiplication of two binomials is such a common operation that a special procedure has been devised to make it easy to do mentally.

Consider the product of two binomials:

Call A and C the First terms of the binomials.
Call A and D the Outer terms.
Call B and C the Inner terms.
Call B and D the Last terms.

The product can be found by following the acronym FOIL.
For example, to multiply $(2x + 3)(x + 4)$:

Multiply the First terms: $(2x)(x) = 2x^2$.
Multiply the Outer terms: $(2x)(4) = 8x$.
Multiply the Inner terms: $(3)(x) = 3x$.
Multiply the Last terms: $(3)(4) = 12$.

Since the Outer product and the Inner product are similar terms, combine them and write the answer:

$$2x^2 + 11x + 12$$

Three products occur frequently and deserve special attention:

Sum and difference binomials: $(A + B)(A - B) = A^2 - B^2$

Square of a binomial: $(A \pm B)^2 = A^2 \pm 2AB + B^2$

Cube of a binomial: $(A \pm B)^3 = A^3 \pm 3A^2B + 3AB^2 \pm B^3$

EXAMPLES

1. $(3x - 5)(3x + 5) = 9x^2 - 25$
2. $(5x - 2y)^2 = 25x^2 - 20xy + 4y^2$
3. $(x + 4)^3 = x^3 + 12x^2 + 48x + 64$

EXERCISES

Perform the indicated operations. Express each answer in the order of descending degree in some variable.

1. $(5x + 3xy - 8y) - (y - 6yx + 2x)$
2. $(2x - 3) - [(4x + 7) - (5x - 2)]$
3. $-3ab(4a^2 - 5ab + 2b^2)$
4. $(2x - 3)(4x^2 + 6x + 9)$
5. $(x + 3)(x - 5)$
6. $(3x + 1)(2x + 5)$
7. $(3x + 5)^2$
8. $(2a - b)^3$

Solutions

1. $(5x + 3xy - 8y) - (y - 6yx + 2x)$
   $= 5x + 3xy - 8y - y + 6yx - 2x$
   $= 3x + 9xy - 9y$
2. $(2x - 3) - [(4x + 7) - (5x - 2)]$ Do inner grouping
   $= (2x - 3) - [4x + 7 - 5x + 2]$ symbols first.
   $= 2x - 3 - 4x - 7 + 5x - 2$
   $= 3x - 12$
3. $-3ab(4a^2 - 5ab + 2b^2)$
   $= -12a^3b + 15a^2b^2 - 6ab^3$
4. Multiply each term of the second polynomial first by $2x$ and then by -3:
   $(2x - 3)(4x^2 + 6x + 9)$
   $= 8x^3 + 12x^2 + 18x - 12x^2 - 18x - 27$
   $= 8x^3 - 27$
5. $(x + 3)(x - 5)$ Use FOIL.
   $= x^2 - 5x + 3x - 15$ Try not to write this line.
   $= x^2 - 2x - 15$

6. $(3x + 1)(2x + 5)$ Use FOIL. Do the
    $= 6x^2 + 17x + 5$ Outer and Inner mentally.

7. $(3x + 5)^2$ This is a binomial square. The middle term is 2 times
    $= 9x^2 + 30x + 25$ the product of the terms of the binomial.

8. $(2a - b)^3$
    $= 8a^3 + 3(2a)^2(-b) + 3(2a)(-b)^2 + (-b)^3$
    $= 8a^3 - 12a^2b + 6ab^2 - b^3$

Factoring

The process of factoring involves changing an expression from addition or subtraction to multiplication—creating factors. The property underlying all factoring rules is the distributive property:

$$ab + ac = a(b + c)$$

Notice that the left has the *sum* of terms, while the right has the *product* of factors.

If an expression has a *common factor* other than 1 in all of its terms, factor it out. Here are some examples:

- $4ab^2 + 2a^2b = 2ab(2b + a)$
- $39x^5y^3 - 26x^7y^2 + 52x^8y^5$ The common factor chosen should
  $= 13x^5y^2(3y - 2x^2 + 4x^3y^3)$ be the greatest common factor of the terms. Choose the exponent on each variable to be the smallest exponent on that variable in the expression.

- $-25x^3y^2 - 20x^4y^3 + 15x^5y^4 - 50x^6y^2$ If the first term is negative,
  $= -5x^3y^2(5 + 4xy - 3x^2y^2 + 10x^3)$ choose a negative common factor.

- $(x + 5)(x - 6) + (x + 5)(x - 1)$ The common factor is the
  $= (x + 5)[(x - 6) + (x - 1)]$ binomial $(x + 5)$.
  $= (x + 5)(2x - 7)$

- $pq + 3rq + pm + 3rm$ The trick is to group so that
  $= (pq + 3rq) + (pm + 3rm)$ each group has a common
  $= q(p + 3r) + m(p + 3r)$ factor.
  $= (p + 3r)(q + m)$

- $8x^2 + 6xy - 12xy - 9y^2$
  $= (8x^2 + 6xy) - (12xy + 9y^2)$ Be very careful of signs.
  $= 2x(4x + 3y) - 3y(4x + 3y)$
  $= (4x + 3y)(2x - 3y)$

PRACTICE EXERCISES

Factor completely.

1. $8x^3y^3 - 12x^2y^2$
2. $28a^2b - 14ab^2 + 7ab$
3. $-6a^5b^5 - 8a^4b^4 + 4a^3b^2$
4. $7m^3n^3 + 6$
5. $9x(3x + 2y) - 5y(3x + 2y)$
6. $5x^2y^2 + 10x^2 - 7y^2 - 14$

Solutions

1. $4x^2y^2(2xy - 3)$
2. $7ab(4a - 2b + 1)$ The 1 is easy to miss but very important.
3. $-2a^3b^2(3a^2b^3 + 4ab^2 - 2)$
4. The terms of the binomial have no common factor other than 1. It is not factorable. A nonfactorable polynomial is said to be prime.
5. $(3x + 2y)(9x - 5y)$
6. $5x^2y^2 + 10x^2 - 7y^2 - 14$
   $(5x^2y^2 + 10x^2) - (7y^2 + 14)$ Group, being careful of signs.
   $= 5x^2(y^2 + 2) - 7(y^2 + 2)$
   $= (y^2 + 2)(5x^2 - 7)$

Difference of Squares, Sum and Difference of Cubes

The following products are the bases for factoring special types of binomials:

$(a + b)(a - b) = a^2 - b^2$ Difference of squares.

$(a + b)(a^2 - ab + b^2) = a^3 + b^3$ Sum of cubes.

$(a - b)(a^2 + ab + b^2) = a^3 - b^3$ Difference of cubes.

Here is an example of each type:

- $25 - 49x^2 = (5 + 7x)(5 - 7x)$ Difference of squares.
- $x^3 + 8 = (x + 2)(x^2 - 2x + 4)$ Sum of cubes. Watch signs carefully.
- $125x^3 - 64y^3$ Difference of cubes.
  $= (5x - 4y)(25x^2 + 20xy + 16y^2)$

Factoring Trinomials of the Type $x^2 + Bx + C$

When two binomials of the type $(x + a)(x + b)$ are multiplied, a trinomial of the type $x^2 + Bx + C$ results, in which C is the product of a and b and B is the sum of a and b. To factor such a trinomial, look for two factors of C whose sum is B.

EXAMPLES

Factor each of the following.
1. $x^2 + 7x + 12$ Search the factors of 12 to find a pair whose sum is 7. The factors of 12 in pairs are 1, 12; 2, 6; and 3, 4. The sum is 7. The factors are $(x + 3)(x + 4)$.
2. $x^2 - 8x + 15$ The factors of 15 are 1 and 15 or 3 and 5. The factors are $(x - 3)(x - 5)$.
3. $x^2 - 3x - 40$ Since the sign of the third term is negative, the signs in the two binomials are different, and the middle term is the sum of two numbers with different signs. Search for a pair of factors so that the difference is 3, and adjust signs. The answer is $(x - 8)(x + 5)$.
4. $x^2 + 5x - 66$ Look for two factors of 66 whose difference is 5: 6, 11. The answer is $(x - 6)(x + 11)$.

Factoring Trinomials of the Type $Ax^2 + Bx + C$

The leading coefficient of this type of polynomial is always something other than 1. The procedure is to multiply the coefficients of the first and third terms and look for a pair of factors of that number whose sum or difference is the second coefficient. Rewrite the second term using those numbers, then group and factor.

EXAMPLES

1. $2x^2 + 5x - 12$ Multiply 2 times 12. Look for two factors of 24 whose difference (because the 12 is negative) is 5. $24 = (3)(8)$

$2x^2 + 8x - 3x - 12$ Rewrite 5x using the numbers above.

$(2x^2 + 8x) - (3x + 12)$ Group.
$2x(x + 4) - 3(x + 4)$ Factor out the common factor in each group.

$(x + 4)(2x - 3)$ Factor out the common factor $(x + 4)$.

2. $24x^2 - 14x - 3$ $24 \cdot 3 = 72$
$24x^2 - 18x + 4x - 3$ $72 = 18 \cdot 4$
$(24x^2 - 18x) + (4x - 3)$
$6x(4x - 3) + 1(4x - 3)$
$(4x - 3)(6x + 1)$

3. $24x^2 - 34x + 5$ $24 \cdot 5 = 120$
   $24x^2 - 4x - 30x + 5$ $120 = \ 30 \cdot 4$
   $(24x^2 - 4x) - (30x - 5)$
   $4x(6x - 1) - 5(6x - 1)$
   $(6x - 1)(4x - 5)$

This type of trinomial can also be factored by a method best described as "trial and error." Given a trinomial of the appropriate type, begin with either the first or third term (whichever one has fewer factors). Look for obvious factors of that number to place in the binomial factors.

4. $6x^2 + 19x + 10$ There are two possibilities for the first
   $(2x \quad)(3x \quad)$ terms of the binomials. Guessing that

2	5	
5	2	←
1	10	
10	1	

the correct choice is $2x$ and $3x$, list the factors of 10 and check them, adding the outer and inner products in the hope of getting $19x$. The answer is $(2x + 5)(3x + 2)$.

5. $8x^2 - 2x - 3$ There are two possibilities for the first
   $(\quad 1)(\quad 3)$ terms of the binomials and only one for

2x	4x	←
4x	2x	
x	8x	
8x	x	

the second terms, so begin there, and list the factors of $8x$. Since the sign of the third term is negative, subtract the outer and inner products in the hope of getting $2x$. Then adjust the signs to make the middle term negative. The answer is $(2x + 1)(4x - 3)$.

Perfect Square Trinomials

If the first and last terms of a trinomial are squares, it is worth considering the special form of a perfect square trinomial:

$$a^2 + 2ab + b^2 = (a + b)^2$$

For example, $x^2 + 10x + 25$ is a perfect square trinomial. The correct factorization is $(x + 5)^2$. [The factorization $(x + 5)(x + 5)$ is also correct.]

General Strategy for Factoring a Polynomial

1. If a polynomial has a common factor, *always* factor that first.
2. If there is no common factor (or if the common factor has already been factored out):
   - factor a binomial according to the rule for the difference of squares or the sum or difference of cubes;

- factor a trinomial according to the appropriate rule;
- consider factoring by grouping if there are more than three terms.

3. Look for tricks. Here are some examples:

- $250x^3 + 54y^3$
  $= 2(125x^3 + 27y^3)$
  $= 2(5x + 3y)(25x^2 - 15xy + 9y^2)$

  There is a common factor of 2. In the parentheses is a sum of cubes. Be sure the common factor appears in the answer.

- $-288x^2 + 8y^4$
  $= -8(36x^2 - y^4)$
  $= -8(6x - y^2)(6x + y^2)$

  The common factor is -8. In the parentheses is the difference of squares. By reversing the terms, a correct answer would also be obtained: $8(y^2 - 6x)(y^2 + 6x)$.

- $4x^4 - 5x^2 + 1$
  $= (4x^2 - 1)(x^2 - 1)$
  $= (2x - 1)(2x + 1)(x - 1)(x + 1)$

  There is no common factor. Factor the trinomial. Now each binomial is the difference of squares.

- $9x^2y^2 - 6xy + 1 = (3xy - 1)^2$

  This is a perfect square trinomial.

- $3ab + a - 3b^2 - b$
  $= (3ab + a) - (3b^2 + b)$
  $= a(3b + 1) - b(3b + 1)$
  $= (3b + 1)(a - b)$

  Try grouping.

PRACTICE EXERCISES

Factor completely.

1. $5x^2y^2 - 10xy$
2. $2x^2 - x - 10$
3. $-5x^2 - 15xy + 50y^2$
4. $8a^3 - b^3$
5. $9x^2 + 30xy + 25y^2$
6. $16u^4 - v^4$
7. $6x^2 - 14xy - 21xy + 49y^2$

Solutions

1. $5x^2y^2 - 10xy = 5xy(xy - 2)$
2. $2x^2 - x - 10$ Multiply 2 times 10. Look for factors of 20 whose difference is 1. Rewrite $-x$ using those two numbers. Group and find common factors in each group.

    $2x^2 - 5x + 4x - 10$

    $x(2x - 5) + 2(2x - 5)$

    $(2x - 5)(x + 2)$

3. $-5x^2 - 15xy + 50y^2$

    $= -5(x^2 + 3xy - 10y^2)$ -5 is the common factor.

    $= -5(x + 5y)(x - 2y)$

4. $8a^3 - b^3$

    $= (2a - b)(4a^2 + 2ab + b^2)$ Difference of cubes.

5. $9x^2 + 30xy + 25y^2$

    $= (3x + 5y)^2$ A perfect square trinomial.

6. $16u^4 - v^4$

    $= (4u^2 + v^2)(4u^2 - v^2)$ Two layers of difference

    $= (4u^2 + v^2)(2u + v)(2u - v)$ of squares.

7. $6x^2 - 14xy - 21xy + 49y^2$

    $= (6x^2 - 14xy) - (21xy - 49y^2)$ Grouping.

    $= 2x(3x - 7y) - 7y(3x - 7y)$

    $= (3x - 7y)(2x - 7y)$

Quadratic Equations

An equation is called *quadratic* if it is equivalent to

$$ax^2 + bx + c = 0, \quad a \neq 0$$

An equation in this form is said to be in *standard* form.

    An important rule used in the solution of quadratic equations is sometimes called the Zero Product Principle:

$$\text{If } AB = 0, \quad \text{then} \quad A = 0 \quad \text{or} \quad B = 0.$$

EXAMPLES

        Solve each of the following:

• $x^2 + 8x + 15 = 0$ Factor.

        $(x + 5)(x + 3) = 0$ Zero Product Principle

    $x + 5 = 0$ or $x + 3 = 0$

        $x = -5$ or $x = -3$

    The solution set is $\{-5, -3\}$.

- $$3x^2 + 5 = 2x$$

$3x^2 - 2x + 5 = 0$	Standard form.
$(3x - 5)(x + 1) = 0$	Factor.
$3x - 5 = 0$ or $x + 1 = 0$	Zero Product Principle
$x = \dfrac{5}{3}$ or $x = -1$	Solve each linear equation.

The solution set is $\left\{\dfrac{5}{3}, -1\right\}$.

If the coefficient of the linear term in the standard form of the quadratic equation is zero ($b = 0$), it is easier to solve the equation by isolating x^2 and taking the square root of both sides, remembering that there are two solutions to such an equation—one positive and the other negative.

- $2x^2 - 10 = 0$

$$2x^2 = 10$$

$$x^2 = 5$$

$$x = \pm\sqrt{5}.$$

The solution set is $\{\sqrt{5}, -\sqrt{5}\}$.

The Quadratic Formula

All quadratic equations can always be solved by using the quadratic formula:

$$x = \frac{-b \pm \sqrt{b^2 - 4ac}}{2a}$$

PRACTICE EXERCISES

Solve the following quadratic equations:

1. $x^2 - 3x - 4 = 0$
2. $x^2 + 9 = 6x$
3. $2x^2 + 5x = 0$

Solutions

1. $x^2 - 3x - 4 = 0$

$(x - 4)(x + 1) = 0$	Factor the left side.
$x - 4 = 0$ or $x + 1 = 0$	
$x = 4$ $x = -1$	Set each factor equal to zero.
	Solve each equation.

The solution set is $\{4, -1\}$.

2. $x^2 + 9 = 6x$

    $x^2 - 6x + 9 = 0$ The equation is in standard form.

    $(x - 3)^2 = 0$ Factor.

    $x - 3 = 0$ Set factor equal to zero.

    $x = 3$ Solve.

The solution set is {3}.

3. $2x^2 + 5x = 0$

    $2x(x + 5) = 0$ Factor.

    $2x = 0$ or $x + 5 = 0$ Set each factor equal to zero.

    $x = 0$ $x = -5$ Solve.

    The solution set is {0, -5}.

Algebraic Fractions

Algebraic fractions can be reduced by using the Fundamental Principle of Fractions:

$$\frac{a}{b} = \frac{ak}{bk}, \, b, k \neq 0$$

Multiplication and Division

Multiplication and division of fractions are merely extensions of the same procedure. It is important to factor all expressions first and to cancel only common *factors* from any numerator and any denominator. Most errors are made by attempting to cancel *terms,* not factors.

EXAMPLES ▬▬▬▬▬▬▬▬▬▬▬▬▬▬▬▬▬▬▬▬▬▬▬▬▬▬▬▬▬▬▬

- Reduce: $\dfrac{15x + 7x^2 - 2x^3}{x^2 - 8x + 15}$

                 $\dfrac{x(5 - x)(3 + 2x)}{(x - 3)(x - 5)}$ Factor.

                    $\dfrac{-x(3 + 2x)}{(x - 3)}$

The factors $(x - 5)$ and $(5 - x)$ are not equal, but they are opposites. Therefore, when canceled, these factors yield -1.

- Multiply:

$$\frac{a^3 + a^2b}{5a} \cdot \frac{25}{3a + 3b}$$

$$\overset{a}{\frac{\cancel{a^2}(a+b)}{\cancel{5a}}} \cdot \frac{\cancel{25}\,^5}{3(a+b)} \qquad \text{Cancel } a, (a+b), \text{ and } 5.$$

$$\frac{a}{1} \cdot \frac{5}{3}$$

$$\frac{5a}{3}$$

Addition and Subtraction

The same rules for addition and subtraction that are used in arithmetic apply to the addition and subtraction of algebraic fractions.

$$\frac{a}{b} \pm \frac{c}{b} = \frac{a \pm c}{b}, b \neq 0$$

EXAMPLE

- Subtract: $\dfrac{3}{x^2 - 5x + 6} - \dfrac{2}{x^2 - x - 2}$

Factor each denominator: $(x - 2)(x - 3)$
$(x - 2)(x + 1)$

Therefore the LCD is $(x - 2)(x - 3)(x + 1)$. The numerator and denominator of the first fraction must be multiplied by the factor $(x + 1)$, and those in the second fraction by $(x - 3)$.

$$\frac{3(x + 1)}{(x - 2)(x - 3)(x + 1)} - \frac{2(x - 3)}{(x - 2)(x - 3)(x + 1)}$$

$$= \frac{3(x + 1) - 2(x - 3)}{(x - 2)(x - 3)(x + 1)}$$

$$= \frac{3x + 3 - 2x + 6}{(x - 2)(x - 3)(x + 1)}$$

$$= \frac{x + 9}{(x - 2)(x - 3)(x + 1)}$$

PRACTICE EXERCISES

Perform the indicated operations and simplify.

1. $\dfrac{z^2 - z - 6}{z - 6} \cdot \dfrac{z^2 - 6z}{z^2 + 2z - 15}$

2. $\dfrac{a^3 - b^3}{a^2 - b^2} \div \dfrac{a^2 + ab + b^2}{a^2 + ab}$

3. $\dfrac{2}{x + 1} + \dfrac{6}{x - 1}$

4. $\dfrac{2x}{2x^2 - x - 1} - \dfrac{3x}{3x^2 - 5x + 2}$

Solutions

1. $\dfrac{(z - 3)(z + 2)}{z - 6} \cdot \dfrac{z(z - 6)}{(z + 5)(z - 3)}$

$= \dfrac{z + 2}{1} \cdot \dfrac{z}{z + 5}$

$= \dfrac{z(z + 2)}{z + 5}$

2. $\dfrac{(a - b)(a^2 + ab + b^2)}{(a - b)(a + b)} \cdot \dfrac{a(a + b)}{a^2 + ab + b^2}$

$= \dfrac{1}{1} \cdot \dfrac{a}{1} = a$

3. The LCD is $(x + 1)(x - 1)$.

$\dfrac{2(x - 1)}{(x + 1)(x - 1)} + \dfrac{6(x + 1)}{(x + 1)(x - 1)}$

$= \dfrac{2x - 2 + 6x + 6}{(x + 1)(x - 1)}$

$= \dfrac{8x + 4}{(x + 1)(x - 1)}$

4. Factor each denominator:

$$(2x + 1)(x - 1)$$
$$(3x - 2)(x - 1)$$

The LCD is $(2x + 1)(3x - 2)(x - 1)$.

$$\frac{2x(3x - 2)}{(2x + 1)(3x - 2)(x - 1)} - \frac{3x(2x + 1)}{(2x + 1)(3x - 2)(x - 1)}$$

$$= \frac{2x(3x - 2) - 3x(2x + 1)}{(2x + 1)(3x - 2)(x - 1)}$$

$$= \frac{6x^2 - 4x - 6x^2 - 3x}{(2x + 1)(3x - 2)(x - 1)}$$

$$= \frac{-7x}{(2x + 1)(3x - 2)(x - 1)}$$

Word Problems

Word problems can seem difficult, but not if you follow these key points:

1. *Read the problem carefully,* often several times until the meaning of the problem is clear.
2. *Make a sketch or diagram* if it would help make the problem clear.
3. Choose a variable to represent an unknown quantity in the problem. Many times it is helpful to put the variable where the question is.
4. *Represent all other unknown quantities* in terms of the chosen variable.
5. *Write an equation.* Many times a well-known formula can be used. Other times a literal translation of the problem leads to the equation. This is the most difficult step in the procedure.
6. *Solve the equation.*
7. *Answer the question.*

Here are some typical word problems found in most algebra courses.

PROBLEM 1

Two-thirds of the graduating class of Limerick Avenue Elementary School are girls, and 25% of the girls are also in the band. If there are eight graduating girls in the band, how many are in the graduating class?

If 25% $= \frac{1}{4}$ of the girls are in the band, and that number is eight, then there must be $4 \cdot 8 = 32$ girls in the graduating class. The number of girls in the graduating class represents $\frac{2}{3}$ of all the graduating students. Let x equal the number of students in the graduating class. Then:

$$\frac{2}{3}x = 32 \qquad \text{Multiply both sides by } \frac{3}{2}.$$

$$\frac{3}{2} \cdot \frac{2}{3}x = 32 \cdot \frac{3}{2}$$

$$x = 48 \qquad \text{There are 48 in the graduating class.}$$

PROBLEM 2

The average cost of three books for Jason's classes is $74.16. What should the average cost of the next two books that he buys be so that his average for all five books is $90?

If the average cost of three books is $74.16, it's as if each book cost exactly that amount. If x represents the average cost of the next two books, then:

$$\frac{3(74.16) + 2x}{5} = 90$$ Multiply both sides by 5.

$$222.48 + 2x = 450$$ Subtract 222.48 from both sides.

$$2x = 227.52$$

$$x = 113.76$$ The average cost of the next two books is $113.76.

PROBLEM 3

Linda commutes a one-way total of 40 miles to work each day—part by car and part by train. If the ratio of the distance traveled by car to the distance traveled by train is 1 to 9, how far does she ride on the train?

Suppose she divides her total trip of 40 miles into 10, $(1 + 9)$, equal parts of 4 miles each. Then she drives her car for one of them and rides the train for nine of them. Therefore, she rides the train 36 miles.

This problem could also be solved by using an equation:

$$x + 9x = 40$$

Laws of Exponents

The following laws of exponents apply to all real-number exponents:

1. $x^m \cdot x^n = x^{m+n}$

2. $(x^m)^n = x^{mn}$

3. $(xy)^m = x^m \cdot y^m$

4. $\dfrac{x^m}{x^n} = x^{m-n}, x \neq 0$

5. $\left(\dfrac{x}{y}\right)^m = \dfrac{x^m}{y^m}, y \neq 0$

6. $x^0 = 1, x \neq 0$

7. $x^{-m} = \dfrac{1}{x^m}, x \neq 0$

   a. $\left(\dfrac{x}{y}\right)^{-m} = \left(\dfrac{y}{x}\right)^m, x, y \neq 0$

   b. $\dfrac{a}{x^{-m}} = ax^m, x \neq 0$

Here are some examples:

- $x^{5/3} \cdot x^{-2/3} = x^{3/3} = x^1 = x$
- $(x^{3/2})^4 = x^6$
- $(x^3 y)^3 = x^9 y^3$
- $\dfrac{x^5}{x^6} = x^{-1} = \dfrac{1}{x^1} = \dfrac{1}{x}$

- $\dfrac{a^3 b}{a^{-2} a^2} = a^{3-(-2)} b^{1-2} = a^5 b^{-1} = \dfrac{a^5}{b}$

- $\left(\dfrac{x^2}{y^4}\right)^{-3} = \left(\dfrac{y^4}{x^2}\right)^3 = \dfrac{y^{12}}{x^6}$

- $\dfrac{3^{-2}}{3^{-3}} = 3^{-2-(-3)} = 3^1 = 3$

PRACTICE EXERCISES

Simplify and write without negative exponents. Assume no denominator is zero.

1. $\dfrac{x^{10}}{x^4}$

2. $\left(\dfrac{4x^3}{y^2}\right)^3$

3. $\left(\dfrac{a^2 b^3}{2a^{-2} b}\right)^{-2}$

4. $\dfrac{2}{a^{-7}}$

5. $\left(\dfrac{3}{2}\right)^0$

6. $3x^0$

7. $4x^{-2}$

Solutions

1. $\dfrac{x^{10}}{x^4} = x^{10-4} = x^6$

2. $\left(\dfrac{4x^3}{y^2}\right)^3 = \left(\dfrac{4^3 x^9}{y^6}\right) = \left(\dfrac{64x^9}{y^6}\right)$

3. $\left(\dfrac{a^2b^3}{2a^{-2}b}\right)^{-2} = \left(\dfrac{2a^{-2}b}{a^2b^3}\right)^2 = \dfrac{2^2a^{-4}b^2}{a^4b^6}$

$$= 4a^{-4-4}b^{2-6} = 4a^{-8}b^{-4} = \dfrac{4}{a^8b^4}$$

4. $\dfrac{2}{a^{-7}} = 2a^7$

5. $\left(\dfrac{3}{2}\right)^0 = 1$

6. $3x^0 = 3(1) = 3$ An exponent applies only to the immediately preceding symbol.

7. $\dfrac{4}{x^2}$ Not $\dfrac{1}{4x^2}$. The exponent applies only to x.

Roots and Fractional Exponents

The definition of an nth root is as follows:

a is an nth root of b if and only if $a^n = b$.

The symbol for the nth root of b is $\sqrt[n]{b}$. According to the definition, this is the number that, when raised to the nth power, yields b. If n is even and b is negative, the nth root of b is not a real number.

Simplest Radical Form

A radical expression is said to be in simplest radical form (SRF) if the following conditions are met:

1. The radicand has no perfect nth-power factors.
2. There are no fractions in the radicand.
3. There are no radicals in a denominator.

Here are examples of these rules:

- $\sqrt{12}$ is not in simplest radical form because the radicand has $4 = 2^2$ as a factor. To put $\sqrt{12}$ in SRF, factor the radicand so that one factor is the largest square factor of the radicand. Then use the rule of radicals.

$$\sqrt[n]{xy} = (\sqrt[n]{x})(\sqrt[n]{y}) \quad \text{for all defined radicals.}$$

The square factor can be extracted from the radical.

$$\sqrt{12} = \sqrt{4 \cdot 3} = \sqrt{4} \cdot \sqrt{3} = 2\sqrt{3}$$

- $\sqrt[3]{32x^3y^8} = \sqrt[3]{(8x^3y^6)(4y^2)}$ Separate the radic and into cube and noncube parts.

$$= \sqrt[3]{8x^3y^6} \cdot \sqrt[3]{4y^2}$$

$$= 2xy^2 \sqrt[3]{4y^2}$$

- $\sqrt{\dfrac{5}{8}}$ is not in SRF because of rule 2 above. To simplify, multiply the numerator and denominator by some number in order to make the denominator a perfect square. Then use the rule of radicals

$$\sqrt[n]{\frac{x}{y}} = \frac{\sqrt[n]{x}}{\sqrt[n]{y}} \quad \text{for all defined radicals.}$$

$$\sqrt{\frac{5}{8}} = \sqrt{\frac{5 \cdot 2}{8 \cdot 2}} = \sqrt{\frac{10}{16}} = \frac{\sqrt{10}}{\sqrt{16}} = \frac{\sqrt{10}}{4}$$

- $\dfrac{7}{\sqrt[3]{12}}$ is not in SRF because of rule 3 (see page 111). To simplify, multiply the numerator and denominator by an appropriate radical to make the bottom radicand a perfect nth power.

$$\frac{7}{\sqrt[3]{12}} = \frac{7\sqrt[3]{18}}{\sqrt[3]{12}\sqrt[3]{18}} = \frac{7\sqrt[3]{18}}{\sqrt[3]{216}} = \frac{7\sqrt[3]{18}}{6}$$

Since $12 = 2 \cdot 2 \cdot 3$, one more 2 and two 3's are needed to make a perfect cube. Multiply by $2 \cdot 3 \cdot 3 = 18$ in the radical.

- $\dfrac{2}{3 - \sqrt{2}}$ is not in SRF because of rule 3 above. To simplify, multiply by an appropriate radical expression, sometimes called the *conjugate* of the denominator. In this case, multiply the numerator and denominator by $3 + \sqrt{2}$.

$$\frac{2(3 + \sqrt{2})}{(3 - \sqrt{2})(3 + \sqrt{2})} = \frac{2(3 + \sqrt{2})}{9 - 2} = \frac{2(3 + \sqrt{2})}{7} = \frac{6 + 2\sqrt{2}}{7}$$

PRACTICE EXERCISES

Simplify. Assume all variables are nonnegative.

1. $2^{1/3} \cdot 2^{1/4}$

2. $\dfrac{1}{8^{-4/3}}$

3. $\sqrt{500}$

4. $\sqrt{20x^6}$

5. $\sqrt[4]{x^5 y^7}$

6. $\sqrt{\dfrac{5}{12}}$

7. $\dfrac{6}{\sqrt{3}}$

8. $\dfrac{4}{\sqrt{6} - 4}$

Solutions

1. $2^{1/3} \cdot 2^{1/4} = 2^{1/3 + 1/4} = 2^{7/12}$

2. $\dfrac{1}{8^{-4/3}} = 8^{4/3} = \left(\sqrt[3]{8}\right)^4 = 2^4 = 16$

3. $\sqrt{500} = \sqrt{(100 \cdot 5)} = \sqrt{100} \cdot \sqrt{5} = 10\sqrt{5}$

4. $\sqrt{20x^6} = \sqrt{(4x^6)(5)} = \sqrt{4x^6}\,\sqrt{5} = 2x\sqrt[3]{5}$

5. $\sqrt[4]{x^5 y^7} = \sqrt[4]{(x^4 y^4)(xy^3)}$

$$= \sqrt[4]{x^4 y^4} \cdot \sqrt[4]{xy^3} = xy\sqrt[4]{xy^3}$$

6. $\sqrt{\dfrac{5}{12}} = \sqrt{\dfrac{15}{36}}$ 　　　　Multiply by $\dfrac{3}{3}$ to make the denominator a square.

$$= \dfrac{\sqrt{15}}{\sqrt{36}} = \dfrac{\sqrt{15}}{6}$$

7. $\dfrac{6}{\sqrt{3}} = \dfrac{6\sqrt{3}}{\sqrt{9}}$ 　　　　Multiply by $\dfrac{\sqrt{3}}{\sqrt{3}}$ to make the denominator a square.

$$= \dfrac{6\sqrt{3}}{3} = 2\sqrt{3}$$

8. $\dfrac{4}{\sqrt{6}-4}$ 　　　　Multiply the numerator and denominator by the conjugate of the denominator.

$$= \dfrac{4(\sqrt{6} + 4)}{(\sqrt{6} - 4)(\sqrt{6} + 4)}$$

$$= \dfrac{4(\sqrt{6} + 4)}{6 - 16}$$

$$= \dfrac{4(\sqrt{6} + 4)}{-10} = \dfrac{-2(\sqrt{6} + 4)}{5} = \dfrac{-2\sqrt{6} - 8}{5}$$ 　　Reduce the fraction.

Operations with Radicals

All of the following discussion assumes that the radicals represent real numbers, that is, there are no even roots of negative numbers.

Any radicals with the same index may be multiplied or divided according to the following rules:

$$\sqrt[n]{x}\,\sqrt[n]{y} = \sqrt[n]{xy} \quad \text{and} \quad \frac{\sqrt[n]{x}}{\sqrt[n]{y}} = \sqrt[n]{\frac{x}{y}}$$

Radicals may be added and subtracted only if both the indices and the radicands are the same.

$$a\sqrt[n]{x} \pm b\sqrt[n]{x} = (a \pm b)\sqrt[n]{x}$$

PRACTICE EXERCISES

Perform the indicated operations and simplify. Assume all variables are non-negative.

1. $5\sqrt{8} - 3\sqrt{72} + 3\sqrt{50}$
2. $6\sqrt[3]{128m} - 3\sqrt[3]{16m}$
3. $\sqrt{2}\,(\sqrt{32} - \sqrt{9})$
4. $(\sqrt{7} + \sqrt{3})(\sqrt{7} - \sqrt{3})$
5. $(4\sqrt{5})^2$

Solutions

1. $5\sqrt{8} - 3\sqrt{72} + 3\sqrt{50}$

   Simplify each radical term first.

   $5\sqrt{8} = 5 \cdot 2\sqrt{2} = 10\sqrt{2}$
   $3\sqrt{72} = 3 \cdot 6\sqrt{2} = 18\sqrt{2}$
   $3\sqrt{50} = 3 \cdot 5\sqrt{2} = 15\sqrt{2}$
   $10\sqrt{2} - 18\sqrt{2} + 15\sqrt{2} = 7\sqrt{2}$

2. $6\sqrt[3]{128m} - 3\sqrt[3]{16m}$

   $6\sqrt[3]{128m} = 6\sqrt[3]{(64)(2m)}$

   $\qquad\qquad = 6 \cdot 4\sqrt[3]{2m} = 24\sqrt[3]{2m}$

   $3\sqrt[3]{16m} = 3\sqrt[3]{(8)(2m)}$

   $\qquad\qquad = 3 \cdot 2\sqrt[3]{2m} = 6\sqrt[3]{2m}$

   $24\sqrt[3]{2m} - 6\sqrt[3]{2m} = 18\sqrt[3]{2m}$

3. $\sqrt{2}(\sqrt{32} - \sqrt{9})$ Apply the distributive property.

   $= \sqrt{64} - \sqrt{18}$

   $= 8 - \sqrt{9 \cdot 2} = 8 - 3\sqrt{2}$

4. $(\sqrt{7} + \sqrt{3})(\sqrt{7} - \sqrt{3})$

   $= \sqrt{49} - \sqrt{9}$ This is the same FOIL for binomials.

   $= 7 - 3 = 4$

5. $(4\sqrt{5})^2 = 16\sqrt{25}$ Square each factor.

   $= 16 \cdot 5 = 80$

Distance Formula

The distance between two points (x_1, y_1) and (x_2, y_2) in the plane can be found by the distance formula, which is a result of the Pythagorean Theorem:

$$d = \sqrt{(x_2 - x_1)^2 + (y_2 - y_1)^2}$$

Midpoint Formula

The midpoint of the segment between two points $A\ (x_1, y_1)$ and $B\ (x_2, y_2)$ is found by averaging the x-coordinates and the y-coordinates.

$$\text{midpoint of } \overline{AB}: \left(\frac{x_1 + x_2}{2}, \frac{y_1 + y_2}{2} \right)$$

PRACTICE EXERCISES

1. Find the distance between the following points in the plane:
   a.   (2, 5) and (5, 9)
   b.   (−4, 8) and (6, 1)
2. Find the midpoint of the segment between each pair of points in problem 1 above.

Solutions

1. a. $d = \sqrt{(5 - 2)^2 + (9 - 5)^2} = \sqrt{3^2 + 4^2} = \sqrt{9 + 16} = \sqrt{25} = 5$

   b. $\sqrt{[6 - (-4)]^2 + (1 - 8)^2} = \sqrt{10^2 + (-7)^2} = \sqrt{100 + 49} = \sqrt{149}$

2. a. $\left(\dfrac{2 + 5}{2}, \dfrac{5 + 9}{2} \right) = \left(\dfrac{7}{2}, 7 \right)$

   b. $\left(1, \dfrac{9}{2} \right)$

Linear Equations

The graph of every linear equation is a line in the rectangular coordinate system. A linear equation is one that is equivalent to $Ax + By = C$ in which not both A and B are zero. A linear equation written in the form $Ax + By = C$ is in *standard form*.

The two ordered pairs obtained by choosing each variable in turn to be 0 are the coordinates of the intercepts of the graph of a linear equation. In other words, by choosing $x = 0$, one obtains the ordered pair $(0, b)$, the y-intercept. The ordered pair $(a, 0)$ is the x-intercept.

For any two ordered pairs (x_1, y_1) and (y_2, y_2) on the graph of a linear equation, the following is called the *slope formula*:

$$m = \frac{y_2 - y_1}{x_2 - x_1} \quad \text{if } x_1 \neq x_2$$

If $x_1 = x_2$ and $y_1 \neq y_2$, then the line is vertical, and it has no slope. If $y_1 = y_2$ and $x_1 \neq x_2$ then the line is horizontal, and it has slope 0. Zero slope is very different from no slope.

A linear equation written in the form

$$y = mx + b$$

is said to be in *slope-intercept* form because the coefficient of x is the slope m of the line and b is the y-intercept. This form is most useful for determining the slope of a line, given its equation.

When an equation is written in this form, the right side of the equation may be entered into a graphing calculator. By choosing an appropriate viewing window, you can graph the equation on the calculator screen. Then by using the *trace* function on the calculator, you can find specific ordered pairs on the graph. Equations whose graphs are vertical lines cannot be graphed on a graphing calculator. The equations of all vertical lines are of the type $x = constant$, so there is no way to solve for the variable y.

We derive the *point-slope* form of the equation of the line from the slope formula:

$$y - y_1 = m(x - x_1)$$

in which m is the slope and (x_1, y_1) is a given fixed point on the line. This form is most useful for determining the equation of a line with certain given characteristics.

PRACTICE EXERCISES

Find the slope of the line:

1. through (2, 3) and (−1, 5)
2. with equation $2x - 3y = 5$

Find the standard form of the equation of the line:

3. through (−3, 4) with slope $m = \dfrac{5}{8}$

4. through (−8, 1) and (3, 5)

Solutions

1. $\dfrac{y_2 - y_1}{x_2 - x_1} = \dfrac{5 - 3}{-1 - 2} = \dfrac{2}{-3} = \dfrac{-2}{3}$

2. Solve the equation for y: $y = \dfrac{2}{3}x - \dfrac{5}{3}$.

The slope is the coefficient of x: $\dfrac{2}{3}$.

3. Plug the slope and the coordinates of the fixed point into the point-slope form:

$$y - 4 = \frac{5}{8}\,[x - (-3)]$$

$$y - 4 = \frac{5}{8}\,(x + 3) \qquad \text{Multiply by 8.}$$

$$8y - 32 = 5(x + 3)$$
$$8y - 32 = 5x + 15$$
$$-5x + 8y = 47$$

or

$$5x - 8y = -47 \qquad \text{If both sides are multiplied by } -1.$$

4. First find the slope: $m = \dfrac{5 - 1}{3 - (-8)} = \dfrac{4}{11}$.

Choose either ordered pair, and plug into the point-slope form:

$$y - 5 = \frac{4}{11}(x - 3)$$

$$11y - 55 = 4(x - 3)$$
$$11y - 55 = 4x - 12$$
$$-4x + 11y = 43$$

or

$$4x - 11y = -43$$

Circle

The equation of the circle in the plane comes from the distance formula:

$$(x - h)^2 + (y - k)^2 = r^2$$

For an equation in this form the center of the circle is (h, k), and its radius is r.

Ellipse

The equation of an ellipse is:

$$\frac{x^2}{a^2} + \frac{y^2}{b^2} = 1 \quad \text{or} \quad \frac{x^2}{b^2} + \frac{y^2}{a^2} = 1$$

Center at the origin. The larger denominator is always a^2.

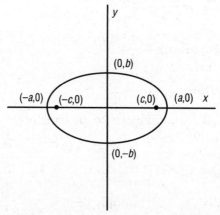

The major axis is a segment of length $2a$, and the minor axis is $2b$. The foci are located along the major axis at a distance $c = \sqrt{a^2 - b^2}$ from the center.

If the center is not at the origin, the equation of an ellipse with major axis oriented horizontally is

$$\frac{(x - h)^2}{a^2} - \frac{(y - k)^2}{b^2} = 1$$

The center is at (h, k).

If the larger denominator is under the variable y, then the major axis is vertical, and the foci are located c units from the center in a vertical direction.

Parabola

The equation of a parabola is either

$$y - k = a(x - h)^2 \quad \text{or} \quad x - h = a(y - k)^2$$

In both cases the vertex is at the point (h, k). In the first case the parabola is oriented vertically, so that there is a maximum or a minimum point, depending on whether a is negative or positive, respectively. In the second case the parabola is oriented horizontally, and there is a point farthest to the left or farthest to the right depending on whether a is positive or negative.

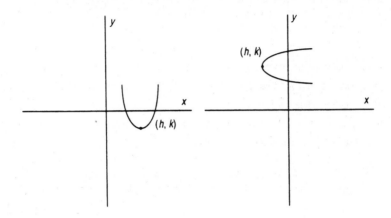

Hyperbola

The equation of a hyperbola is:

$$\frac{x^2}{a^2} - \frac{y^2}{b^2} = 1 \quad \text{or} \quad \frac{y^2}{a^2} - \frac{x^2}{b^2} = 1$$

Center at the origin. The positive term identifies a^2. It is not the larger value as with an ellipse.

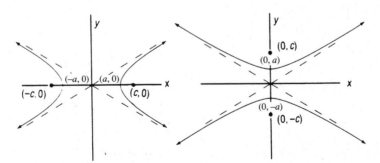

The segment of length $2a$ between the intercepts is called the *transverse axis*. The segment perpendicular to the transverse axis at its midpoint (the center of the hyperbola) of length $2b$ is called the *conjugate axis*.

If the positive term contains the y-variable, then the transverse axis is vertical and the conjugate axis is horizontal.

The foci of the hyperbola are located along the line containing the transverse axis at a distance $c = \sqrt{a^2 + b^2}$ from the center.

The asymptotes of a hyperbola with a horizontal transverse axis are two lines that intersect at the center of the hyperbola and have equations

$$\frac{x}{a} + \frac{y}{b} = 0 \text{ and } \frac{x}{a} - \frac{y}{b} = 0$$

The easiest way to find these equations is to factor the left side of the equation in standard form and set each factor equal to zero. (The left side will always be a difference of squares.)

If the center is not at the origin [at some point (h, k)], then the equation of a hyperbola with a horizontal transverse axis is

$$\frac{(x - h)^2}{a^2} - \frac{(y - k)^2}{b^2} = 1$$

PRACTICE EXERCISES

Discuss the graph of each equation.

1. $x^2 + y^2 - 10x - 4y - 7 = 0$
2. $x - 2 = (y - 1)^2$
3. $\dfrac{(x - 3)^2}{25} + \dfrac{(y + 4)^2}{16} = 1$

Solutions

1. $x^2 + y^2 - 10x - 4y - 7 = 0$ Complete the square in each variable:

$$x^2 - 10x \quad + y^2 - 4y \quad = 7$$

Take half of the coefficient of each linear term, square it, and add the result to both sides of the equation.

$$x^2 - 10x + 25 + y^2 - 4y + 4 = 7 + 25 + 4$$
$$(x - 5)^2 + (y - 2)^2 = 36 \qquad \text{Standard form.}$$

The graph is a circle with center at (5, 2) and radius 6.

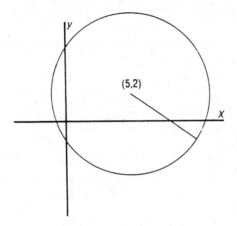

2. Written as $x - 2 = (y - 1)^2$, this equation is the standard form of the equation for a parabola oriented horizontally with a vertex at (2, 1), which happens to be the point farthest to the left. Locating a couple of other points gives the graph.

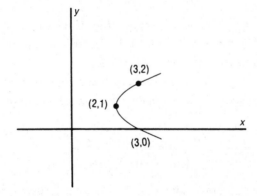

3. $\dfrac{(x - 3)^2}{25} + \dfrac{(y + 4)^2}{16} = 1$ This is the standard form of an equation of an ellipse with major axis horizontal, of length $2a = 10$, minor axis of length $2b = 8$, and center at point (3, −4).

The foci are located $c = \sqrt{5^2 - 4^2} = \sqrt{9} = 3$ units horizontally from the center, $(3 + 3, -4)$ and $(3 - 3, -4)$.

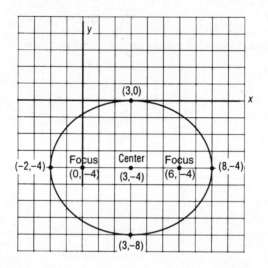

Functions

A function is a set of ordered pairs of real numbers in which no two ordered pairs have the same first component.

An example of a function according to this definition is

$$f = \{(1, 1),(2, 4)(3, 9)(4, 16)(5, 25)\}$$

The equation $f(x) = y$, read as "f of x equals y," is special notation for functions to indicate that the ordered pair, (x, y), is in the function. In the example, $f(4) = 16$ conveys the same information as $(4, 16) \in f$.

The *domain* of a function is the set of all first components of the ordered pairs in the function. The *range* is the set of all second components of the ordered pairs. In the example:

$$\text{Domain} = \{1,2,3,4,5\}$$
$$\text{Range} = \{1,4,9,16,25\}$$

Many times a function is given by the rule that generates the ordered pairs, rather than by the ordered pairs themselves. For example, $g(x) = x^2$. The domain in this case should always be chosen to be the largest set of real numbers for which the defining rule makes sense—no division by 0 or square roots of negative numbers. The range is usually a more difficult question; it can be determined by examining the rule itself or by observing the graph of the function.

PRACTICE EXERCISES

Find the domain and range of each function.

1. $f(x) = x^2 + 1$

2. $g(x) = \dfrac{1}{x}$

3. $h(x) = \sqrt{x - 1}$

Solutions

1. Domain: R
   Range: $\{y | y \in R \text{ and } y \geq 1\}$
2. Domain: $\{x | x \in R \text{ and } x \neq 0\}$
   Range: $\{y | y \in R \text{ and } y \neq 0\}$
3. Domain: $\{x | x \in R \text{ and } x \geq 1\}$
   Range: $\{y | y \in R \text{ and } y \geq 0\}$

Exponential and Logarithmic Functions

An *exponential function* is any function of the type

$$f(x) = a^x \quad \text{for any positive number } a, \quad a \neq 1.$$

The following is a definition of a *logarithmic function*:

$$y = \log_a x \quad \text{if and only if} \quad x = a^y.$$

Six fundamental properties of logarithms are easily derived from the definition given above:

1. $\log_a (xy) = \log_a x + \log_a y$ The logarithm of a product is the sum of the logarithms.

2. $\log_a \left(\dfrac{x}{y}\right) = \log_a x - \log_a y$ The logarithm of a quotient is the difference of the logarithms.

3. $\log_a x^n = n \log_a x$ The logarithm of a power is that power multiplied by the logarithm.

4. $\log_a a^x = x \text{ and } a^{\log_a x} = x$
5. $\log_a 1 = 0$
6. $\log_a a = 1$

When no base is indicated, the base is understood to be 10. Base 10 logarithms are called common logs.

PRACTICE EXERCISES

1. Write as a logarithmic equation:

    $$8^{-(1/3)} = \frac{1}{2}$$

2. Write as an exponential equation:

    $$\log_{1/4} 16 = -2$$

    Evaluate.

3. $\log_3 \dfrac{1}{9}$

4. $\log_3 \sqrt{3^5}$

5. $\log_3 27^{1/2}$

    Solve (6–8).

6. $\log_x 125 = -3$

7. $\log_x 4 = 1$

8. $\log_5 x = 0$

Solutions

1. $\log_8 \dfrac{1}{2} = -\dfrac{1}{3}$

2. $\left(\dfrac{1}{4}\right)^{-2} = 16$

3. $\log_3 \dfrac{1}{9} = x$

    $3^x = \dfrac{1}{9} = 9^{-1} = \left(3^2\right)^{-1} = 3^{-2}$ So $x = -2$.

4. $\log_3 \sqrt{3^5} = x$

    $3^x = \sqrt{3^5} = \left(3^5\right)^{1/2} = 3^{5/2}$ So $x = \dfrac{5}{2}$.

5. $\log_3 27^{1/2} = x$

    $3^x = 27^{1/2} = \left(3^3\right)^{1/2} = 3^{3/2}$ So $x = \dfrac{3}{2}$.

6. $\log_x 125 = -3$ Write the equation in exponential form.

    $x^{-3} = 125$ Raise both sides to the $-\dfrac{1}{3}$ power.

    $x = 125^{-(1/3)}$

    $= \sqrt[3]{\dfrac{1}{125}} = \dfrac{1}{5}$

7. $\log_x 4 = 1$ $x^1 = 4$ A rule is $\log_b b = 1$. The logarithm
$x = 4$ of the base is always 1.

8. $\log_5 x = 0$ $5^0 = x$ A rule is $\log_b 1 = 0$. The logarithm
$x = 1$ of 1 in any base is 0.

The Binomial Theorem

The expression $n!$ (read as "n factorial") is defined as follows:

$$n! = n(n - 1)(n - 2)(n - 3) \cdots 2 \cdot 1$$
$$1! = 1$$
$$0! = 1$$

Factorials allow easy counting of arrangements (or permutations) and combinations. The number of permutations of n things taken r at a time is

$$_nP_r = \frac{n!}{(n - r)!} \quad \text{(The notations } P_{n,r} \text{ is also used.)}$$

For example, if one has 20 different books and a shelf that will hold 8 of them, how many different arrangements of those books on the shelf are possible?

$$_{20}P_8 = \frac{20!}{(20 - 8)!} = 20 \cdot 19 \cdot 18 \cdots \cdot 13$$
$$= 5,079,110,400$$

The number of combinations of n things taken r at a time is

$$_nC_r = \frac{n!}{r!\,(n - r)!} \quad \text{(The notations } C_{n,r} \text{ and } \binom{n}{r} \text{ are also used.)}$$

The difference is that permutations are concerned with order, whereas combinations are not. For example, the number of different combinations of the 20 books on the shelf that will hold 8 books is

$$_{20}C_8 = \frac{20!}{8!12!}$$
$$= 125,970$$

The combination numbers turn out to be useful in the formula to raise a binomial to a power. This formula is known as the Binomial Theorem.

$$(a + b)^n = {}_nC_0a^n + {}_nC_1a^{n-1}b^1 + {}_nC_2a^{n-2}b^2 + \cdots$$
$$+ {}_nC_ra^{n-r}b^r + \cdots + {}_nC_nb^n$$

The coefficients of the terms in the Binomial Theorem are found in the nth row of Pascal's triangle, an array of numbers in which each entry other than the 1 at the end of each row is found by adding the two numbers immediately above it.

1		Row 0
1 1		Row 1
PASCAL'S	1 2 1	Row 2
TRIANGLE	1 3 3 1	.
1 4 6 4 1	.
1 5 10 10 5 1	.
1 6 15 20 15 6 1	

Using Pascal's triangle, we can easily write the expansion of $(x + y)^6$ as follows:

$$(x + y)^6 = 1x^6 + 6x^5y + 15x^4y^2 + 20x^3y^3 + 15x^2y^4 + 6xy^5 + 1y^6$$

PRACTICE EXERCISES

Evaluate.

1. $7!$ **2.** $_8P_3$ **3.** $_{10}C_4$
4. Write the expansion of $(a - b)^4$

Solutions

1. $7! = 7 \cdot 6 \cdot 5 \cdot 4 \cdot 3 \cdot 2 \cdot 1 = 5040$

2.
$$_8P_3 = \frac{8!}{(8-3)!}$$
$$= \frac{8 \cdot 7 \cdot 6 \cdot 5 \cdot 4 \cdot 3 \cdot 2 \cdot 1}{5 \cdot 4 \cdot 3 \cdot 2 \cdot 1}$$
$$= 8 \cdot 7 \cdot 6 = 336$$

3.
$$_{10}C_4 = \frac{10!}{4!(10 - 4)!}$$
$$= \frac{10!}{4!6!} \qquad \text{Cancel } 6!.$$
$$= \frac{10 \cdot \cancel{9} \cdot \cancel{8} \cdot 7}{\cancel{4} \cdot \cancel{3} \cdot \cancel{2} \cdot 1} \qquad \text{Cancel common factors.}$$
$$= 10 \cdot 3 \cdot 1 \cdot 7 = 210$$

4. $(a - b)^4 = (a + (-b))^4$

$$= {}_4C_0a^4(-b)^0 + {}_4C_1a^3(-b)^1 + {}_4C_2a^2(-b)^2$$
$$+ {}_4C_3a^1(-b)^3 + {}_4C_4a^0(-b)^4$$
$$= a^4 - 4a^3b + 6a^2b^2 - 4ab^3 + b^4$$

Complex Numbers

A complex number is any number in the form $a + bi$, in which a and b are real numbers and $i = \sqrt{-1}$.

$$a + bi = c + di \quad \text{if and only if} \quad a = c \text{ and } b = d$$

The following are the definitions of operations involving complex numbers:

- **Absolute value:** $|a + bi| = \sqrt{a^2 + b^2}$ (Note that i is not used in the radicand.) The absolute value of a complex number is called its modulus.
- **Conjugate:** The conjugate of $a + bi$ is $a - bi$. (Change the sign of the imaginary part.)
- **Addition:** $(a + bi) + (c + di) = (a + c) + (b + d)i$ (Add the real parts and add the imaginary parts separately.)
- **Subtraction:** $(a + bi) - (c + di) = (a - c) + (b - d)i$ (Subtract the real parts and subtract the imaginary parts.)
- **Multiplication:** $(a + bi)(c + di) = (ac - bd) + (ad + bc)i$ (Rather than use the definition, it is common to treat the complex numbers like binomials and multiply by the FOIL method.)
- **Division:** $\dfrac{a + bi}{c + di} = \dfrac{(a + bi)(c - di)}{(c + di)(c - di)}$ (Multiply the numerator and denominator by the conjugate of the denominator.)

PRACTICE EXERCISES

Perform the indicated operations. Express answers in the standard form, $a + bi$.

1. $\sqrt{-125}$

2. $\sqrt{-9} \cdot \sqrt{-36}$

3. $(-3 + 2i) + (4 + 5i)$

4. $(-3 - 4i) - (-1 - i)$

5. $2i(4 - 3i)$

6. $(7 + 3i)(-5 + i)$

7. $\dfrac{4i}{1 - i}$

Solutions

1. $\sqrt{-125} = \sqrt{(-1)(25)(5)} = \sqrt{-1} \cdot \sqrt{25} \cdot \sqrt{5}$
   $= i \cdot 5 \cdot \sqrt{5} = 5i\sqrt{5}$

2. $\sqrt{-9}\,\sqrt{-36} = (3i)(6i) = 18i^2 = 18(-1) = -18$

   (The rule from algebra, $\sqrt{ab} = \sqrt{a}\,\sqrt{b}$, does not apply to this problem because the factors are not real numbers.)

3. $(-3 + 2i) + (4 + 5i) = 1 + 7i$

4. $(-3 - 4i) - (-1 - i) = -2 - 3i$

5. $2i(4 - 3i) = 8i - 6i^2 = 8i - 6(-1)$
   $\qquad\qquad = 8i + 6 = 6 + 8i$

6. $(7 + 3i)(-5 + i) = -35 + 7i - 15i + 3i^2$
   $\qquad\qquad\qquad = -35 - 8i + 3(-1)$
   $\qquad\qquad\qquad = -35 - 8i - 3 = -38 - 8i$

7. $\dfrac{4i}{1 - i} = \dfrac{4i(1 + i)}{(1 - i)(1 + i)} = \dfrac{4i - 4}{1 - i^2}$

   $\qquad = \dfrac{-4 + 4i}{2} = -2 + 2i$

GEOMETRY

Angles

An *angle* is the union of two rays with a common endpoint.

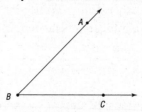

The angle shown above consists of $\overrightarrow{BA}$ and $\overrightarrow{BC}$. The common endpoint B is called the *vertex*.

Two angles that have the same measure are called *congruent*.

Angles can be classified according to their measure.

- The measure of an *acute angle* is between 0° and 90°.
- A *right angle* measures 90°.
- The measure of an *obtuse angle* is between 90° and 180°.
- A *straight angle* measures 180°.

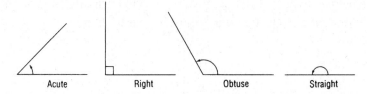

| Acute | Right | Obtuse | Straight |

Two angles are called *adjacent* if they have a common side and the interiors of the angles do not intersect.

A segment, a ray, or a line that contains the vertex of an angle such that it forms two congruent adjacent angles with the sides of the angle is called an *angle bisector*.

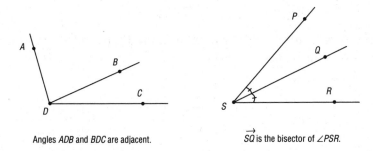

Angles *ADB* and *BDC* are adjacent.

$\overrightarrow{SQ}$ is the bisector of ∠*PSR*.

There are always two pairs of *vertical angles* formed by the intersection of two lines. In the figure shown below, angles *AEB* and *DEC* are vertical angles, and angles *AED* and *BEC* are also vertical angles.

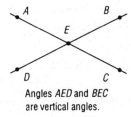

Angles *AED* and *BEC*
are vertical angles.

Two angles are *complementary* if their sum is 90°. Two angles are *supplementary* if their sum is 180°. Notice that both definitions specify two angles. These definitions do not apply to three or more angles.

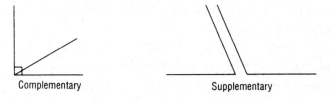

| Complementary | Supplementary |

Perpendicular lines are two lines that intersect to form a right angle. Of course, if there is one right angle, then there must be four of them.

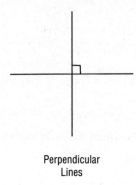

Perpendicular
Lines

If two parallel lines are intersected by a third line (called the *transversal*), then the following angles are congruent:

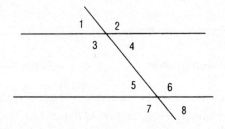

Corresponding angles: 1 and 5, 2 and 6, 3 and 7, 4 and 8

Alternate interior angles: 3 and 6, 4 and 5

Alternate exterior angles: 1 and 8, 2 and 7

Vertical angles: 1 and 4, 2 and 3, 5 and 8, 6 and 7

Interior angles on the same side of the transversal are supplementary. Angles 4 and 6 are supplementary, and 3 and 5 are supplementary. Exterior angles on the same side of the transversal are also supplementary: 2 and 8, 1 and 7.

Polygons

Triangles

A triangle is a polygon with three sides. Triangles may be classified according to the lengths of their sides.

- An **equilateral triangle** has three congruent sides.
- An **isosceles triangle** has at least two congruent sides.
- A **scalene triangle** has no two congruent sides.

A triangle may also be classified according to the measure of its angles.
- An **equiangular triangle** has three congruent angles.
- An **acute triangle** has all acute angles.
- A **right triangle** has one right angle.
- An **obtuse triangle** has one obtuse angle.

An *altitude* of a triangle is a segment from a vertex perpendicular to the opposite side (the base). Each triangle has three altitudes, and the lines that contain all three intersect at a point. The area of any triangle is $\frac{1}{2}$ of the product of the length of an altitude and the length of the base to that altitude:

$$A = \frac{1}{2}bh$$

The following are important properties of triangles:

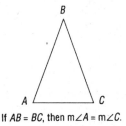

1. Base angles of an isosceles triangle are congruent. (If two sides are the same length, then the angles opposite those sides are congruent.)

2. The sum of the measures of the angles of any triangle is 180°. Therefore the sum of the measures of the angles of an *n*-sided polygon is $(n - 2)(180°)$.

If $AB = BC$, then $m\angle A = m\angle C$.

3. The angles of an equilateral triangle are congruent. They each have measure 60°.

4. The sum of the exterior angles of a triangle (taking one at each vertex) is 360°. An exterior angle is formed by extending one side of a triangle through the vertex.

5. If the sides of a right triangle have lengths a, b, and c (c is the length of the hypotenuse), then these numbers satisfy the Pythagorean Theorem:

$$a^2 + b^2 = c^2$$

Quadrilaterals

A quadrilateral is a polygon with four sides. The following are definitions of certain quadrilaterals with special characteristics:

- A **trapezoid** has one pair of opposite sides parallel.

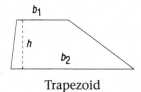

Trapezoid

- A **parallelogram** has both pairs of opposite sides parallel.

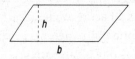

Parallelogram

- A **rectangle** is a parallelogram with a right angle (and, hence, four right angles).

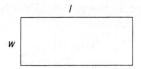

Rectangle

- A **square** is an equilateral rectangle or a regular quadrilateral.

Square

- A **rhombus** is an equilateral parallelogram.

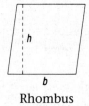

Rhombus

Areas of Quadrilaterals

The following are area formulas for the quadrilaterals defined above:

Trapezoid: $A = \dfrac{1}{2}h(b_1 + b_2)$

Parallelogram: $A = hb$

Rectangle: $A = lw$

Square: $A = s^2$

Rhombus: $A = hb = \dfrac{1}{2}(\text{product of diagonals})$

Circles

A circle is the set of points in a plane that are a given fixed distance from a given point. The given distance is called the *radius* and the fixed point is the *center*. A segment whose endpoints are on the circle is called a *chord*. A chord that also contains the center is a *diameter* (the longest chord). A line that contains a chord of a circle is a *secant line*. A line that contains only one point of a circle is a *tangent line*.

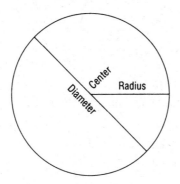

The length around a circle is called its *circumference*. The formula for the circumference is

$$C = \pi d \quad (\pi \text{ times diameter}) \quad \text{or} \quad C = 2\pi r \quad (2\pi \text{ times radius})$$

The area formula for a circle is

$$A = \pi r^2$$

A *central angle* is an angle with its vertex at the center of a circle. The measure of a central angle is the same as the measure of its intercepted arc. Thus there are 360° of arc in a circle.

An *inscribed angle* is an angle formed by two chords of a circle; its vertex is on the circle. The measure of an inscribed angle is one-half the measure of its intercepted arc.

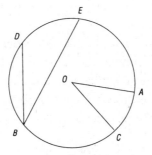

Angle *AOC* is a central angle.
Angle *DBE* is inscribed.

PRACTICE EXERCISES

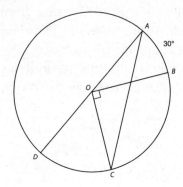

In circle with center O, m($\widehat{AB}$) = 30° and $\overline{OB} \perp \overline{OC}$. What is the measure of:

1. $\widehat{CD}$ 3. $\angle CAD$

2. $\angle COD$ 4. $\angle ACO$

Solutions

1. A central angle has the same measure as its intercepted arc, m($\widehat{BC}$) = 90°. AD is a diameter; therefore the sum of arcs AB, BC, and DC is 180°. Therefore m($\widehat{CD}$) = 60°

2. m($\angle COD$) = m($\widehat{CD}$) = 60°

3. Inscribed angle CAD is half the measure of its intercepted arc. m($\angle CAD$) = 30°.

4. $\triangle ACO$ is an isosceles triangle. Base angles of an isosceles triangle have the same measure. m(ACO) = 30°.

TRIGONOMETRY

Angles

An angle is in standard position if its initial side is the positive x-axis and the vertex is at the origin. If the terminal side of the angle then lies in quadrant I, the angle is called a quadrant I angle; if it lies in quadrant II, it is called a quadrant II angle; etc. A positive angle is measured counterclockwise, and a negative angle is measured clockwise from the positive x-axis.

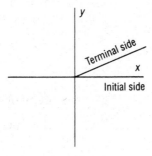

Standard Position

There are several measurement systems for angles. Two of them will be reviewed here.

1. Degree-minute-second:

$$1 \text{ degree} = 1° = \frac{1}{360} \text{ of a revolution}$$

$$1 \text{ minute} = 1' = \frac{1}{60}°$$

$$1 \text{ minute} = 1'' = \frac{1}{60}'$$

2. Radians: 1 radian is the central angle subtended by an arc equal in length to the radius of the circle.

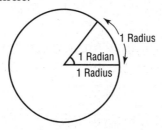

The formula for the circumference of a circle, $C = 2\pi r$, shows that there are 2π radii in the circumference of a circle. Therefore there are 2π radians in one complete revolution.

2π radians $= 360°$ (The equal sign is used here to mean that the two numbers measure the same angle.)

Therefore:

π radians $= 180°$

$\frac{\pi}{2}$ radians $= 90°$

$\frac{\pi}{3}$ radians $= 60°$

Most angles of interest are multiples of these five. Memorize them.

$$\frac{\pi}{4} \text{ radians} = 45°$$

$$\frac{\pi}{6} \text{ radians} = 30°$$

Generally, to convert an angle measurement from degrees to radians, multiply the number of degrees by $\frac{\pi}{180}$. The measurement of an angle in radians is commonly expressed in terms of π. ($1° = \frac{\pi}{180}$ radians.)

To convert an angle measurement from radians to degrees, multiply the number of radians by $\frac{180°}{\pi}$. The π normally cancels. (1 radian = $\frac{180°}{\pi}$.)

Any statement made below, even though it may be phrased with the angles measured in degrees, will be true also if the angles are measured in radians.

If two different angles in standard position have the same terminal side, the angles are called *coterminal*. Coterminal angles can be found by adding or subtracting multiples of 360° or 2π to or from the original angle.

The acute angle formed by the terminal side of the angle and the nearer portion of the x-axis is called the *reference* angle.

PRACTICE EXERCISES

Convert from degree measure to radian measure.

1. 210°
2. −540°

Convert from radian measure to degree measure.

3. $\frac{5\pi}{4}$

4. $\frac{7\pi}{9}$

Find: a. The smallest positive angle that is coterminal with the given angle
   b. The reference angle

5. 478°
6. −815°
7. $\frac{11\pi}{3}$

Solutions

1. $210\left(\dfrac{\pi}{180}\right) = \dfrac{7\pi}{6}$

2. $-540\left(\dfrac{\pi}{180}\right) = -3\pi$

3. $\dfrac{5\pi}{4}\left(\dfrac{180}{\pi}\right) = 225$

4. $\dfrac{7\pi}{9}\left(\dfrac{180}{\pi}\right) = 140$

5. a. $478 - 360 = 118$
  $118°$ is in quad. II.
  b. $180 - 118 = 62$

6. a. $-815 + 3(360) = -815 + 1080 = 265$
  $265°$ is in quad. III.
  b. $265 - 180 = 85$

7. a. $\dfrac{11\pi}{3} - 2\pi = \dfrac{11\pi}{3} - \dfrac{6\pi}{3} = \dfrac{5\pi}{3}$

  $\dfrac{5\pi}{3}$ is in quad. IV.

  b. $2\pi - \dfrac{5\pi}{3} = \dfrac{6\pi}{3} - \dfrac{5\pi}{3} = \dfrac{\pi}{3}$

Definitions of Trigonometric Functions

Choose a point, (x, y), on the terminal side of an angle, θ, in standard position. The distance from the origin is $r = \sqrt{x^2 + y^2}$.

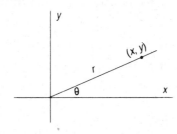

$\sin \theta = \dfrac{y}{r}$ Sine

$\cos \theta = \dfrac{x}{r}$ Cosine

$$\tan \theta = \frac{y}{x}, \quad x \neq 0, \theta \neq 90° \pm 180n° \qquad \text{Tangent}$$

$$\csc \theta = \frac{r}{y}, \quad y \neq 0, \theta \neq \pm 180n° \qquad \text{Cosecant}$$

$$\sec \theta = \frac{r}{x}, \quad x \neq 0, \theta \neq 90° \pm 180n° \qquad \text{Secant}$$

$$\cot \theta = \frac{x}{y}, \quad y \neq 0, \theta \neq \pm 180n° \qquad \text{Cotangent}$$

In each case above, $n = 0, 1, 2, \ldots$.

This information should be memorized for the four quadrants:

   I: All positive.

  II: Sine and cosecant positive, others negative.

 III: Tangent and cotangent positive, others negative.

 IV: Cosine and secant positive, others negative.

ASTC is a helpful mnemonic aid.

A function of any angle is equal to $\pm$ the same function of the reference angle. The sign of the function value is determined by ASTC.

PRACTICE EXERCISES

Name the six trigonometric function values for the angle θ in standard position with the given point on the terminal side.

1. $(-3, 4)$
2. $(-2, -6)$

Name the quadrant in which the angle θ must lie for the following to be true:

3. $\sin \theta > 0$ and $\tan \theta < 0$
4. $\cos \theta < 0$ and $\csc \theta > 0$
5. $\cot \theta > 0$ and $\sec \theta < 0$
6. $\sec \theta > 0$ and $\sin \theta < 0$

Find the remaining five function values, given the following information:

7. $\tan \theta = \frac{1}{2}$ and $\sin \theta$ is negative

Solutions

1. First $r = \sqrt{(-3)^2 + 4^2} = \sqrt{25} = 5$

$$\sin \theta = \frac{4}{5} \qquad \csc \theta = \frac{5}{4}$$

$$\cos \theta = \frac{-3}{5} \qquad \sec \theta = \frac{-5}{3}$$

$$\tan \theta = \frac{-4}{3} \qquad \cot \theta = \frac{-3}{4}$$

2. $r = \sqrt{(-2)^2 + (-6)^2} = \sqrt{40} = 2\sqrt{10}$

$$\sin \theta = \frac{-6}{2\sqrt{10}} = \frac{-3\sqrt{10}}{10}$$

$$\cos \theta = \frac{-2}{2\sqrt{10}} = \frac{-\sqrt{10}}{10}$$

$$\tan \theta = \frac{-6}{-2} = 3$$

$$\csc \theta = \frac{2\sqrt{10}}{-6} = \frac{-\sqrt{10}}{3}$$

$$\sec \theta = \frac{-2\sqrt{10}}{2} = -\sqrt{10}$$

$$\cot \theta = \frac{-2}{-6} = \frac{1}{3}$$

3. ASTC indicates that the sine is positive in quads. I and II, while the tangent is negative in quads. II and IV. Both are true only in quad. II.

4. $\cos \theta < 0$ in II and III
   $\csc \theta > 0$ in I and II
   Both are true only in quad. II.

5. $\cot \theta > 0$ in I and III
   $\sec \theta < 0$ in II and III
   Both are true only in quad. III.

6. $\sec \theta > 0$ in I and IV
   $\sin \theta < 0$ in III and IV
   Both are true only in quad. IV.

7. Since $\tan \theta = \dfrac{1}{2}$ (>0) and $\sin \theta < 0$, angle θ must be in quad III.

And since $\tan \theta = \dfrac{y}{x} = \dfrac{1}{2} = \dfrac{-1}{-2}$ choose a point $(-2, -1)$ on the terminal side of θ.

$$r = \sqrt{2^2 + 1^2} = \sqrt{5}$$

$$\sin \theta = \frac{-1}{\sqrt{5}} = \frac{-\sqrt{5}}{5}$$

$$\cos \theta = \frac{-2}{\sqrt{5}} = \frac{-2\sqrt{5}}{5}$$

$\tan \theta$ is given.

$$\csc \theta = \frac{\sqrt{5}}{-1} = -\sqrt{5}$$

$$\sec \theta = \frac{-\sqrt{5}}{2}$$

$$\cot \theta = \frac{2}{1} = 2$$

Identities

An identity is an equation that is true for all elements in the domains for which the functions involved are defined. There are many identities in trigonometry. Memorize these:

- **Reciprocal identities**

$$\sin x = \frac{1}{\csc x} \qquad \csc x = \frac{1}{\sin x}$$

$$\cos x = \frac{1}{\sec x} \qquad \sec x = \frac{1}{\cos x}$$

$$\tan x = \frac{1}{\cot x} \qquad \cot x = \frac{1}{\tan x}$$

- **Quotient identities**

$$\tan x = \frac{\sin x}{\cos x} \qquad \cot x = \frac{\cos x}{\sin x}$$

- **Pythagorean identities**

$$\sin^2 x = \cos^2 x = 1 \qquad \text{Note that } \sin^2 x = (\sin x)^2 \cdot$$

$$\tan^2 x + 1 = \sec^2 x$$

$$1 + \cot^2 x = \csc^2 x$$

- **Sum and difference identities**

    ($\pm$ and $\mp$ are different; if one is $-$, the other is $+$.)

    $\cos (A \pm B) = \cos A \cos B \mp \sin A \sin B$

    $\sin (A \pm B) = \sin A \cos B \pm \sin B \cos A$

    $\tan (A \pm B) = \dfrac{\tan A \pm \tan B}{1 \mp \tan A \tan B}$

- **Double-angle identities**

    $\sin 2A = 2 \sin A \cos A$

    $\cos 2A = \cos^2 A - \sin^2 A = 2 \cos^2 A - 1 = 1 - 2 \sin^2 A$

    $\tan 2A = \dfrac{2 \tan A}{1 - \tan^2 A}$

- **Half-angle identities**

    $\sin \dfrac{A}{2} = \pm \sqrt{\dfrac{1 - \cos A}{2}}$

    $\cos \dfrac{A}{2} = \pm \sqrt{\dfrac{1 + \cos A}{2}}$

    $\tan \dfrac{A}{2} = \pm \sqrt{\dfrac{1 - \cos A}{1 + \cos A}} = \dfrac{\sin A}{1 + \cos A} = \dfrac{1 - \cos A}{\sin A}$

PRACTICE EXERCISES

Use the identities above to find each function value.

1. $\cos 15°$
2. $\tan 75°$
3. $\sin 195°$
4. $\cos \dfrac{\pi}{8}$
5. $\sin 2A$, given that $\sin A = \dfrac{3}{4}$ and a is in quadrant I.

Solutions

1. Find two angles whose difference is 15° (45° and 30° will do).

$$\cos 15° = \cos (45 - 30)°$$
$$= \cos 45 \cos 30 + \sin 45 \sin 30$$
$$= \left(\frac{\sqrt{2}}{2}\right)\left(\frac{\sqrt{3}}{2}\right) + \left(\frac{\sqrt{2}}{2}\right)\left(\frac{1}{2}\right)$$
$$= \frac{\sqrt{6}}{4} + \frac{\sqrt{2}}{4}$$
$$= \frac{\sqrt{6} + \sqrt{2}}{4}$$

2. Several choices are possible. Choose the half-angle tangent formula.

$$\tan 75° = \tan \frac{1}{2}(150°) = \frac{\sin 150°}{1 + \cos 150°}$$
$$= \frac{\frac{1}{2}}{1 + \frac{-\sqrt{3}}{2}}$$
$$= \frac{1}{2 - \sqrt{3}} = 2 + \sqrt{3}$$

3. $$\sin 195° = \sin (150 + 45)°$$
$$= \sin 150 \cos 45 + \sin 45 \cos 150$$
$$= \left(\frac{1}{2}\right)\left(\frac{\sqrt{2}}{2}\right) + \left(\frac{\sqrt{2}}{2}\right)\left(\frac{-\sqrt{3}}{2}\right)$$
$$= \frac{\sqrt{2}}{4} + \frac{-\sqrt{6}}{4} = \frac{\sqrt{2} - \sqrt{6}}{4}$$

4. $$\cos \frac{\pi}{8} = \cos \frac{\left(\frac{\pi}{4}\right)}{2} = \pm\sqrt{\frac{1 + \cos\left(\frac{\pi}{4}\right)}{2}}$$
$$= \pm\sqrt{\frac{1 + \frac{\sqrt{2}}{2}}{2}}$$
$$= \pm\sqrt{\frac{2 + \sqrt{2}}{4}} \qquad \text{Choose the positive sign}$$
$$= \frac{\sqrt{2 + \sqrt{2}}}{2} \qquad \text{because } \frac{\pi}{8} \text{ is in quad. I.}$$

5. Since $\sin A = \dfrac{3}{4}$ and A is in quad. I,

$$\sin^2 A + \cos^2 A = 1$$

$$\left(\frac{3}{4}\right)^2 + \cos^2 A = 1$$

$$\frac{9}{16} + \cos^2 A = 1$$

$$\cos^2 A = \frac{7}{16}$$

$$\cos A = \frac{\sqrt{7}}{4} \qquad \text{Choose the positive sign.}$$

So $\sin 2A = 2 \sin A \cos A = 2\left(\dfrac{3}{4}\right)\left(\dfrac{\sqrt{7}}{4}\right) = \dfrac{3\sqrt{7}}{8}.$

Preparing for the Reading Test

4

DESCRIPTION OF THE READING TEST

The ACT Reading Test contains reading passages from four content areas:

Content Area	Subject	# of Questions	% of Test
1. Prose Fiction	novel or short story	10	25
2. Social Studies	anthropology, archaeology, business, economics, education, geography, history, political science, psychology, and sociology	10	25
3. Humanities	architecture, art, dance, ethics, film, language, literary criticism, music, philosophy, radio, television, and theater	10	25
4. Natural Science	anatomy, astronomy, biology, botany, chemistry, ecology, geology, medicine, meteorology, microbiology, natural history, physiology, physics, technology, and zoology	10	25
Scoring: Two subscores reported: 1) Prose Fiction and Humanities — 20 questions; 2) Social Studies and Natural Science — 20 questions			

Each passage is about 750 words, or roughly two pages of a typical book. On a given ACT, the prose fiction passage may be first, second, third, or fourth. The same holds true for the other passages. The order is not announced ahead of time.

Each passage is followed by 10 multiple-choice questions—40 questions in all. Fourteen of the questions test what the passages say explicitly. Many more of the questions—almost twice as many—ask what the passage implies or suggests.

𝔸⟶🗝 TEST-TAKING TIPS

You've probably observed that people cope with tests in a variety of ways. In fact, the manner in which you take a test is as individual as your DNA.

Considering the variety of test-taking styles, it would take a very long list to describe every tactic that has helped other students taking the ACT Reading Test. What works for them may not work for you and vice versa. Nevertheless, some tactics help everyone, regardless of ability or test-taking style. Many of the following tactics can improve your score. Give them an honest chance to work for you.

1. **Pace yourself.** You have less than nine minutes per passage. If you spend five minutes reading a passage, you still have four minutes left to answer ten questions, or almost 25 seconds per question.

2. **Understand the test directions.** Know what the directions say before you walk into the exam room. They will be similar to the following:

> _Directions:_ This test consists of four passages, each followed by ten multiple-choice questions. Read each and then pick the best answer for each question. Fill in the spaces on your answer sheet that correspond to your choices. Refer to the passage as often as you wish while answering the questions.

3. **Decide on a reading technique.** On the ACT, different approaches to a reading passage carry different gains and losses.
   - **Read the passage carefully from start to finish.** Don't try to remember every detail. As you read, ask yourself, "What is this passage really about?" You can usually get the general idea in two or three lines.
   - **Skim the passage for its general idea.** Read faster than you normally would to figure out the type of passage it is. Don't expect to keep details in mind. Refer to the passage as you answer the questions.
   - **Skim the passage to get its general meaning; then go back and read it more thoroughly.** Two readings, one fast and one slow, enable you to grasp the passage better than if you read it only once.
   - **Read the questions first; then read the passage.** Alerts you to the content of the passage.

4. **Concentrate on paragraph openings and closings.** Knowing how passages are constructed can speed up your reading and also guide your search for answers to the questions. When reading quickly for the gist of a passage,

for instance, focus on paragraph openings and closings. Skip the material in between until you need the details to answer certain questions.

5. **Use paragraphs as clues to help you understand the passage.** Writers generally take pains to organize their material. They decide what goes first, second, third. Usually, the arrangement follows a logical order, although sometimes material is arranged to build suspense or to surprise the reader. Most often, though, paragraphs are used to build the main idea of a passage. Each paragraph in some way reinforces the author's point.

6. **Decide whether to use an underlining technique.**
   • **Underline key ideas and phrases.** Since you have a pencil in your hand during the ACT, use it to highlight the important points of a reading passage. When you come to an idea that sounds important, quickly draw a line under it or put a checkmark next to it in the margin.
   • **Don't underline anything.** The rationale here is that, without having read the passage at least once, you can't know what's important. Furthermore, underlining takes time and you may be wasting seconds drawing lines under material that won't help you answer the questions. The time you spend underlining might better be spent rereading the passage or studying the questions.
   • **Underline answers only.** After you have read the questions and returned to the passage, use your pencil to identify tentative answers to the questions.

7. **Decide when to read the questions.**
   • **Read the questions before you read the passage.** When you know the questions beforehand, you can read a passage more purposefully. Instead of reading for a general impression, you can look for the main idea of the passage, seek out specific details, and locate the meaning of a phrase or idea. When a question refers to a specific line number, go directly to the passage and mark that line with a check or asterisk. Better still, write the number of the question in the margin (e.g., #3, #8). Later, when you read the passage, you'll know instantly that you must read that line attentively because it may give you, or at least strongly suggest, the right answer.
   • **Read the questions after you read the passage.** With the passage fresh in your mind, you can probably answer two or three questions immediately. With a few questions and choices eliminated, direct your second reading of the passage to the remaining questions.

- **Read the questions one by one, not as a group.** After reading the passage, start with the first question and answer it by referring to the passage. Then go on to the next question. Don't be a slave to the order of the questions. If you can't answer a question, skip it for the time being and go on to the next one. Go back later if you have time.

8. **Suspend your prior knowledge.** Occasionally, a reading passage may deal with a subject you know about. Because all the questions are derived from the passage in front of you, all your answers should be, too. Cast aside your prior knowledge and read both passage and questions with an open mind.

9. **Identify each question by type.** Usually the wording of a question will tell you whether you can find the answer by *referring* directly to the passage or by using your *reasoning* powers. Once you know how to distinguish between them, you can vary your approach to find the right answers. For example, when a question asks you to identify what the author of the passage says, you'll know instantly that you are dealing with a factual question and that you should search the passage for explicit material. In contrast, a question that asks about the main thought of a passage calls for a different approach, perhaps rereading the passage's opening and closing paragraphs and inferring the author's purpose.

10. **Answer general questions before detail questions.** General questions usually ask you to identify the author's point of view or the main idea of the passage. Get the easier questions out of the way before tackling the more time-consuming ones.

11. **Do the easy passages first.** If you've always experienced success with natural science passages, and you have trouble with fiction, go first to the natural science passage even if it's last on the test. Likewise, if you have a knack for the arts, turn first to the humanities passage. In other words, lead with your strength, whatever it may be. If you're equally good in everything, then stick with the order of the test.

12. **Stay alert for "switchbacks."** These are the words and phrases frequently used to alert you to shifts in thought. The most common switchback word is *but*. Other switchback words and phrases that function like *but* include *although, however, nevertheless, on the other hand, even though, while, in spite of, despite, regardless of.*

PROSE FICTION

Fiction comes in many forms and styles, from simple folk stories and fairy tales to confusing, nearly impenetrable novels and short stories. On the ACT the passage is straightforward, and you are asked to demonstrate that you can use clues found in the text to determine where and when the action takes place, to understand what is happening in the story, and to recognize the human emotions or conflicts that motivate the characters.

Here, for example, is a prose passage consisting only of dialogue.* As you read it, identify the characters, the time and place, and the situation:

"I'd like you to do that assignment before you leave today."

"I can't. I have to go home. My mother wants me to shovel the walk."

"But I insist. You have to do it."

"I'm not going to."

(5)   "Listen, Charles, you were absent all last week with an earache and runny nose. Now you have to make up the work. I've put the assignment on the board."

"No!"

"Yes."

"Make me. I dare you."

(10) "Oh, Charles, dear, I can't make you. You know that, but I just want you to do well in my class. Don't you understand?"

"I don't care. Math is so stupid."

"Math isn't stupid."

"It is!"

(15) "Look, Charles, I can't stay here all day and argue. I have to eat. After lunch I'm going to call your mother and ask her if you can stay."

"Don't."

"Why not?"

"Just don't."

(20) "But why?"

"Just don't call her. I'll stay, O.K."

"You mean you don't want to get into trouble?"

"She'll get mad and won't let me play."

"Play what?"

(25) "With my friends."

"Why?"

·   "Just forget it, O.K.? I'll stay and do math."

"Good, Charles. I knew you'd see it my way. I'll see you at three o'clock."

---

*The passages used for illustration and practice exercises in this chapter may be shorter or longer than the 750 words typical of ACT passages. Accordingly, you should not be concerned with time when doing the practice exercises.

Analysis

Although the author doesn't tell you who is talking in the dialogue, it's pretty obvious after a line or two. Nor are you told the place, the time, the season, and the circumstances of the conversation, but you can deduce all those details by paying attention to the speakers' words. Likewise, you should be able to tell Charles's approximate age and whether the teacher is a man or a woman. You may also conclude that Charles is a stubborn little kid, but one who knows when he's beaten. Perhaps you've inferred, too, that the teacher has a mean streak, not because she forces Charles to stay after school, but because she insists on having the last word. She provokes Charles, trying to prove that she's the boss.

A typical prose fiction passage consists of both dialogue and narration. Questions often pertain to the *narrator, setting, character, tone,* and *use of language* in a passage. You may also be asked to *identify main ideas, draw inferences about the relationship of characters, speculate on events that may have preceded or will follow the passage,* and much more. In short, you may expect questions on anything that the author has done to convey meaning or create an effect.

Prose fiction passages come from contemporary novels and stories, and also, as in the following instance, from works written generations ago.

In this well-known Civil War tale, a Southerner, Peyton Farquhar, is about to be hanged as a spy. The action takes place as he stands on a railroad bridge with a noose around his neck.

He closed his eyes in order to fix his last thoughts upon his wife and children. The water, touched to gold by the early sun, the brooding mists under the banks at some distance down the stream, the fort, the soldiers, the piece of drift—all had distracted him. And now he became conscious of a new
(5) disturbance. Striking through the thought of his dear ones was a sound which he could neither ignore nor understand, a sharp, distinct, metallic percussion like the stroke of a blacksmith's hammer upon the anvil; it had the same ringing quality. He wondered what it was, and whether immeasurably distant or near by—it seemed both. Its recurrence was regular, but as slow as the tolling of a
(10) death knell. He awaited each stroke with impatience and—he knew not why—apprehension. The intervals of silence grew progressively longer; the delays became maddening. With their greater infrequency the sounds increased in strength and sharpness. They hurt his ear like the thrust of a knife; he feared he would shriek. What he heard was the ticking of his watch.

Ambrose Bierce, *An Occurrence at Owl Creek Bridge*

1. The passage indicates that, just before being put to death, Farquhar tries to think about:

   A. the beauty of his surroundings.
   B. anything other than his impending doom.
   C. his family.
   D. why this is happening to him.

To answer this question, skim the passage in search of words that correspond to each choice. Sometimes a choice will repeat the words in the passage, but be wary of such duplication. The repetition may be a trap. More than likely, the choices will paraphrase or summarize ideas in the passage. Where you find a thought or idea that seems closely related to the choice, read it carefully to determine whether it's the answer you need.

Choice A summarizes in a phrase all the beauty that Farquhar sees. If you read the second sentence to its end, however, you see that the beauty of nature has distracted him from what he really wants to think about. B refers to an idea not mentioned in the passage. C paraphrases the contents of the first sentence. "Family" is clearly a synonym for "wife and children." Choice C is the correct answer. D refers to an idea not mentioned in the passage.

Question 1 is a relatively easy question. Here is a more challenging one:

2. According to the passage, which emotion did Farquhar NOT experience during the moment before he was hanged?

   F. Frustration
   G. Impatience
   H. Fear
   J. Sorrow

To find the best answer, you must search the entire passage for an example of each emotion that Farquhar feels. The one you *don't* find is the answer. Obviously, it's more of a challenge to find three wrong answers than to find a single correct one. As you did for question 1, skim the passage for words and ideas that correspond to each choice.

Choice F names the emotion that Farquhar experiences as he tries in vain to shut out the pounding in his ears. G names Farquhar's emotion as he waits impatiently for each stroke. H names an emotion that Farquhar feels while resisting the urge to shriek out loud. J refers to an emotion *not* mentioned in the passage. Therefore, J is the correct answer.

3. Based on information in the passage, Farquhar probably "feared he would shriek," because he doesn't want:

   A. his wife and children to hear his screams.
   B. the soldiers to know that he is scared of dying.
   C. to disturb the peacefulness of early morning.
   D. to lose control of himself.

To answer this question, you must infer a reason why Farquhar might want to keep himself from shrieking. Consider the likelihood of each choice:

Choice **A** could not be correct, because Farquhar's family is not at the scene. **B** implies that Farquhar is scared, but nothing in the passage suggests that he is afraid to die. **C** is unrelated to Farquhar's state of mind. **D** is correct. Farquhar, a spy, is portrayed as a highly rational person, one who masters his fears and emotions. It would be out of character, even moments before death, for him to lose his calm.

4. The ticking of the watch in Farquhar's ears signifies:

   F. that each second just before death grows increasingly important.
   G. that the pressure has made Farquhar crazy.
   H. the footsteps of the approaching executioner.
   J. the excited pounding of Farquhar's heart.

To answer this reasoning question, you must interpret the beating sound inside Farquhar's head, using clues from the passage. Examine the possibilities of each choice:

Choice **F** describes Farquhar's condition. Since he has just moments to live, each remaining second of life acquires importance. **F** is the correct answer. **G** raises a valid point. A man on the verge of execution might well lose his mind, but Farquhar shows no symptoms of insanity. **H** contradicts information in the last sentence of the passage, that the beating sound is the tick of Farquhar's watch. **J** may accurately describe Farquhar's physical state. His heart probably is racing, but we are told that the sound comes from the ticking of his watch.

SOCIAL STUDIES

The ACT reading comprehension test includes a passage from Social Studies that may focus on people, usually people in groups. A social scientist may be interested in *anthropology*, the study of society's customs and values and the relationships of people to each other and their environment. *Economics*, or how people earn and spend money, is also a social science, as are *sociology*, the study of society's functions and institutions, and *political science*, the study of people's laws and governments. *Psychology* is also considered a social science, even though psychologists study individual behavior as well as the behavior of groups. Passages in this section of the ACT may also be drawn from the worlds of archaeology, business, education, geography, and history.

The task of answering questions about social studies passages becomes more manageable when you understand the main principles of writing followed by social scientists. More often than not, social scientists write to inform others about their observations, to report on their research, and to expound their theories. Their domain is reality, not the world of the imagination.

For instance, a passage meant to explain the all-too-real phenomenon of poverty reads this way:

> Categorizing people as "in poverty" or "not in poverty" is one way to describe their economic situation. The income-to-poverty ratio and the income deficit (surplus) describe other aspects of economic well-being. Where the poverty rate provides a measure of the proportion of people with a family income that is below
> (5) the established poverty thresholds, the income-to-poverty ratio provides a measure to gauge the depth of poverty and to calculate the size of the population who may be eligible for government-sponsored assistance programs, such as Temporary Assistance to Needy Families (TANF), Medicare, food stamps, and the Low-Income Home Energy Assistance Program (LIHEAP). The income-to-poverty
> (10) ratio is reported as a percentage that compares a family's or an unrelated individual's (people who do not live with relatives) income with their poverty threshold. For example, a family or individual with an income-to-poverty ratio of 110 percent has income that is 10 percent above their poverty threshold.
> The income deficit (surplus) tells how many dollars a family's or an unrelated
> (15) individual's income is below (above) their poverty threshold. These measures illustrate how the low-income population varies in relation to the poverty thresholds.

U.S. Census Bureau

Analysis

This passage may seem hard to follow at first. Although it contains some specialized terms (*income-to-poverty ratio, income deficit, poverty thresholds*), the terms aren't so technical that you can't figure them out. Be assured that the passage makes sense and can be understood even by readers not well versed in economics and other social sciences. The author of the passage is attempting to spell out guidelines for an official definition of poverty, a yardstick used in determining who is eligible for certain kinds of government assistance and who is not.

To deal with a passage such as this on the ACT, you don't need extensive preparation in the social sciences. All the information you need is provided. Your job is simply to read the passage thoroughly and to answer the questions.

In the following passage, the author discusses the dynamics of social exchange between individuals—in other words, how people talk to each other. The author doesn't intend to provoke an argument or espouse a point of view. Rather, he spells out the observations of a social theorist. Although you should read the passage as though it were fact, be aware that it is mostly opinion. ACT questions on this passage would test whether you understood the author's ideas, not whether you agree with them.

> The key task of sociology . . . is to analyze social associations, which are based on the fact that both parties to an exchange can often benefit. But this does not mean that the parties to an exchange benefit equally, that they have complete information about the exchange, or that each exchange occurs in a vacuum
> (5) isolated from other commitments the parties may have. Often one individual is able to get more from an exchange than the other person does, because he or she has more power of one kind or another.
> People are attracted to others if they expect exchanges with them to be rewarding and they need to become attractive to the others in order to develop an
> (10) enduring association. Often a person wants something from another but has nothing to give in return that the other wants. A person in this uncomfortable situation has three basic alternatives. First, it may be possible to force the other person to give the desired item, perhaps by threat of violence or outright theft. Second, it may be possible to find another person who can provide the item.
> (15) Third, the person may subordinate himself or herself to the person who has the item, giving that person power. Thus, in the course of a large number of social exchanges, some individuals come to have power over others.

William Sims Bainbridge, *Sociology*, Barron's (1997), pp. 26–27

Analysis

You probably noticed that this passage is impersonal, serious, analytical. It doesn't define terms because the author assumes that readers will understand the ideas it contains. Clearly, it's not meant for readers unaccustomed to abstract concepts about human behavior. It is written in the style of much social science literature and would sound familiar to professionals in the field. To some extent it's "in" talk. Yet, it's not so far "in" that an outsider like you cannot grasp its meaning.

Sample Questions

Seven of the ten questions that follow the Social Studies passage on the ACT will ask you to reason out the answers. The remaining three questions ask you about material explicitly stated in the passage.

Answer the four sample questions following this passage about terrorism. Techniques for answering these questions are similar to those you used for Prose Fiction.

Democracies have always been subject to terrorist attacks. Our constitutional rights, the restrictions set on police power, and our citizens' enjoyment of due process of the law—the very qualities of our society that terrorists despise—are the same qualities that for years made us easy prey. Although many people view
(5)   this as a cruel irony, we have within our free society the tools with which not only to fight and destroy terrorists but to keep them at bay. Following the attacks of September 11, 2001, America went to war against terrorism. A federal Department of Homeland Security was created. The citizenry was put on alert. Our superbly trained law enforcement people at every level of government began to coordinate
(10) their efforts as never before. The courts granted more liberal use of wiretap surveillance and search warrants, and a system of laws was introduced to fight terrorism as both a crime and a military assault instead of merely a political act. Terrorists from foreign lands were put on notice that they faced prosecution in military tribunals, and American citizens who chose to terrorize their own country
(15) faced the maximum penalties allowed by criminal law.
      In order to preserve our basic freedoms and way of life, we must never cave in to the fear of terrorism. We must depend on the strength of our system to protect us. If we allow dread, as intense as it may be, to control our actions, we will lose our strongest defense against terrorism. The demise of terrorism will be hastened
(20) when all freedom-loving countries join us in sending out a strong and clear message to the world's terrorists that terror, like other crime, shall not pay!

1. According to the passage, U.S. citizens are popular targets for terrorists because they:

  A. usually don't carry firearms.
  B. represent everything that terrorists hate.
  C. are not accustomed to worrying about their personal safety.
  D. are rich and arrogant.

Before you skim the passage to find the location of the answer, identify what you will look for as your eyes move quickly through the text. Since the question asks why terrorists like to pick on Americans, keep the phrase "popular targets" in mind. Within a few seconds you may pick out "easy prey" (line 4), an idea that may well explain why Americans are "popular targets." Where you found "easy prey," then, is the section of the passage to reread in search of the correct answer.

Choice A may be true most of the time, but no such idea is stated in the passage. B reiterates a phrase in the passage, "qualities of our society that terrorists despise." Therefore, B is correct. C and D are not mentioned in the passage.

2. According to the passage, the terrorist attacks of September 11, 2001, brought about all of the following changes EXCEPT:

F. an expansion of police powers.
G. an overall restructuring of the federal government.
H. the introduction of military courts to prosecute foreign terrorists.
J. an expanded public awareness of terrorist threats.

Before skimming the passage for the location of the answer, identify the key words in the question, most likely "attacks of September 11, 2001" and "changes." Where you find these or related words and phrases (lines 6–15) is the section to reread. Because this question asks you to identify an idea that is NOT stated in the passage, search for references to each of the four choices.

Choice **F** is covered by the idea that the courts authorized wider use of wiretaps and search warrants. **G** alludes indirectly to the creation of a Department of Homeland Security, but the passage does not indicate that the founding of such an agency is equivalent to an overall restructuring of the federal government. Choice **H** restates the reference to military tribunals for foreign terrorists, and **J** paraphrases the idea that the citizenry was put on alert. **G**, therefore, is the best answer.

3. The phrase *enjoyment of due process of the law* (second sentence) means that citizens:

A. have a basic right to pursue pleasure and happiness.
B. may protest against distasteful laws.
C. are protected by the laws of our society.
D. can sue the government to redress grievances.

To figure out the answer, find the phrase in the passage and look for contextual clues. The phrase is included as one of three fundamental rights that belong to citizens in a democracy. *"Enjoyment"* is not used in its usual sense, but rather in the sense of *having* or *being in possession of.* Our citizens, the passage says, *have* or *possess* "due process of the law." Review each choice for the best definition.

Choice **A** is the right of every citizen, but it is not the right of "due process." **B** is a right, but our right to protest is not the equivalent of "due process of the law." **C** is a fundamental right that lawbreaking terrorists naturally despise. **C** is the correct answer. **D** is the right of every citizen, but it is not on the same level of importance as the others mentioned in the passage.

4. Which of the following ideas most accurately states the main point of the passage?

    F. Terrorists feel a particular hatred for democratic countries.
    G. Our system of government serves as the best deterrent to terrorism.
    H. Countries must never give in to terrorist demands.
    J. Cooperation by the free countries of the world can stop terrorism.

To answer main-idea questions, you need an overview of the whole passage. Each of the four possible answers may be inferred from the passage, but only one of them encompasses more of the passage than the others. Although counting the number of sentences devoted to a particular subject may reveal the main idea, just as often the main idea may be stated briefly or not at all. Therefore, rely on your sense of the entire passage to find the answer.

Choice **F** is too insignificant to be the main idea. **G** summarizes much of the first paragraph. The idea is reiterated in a slightly different form in the second paragraph. **G** is the correct answer. **H** and **J** are too limited to be the main idea.

HUMANITIES

The humanities passage on the ACT relates to such creative and cultural disciplines as art, music, architecture, theater, dance, and even history. The passage may discuss Impressionist painting or the origins of jazz. It could be a portrait of Lady Gaga, an analysis of current sci-fi films, or a critique of modern dance— almost any sort of passage on a multitude of topics.

A passage about a cultural matter will sometimes consist only of *facts*. Consider this brief history of ballet costumes:

> Early in the history of ballet, dancers wore bulky but elaborate costumes on the stage. As dancers' technique improved, however, costumes were redesigned. They became lighter and revealed the movement and steps of the performers. By the start of the 18th century, ballet skirts had risen above the ankles, and heels had been removed from dancing slippers. Over time, as dancers developed spectacular movements and jumps, costumes continued to grow simpler, less cumbersome, and more revealing. Today, most ballet costumes weigh but a few ounces and cling tightly to the body of the dancers.

(5)

Analysis

This passage is a factual chronology, sweeping across centuries in just a few sentences. As often as including a totally factual passage, the ACT will include a passage of interpretation dressed up as fact. A passage that after a quick reading may seem factual and objective may actually be full of opinions. Take this one, for instance, about Johann Strauss, the nineteenth-century composer known as the "Waltz King":

> Perhaps the Vienna that Johann Strauss immortalized in his waltzes never did exist, but the Viennese waltz as he perfected it became the symbol for millions at a time when the world was young and gay—a symbol of romance projected through the magic of three-four time.
> (5)　　The great waltzes—Blue Danube, Wine, Women and Song, Artist's Life and the rest—are more than mere ballroom dances. They are an idealization of the spirit of the dance. Their flowing measures—by turn capricious, nostalgic, gay—capture the poetry of the waltz. . . .
>
> Joseph Machlis, *Johann Strauss*

Everyone who reads this excerpt may agree fully with the author's statements about Strauss's music. Yet, the content is mostly interpretive. The only hard fact in the text is that Strauss wrote waltzes entitled "Blue Danube," "Wine, Women and Song," and "Artist's Life." Frequently on the ACT you are asked to distinguish between fact and opinion.

Sample Questions

After reading the following passage about the American poet Robert Frost, answer the sample questions.

> Louis Untermeyer in his introduction to a book of Frost's poems wrote that the character as well as the career of Robert Frost gives the lie to the usual misconceptions of the poet. Frost has been no less the ordinary man for being an extraordinary creator. The creator, the artist, the extraordinary man, is merely the
> (5)　　ordinary man intensified; a person whose life is sometimes lifted to a high pitch of feeling and who has the gift of making others share his excitement.
> 　　There are curious contradictions in the life of Robert Frost. Though his ancestry was New England he was born in California; the most American of poets, he was first recognized in England and not in the U.S.; not believing in competitions he
> (10)　　never entered them, yet he won the Pulitzer Prize four times; the "rough conversational tones" of his blank verse are remarkable for their lyrical music. Though he has chosen one part of the country on which to focus his poetry, no poetry so regional has ever been so universal.
>
> Ruth Levin, *Ordinary Heroes: The Story of Shaftsbury*

1. According to the passage, a distinctive quality of Frost's poetry is its:

    A. obvious symbolism.
    B. spirituality.
    C. unusual rhymes.
    D. association with one section of the country.

To answer this referring question, you must find words, phrases, and ideas in the passage that are similar in meaning to each of the choices. Skim the passage and notice that most of the first paragraph is about poets, while most of the second paragraph pertains to Frost's life and poetry. Therefore, look for the answer in the second paragraph.

Choice **A** refers to a quality not mentioned in the passage. **B** brings up an idea not discussed in the passage. **C** contradicts the passage, which states that Frost wrote blank verse, or poetry without rhyme. **D** paraphrases part of line 17. **D**, therefore, is correct.

2. According to the passage, Robert Frost could be considered "the most American of poets" for all of the following reasons EXCEPT that:

    F. his verses are often patriotic.
    G. his poetry often sounds like everyday American speech.
    H. his background is American.
    J. he focused his poetry on a specific section of America.

To answer this question, you must reread the passage and locate references to the four choices. The one you *don't* find is the correct answer. This variation in ACT questions calls for close reading and takes longer than single-choice answers, especially when you have to find material scattered throughout a full-length passage. In this question, though, all the references to "the most American of poets" are concentrated in the second paragraph.

Choice **F** refers to an idea *not* mentioned in the passage. **F** is correct. **G** is a reference to the "rough conversational tones" of Frost's poetry. **H** refers to the fact that his family came from New England. **J** alludes to the regionalism of Frost's poetry, mentioned in lines 11–12 of the passage.

3. The author of the passage apparently believes that Robert Frost's life was:

    A. typical of a poet's life.
    B. extraordinary.
    C. rather ordinary.
    D. no different from that of farmers in Vermont.

Material that discusses the quality of Frost's life is found in lines 3–5. Look there to figure out which of the four choices most accurately describes the author's intent. Draw your conclusion only after you've carefully reread the entire paragraph and considered each choice separately.

Choice **A** is contradicted by line 2 of the paragraph. Frost's life "gives the lie" to stereotypical images of poets. **B** seems to correspond with the author's intent. Frost is called both "an extraordinary creator" and an "extraordinary man." **B** is correct. **C** seems like a possible answer, but since Frost is called an "ordinary man intensified," he must be considered extraordinary. **D** is not related to material in the passage.

4. The passage suggests that a successful poet must:
   - **F.** be misunderstood by society.
   - **G.** avoid acting like an ordinary man.
   - **H.** endow ordinary matters with excitement.
   - **J.** invent new forms and styles of expression.

The correct answer to this reasoning question must be inferred from the first paragraph of the passage, where the author generalizes about successful poets.

Choice **F** may accurately describe many poets, but it brings up an idea not discussed in the passage. **G** may describe the behavior of some poets, but it is a generalization outside the scope of the passage. **H** closely resembles the description of a creative artist found in lines 4–6. **H** is correct. **J** raises a matter not discussed in the passage.

NATURAL SCIENCE

Out of a flood of publications by biologists, ecologists, chemists, physicists, geologists, and other natural scientists, the ACT questioners pick one passage. It comes from a textbook or an article, a research or lab report—from almost any scientific writing. The only certainty is that it pertains to the natural world.

A passage of scientific writing can be a wide-ranging story about the world's endangered species. Or it can be an excerpt from a report on hypothermia, or the greenhouse effect, or volcanoes, or brain waves. Whatever the topic, the passage will probably contain many factual statements, along with statistics and other data, all intended to give an accurate account of reality. There is no science fiction on this part of the ACT.

Science writers usually adopt a serious tone. They write dispassionately, because personal feelings have little place in scientific reporting. Yet, in the following passage, the writer seems almost unable to suppress his admiration for the methods that science has devised for collecting and storing huge amounts of gene- and genome-related data.

For most of its history, biology managed to amass its data mostly with the help of plain old arithmetic. By contrast, today's genetic research creates too much data for one person, or even a scientific team, to understand. New technologies are needed to manage this huge amount of data.

(5)   Consider this: Gene-sequencing machines can read hundreds of thousands of nucleotides a day. Gene chips are even faster. The information in GenBank, a widely used database of all known DNA sequences, now doubles in just three years. A single laboratory doing cutting-edge research can generate hundreds of gigabytes of data a day, every day. For comparison, 100 gigabytes could hold an

(10)   entire floor of journals in an academic library.

How can anyone make sense of all this information? The only way is to enlist the aid of computers and software that can store the data and make it possible for researchers to organize, search, and analyze it. In fact, many of today's challenges in biology, from gene analysis to drug discovery, are really challenges

(15)   in information technology. This is not surprising when you remember that DNA is itself a form of information storage.

Where are genetic and genomic data stored? One of the first biological databases was created to store the huge volume of data from experiments with the fruit fly *Drosophila melanogaster*.

(20)   Called Flybase, it has grown into a huge, comprehensive, international electronic repository for information on *Drosophila* genetics and molecular biology, run by scientists for scientists. The information spans a century's worth of published scientific literature on *Drosophila melanogaster* and its relatives, including their complete genome sequence.

(25)   Several other communities of researchers have created their own databases, including those dedicated to investigation of the roundworm *Caenorhabditis elegans* (Wormbase), the soil-dwelling amoeba *Dictyostelium discoideum* (*DictyBase*) and the strain of yeast used for many laboratory studies (*Saccharomyces* Genome Database).

(30)   A key goal is to make sure that all these databases can "talk" to each other. For database communication to work, researchers in different fields must use the same terms to describe biological processes. The development and use of such universal "ontology"—a common language—is helping scientists analyze the complex network of biology that underlies our health.

The New Genetics, published by the
National Institute of General Medical Sciences,
National Institutes of Health, 2010

Analysis

If the preceding excerpt appeared on the ACT, it would have been introduced, like all reading passages on the exam, by a short description of its origin. Knowing that it came from the National Institutes of Health, you may have anticipated that its tone would be serious and its information, dated 2010, mostly up to date.

Chances are that on the ACT you'd be asked about the main idea of the passage. If you picked an answer that alluded to the necessity of researchers to employ information technology (in the third paragraph), you'd be 100% right. Other questions could pertain to the history, usefulness, and distribution of genetic data as well as recent changes in the way data is gathered, stored, and shared among scientists.

Perhaps you studied genetics in your high school biology class. If so, this passage may not have told you anything new. But don't rely totally on what you learned in school. Although prior knowledge may convince you that you know all the answers, don't pick them unless they're supported by evidence in the passage.

Another type of writing from the natural sciences is meant to alert readers to a problem. Few published works about the deteriorating environment, for example, are strictly informative. Lethal air and filthy water are not subjects to be unemotional about. Notice that the following passage, while informative, also holds a warning about contaminating one of the earth's major sources of clean water:

Most groundwater originates as precipitation, percolates into the soil much as water fills a sponge, and moves from place to place along fractures in rock, through sand and gravel, or through channels in formations such as cavernous limestone. Constantly encountering resistance from the surrounding material,

(5) groundwater moves in a manner considerably different from that of surface water. Varying with the type of formation, its flow ranges from a fraction of an inch to a few feet per day. These movement characteristics are important to an understanding of groundwater contamination, since concentrations of pollutants called plumes will also move very slowly, with little dilution or dispersion.

(10) "Unconfined" aquifers are the most susceptible to contamination. These aquifers are not protected by an overlying layer of impermeable material and may occur fairly close to the land surface. The volume of water available in unconfined aquifers will fluctuate with usage and with seasonal replenishment or "recharging" of the source of precipitation.

(15) In contrast to this type of aquifer is the "confined" aquifer which is bounded on top and below by layers of relatively impermeable material. Confined aquifers generally occur at greater depths and their impermeable layers may offer a certain measure of protection from contamination. Some confined aquifers have no recharge zone at all and must be recognized as a finite resource which cannot

(20) be replenished.

Concern, Inc., *Groundwater*

Analysis

Unlike the author who wrote about genetics, this one doesn't hand you the main point of the passage. Rather, the idea that groundwater must be understood in order to keep it pure is dispersed throughout the discussion. In addition to being aware of the writer's point of view about groundwater, you may be required to know the differences between confined and unconfined aquifers, to have a general idea of how water moves underground, and to recognize how aquifers become polluted.

The passage contains some specialized language. The word *aquifer* is used several times, so often in fact, that it's hard not to know what it means by the end of the passage. The word *plumes* appears in the first paragraph, but the writer defines it. Percolates is also defined. *Impermeable*, while not a technical word, can give you trouble. Since *impermeable* material is contrasted with spongy material, the meaning becomes apparent.

Required reading in most school science courses is often far more exacting than the science passage on the ACT. While taking chemistry or earth science in school, you are immersed in the subject, and your teachers and texts take you deep into its contents. The natural science passage on the ACT, on the other hand, is accessible to the general reader. The two samples of science writing you've seen so far offer no insurmountable challenges to an alert college-bound student. But you must also be ready for more difficult reading, a passage taken from the literature of scientific research, for example. Researchers often fill their reports with the technical terms of their disciplines. Don't get stuck on these specialized words and phrases. Your aim is to discover the general message of the passage. No passage on the ACT will be beyond reach.

Sample Questions

Answer the questions after you read this passage on whales.

No animal in prehistoric or historic times has ever exceeded the whale, in either size or strength, which explains perhaps its survival from ancient times. Few people have any idea of the relative size of the whale compared with other animals. A large specimen weighs about ninety tons, or thirty times as much as

(5) an elephant, which beside a whale appears about as large as a dog compared to an elephant. It is equivalent in bulk to one hundred oxen, and outweighs a village of one thousand people. If cut into steaks and eaten, as in Japan, it would supply a meal to an army of one hundred and twenty thousand men.

Whales have often exceeded one hundred feet in length, and George Brown

(10) Goode, in his report on the United States Fisheries, mentions a finback having been killed that was one hundred and twenty feet long. A whale's head is

sometimes thirty-five feet in circumference, weighs thirty tons, and has jaws twenty feet long, which open thirty feet wide to a mouth that is as large as a room twenty feet long, fifteen feet high, nine feet wide at the bottom, and two feet wide
(15) at the top. A score of Jonahs standing upright would not have been unduly crowded in such a chamber.

The heart of a whale is the size of a hogshead. The main blood artery is a foot in diameter, and ten to fifteen gallons of blood pour out at every pulsation. The tongue of a right whale is equal in weight to ten oxen, while the eye of all whales
(20) is hardly as large as a cow's, and is placed so far back that it has in direction but a limited range of vision. The ear is so small that it is difficult to insert a knitting needle, and the brain is only about ten inches square. The head, or "case" contains about five hundred barrels, of ten gallons each, of the richest kind of oil, called spermaceti.

Whale Fishery of New England

1. According to the passage, whales, in addition to being unusually large creatures, are also distinctively:

   A. fast swimmers.
   B. powerful.
   C. adaptable to their environment.
   D. intelligent.

As suggested for previous referring questions, skim the passage for thoughts and ideas that refer specifically to each choice.

Choice **A** is not mentioned in the passage. **B** corresponds to information about the strength of whales in the first sentence of the passage. **B** is correct. **C** is not discussed in the passage. **D** contradicts the information in line 22 about the very small size of a whale's brain.

2. According to the passage, all parts of a whale are physically huge EXCEPT its:

   F. heart.
   G. mouth.
   H. eyes.
   J. tongue.

To answer this question, find a reference to each body part of the whale. If the passage doesn't mention that part or if it fails to say how big it is, you have probably found the answer.

Choice **F** is described in line 17. The heart is the "size of a hogshead." If you don't know the dimension of a hogshead, you can infer it from the next sentence, which tells you about the one-foot diameter of a whale's main artery. **G** is described in lines 13–14. The mouth is the size of a large room. **H** is discussed in lines 19–20. The whale's eye is "hardly as large as a cow's." **H** is the correct answer. **J** is described in lines 18–19. The tongue of a right whale weighs as much as ten oxen.

3. It can reasonably be inferred from the passage that it is not uncommon for whales to grow as long as:

   A. 35 feet.
   B. 100 feet.
   C. 120 feet.
   D. 185 feet

Answer this question as you did previous reasoning questions. From information in the passage, draw a reasonable conclusion about the usual size of whales.

Choice **A** is smaller than any whale mentioned in the passage. **B** is a reasonable answer based on the fact that whales "have often exceeded one hundred feet in length" (line 9). **B** is correct. **C** describes the size of a whale cited as an exceptionally long one. **D** is larger than any whale mentioned in the passage.

4. The passage suggests that people have used whales in all of the following ways EXCEPT:

   F. as a source of oil.
   G. for sport fishing.
   H. as food.
   J. as a subject for stories.

Notice that the question uses the word "suggests." That means you probably won't find specific material in the passage about people's use of whales. Look for implications. The correct answer will be the implication that is *not* in the passage.

Choice **F** refers to material at the end of the passage. People use the "richest kind of oil, called spermaceti." **G** is not in the passage. **G** is the correct answer. **H** refers to a statement in line 7 that whalesteak is eaten in Japan. **J** alludes to the biblical story of Jonah and the whale, mentioned in lines 15–16.

SAMPLE READING TEST

Now that you are acquainted with the various types of reading passages and questions on the ACT, see whether you can apply what you have learned. This exercise consists of four passages, each accompanied by ten questions. Because the passages in this Sample Test vary in length from those on the ACT Reading Test, you may wish to allow yourself about 45 minutes, rather than the 35 minutes allotted on the ACT, to complete the exercise. Don't let yourself be distracted by the time limit, however. For the moment, devote yourself to recalling and using the test-taking tactics suggested throughout this chapter.

> *Directions:* This test consists of four passages, each followed by ten multiple-choice questions. Read each passage and then pick the best answer for each question. Refer to the passage as often as you wish while answering the questions.

Passage 1

PROSE FICTION: *This passage is adapted from William Dean Howells' The Rise of Silas Lapham (1885). In this excerpt, the protagonist, a newly rich self-made business man, is about to be interviewed by a newspaper reporter.*

When Bartley Hubbard went to interview Silas Lapham for the "Solid Men of Boston" series, Lapham received him in his private office by previous appointment.

"Walk right in!" he called out to the journalist, whom he caught sight of through the door of the counting room.

(5) He did not rise from the desk at which he was writing, but he gave Bartley his left hand for welcome, and he rolled his large head in the direction of a vacant chair. "Sit down! I'll be with you in just half a minute."

"Take your time," said Bartley, with the ease he instantly felt. "I'm in no hurry." He took a note-book from his pocket, laid it on his knee, and began to sharpen a

(10) pencil.

"There!" Lapham pounded with his great hairy fist on the envelope he had been addressing. "William!" he called out, and he handed the letter to a boy who came to get it. "I want that to go right away. Well, sir," he continued, wheeling round in his leather-cushioned swivel chair, and facing Bartley, seated so near that their

(15) knees almost touched, "so you want my life, death, and Christian sufferings, do you, young man?"

"That's what I'm after," said Bartley. "Your money or your life."

"I guess you wouldn't want my life without the money," said Lapham, as if he were willing to prolong these moments of preparation.

(20) "Take 'em both," Bartley suggested. "Don't want your money without your life, if you come to that. But you're just one million times more interesting to the public than if you hadn't a dollar; and you know that as well as I do, Mr. Lapham. There's no use beating around the bush."

"No," said Lapham, somewhat absently. He put out his huge foot and pushed

(25) the ground-glass door shut between his little den and the book-keepers, in their larger den outside.

"In personal appearance," wrote Bartley in the Sketch for which he now studied his subject, "Silas Lapham is a fine type of successful American. He has a square, bold chin, only partly concealed by the short reddish-grey beard, growing to the

(30) edges of his firmly closing lips. His nose is short and straight; his forehead good, but broad rather than high; his eyes blue, and with a light in them that is kindly or sharp according to his mood. He is of medium height, and fills an average armchair with a solid bulk, which on the day of our interview was unpretentiously clad in a business suit of blue serge. His head droops somewhat from a short

(35) neck, which does not trouble itself to rise far from a pair of massive shoulders."

"I don't know as I know just where you want me to begin," said Lapham.

"Might begin with your birth; that's where most of us begin," replied Bartley.

A gleam of humorous appreciation shot into Lapham's blue eyes.

"I didn't know whether you wanted me to go quite so far back as that," he said.

(40) "But there's no disgrace in having been born, and I was born in Vermont up near Canada—so well up, in fact I came very near being an adoptive citizen; for I was bound to be an American of *some* sort, from the word Go! That was about—well, let me see!—pretty near sixty years ago: this is '75, and that was '20. Well, say I'm fifty-five years old; and I've *lived* 'em too; not an hour of waste time about *me*,

(45) anywheres! I was born on a farm, and—"

"Worked in the fields summers and went to school winters: regulation thing?" Bartley cut in.

"Regulation thing," said Lapham, accepting this irreverent version of his history somewhat dryly.

(50) "Parents poor, of course," suggested the journalist. "Any barefoot business? Early deprivations of any kind, that would encourage the youthful reader to go and do likewise? Orphan myself, you know," said Bartley, with a smile of cynical good-comradery.

Lapham looked at him silently, and then said with quiet self-respect, "I guess if

(55) you see these things as a joke, my life won't interest you."

"Oh yes, it will," returned Bartley, unabashed. "You'll see; it'll come out all right." And in fact it did so, in the interview which Bartley printed.

"Mr. Lapham," he wrote, "passed rapidly over the story of his early life, its poverty and its hardships, sweetened, however, by the recollections of a devoted

(60) mother, and a father who, if somewhat her inferior in education, was no less ambitious for the advancement of his children. They were quiet, unpretentious people, religious, after the fashion of that time, and of sterling morality, and they taught their children the simple virtues of the *Old Testament* and *Poor Richard's Almanac*."

(65) Bartley could not deny himself this gibe; but he trusted to Lapham's unliterary habit of mind for his security in making it, and most other people would consider it sincere reporter's rhetoric.

1. Bartley's main interest in writing a newspaper story about Lapham is to:

   A. honor one of Boston's most successful businessmen.
   B. increase the circulation of his newspaper.
   C. prove to his boss that he is a good journalist.
   D. attract readers to the "Solid Men of Boston" series.

2. The narrator includes the fact that Lapham met Bartley "in his private office by previous appointment" to suggest that Lapham:

   F. managed to squeeze Bartley into a busy schedule of appointments.
   G. has hired an office staff to attend to the details of the business.
   H. wishes to enhance his image and status.
   J. knows that Bartley plans to ask him personal questions.

3. Lapham's reaction to Bartley's arrival in his office (lines 2–4) can best be described as:

   A. antagonistic; he takes an instant dislike to Bartley.
   B. casual; he wants to appear an easygoing fellow and laid back.
   C. cordial; he treats Bartley like a welcome guest.
   D. indifferent; he has more pressing matters to attend to.

4. The passage describes Lapham's workplace as:

   F. streamlined, up-to-date quarters.
   G. a luxurious, comfortable office.
   H. a cramped suite of rooms.
   J. a shabby space in need of renovation.

5. From the dialogue that takes place in lines 46–56, it is reasonable to infer that Bartley has all of the following characteristics EXCEPT:

   A. he has a knack for reading other people's minds.
   B. he has heard many other stories like Lapham's.
   C. he composes stories mentally before putting words on paper.
   D. his main interest is the story he expects to write, not Lapham, the person.

6. Bartley informs Lapham that he is an orphan himself (line 52) for all of the following reasons EXCEPT:

   F. to insinuate that Lapham's deprivations were not unique.
   G. to win Lapham's sympathy.
   H. to establish rapport with Lapham.
   J. to lighten up the conversation.

7. The passage indicates that Lapham's physical features include:

   A. a ruddy complexion.
   B. large hands and feet.
   C. cold, steely blue eyes.
   D. hair loss.

8. According to Bartley's sketch of Lapham, Silas credits his parents with:

   F. bestowing on him an honest and open personality.
   G. motivating him to succeed in life.
   H. exposing him to the *Old Testament* and *Poor Richard's Almanac*.
   J. toughening him up for a career as a businessman.

9. As it is used in the passage (line 48), the word *irreverent* most nearly means:

   A. commonplace.
   B. unacceptable.
   C. disrespectful.
   D. destructive.

10. Throughout the passage, Bartley's attitude toward Lapham can best be described as one of:

   F. cynicism.
   G. resentment.
   H. contempt.
   J. ingratitude.

Passage 2

SOCIAL STUDIES: *This passage is an excerpt adapted from an article that discusses a method that modern anthropologists use to study a Native American tribe of the distant past.*

At the end of the eighteenth century the Omaha Indian tribe controlled the fur trade on the upper Missouri River. Without the say-so of Chief Blackbird, French and Spanish fur traders could not do business with tribes farther up the Missouri. Under Blackbird's leadership the Omaha gained wealth, political prestige, and
(5) military strength. But in 1800, the tribe was ravaged by smallpox, one of the diseases that accompanied Europeans. The epidemic killed as many as one-third of the Omaha, including Blackbird. By the time Lewis and Clark visited in 1804, the Omaha culture that survived was decidedly different from the one first encountered by Europeans in 1750.
(10) More than ten thousand objects taken from the gravesites of about one hundred members of the tribe have shed light on the life of the tribe in the late 1700s. Within the few decades after the Omaha settled in 1775 at Big Village or Ton won

tonga, (what is now northeastern Nebraska near the town of Homer), the
community changed dramatically—particularly in its economic roles—and the
(15)   bones of its people offer clues to how and why.

     "The most revealing discovery," says Karl J. Reinhard at the University of
Nebraska, "is that the Omaha were fully equestrian buffalo hunters by 1770. That
makes them the first documented equestrian culture in the Northern Plains. This
is nearly one hundred years earlier than the Dakotas." Reinhard documents this
(20)   by finding similar bone patterns between the Omaha and those of the English
cavalry. But a key piece of evidence is unique to the Omaha. "The Omaha used
a 'toe stirrup,' which was essentially a thong that went around the big toe,"
Reinhard explains. "Because riding, mounting, and dismounting puts pressure
on the toes, the first toe joints went arthritic prematurely."

(25)   Reinhard and his team have been studying the ancestral remains in the context
of their cultural and historical significance. "Human skeletons make a kind of
record of the life of each person," Reinhard says. "Skeleton study reveals aspects
of life such as occupation, disease, age, sex, and sometimes cause of death. By
combining the information from skeletons with artifacts from the burials, the role
(30)   of each person in the society can be seen."

     The remains of a fifty-year-old woman tell about the daily life of an Omaha
woman before 1800. For instance, the bones reveal severe arthritis in her right
elbow, probably caused by repeatedly performing tasks such as wood chopping,
farming, and food grinding. "Before the epidemic struck, the women seemed to
(35)   have had long lives," Reinhard says. "They were having many children and were
as healthy as and tended to live as long as the men. But after the epidemic, the
women took on more of the responsibility for manufacturing, and this wore them
down. We can see that in the bones. There was a constant bending over and
scraping the hides that stressed the lower back. And when we look at the teeth of
(40)   the women, we see that they're very badly worn from chewing hides to prepare
them for trade.

     "None of them lived past the age of thirty," he says about the women buried
after 1800. "They weren't living long enough to regenerate the population. There
weren't enough children born to keep the Omaha population viable, so the
(45)   population was definitely in a decline."

     The artifacts show that there were many more roles for men than there were for
women, especially before the 1800 smallpox epidemic. Specific bone formations
and varied artifacts point to men who were archers, warriors, gunsmiths, and
merchants. Ceremonial roles apparently were exclusive to men. The remains of
(50)   four men between the ages of twenty and fifty were found buried with bundles of
animal bone and other items of ceremonial significance. One was buried with a
drumstick. "These artifacts indicate that the formal religious system involved
men," Reinhard notes. "Because some of these men died as young adults,
ceremonial roles could be assigned to individuals early in adult life."

(55)   "The death of Chief Blackbird brought an end to the traditional Omaha society in
which men had more roles than women," Reinhard says. "After that period, there

seems to have been more social mobility. Virtually no silver artifacts were found with women before Lewis and Clark visited in 1804. After Lewis and Clark, most of the expensive silver ornaments were found with women." The change in the
(60) Omaha culture resulted not just from disease, which forced the remaining Omaha to take on new roles, Reinhard says, but also a change in economics.

The nature of trade after Chief Blackbird's time was markedly different. "The trade until 1800 was largely in arms and ornaments," Reinhard says. After they began trading under the auspices of the United States "there was an influx in
(65) trade in tools and clothing such as scissors, axes, top hats, and buttons.

> Paulette W. Campbell, "Ancestral Bones: Reinterpreting the Past of the Omaha, *Humanities*, November/December, 2002.

11. In the history of the Omaha people, the most significant societal changes seem to have occurred:

   A. at the time of Lewis and Clark's visit.
   B. between 1750 and 1775.
   C. between 1775 and 1800.
   D. after 1800.

12. The facts in the passage indicate that Omaha Indians became infected with smallpox as a result of:

   F. an increase in the fur trade.
   G. contact with foreigners.
   H. spreading of the disease throughout the upper Missouri River area.
   J. their dealings with Lewis and Clark.

13. It may be inferred from the passage that Blackbird's leadership of the Omaha is best characterized by a kind of:

   A. conservatism; he labored to keep tribal customs and traditions intact.
   B. democracy; he gave his people a role in governing the tribe.
   C. benevolence; he worked in behalf of his people's well-being.
   D. fearlessness; he refused to be intimidated by neighboring tribes.

14. According to the passage smallpox changed the Omaha society in all of the following ways EXCEPT:

   F. the tribe stopped trading furs with Europeans.
   G. the tribe's population declined.
   H. the tribe lost its chief.
   J. some male roles were taken over by females.

15. As used in line 44, the word *viable* means:

    A. feasible.
    B. employed.
    C. growing.
    D. functioning.

16. In determining that the Omaha hunted buffalo on horseback, Reinhard and his colleagues were aided by:

    F. deformed bones.
    G. unearthed artifacts.
    H. the relation between the Omahas and the Dakotas.
    J. their awareness of the dangers of hunting buffalo on foot.

17. Modern anthropologists have been able to infer details about the lives of long-dead Omaha tribesmen because:

    A. bones reveal the cause of death.
    B. the remains have been well preserved.
    C. the Omaha buried their dead with artifacts.
    D. their bones resemble those of other Indian tribes.

18. It may reasonably be inferred that the smallpox epidemic shortened the lives of Omaha women because:

    F. they assumed the responsibilities of the men who had perished.
    G. they began to die in greater numbers during childbirth.
    H. they were deprived of ceremonial or religious functions.
    J. the reduced population left women unprotected when men went out to hunt or to trade with Europeans.

19. The author's statement that after 1775, "the community changed dramatically— particularly in its economic roles" (lines 13–14) is supported elsewhere in the passage by the discussion of:

    A. Chief Blackbird's relationship with French and Spanish fur traders (first paragraph, lines 1–9).
    B. the use of the "toe stirrup" (third paragraph, lines 21–24).
    C. studying the bones of women (fifth paragraph, lines 31–41).
    D. the ceremonial functions of Omaha males (seventh paragraph, lines 49–54).

20. The passage suggests that the Omaha were introduced to tools and other manufactured goods partly as a result of:

    F. Lewis and Clark's visit.
    G. Chief Blackbird's death.
    H. the signing of a peace treaty with the United States government.
    J. the development of a barter system.

Passage 3

HUMANITIES: *This passage is adapted from an essay written by the American author, Jack London, who, about 100 years ago, laid plans to build a new house in California.*

Last year I started to build a barn. A man who was a liar undertook to do the stonework and concrete work for me. He could not tell the truth to my face; he could not tell the truth in his work. I was building for posterity. The concrete foundations were four feet wide and sunk three and one-half feet into the earth.

(5) The stone walls were two feet thick and nine feet high. Upon them were to rest the great beams that were to carry all the weight of hay and forty tons of roof. The man who was a liar made beautiful stone walls. I used to stand alongside of them and love them. I caressed their massive strength with my hands. I thought about them in bed before I went to sleep. And they were lies.

(10) Came the earthquake. Fortunately the rest of the building of the barn had been postponed. The beautiful stone walls cracked in all directions. I started to repair and discovered the whole enormous lie. The walls were shells. On each face were beautiful, massive stones—on edge. The inside was hollow. This hollow in some places was filled with clay and loose gravel. In other places it was filled with air

(15) and emptiness, with here and there a piece of kindling wood or dry-goods box to aid in the making of the shell. The walls were lies. They were beautiful, but they were not useful. Construction and decoration had been divorced. The walls were all decoration. They hadn't any construction in them. "As God lets Satan live," I let that lying man live, but—I have built new walls from the foundation up.

(20) And now to my own house beautiful, which I shall build some seven or ten years from now. I have a few general ideas about it. It must be honest in construction, material, and appearance. If any feature of it, despite my efforts, shall tell lies, I shall remove that feature. Utility and beauty must be indissolubly wedded. Construction and decoration must be one. If the particular details keep true to

(25) these general ideas, all will be well.

I have not thought of many details. But here are a few. Take the bathroom, for instance. It shall be as beautiful as any room in the house, just as it will be as useful. The chance is that it will be the most expensive room in the house. No delights of the bath shall be lacking. Also a large part of the expensiveness will

(30) be due to the use of material that will make it easy to keep the bathroom clean and in order. Why should a servant toil unduly that my body may be clean? On the other hand, the honesty of my own flesh and the square dealing I give it, are more important than all the admiration of my friends for expensive decorative schemes and magnificent trivialities. More delightful to me is a body

(35) that sings than a stately and costly grand staircase built for show. Not that I like grand staircases less, but that I like bathrooms more.

One chief aim in the building of my house beautiful will be to have a house that will require the minimum of trouble and work to keep clean and orderly. I live in California where the days are warm. I'd prefer that the servants had three hours to

(40) go swimming (or hammocking) than be compelled to spend those three hours in

keeping the house clean. Therefore, I have resolved to build a house that can be kept unsoiled without the need of those three hours.

(45) For countless thousands of years my ancestors have lived and died and drawn all their breaths in the open air. It is only recently that we have begun to live in houses. The change is a hardship, especially on the lungs. I've got only one pair of lungs, and I haven't the address of any repair shop. Therefore, I stick to the open air as much as possible. For this reason my house will have large verandas, and, near to the kitchen, there will be a veranda dining room. Also, there will be a veranda fireplace, where we can breathe fresh air and be comfortable when the

(50) evenings are touched with frost.

I have a plan for my own bedroom. I spend long hours in bed, reading, studying, and working. I have tried sleeping in the open, but the lamp attracts all the creeping, crawling, butting, flying, fluttering things to the pages of my book, into my ears and blankets, and down the back of my neck. So my bedroom shall be

(55) indoors.

But it will not be of indoors. Three sides of it will be open. The fourth side will divide it from the rest of the house. The three sides will be screened against the creeping, fluttering things, but not against the good fresh air and all the breezes that blow. For protection against storm, to keep out the driving rain, there will be a

(60) sliding glass, so made that when not in use it will occupy small space and shut out very little air.

"The House Beautiful" (1906)

21. The mason who did the stonework is called a "liar" because he:

    A. concealed his defective work from view.
    B. used cheap materials.
    C. failed to build what he had promised.
    D. ignored the plans drawn up for the foundation.

22. By saying that he "was building for posterity" in line 3, the author means that he:

    F. had drawn up plans for a beautiful structure.
    G. ordered special concrete for the foundation.
    H. expected the foundation to last a long time.
    J. made plans for an oversize foundation.

23. According to the passage, the author's discovery of defects in the foundation wall took place after:

    A. an earthquake destroyed the wall.
    B. construction of the barn was delayed.
    C. he attempted to repair some cracks.
    D. he stroked the wall with his hands.

24. According to the passage, the foundation wall was flawed in all of the following ways EXCEPT:

   F. its beauty was only skin deep.
   G. the interior contained building debris.
   H. stones had not been laid flat.
   J. it was solid in only a few places.

25. It may reasonably be inferred from the passage that foundation walls should be solid because they must:

   A. withstand damage caused by earthquakes.
   B. carry the weight of structures that rest upon them.
   C. be at least as strong as the earth on which they are built.
   D. resist groundwater from seeping in.

26. In the passage the author discusses the building of the barn before he begins to describe his "house beautiful" mainly to:

   F. illustrate that building can be hazardous and back-breaking work.
   G. warn readers to be wary of dishonest builders.
   H. impress readers with his expertise as a builder.
   J. introduce the design and construction principles he intends to follow.

27. The author states a preference for building a bathroom instead of a constructing a grand staircase (lines 34–36) to suggest that:

   A. an elegant stairway is inappropriate in a modest house.
   B. it's easier to clean a bathroom than a fancy set of stairs.
   C. he values usefulness more than beauty.
   D. his friends will be indifferent to a showy staircase.

28. It may be inferred from the principles of home design espoused by the author that:

   F. he once held a job as a servant.
   G. he is concerned about the cost of building a new house.
   H. he thinks that housecleaning is a waste of time.
   J. his house will have an ocean view.

29. The author states that he sticks "to the open air as much as possible" (lines 46–47) because:

   A. his ancestors lived outside.
   B. inside air is unhealthy.
   C. he dislikes having a roof over his head.
   D. of the warmth of California.

30. By referring to the home he is planning to build as "my own house beautiful," the author suggests all of the following EXCEPT:

    F. the house will contain no decorative features that lack a function.

    G. the house will be built to please him rather than to impress others.

    H. the architect and the builders will share his vision of what a house should be.

    J. in a house, utility is an aspect of its beauty.

Passage 4

NATURAL SCIENCE: *This passage is from Mark Twain's Life on the Mississippi (1883). In this excerpt Twain describes several features of the river he loved.*

The Mississippi is well worth reading about. It is not a commonplace river, but on the contrary is in all ways remarkable. Considering the Missouri its main branch, it is the longest river in the world—four thousand three hundred miles. It seems safe to say that it is also the crookedest river in the world, since in one part of its
(5) journey it uses up one thousand three hundred miles to cover the same ground as the crow would fly over in six hundred and seventy-five. It discharges three times as much water as the St. Lawrence, twenty-five times as much as the Rhine, and three hundred and thirty-eight times as much as the Thames. No other river has so vast a drainage-basin; it draws its water supply from twenty-eight states and
(10) territories; from Delaware on the Atlantic seaboard, and from all the country between that and Idaho on the Pacific slope—a spread of forty-five degrees of longitude. The Mississippi receives and carries to the Gulf water from fifty-four subordinate rivers that are navigable by steamboats, and from some hundreds that are navigable by flats and keels. The area of its drainage-basin is as great as
(15) the combined areas of England, Wales, Scotland, Ireland, France, Spain, Portugal, Germany, Austria, Italy, and Turkey; and almost all this wide region is fertile; the Mississippi valley, proper, is exceptionally so.

It is a remarkable river in this: that instead of widening toward its mouth, it grows narrower; grows narrower and deeper. From the junction of the Ohio to a
(20) point half-way down to the sea, the width averages a mile in high water; thence to the sea the width steadily diminishes, until, at the "Passes," above its mouth, it is but a little over half a mile. At the junction of the Ohio, the Mississippi's depth is eighty-seven feet; the depth increases gradually, reaching one hundred and twenty-nine just above its mouth.

(25) The difference in rise and fall is also remarkable—not in the upper, but in the lower river. The rise is tolerably uniform down to Natchez (three hundred and sixty miles above its mouth)—about fifty feet. But at Bayou La Fourche the river rises only twenty-four feet; at New Orleans only fifteen, and just above the mouth only two and one-half.

(30) An article in the New Orleans *Times-Democrat*, based upon reports of able engineers, states that the river annually empties four hundred and six million tons of mud into the Gulf of Mexico—which brings to mind Captain Marryat's rude

name for the Mississippi—"the Great Sewer." This mud, solidified, would make a mass a mile square and two hundred and forty-one feet high.

(35)   The mud deposit gradually extends the land—but only gradually; it has extended it not quite a third of a mile in the two hundred years which have elapsed since the river took its place in history.

The belief of the scientific people is that the mouth used to be at Baton Rouge, where the hills cease, and the two hundred miles of land between there and the

(40)   Gulf was built by the river. This gives us the age of that piece of country, without any trouble at all—one hundred and twenty thousand years. Yet it is much the youthfulest batch of country that lies around there anywhere.

The Mississippi is remarkable in still another way—its disposition to make prodigious jumps by cutting through narrow necks of land, and thus

(45)   straightening and shortening itself. More than once it has shortened itself thirty miles at a single jump!

These cut-offs have had curious effects: they have thrown several river towns out into the rural districts, and built up sand-bars and forests in front of them. The town of Delta used to be three miles below Vicksburg; a recent cut-off has

(50)   radically changed the position, and Delta is now *two miles above* Vicksburg.

Both of these river towns have been retired to the country by that cut-off. A cut-off plays havoc with boundary lines and jurisdictions: for instance, a man is living in the state of Mississippi today, a cut-off occurs tonight, and tomorrow the man finds himself and his land over on the other side of the river, within the boundaries

(55)   and subject to the laws of the state of Louisiana! Such a thing, happening in the upper river in the old times, could have transferred a slave from Missouri to Illinois and made a free man of him.

The Mississippi does not alter its locality by cut-offs alone: it is always changing its habitat *bodily*—is always moving bodily *sidewise*. At Hard Times, Louisiana,

(60)   the river is two miles west of the region it used to occupy. As a result, the original *site* of that settlement is not now in Louisiana at all, but on the other side of the river, in the state of Mississippi. *Nearly the whole of that one thousand three hundred miles of old Mississippi river which La Salle floated down in his canoes, two hundred years ago, is good solid dry ground now.* The river lies to the right of

(65)   it, in places, and to the left of it in other places.

31. The author's attitude toward the Mississippi River is best characterized as one of:

A. deliberate indifference.
B. enthusiastic wonder.
C. scientific impartiality.
D. uncontrollable passion.

32. The first paragraph indicates that the Mississippi River is most notable for its:

F. navigability.
G. size.
H. rate of flow.
J. width.

33. The "subordinate rivers" referred to in line 13 are:

    A. the St Lawrence, the Rhine, and the Thames.
    B. rivers less navigable than the Mississippi.
    C. tributaries to the Mississippi.
    D. rivers that empty into the Atlantic Ocean.

34. It can reasonably be inferred from the passage that most rivers:

    F. grow wider as they approach the sea.
    G. maintain roughly the same width for most of their length.
    H. flow faster upstream than at their mouth.
    J. are deeper where they intersect with other rivers.

35. The passage suggests that mud deposited in the Gulf of Mexico:

    A. consists mostly of sewage dumped into the river upstream.
    B. adds a square mile to the country's land mass every year.
    C. diminishes the fertile soil of the Mississippi valley.
    D. accounts for shifts in the shape and location of the coastline.

36. The passage indicates that *cut-offs* occur when the river:

    F. slices through a slender piece of land.
    G. temporarily reverses course.
    H. moves sideways.
    J. floods low-lying areas of nearby land.

37. According to the passage, the Mississippi follows a route that:

    A. never varies.
    B. puzzles scientists and engineers.
    C. is unpredictable.
    D. straightens as it approaches the sea.

38. The passage indicates that the Mississippi River's disposition to cut through narrow necks of land may do all of the following EXCEPT:

    F. alter the topography of the land.
    G. change the location of towns relative to the river.
    H. convert river towns into country towns.
    J. reduce the value of riverfront property.

39. That "Delta is now *two miles above* Vicksburg" (line 50) indicates that:

    A. the towns have swapped names.
    B. Delta is two miles higher than Vicksburg.
    C. Vicksburg is located downstream from Delta.
    D. Vicksburg and Delta are closer to each other than they used to be.

40. The passage implies that the Mississippi River has functioned historically as a:

    F.   symbolic barrier between Easterners and Westerners.

    G. geographical boundary line.

    H. route between the Eastern seaboard and some Western states.

    J.   source of livelihood for many people.

Answer Key

1. D	11. C	21. A	31. B
2. H	12. G	22. H	32. G
3. D	13. C	23. C	33. C
4. H	14. F	24. J	34. F
5. A	15. D	25. B	35. D
6. G	16. F	26. J	36. F
7. B	17. C	27. C	37. C
8. G	18. F	28. H	38. J
9. C	19. C	29. B	39. C
10. F	20. G	30. H	40. G

Answer Explanations

1. **(D)**

The first paragraph of the passage indicates the purpose of the interview. A holds promise as a correct answer, but Bartley's cynicism would keep him from writing a piece that honors a man he barely respects. B and C apply generally to all newspaper reporters, but the passage mentions neither idea.

2. **(H)**

The phrase rings of pretentiousness that might appeal to a proud, self-made man like Lapham. Choice F may be true, but there is no evidence that Lapham has additional appointments. If G had validity, Lapham would not have been addressing an envelope, customarily a clerk or secretary's job. Choice J is unrelated to the point of the question.

3. **(D)**

Choice D is the best answer because Lapham offers Bartley his left hand, remains seated, and nods to the vacant chair with his head—all signs of indifference. Eliminate A because nothing suggests that Lapham dislikes his visitor. The intensity of Lapham's behavior and the manner in which he addresses William contradict B, and C overstates the type of welcome that Bartley receives.

4. **(H)**

In the tiny office, called a "little den" in line 25, the two men's knees almost touch (lines 14–15). A larger den, the "counting room," completes the layout of Lapham's office. No other choice applies.

5. **(A)**

The dialogue reveals that Bartley is accustomed to hearing stories of childhood deprivation and hardship B.. It also suggests that Bartley is searching for compelling words and ideas to attract readers and perhaps inspire poverty-stricken youngsters to succeed in life (C and D). Only A is not an issue in the passage.

6. **(G)**

The best answer is choice G because Bartley has no reason to win Lapham's sympathy. Bartley discloses that he is an orphan as a not-too-subtle hint that Lapham isn't the only man to have suffered through a deprived childhood (choice F). The disclosure helps Bartley to break down the natural barrier between the businessman and the journalist H.. Bartley's words are said with humor J., but Lapham assumes that Bartley is teasing him and doesn't like it.

7. **(B)**

Lapham has a "great hairy fist" (line 11) and a "huge foot" (line 24). Choices A and D are not mentioned in the passage. C is only partly correct; Lapham's eyes are blue but never cold or steely.

8. **(G)**

Lines 60–64 indicate that both of Lapham's parents had been ambitious for his advancement. F should be discarded because Bartley fails to mention Lapham's personality. Rule out H because Bartley never says that Lapham ever read either book but that his parents taught him the simple virtues espoused by the *Old Testament* and *Poor Richard's Almanac*. J alludes to something not discussed in the passage.

9. **(C)**

Bartley derides Lapham's story. To him, tales of poor boys who make something of themselves are clichés, not worth taking seriously.

10. **(F)**

Bartley is portrayed as a seasoned and cynical reporter unimpressed by Lapham as a person but aware that readers like stories about rich people (lines 21–22). Bartley belittles Lapham's story of childhood deprivation; he's heard it all before and sarcastically asks questions about poor parents and "barefoot business" (line 50) that he might use in his article. Rule out choices G and J because Bartley shows neither resentment nor ingratitude. H may have some appeal as the answer because it is clear that Bartley has no affection or admiration for Lapham. But to call his attitude contemptuous is an overstatement.

11. **(C)**

Researchers found that the most dramatic changes took place in the decades following 1775 (lines 12–15).

12. **(G)**

Choices F and H may have contributed to the epidemic, but lines 5–7 say that Europeans brought smallpox directly to the tribe. J is unrelated to the spread of smallpox.

13. **(C)**

Based on the first paragraph, the Omaha thrived under Blackbird's leadership. He provided "wealth, political prestige, and military strength." Choices A, B, and D may be valid to some extent, but the preponderance of evidence in the passage suggest C as the best answer.

14. **(F)**

Choice G is supported by the statement that smallpox killed "as many as one-third of the Omaha" (lines 6–7). Evidence of H can be found in line 7. The change in roles caused by the smallpox epidemic—choice J—is discussed in lines 31–41. The passage does not discuss the impact of smallpox on the fur trade, making F the best answer.

15. **(D)**

Synonyms for *viable* include "workable," "conceivable," and "practicable." Therefore, D most closely approximates the meaning in the passage. The loss of population prevented the Omahas from functioning as they had before the smallpox epidemic.

16. **(F)**

Evidence that the Omaha hunted buffalo on horseback lay in the arthritic toes of the Omaha's skeletons (lines 21–24). Discussion of G, H, and J are absent from the passage.

17. **(C)**

According to Reinhard, data about the Omaha were derived from both the skeletons and artifacts (lines 25–30). Choice A is only occasionally true, according to line 28. Neither B nor D is discussed in the passage.

18. **(F)**

Based on the discussion of women's bones, stressful manufacturing jobs formerly done by men shortened women's lives. Before 1800, women may have lived fifty years, afterwards only thirty. Choice G may have resulted from women's weakened condition but is not discussed in the passage. Nor do H and J relate to the contents of the passage.

19. **(C)**

From the bones of women, Reinhard and his team realized that before the smallpox epidemic women's work consisted of "wood chopping, farming, and food grinding." Afterward, women "took on more of the responsibility for manufacturing." Choices A, B, and D are unrelated to changing "economic roles."

20. **(G)**

After 1800 an "influx in trade in tools and clothing" occurred that the last two paragraphs attribute to a change in traditional trading practices brought on by the death of Chief Blackbird. Eliminate choice F because Lewis and Clark's visit had nothing to do with this change. Although trade functioned under the auspices of the United States—mentioned in choice H—nothing in the passage refers to a peace treaty. Rule out J because trade had been conducted by barter long before 1800.

21. **(A)**

The mason is a "liar" because "he could not tell the truth in his work." In other words, his work was a deception. Choices B, C, and D are not discussed in the passage.

22. **(H)**

You may know that *posterity* means "generations of the distant future," making H the best answer. J may be suggested by the fact that the "foundations were four feet wide and sunk three and one-half feet into the earth." But wouldn't it be bizarre to build an oversize foundation just to have an oversize foundation? The author must have had another motive. Neither F nor G explain what the author had in mind.

23. **(C)**

In lines 11–12 the author states that he discovered the lie when he started to repair cracks in the wall caused by an earthquake. Choice A overstates the impact of the earthquake on the foundation wall. B and D occurred in the passage but are unrelated to the discovery of the wall's deficiencies.

24. **(J)**

The second paragraph cites all the defects listed by choices F, G, and H. Only J is missing.

25. **(B)**

Lines 4–9 imply the need for a sturdy foundation wall. Choices A, C, and D name other functions of a foundation wall, but they are not implied or stated in the passage.

26. **(J)**

The author's main purpose is to acquaint readers with principles of design and construction that he favors. Choices F and G are irrelevant. H may be a by-product of the discussion but is by no means its main purpose.

27. **(C)**

To the author choice B may be a valid statement, but in the context of the passage, the author's main concern is utility vs. stateliness, and in his view, utility should win hands down, making C the best answer. A is not discussed, and D alludes to an idea that the author abhors. After all, he's building a house not for friends but for himself.

28. **(H)**

At least twice (in the fourth and fifth paragraphs) the author discusses the irksomeness of housecleaning. The passage lacks evidence to support F. Rule out G because, except for a brief allusion to the cost of building a bathroom, the passage contains no evidence that the author is concerned about paying for the house. Besides, a man with servants is not likely to worry too much about money. J may be true because the author wants his servants to go swimming, but the passage says nothing about where the house will be located other than "in California."

29. **(B)**

The author believes that living inside causes damage to our lungs (lines 45–46). Choice A is incidental to his preference for outside air. C is an obvious inference—not a fact—to be drawn from the author's stated preference for outside air. D is mentioned earlier in the passage (lines 38–39) but is unrelated to the author's predilection for open air.

30. **(H)**

Choices F, G, and J are stated or implied by the second and third paragraphs of the passage. Although H may be desirable, the author doesn't discuss the need for a shared vision.

31. **(B)**

A host of "remarkable" qualities has left the author marveling about this extraordinary waterway. Choice A totally misrepresents the author's feelings. C ignores Twain's affection for the river, and D is hyperbolic; the river may impress Twain, but he shows no signs of uncontrollable passion.

32. **(G)**

The text of the first paragraph emphasizes the river's length, number of tributaries, vastness of its drainage basin, and other size-related features.

33. **(C)**

The phrase refers the hundreds of rivers from which the Mississippi receives its supply of water. Choice C, therefore, is the best answer. B should be ruled out because some rivers that feed the Mississippi carry steamboats (lines 13–14) and are equally navigable. Discard A because such distant rivers could not possibly be tributaries of the Mississippi. Eliminate D because the passage makes no reference to rivers emptying into the Atlantic.

34. **(F)**

Lines 18–19 point out a "remarkable" feature of the river: it narrows as it gets closer to its mouth, suggesting that other rivers widen as they approach the sea. G is contradicted by the variations in width pointed out in lines 20–22. Eliminate H because the rate of flow is not discussed. J is ambiguous at best because the water depth is discussed only as it pertains to the confluence of the Mississippi and Ohio Rivers. Whether water deepens at other intersections is left unclear.

35. **(D)**

Lines 35–41 explain that over many centuries the mud has caused land that once lay by the sea to now be located 200 miles inland. Both choices A and C are wrong because the passage does not discuss the origin of the Mississippi's mud. B describes only a hypothetical mass of mud that if solidified would add to the land mass.

36. **(F)**

This choice coincides with the description of the river's "disposition to make prodigious jumps by cutting through narrow necks of land" (lines 43–45). G may be a tempting answer based on the changes that a cut-off recently brought to Delta and Vicksburg (lines 47–50), but there is no indication that the river suddenly flowed backward. The explanation of the river's sidewise movement (choice H) does not mention cut-offs. Rule out J because the passage does not discuss floods.

37. **(C)**

Choice A is incorrect because the passage describes the Mississippi unexpectedly moving sideways, crossing spits of land and straightening itself. Eliminate B because scientists and engineers, while fascinated by the river, do not seem puzzled by it. As for D, the river does, in fact, straighten itself but not necessarily as it gets closer to the sea. C is the best answer.

38. **(J)**

All choices except J name a consequence of cut-offs. The passage makes no mention of property values along the river.

39. **(C)**

Before a recent cut-off (lines 47–50), the river flowed past Vicksburg before it flowed past Delta. Now it reaches Delta first. There is nothing in the passage to support A or B. Choice D is supported only insofar as distance is measured by river miles; the towns themselves obviously have not moved.

40. **(G)**

Based on the material in the last two paragraphs, the shifting of the river's path altered borders between states. Choice F may be true in reality, but the passage does not discuss it. Neither H nor J is supported in the passage.

Preparing for the Science Reasoning Test

5

▼▲▼▲▼▲▼▲▼▲▼▲▼▲▼▲▼▲▼▲▼▲▼▲▼▲▼▲▼▲▼▲▼▲▼

DESCRIPTION OF THE SCIENCE REASONING TEST

Be prepared for a science test that is probably different from any you have ever taken. It will draw on your general background in science, but will not ask you to make use of your knowledge of scientific facts. Everything you need to know in order to answer the questions will be given to you. This is a test of science reasoning, not knowledge of subject matter.

All questions are multiple choice. Your choice of answer will be in the form of key letters (either A-B-C-D or F-G-H-J in alternate questions). There are 40 questions altogether, and you have 35 minutes in which to answer them by filling in the appropriate spaces on the answer sheet.

The questions are in seven groups, each group containing five or six questions. Each group starts with a passage of information in the form of graphs, diagrams, paragraphs, or tables. The questions in each group can be answered from the information in the passage.

Testing Reasoning Skills

In the Science Reasoning Test, there are three distinctly different kinds of passages, each testing a different kind of reasoning skill.

- **Data Representation.** Two or three of the seven passages will present you with some sort of graph or chart. The questions that follow will ask you to interpret the information given and to draw conclusions from it.
- **Research Summaries.** Three or four passages will each present you with a description of a scientific experiment and the results of the investigation. You will be asked to evaluate the experimental method, to interpret the results, and to appreciate some of the implications of the experimental findings.
- **Conflicting Viewpoints.** One passage will give you two statements to read. The statements will deal with some controversial scientific question. The scientists who wrote the statements disagree with each other.

You will be asked to evaluate the arguments of each, identify the points of disagreement, and recognize the evidence that each scientist cites in favor of his viewpoint. *You will not be asked to decide who is right.*

Cognitive Levels

Within each group of questions, the level of difficulty is graded. The first questions in the group are the easiest; as you go further into the group, the questions will call for deeper levels of understanding. Three cognitive levels are tested in each group:

- **Understanding.** These questions, about two in each group, test only your ability to know what the passage is saying. If it is a graph, do you know what the variables are and what values of them are presented? If it is an experiment, can you identify the nature of the experimental problem and the kind of data that were taken? If it is a controversy, do you know what are the points at issue?
- **Analysis.** About three questions will ask you to find the deeper meanings in the passage. If it is a graph, can you tell how the variables relate to each other and what is implied by the relationship? If it is an experiment, were controls adequate, and what conclusions logically flow from the data? If it is a controversy, how well do the arguments flow from the facts presented by each scientist?
- **Generalization.** What further study might be suggested by the graph, experiment, or controversy? How do the results impact society at large? What does the study imply for systems that were not part of the study itself?

Improving Your Prospects

The best preparation for the Science Reasoning Test is to do as many comparable tests as you can. The science part of this book will give you carefully analyzed samples of the three kinds of questions. There are also two complete tests to work on.

There is something else you can do that will help. Read about science—not textbooks, but newspaper and magazine articles about new developments. Magazines such as *Science Digest* and *Discover* are excellent sources. Some newspapers have superb science coverage; when you read the daily paper, pay particular attention to articles about new developments in science. The *Los Angeles Times* and *The New York Times* (Tuesday's edition) have extensive specialty coverage of science. For detailed study, select articles that deal with advances in fundamental science, rather than material about new kinds of technology.

In reading such articles, use the same kind of technique that is recommended in taking the ACT. First, read the whole article as quickly as you can, without stopping to understand all the details. Then look at it again and highlight the information that is most crucial to understanding the whole article. In particular, look for the kind of information that is relevant to the three kinds of questions in the Science Reasoning Test:

- **Data Representation:** If there are diagrams or graphs, study them to make sure you know exactly what variables are represented, what values of the variables are given, how these values were obtained, and how they relate to each other.
- **Research Summaries:** If experimental results are quoted, see what experiments were done and what was found. How were measurements made? Were there adequate controls? How does the conclusion follow from the results of the experiment?
- **Conflicting Viewpoints:** A good journalist always tries to present all sides of an issue, and many new discoveries contradict canonical ideas. If scientists disagree with the conclusions reached in the article, what is the nature of the disagreement and what is the evidence that each side brings to uphold its viewpoint?

Finally, always look for suggestions in the article of questions left unanswered, additional data needed, the impact of the new discovery on the future progress in science, and the impact of the discovery on society at large.

TEST-TAKING TIPS

There is a special skill to taking a multiple-choice test. In some cases, there is even a danger of getting the "wrong" answer by knowing too much. This is because it may be possible to read into the question some subtle idea that did not occur to the person who wrote the question. Good item-writers try to avoid this pitfall, but they do make mistakes. In this test, the candidate who gets the right answer is not necessarily the one who knows most about the subject. It is the one who understands the passage thoroughly and *bases the choice of answer strictly on the contents of the passage.* Extraneous information can lead you to confusion and misinterpretation of the question.

A multiple-choice test is highly structured and formalized. To do well in such a test, you must be thoroughly familiar with the mechanics of the test. This is one reason why you should take the Model Examinations in this book under precisely the same conditions that you will meet in the testing room. Time yourself; take no more than 35 minutes for the whole test. Do not use a calculator, or any writing instrument other than a soft lead pencil with an eraser on it.

There is always some anxiety in a testing situation, but you can reduce it by being familiar with the forms of the test in advance. If the test looks familiar, you will not waste time figuring out how to go about answering questions. When you go into the testing room, for example, you should expect to find that in some questions the choices are labeled **A, B, C,** and **D,** while in others your choices will be **F, G, H,** and **J.** You should know what the answer sheet will look like, and that you must mark it with a soft lead pencil. And you must expect to find a group of five to seven questions relating to each passage. With all these mechanical details out of the way, you can go into the testing room ready to work.

Here are some test-taking tactics

- **Start by scanning the passage.** Read the passage or look at the data presentation quickly, just to get a rough idea of what it is all about. This should take no more than 20 seconds. Do not stop to study in detail any part that you do not understand. With this background, you are ready to move into a more careful study of the passage.
- **Read the passage again.** Now you can take as much as a minute or even more to understand the passage thoroughly. Feel free to mark up the test booklet with notes. Underline key words.
- **Answer the first question in the group.** In most tests, it is a good policy to skip questions you cannot answer immediately, but there is an exception in this test. The first question in each group will probably be a simple test of understanding. If you cannot answer it, you may well get the others wrong also. If necessary, go back to the passage to find the answer. If you cannot answer the first question, skip the whole passage and come back to it later.
- **Skip the hard questions.** After you have answered the first question, do not initially spend more than 30 seconds or so on any question. If you have time at the end, you can come back and reread the questions you could not get the first time around.
- **Read all the choices.** If you think you have found the right answer at once, do not stop reading. You may discover that there is some idea that has not appeared in the one you think is right. Think of the process as one of eliminating the incorrect answers, rather than selecting the right one. You may find that you can throw out three of the four choices quite easily.
- **If the answers are numerical, estimate.** Calculation takes time, and you should avoid it whenever possible. You can usually eliminate three obviously wrong choices quite easily. For example, suppose a graph shows

that an object has traveled 32 meters in seven seconds, and you are asked to find its speed. You are given these choices:

A. 220 m/s

B. 40 m/s

C. 4.6 m/s

D. 1.4 m/s

You know that 32 divided by 7 will be a little over 4, so you can pick out **C** as the answer without doing the calculation.

- **Pace yourself.** With 35 minutes to answer the questions for seven passages, you have just five minutes for each passage. If you find yourself spending more than that on one passage, skip it and come back to it later. On average, you should spend about two minutes reading each passage and 30 seconds answering each question.

- **Answer every question.** When you have finished doing the easy questions, go back and try again on some that you skipped. If you have only 30 seconds left at the end, turn to the answer sheet, find those questions you have not answered, and mark them at random. However, be careful not to give more than one answer to any question. There is no penalty for guessing, but an item will be marked wrong if you have given two answers.

DATA REPRESENTATION QUESTIONS

Every experiment and many kinds of theoretical studies present results in some kind of numerical matrix. This can be a data table, the familiar line graph, a bar graph, or any other kind that the author can think up. Three of the passages in the Science Reasoning Test will be some kind of data presentation, and about 15 of the questions will ask you to interpret those passages. You may find that the passage presents you with data in a form that you have never seen before.

Here is a sample Data Representation question. It is a graph showing how the population density of two organisms changes with time, under two different conditions of cultivation. Data always consists of variables. In the graphs on the next page, for example, the variables are species, condition of growth, relative population density, and age. The only numerical variable is age; its unit of measure (days) is marked on the horizontal axis.

Two species of the microorganism *Paramecium* are grown in cultures, and the population density is measured daily. The upper graph shows the results if the two species are raised in separate cultures. The lower graph shows the results if the two species are grown together in a single culture.

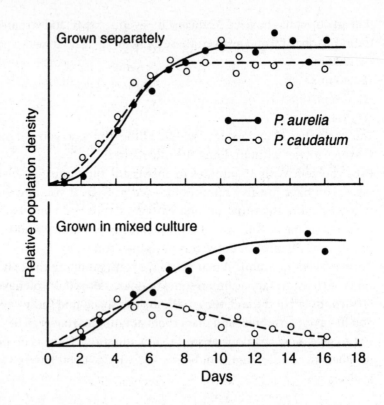

1. When the two species are grown separately,
   A. both species reach maximum population density in 18 days.
   B. both species stop reproducing after 12 days.
   C. populations of both species grow fastest after 3 days.
   D. both species reproduce fastest after 2 days.

   This question is at the *understanding* level of cognition. Both **B** and **D** are wrong because the graphs do not indicate rate of reproduction; the population density depends on other factors in addition to reproduction rate. **A** is wrong because the graph levels off at a maximum at 10 days, not 18. The slope of the graph indicates the rate of increase of the population density, and is greatest just after 3 days; the answer is **C**.

2. When the two species are cultured together,
   F. *P. aurelia* is unaffected, but it inhibits the population of *P. caudatum*.
   G. *P. aurelia* reproduces more rapidly than *P. caudatum*.
   H. it takes about a week for the populations to begin to interfere with each other.
   J. each species inhibits the population growth of the other.

This is an *analysis* question. **G** is wrong because other factors than reproduction rate may affect the population size. **F** is wrong because the population of *P. aurelia* grows more slowly in the presence of *P. caudata* than without it. **H** is wrong because the growth of the *P. caudatum* population starts to diminish in less than 5 days. The answer is **J**.

3. Comparison of the two graphs seems to imply that
   A. the two species of *Paramecium* are competing for the same resources.
   B. no two microorganisms can live successfully in the same culture.
   C. *P. caudatum* could not survive in the wild.
   D. *P. aurelia* is a more common species than *P. caudatum*.

This question calls on you to decide what general conclusion can reasonably be reached from the information given. **B** is wrong because the experiment deals with only two organisms, and says nothing about any other combinations. **C** and **D** are both wrong because conditions in the wild are nothing at all like those in a culture dish. It seems reasonable that *P. caudatum* is losing out in competition with *P. aurelia*; the answer is **A.**

In interpreting any data representation, you must first be sure you understand what the variables are. If they are not numerical, they will simply be named. There will always be numerical variables as well, and you must be able to find their values. These are the things to look for when you come to a Data Representation question:

What are the <u>units</u> *of measure?* These will usually be given along with the name of the variable. In a data chart, they will be at the top of the column. In a graph, they will be stated at the bottom and sides of the graph, along with the name of the variable.

What are the <u>values</u> *of the variables?* In a data chart, the values are entries in the table. In a graph, the values are read off the scales at the bottom and sides of the graph.

Are there any <u>trends</u>? Check to see whether there is an obvious consistent increase or decrease of any values as you move through the chart or graph.

Are there any <u>correlations</u>? If there are trends in any of the variables, how do they relate to trends in other variables? As one variable increases, does another increase or decrease?

These questions are not always applicable, but if they are, it will help you try to find answers to them.

Sample Passages

While any scientist can invent methods of data representation to suit his particular needs, certain kinds are in common use. Here are some examples of forms of numerical data representation that might be encountered.

Data tables. This is the most direct way of presenting data. It is nothing more than a list of the values of the variables. Example: The table below gives the elemental composition of the earth's crust, in two forms:

ABUNDANCE OF THE ATOMS IN THE EARTH'S CRUST. NUMBER OF ATOMS OF EACH ELEMENT PER THOUSAND AND PERCENT BY WEIGHT			
Element	**Symbol**	**No. of Atoms**	**Percent by Weight**
Oxygen	O	533	49.5
Silicon	Si	159	25.7
Hydrogen	H	151	0.9
Aluminum	Al	48	7.5
Sodium	Na	18	2.6
Iron	Fe	15	4.7
Calcium	Ca	15	3.4
Magnesium	Mg	14	1.9
Potassium	K	10	2.4
All others	—	37	1.4
Total		1000	100.0

Variables? There are three: the name of the element and two numerical variables (the number of atoms of each kind in a sample of 1,000 atoms and the relative weight of each). The second column is not an additional variable; it is simply another way of specifying the values of the variable in Column 1.

Units? This question does not apply to Columns 1 and 2, since the entries in these columns are not measurements. In this table, the units are named in the title of the chart and in the head of each column. In Column 3 the unit is the number of atoms of each kind in a sample of 1,000. In Column 4 it is percent by weight, and it does not involve the total number of atoms in the sample.

Values? These are the numbers in the column. In Column 3, for example, we learn that out of every 1,000 atoms, 533 are oxygen. Column 4 tells us that these oxygen atoms constitute 49.5 percent of the weight of the sample.

Trends? There are none. Do not be misled by the fact that the numbers in Column 3 are decreasing. This is only because the person who made the chart elected to list the elements in order of decreasing frequency. There can be no trends because the entries in Column 1 are not numerical.

Correlations? Columns 3 and 4 both show decreasing values going down the column. This only indicates that the element with fewer atoms contributes less to the weight of the sample. The interesting fact here is that there are deviations from the strict order. Hydrogen, for example, is the third most common element, but its weight is less than any of the others. This should tell you that each hydrogen atom weighs far less than any other atom in the group.

Line graphs. This is the most usual way of representing a function of two variables. In scientific graphs, the two variables are measured quantities, and they have units of measure. If there are more than two variables, the graph may contain several curves. The example shown represents the rate of photosynthesis of a red alga, measured as a function of the rate of oxygen production. The other numerical variable is the salinity (salt concentration) of the water. Each of two environments (mangrove estuary and coastline) is represented by two curves, one for summer (s) and one for winter (w).

Variables? There are four; two of them are numerical. On the abscissa, salinity; on the ordinate, rate of photosynthesis. The nonnumerical variables are season and environment; they are indicated by the type of line and the label on the graph.

Units? This applies only to the numerical variables that form the function. Salinity is measured in parts of salt per thousand of water (ppt). Rate of photosynthesis is measured by the rate of oxygen production, in microliters of oxygen per gram of tissue per hour.

Values? Each point on the graph expresses a value of the two variables. For example, the high point on the curve for estuaries in winter is at 5000 microliters of oxygen and 20 parts per thousand of salt.

Trends? Each curve shows that photosynthesis increases with salinity up to some maximum value, and then decreases as the salt concentration goes higher.

Correlations? At all salt concentrations, the rate of photosynthesis is higher in winter than in summer, and higher in estuaries than on the coasts.

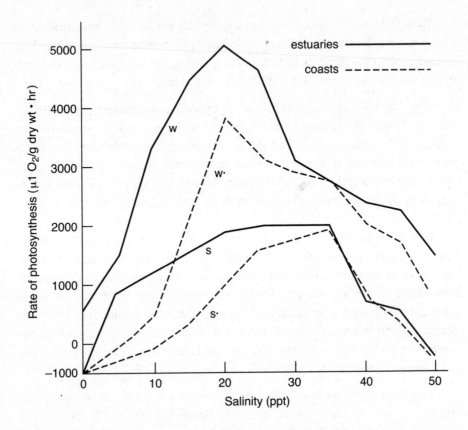

Bar graphs. A bar graph is used to show the distribution of some variable when there is no functional relationship with another variable. If several variables are involved, more than one graph is needed. In the bar graphs shown on the next page, a comparison is made between the skull lengths of European moles before and after two winters.

Variables? In each graph, there are two numerical variables: along the abscissa, skull length (within 0.25 mm); on the ordinate, percent of the total number of moles that fall in each range. The four graphs give data for four groups: males and females before and after the hard winter. The additional information given is the actual number of moles in each of the four groups.

Units? For skull size, millimeters; for the length of each bar, percent of the total.

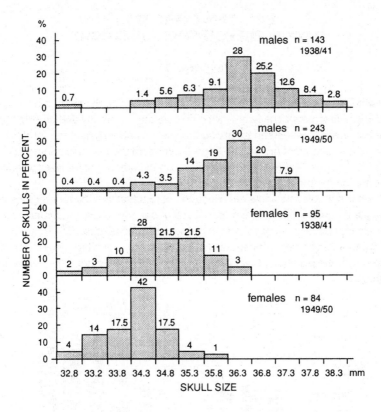

Values? These are read from the ordinate scale, for each size category. In this example, the value of the ordinate is also written in, so that it is unnecessary to read it off the scale. In the top graph (143 males, measured from 1938 to 1941) the bar for the skull length 35.8 mm extends to just under 10% on the ordinate scale; the actual value is given as 9.1%.

Trends? In each of these graphs there is a typical normal distribution, with the largest number of individuals falling near the middle of the distribution and successively smaller numbers on both sides of the center. It is also clear that in both groups, females have smaller skulls than males.

Correlations? At all times, the females' skulls are smaller. Also, the skull lengths were considerably smaller after the hard winter.

PRACTICE EXERCISES:
DATA REPRESENTATION QUESTIONS

Passage 1

A growing plant builds its tissues in four regions: the root, the stem, the leaves, and the seeds (grains). The way in which the resources are divided among these four areas is measured by drying the tissues and weighing the four parts separately. As the plant grows, the apportionment of the new tissue among these four regions changes. It also depends on the amount of fertilizer given to them, and on the presence or absence of parasites.

The charts that follow show the allocation of material into the four regions of wheat plants grown in a square meter of soil under controlled conditions. Separate test plots were given 5 different concentrations of fertilizer, ranging from 0.5 to 4.0 mols per cubic meter. Half of the plots, indicated by [+], were infected with the parasitic plant Striga, and the other half, marked [−], were left uninfected.

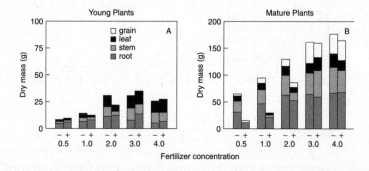

Chart A represents the distribution of mass among the four plant parts 50 days after planting; Chart B gives the same information for wheat 140 days after planting.

1. If a wheat plant infected with Striga is fed with fertilizer concentrated at 2 mols per cubic meter and allowed to grow to maturity, its dry weight would be about:

   A. 30 grams
   B. 80 grams
   C. 130 grams
   D. 160 grams

2. With high fertilizer concentration, the existing parts of a plant that grow most after the first 50 days are the:

   F. roots and leaves.
   G. leaves and grains.
   H. roots and stems.
   J. stems and leaves.

3. When the concentration of the fertilizer is low,

    A. Striga severely restricts the growth of the plants.
    B. no seed is formed in the first 50 days.
    C. Striga does not grow well.
    D. there is little growth after the first 50 days.

4. The parasite does little damage provided that

    F. it attacks only the roots.
    G. does not attack while the plants are young.
    H. the plants are otherwise healthy.
    J. high doses of fertilizer are used.

5. To a wheat farmer, the main benefit from applying high concentrations of fertilizer is:
    A. more resilient root structure.
    B. suppression of the parasite.
    C. increase in grain mass.
    D. increase in overall size of the plants.

Answers and Explanations

1. **(B)**

The bar called for is the one marked + in the 2.0 column of the Mature Plants chart.

2. **(H)**

Between the A and the B charts, the roots quadruple and the stems more than double, with or without the parasite. The leaf mass does not change much, and there are no grains present at 50 days.

3. **(A)**

With 0.5 level of fertilizer, the [−] bar grows from 10 to 70 grams, while the [+] bar is unchanged between the two charts.

4. **(J)**

In the graph for the mature plants, the bars for the 3.0 and 4.0 units of fertilizer are equal whether or not the parasite is present. No information is provided about where the parasite attacks or in what stage of development, or about the health status of the plants.

5. **(C)**

The wheat farmer is in the business of producing grains.

Passage 2

The charts below show the numbers of deaths from three different causes, per hundred thousand of population, plotted against the age of death, separately for men and women, and the total numbers of death at each age.

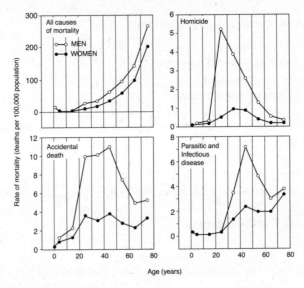

1. The probability that a man in his 40s will die in an accident is about:

    A. one in a thousand.
    B. one in ten thousand.
    C. one in a hundred thousand.
    D. one in a million.

2. One obvious feature of this information is that:

    F. overall, more men die than women.
    G. for men in their 20s death from homicide is about as frequent as death from accident.
    H. more men than women get infectious diseases.
    J. at all ages, the death rate is higher for men.

3. For women in their 60s:

    A. at this age, there is an unusually large rate of accidental death.
    B. most deaths are from causes other than those in this study.
    C. there are more women alive at this age than men.
    D. one woman in 100,000 is murdered.

4. In what way does the curve for infectious disease differ from the curves for homicide and accidental death?

    F. Death rate for both sexes increases after age 60.
    G. Death rates for men and women do not differ until after age 25.
    H. At all ages, more men than women die.
    J. The death rate for men drops sharply after age 40.

5. The data suggest certain sociological generalizations. Which?

    A. Women are better drivers than men.
    B. Young men are inclined to be violent and reckless.
    C. Women commit far fewer murders than men.
    D. At all ages, there are more female than male humans.

Answers and Explanations

1. **(B)**

The data are given in terms of deaths per 100,000 and the data point for men in their 40s is about 10. Ten per 100,000 is one per 10,000.

2. **(J)**

The first chart shows the figures for death rates due to all causes, and the curve for men lies above that for women at all ages. F is wrong; everybody dies. G: note that the scales are not the same in all the graphs; for men in their 20s, homicide rate is about 5; accident is 10. H: more men die from disease than women, but the data say nothing about the rate of infection.

3. **(B)**

The graph for all causes shows about 70 per 100,000 at this age, while the sum of the other causes is only about 5. The rate of accidental death of women is fairly constant from age 20 to about 80. While more men than women have died up to age 60, the data say nothing about number surviving; maybe there were more males to begin with (there were!). The murder rate for women at age 60 is far below 1 per 100,000.

4. **(G)**

The curves for the two sexes run together until age 25, which is not the case for any of the other three. All of the other choices apply also to at least one of the other graphs.

5. **(B)**

The graphs show that young men have a very high rate of death from accident and murder. Choice C is wrong; the data only show that men died of homicide more frequently, but say nothing about who does the killing. A is wrong because automobile accidents are not the only cause of accidental death. D is wrong because no information is given about the relative numbers of boy babies born.

RESEARCH SUMMARIES QUESTIONS

The passage for these questions consists of a description of two or more experiments, followed by a statement of the results of the experiments. Your task is to answer five or six questions based on the results. You will succeed if you know what to look for. For purposes of discussing tactics, one experiment will be exemplified.

Here is a sample of a typical Research Summaries passage, along with a typical question at each of the three cognitive levels:

A series of experiments was done to test the hypothesis that air pollution affects fertility.

Experiment 1

Four groups of female mice, with 40 mice in each group, were mated and then exposed to different diets and concentrations of carbon monoxide in the air. The two diets tested were high protein and low protein. Air was either free of carbon monoxide or contaminated with 65 parts per million of carbon monoxide. This is a pollution level that can be found in cities with heavy traffic. The number of females who became pregnant was then recorded:

High protein, clean air:	38
High protein, polluted air:	36
Low protein, clean air:	19
Low protein, polluted air:	9

Experiment 2

The experiment was repeated, this time using ozone instead of carbon monoxide as the pollutant:

High protein, clean air:	35
High protein, polluted air:	22
Low protein, clean air:	20
Low protein, polluted air:	21

1. Since the problem deals with the effects of polluted air, why were groups of mice exposed to clean air?
   A. to keep a healthy strain of mice going
   B. so that they could be compared with mice exposed to polluted air
   C. so that the effects of protein in the diet could be evaluated
   D. to compare the effects of ozone and carbon monoxide

   This is an *understanding* level question. It asks you to apply your knowledge of the meaning of a control. Unless there was a group given clean air, there is no way of telling whether the pollutants really make a difference in the fertility of the mice. The answer is **B**.

2. Which of the following conclusions is justified by the data?
   F. Carbon monoxide pollution by itself reduces the fertility of mice.
   G. A high protein diet promotes good health in mice.
   H. Proteins protect the fertility of mice against the damage caused by carbon monoxide.
   J. Air pollutants reduce the fertility of mice fed on a low protein diet.

   This is an *analysis* question. You must study the data and find in it an implication that supports one of the offered answers. **F** is probably not a good answer because there is very little difference between the mice in good air and air polluted with carbon monoxide if the diet is high in protein. (You must be prepared to make judgment calls in deciding between two answers.) **G** is wrong because nothing in the experiment deals with the general health of the mice. **J** is wrong because there is no justification for extending the results from the carbon monoxide experiment to pollutants in general; indeed, ozone seems to make very little difference, if the protein level is low. The answer is **H**; fertility is little affected by carbon monoxide if there is plenty of protein, but mice produce very few offspring in air polluted with carbon monoxide if the protein level in the diet is low.

3. Which of the following would be an appropriate response to the results of this experiment?

    A. Start a program to inform women who want to become pregnant that they should move to regions with lower air pollution.

    B. Do a similar experiment on women, to see if their ability to become pregnant is affected by air pollutants.

    C. Start a massive campaign to reduce air pollution, particularly in cities.

    D. Start a research program to find out more about how air pollutants affect the fertility rate in animals.

This *generalization* question requires you to apply the results of the experiment in a broader area. **A** is wrong because mice are not women; there is no evidence that women would react the same way. **B** is wrong; it is good theoretical science, but where would you find women who would volunteer for the experiment? **C** is wrong; while reducing air pollution would probably be a good idea, this experiment does not provide enough evidence to justify such a massive program. **D** is a good idea; with more data in hand, it might be possible to get a better idea of how women might be affected.

⚿ TEST-TAKING TIPS

It is worthwhile to approach the Research Summaries questions in a systematic way. Here are some hints as to the best way to attack these questions, along with a sample passage to show you how these hints apply.

- **Understand the problem.** Each description of an experiment starts with a statement of what the experiment is designed to find out. Read this statement carefully; do not go any further until you are quite sure that you understand exactly what the experimental problem is.

    Here is a sample of such a problem statement:

        A horticulturist investigated the effects of using a high-nitrogen fertilizer on the growth of privet plants.

- **Understand the design.** Next, study the description of the experimental method. It may be accompanied by a diagram. Try to relate the design of the experiment to the problem that the experiment is designed to solve.

    For the sample problem we are considering, the experimental design is as follows:

Fifty 1-year-old privet plants were divided into 10 lots of 5 plants each. All were watered every third day with equal amounts of water. In 9 of the lots, different concentrations of high-nitrogen fertilizer were added to the water once every 2 weeks for a year. The heights of the plants were measured at the end of the year.

- **Identify the variables.** Research problems can fall into two general categories. In some problems, the investigator studies some aspect of the natural world, often making measurements of some kind. By comparing measurements, the scientist hopes to come to some understanding of the nature of the process under study. Generally, there will be two or more variables, and what is being sought is a relationship between the variables. If the research problem you are given is of this kind, your first job is to identify the variables.

  The second category of research is the experiment. Here, the investigator plays a more active part, varying some condition to see what will happen. The independent variable is the quantity that the experimenter adjusts or controls in some way. Presumably, this will make something else change. The something else is the dependent variable. Just as in the other kind of problem, you must first be sure that you understand what the variables are.

  In the sample we are using, the independent variable is the amount of fertilizer, and the dependent variable is the heights of the plants at the end of the year.

- **Identify the controls.** In an experiment, and sometimes in a strictly observational problem, there is always the danger that some unsuspected variable is affecting the outcome. The experimenter must make sure that whatever outcome is observed is due to changes in the independent variable, not in something else. The way to be sure is to include controls in the experiment. Controls are precautions taken to eliminate all variables except the independent variable.

  In our sample experiment, all plants must have identical soil, air, light, and so on. All the plants must be genetically identical. Further, to make sure that the minimum amount of fertilizer has an effect, a special control sample must be included. This is a group of plants that are given no fertilizer. Unless this control group turns out to be different from the experimental groups, there is no way to be sure that the minimum amount of fertilizer is affecting the growth of the plants.

- **Study the results.** The outcome of the experiment may be presented in words, in a diagram, or (most often) in the form of a data table. In such a table, the independent variable appears on the left, and the dependent variable on the right.

  For our experiment, a table of experimental results might look like this:

Fertilizer concentration (g/L)	Average height of plant (cm)
0	22.2
5	25.3
10	29.0
15	28.7
20	29.2
25	29.0
30	28.6
35	20.9
40	16.3
45	13.0

An important control in this experiment is the first data point, when no fertilizer was used. Without this, there would be no way to tell whether 5 g/L of fertilizer had any effect at all.

What trend do you notice in these data? You should see that the fertilizer helps, but that over a wide range the amount is not important. There is no significant difference in plant height between 10 g/L and 30 g/L. However, it is also clear that, if the fertilizer is too concentrated, growth is retarded.

- **Look for flaws in the experiment.** Are the controls adequate? Is the conclusion justified by the data? Are the experimental errors so great as to invalidate the results?

  In the sample experiment, for example, the experimenter did not specify that all the plants be genetically identical. Another flaw is the failure to describe exactly how the height of the plants was measured.

  Once you thoroughly understand the nature of the experiment and the meaning of the results, you should be able to deal with the multiple-choice questions based on the experiment.

Sample Questions

There will be five to seven Research Summaries questions based on a single passage. Look at the following questions, based on the sample experiment. Note the reasoning on which your choice of answer might be based.

1. What is the most efficient rate for a commercial grower to apply fertilizer to the privet plants?

   A. 5 g/L   **C.** 20 g/L

   B. 10 g/L   **D.** 40 g/L

   The answer is **B**. Higher concentrations cost more, but will not produce any further improvement. Furthermore, too much will actually do damage.

2. If a horticulturist is growing chrysanthemums to produce flowers, how would she know how much fertilizer to use?

   F. Perform an identical experiment with chyrsanthemums.

   G. Use 10 g/L of fertilizer.

   H. Perform a similar experiment with chrysanthemums, but use a different dependent variable.

   J. Grow the plants in sunlight because it is known that sunlight stimulates the formation of flowers.

   The answer is **H**. The best fertilizer for privet may not be best for chrysanthemums, so **G** is wrong. The experiment described deals only with growth, not flower formation, so **F** is wrong. **J** tells the horticulturist nothing about how much fertilizer is best. She needs a similar experiment, but with flower formation as the dependent variable.

3. In order for the results of this experiment to be meaningful, which of the following would NOT have to be the same for all the experiment samples?

   A. The soil in which the specimens were planted.

   B. The amount of time it took for the plants to flower.

   C. The particular variety of privet used.

   D. The number of hours of daylight to which the plants were exposed.

   The answer is **B**, since the experimental design proposes only to evaluate rate of growth, not flowering. If none of the other variables were controlled, the experimenter could never be sure whether the differences in growth were due to the fertilizer, or to the soil, the plant variety, or the exposure to daylight.

4. What part of the experimental design was included for the purpose of deter-
mining the smallest concentration of fertilizer that has any effect on growth?
   F. Giving one group water only
   G. Using an interval of 5 g/L between fertilizer concentrations
   H. Including a 10-g/L sample
   J. Using plants from a single genetic stock

   The answer is **F**. This is an important control. Unless there is a different
   outcome between no fertilizer and 5 g/L, there is no evidence that the 5 g/L
   of fertilizer did anything.

5. Which of the following situations would NOT invalidate the results of the
experiment?
   A. Accidental destruction of the sample given 20 g/L of fertilizer
   B. The discovery that half of the plants had been potted in a different soil
   C. The discovery that the water used already contained substantial
      amounts of nitrogen
   D. The discovery that some of the plants had been taken from a different
      variety of privet

   The answer is **A**; results of the experiment are quite clear even without this
   sample. **B** and **D** are wrong because a different soil or a different variety might
   cause differences in the outcome. **C** is wrong because the nitrogen in the water
   has not been taken into account in the effort to find the optimum amount.

6. Which of the following hypotheses is suggested by the data?
   F. High concentrations of fertilizer damage the roots of plants.
   G. Privet plants cannot grow unless there is nitrogen in the soil.
   H. If all other conditions are equal, the amount of fertilizer used does not
      affect plant growth.
   J. Any addition of fertilizer to the soil slows photosynthesis.

   The answer is **F**. **G** is wrong because we have no idea whether there was
   any nitrogen in the soil of the control, where the plants did grow. **H** is wrong
   because the experiment did not test a variety of conditions. **J** is wrong because we would expect slowing down of photosynthesis to retard growth,
   while the experiment shows that moderate amounts of fertilizer increase
   growth. **F** is right because it offers a reasonable explanation for the growth
   retardation produced by 35 g/L of fertilizer.

PRACTICE EXERCISES:
RESEARCH SUMMARIES QUESTIONS

The Research Summaries questions in the test are likely to be more complex than the example given. Try the following questions.

Passage 1

A physicist is investigating the effect that different conditions have on the force of friction. The material used is an ordinary brick, with a mass of 1.8 kg. It is pulled across the surface of a wooden table. Friction is measured by pulling the brick with a string attached to a spring scale, calibrated in newtons (N). When the brick is pulled at constant speed, the reading on the scale is equal to the force of friction between the brick and the table top.

Experiment 1

The brick is placed on the table in three different positions. First, it is allowed to rest on its broad face (area = 180 cm²), then on its side (area = 130 cm²), and finally on its end (area = 56 cm²).

Table 1

Area (cm²)	Friction (N)
180	7.1
130	7.3
56	7.2

Experiment 2

A wooden block of mass 0.6 kg is made to the same dimensions as the brick, and the experiment is repeated.

Table 2

Area (cm²)	Friction (N)
180	1.2
130	1.1
56	1.2

Experiment 3

This time, the wooden block is loaded by adding 1.2 kg of extra mass on top of it, to give it the same weight as the brick.

Table 3

Area (cm²)	Friction (N)
180	3.5
130	3.6
56	3.7

1. From Experiment 1, it would be reasonable to hypothesize that:

   A. the surface area of contact does not affect the amount of friction.
   B. friction is large in a brick-to-wood contact.
   C. the amount of friction depends on the way the weight of the object is distributed.
   D. heavy objects have more friction than light ones.

2. Which combination of experiments shows that the amount of friction depends on the weight of the object?

   F. Experiment 1 and Experiment 2
   G. Experiment 1 and Experiment 3
   H. Experiment 2 and Experiment 3
   J. Experiment 1, Experiment 2, and Experiment 3

3. In doing Experiment 3, what was the purpose of adding enough weight to the wooden block to make its weight equal to that of the brick?

   A. To test the hypothesis that adding weight increases friction
   B. To find the relationship between surface area of contact and friction
   C. To find out whether the density of the material influences the amount of friction
   D. To control other factors and test the effect of the nature of the materials in contact

4. The experimenter repeated the experiment with the unloaded wooden block mounted on three tiny wooden points, which were the only contact with the table top. If the results of all these experiments hold good for extreme values of the experimental variables, about how much would the friction be?

   F. About 0.4 N
   G. Substantially less than 1.2 N
   H. About 1.2 N
   J. Substantially more than 1.2 N

5. Common experience indicates that it is much harder to slide some boxes across a floor than others. Which of the following reasons why this is true is demonstrated in these experiments?

   A. Friction is greater if there is more surface in contact.
   B. A heavy box will have more friction against the floor than a light one.
   C. Objects of irregular shape have more friction because they dig into the floor.
   D. The amount of friction depends on how the weight of the object is distributed.

6. The results of these experiments suggest that, if three bricks were piled up and pulled along as before, the amount of friction would be about:

   F. 3.6 N.
   G. 7.2 N.
   H. 14.4 N.
   J. 22.6 N.

Answers and Explanations

1. **(A)**

In spite of the fact that one surface is almost three times as great as another, there is no substantial difference in the amount of friction. The small differences are surely due to experimental variation. This is obvious when it is noted that the value obtained for the 56-cm² surface is a little larger than that for the 180-cm² surface. **B** is wrong because there is no comparison with other readings to decide what constitutes large friction. **C** is wrong because the experiment did not vary weight distribution. **D** is wrong because in this experiment the same object was used throughout.

2. **(H)**

In these two experiments, both the surface area of contact and the kind of materials in contact are the same, and the only difference is in the weight. The other three choices all include Experiment 1, in which a different kind of material is in contact with the surface, and this might be the reason for the difference in results.

3. **(D)**

With the weight added, all other variables are controlled and the only difference between the brick and the wooden block, as far as contact with the table top is concerned, is in the nature of the material. The other choices are wrong because the experiment makes no comparison of different weights, surface areas, or densities.

4. **(H)**

The data indicate that friction does not depend on surface area of contact. This is tested to extreme limits by repeating the experiment with a very small surface area. If the relationships hold up for extreme values, the friction should be the same for a very small area as for a large one.

5. **(B)**

Comparing Experiment 2 with Experiment 3 shows that, even if the materials and the surface area in contact are the same, friction is greater when the weight of the object is greater. There is no evidence in these experiments that shape or weight distribution affects friction. Choice **A** is wrong because the experiments do not show any difference due to surface area.

6. **(J)**

Experiments 2 and 3 show that, when the effective weight of the wooden block is increased by raising the mass from 0.6 kg to 1.8 kg, the friction triples. This suggests that friction is proportional to the weight of the object. Since three bricks weigh three times as much as one, the friction with three bricks ought to be three times as great as with a single brick.

Passage 2

A bacteriologist cultures a blood specimen and finds that it produces two kinds of bacterial colonies. One kind of bacteria, designated R, grows in red colonies; the other, called Y, produces yellow colonies. To study the metabolism of these bacteria, she performs the following experiments:

Experiment 1

The R strain is cultivated on three media, each containing a different supply of nutrients, and the amount of growth is noted:

Medium	Growth
glucose	very good
amino acids	poor
glucose and amino acids	very good

Experiment 2

The experiment is repeated in Y strain:

Medium	Growth
glucose	poor
amino acids	none
glucose and amino acids	good

Experiment 3

Is this experiment, two strains of bacteria are cultivated together to the same petri dish:

Medium	Growth of R	Growth of Y
glucose	good	none
amino acids	poor	none
glucose and amino acids	none	excellent

1. Which statement is true about the nutritional requirements of the *R* bacteria?

    A. They need both glucose and amino acids in order to grow vigorously.
    B. They can survive and prosper on glucose alone.
    C. Amino acids tend to retard their growth.
    D. They cannot grow without glucose.

2. Which statement is true about the nutritional requirements of the *Y* bacteria?

    F. They cannot survive without both glucose and amino acids.
    G. They can survive without glucose, but must have amino acids.
    H. They can survive without amino acids, if they have glucose.
    J. If they have glucose, the presence of amino acids is irrelevant.

3. Which hypothesis best explains the results obtained when both bacteria are grown together on a glucose-only medium?

    A. The *Y* bacteria do not survive because they need amino acids.
    B. The *Y* bacteria produce some substance that promotes the growth of *R* bacteria.
    C. The *R* bacteria grow vigorously and win out in competition with the *Y* bacteria.
    D. The *R* bacteria promote the growth of the *Y* bacteria.

4. Under what circumstances do the *Y* bacteria produce a substance that prevents the growth of the *R* bacteria?

    F. When there is an adequate supply of glucose
    G. When the *R* bacteria are weakened because of a shortage of amino acids
    H. When the *Y* bacteria have a plentiful supply of amino acids
    J. When the *Y* bacteria have both glucose and amino acids available

5. In another experiment, both kinds of bacteria were cultured on a medium containing glucose, amino acids, and ethyl alcohol. The *R* bacteria grew, but the *Y* bacteria did not. Which of the following hypotheses could NOT explain these results?

    A. Ethyl alcohol is poisonous to *Y* bacteria, but not to *R* bacteria.
    B. In the presence of ethyl alcohol, *R* bacteria produce a substance that is poisonous to *Y* bacteria.
    C. Ethyl alcohol is necessary for the growth of *R* bacteria, but not *Y* bacteria.
    D. Ethyl alcohol prevents *Y* bacteria from making use of glucose.

6. What steps might an experimenter take to see whether any practical outcome might be realized from these experiments?

    F. Test the *Y* bacteria to see whether they can inhibit the growth of many other kinds of bacteria.
    G. Test the *Y* bacteria to see whether they can grow on a different combination of amino acids.
    H. Test the *R* bacteria to see whether an increased concentration of amino acids will enhance their growth.
    J. Test the *R* bacteria to see whether they can grow on other sugars besides glucose.

Answers and Explanations

1. **(B)**

Experiment 1 showed that they grow well on glucose alone. Choice **A** is wrong because there is nothing in the results to indicate that amino acids improved their growth. **C** is wrong because they did well when amino acids were added to the glucose; with amino acids alone, they did poorly because they had no glucose. **D** is wrong because they survived, although weakly, on amino acids alone.

2. **(H)**

The Y bacteria grew, weakly, on a medium with glucose but no amino acids. That is why **F** and **G** are wrong. **J** is wrong because they did much better when amino acids were added.

3. **(C)**

The R bacteria grow well, but they have completely suppressed the growth of the Y bacteria. A is wrong because experiment 2 showed that the Y bacteria can survive, although poorly, on glucose alone. B is wrong because the Y bacteria are not growing at all and so cannot produce anything. D is wrong; the Y bacteria do not grow at all when there are R bacteria present.

4. **(J)**

When both nutrients are available, the Ys completely eliminate the Rs. With glucose alone, it is the Rs that win. **H** is wrong because the Ys need glucose as well as amino acids.

5. **(C)**

Experiment 1 shows that the Rs grow quite well without ethyl alcohol. The other choices could easily explain the lack of R bacteria.

6. **(F)**

The discovery that the Y bacteria could eliminate many kinds of bacteria might well lead to the discovery of a new antibiotic. All the other choices might be of interest, but do not seem to point in the direction of anything useful.

CONFLICTING VIEWPOINTS QUESTIONS

Scientific information is never complete. While ideas and theories are developing, scientists will continue to disagree with each other. It is these disagreements that provide the spur for research. Experiments and other forms of investigation are specifically designed to resolve points at issue. It is through this dialogue of scientists with each other and with nature that consensus is eventually reached.

In the Conflicting Viewpoints questions, you will be given short paragraphs representing the ideas of two scientists. They will disagree with each other. Your job is to analyze the arguments and information in the two paragraphs. You will be asked to identify the nature of the disagreement, to tell why each of the scientists has arrived at the opinion expressed, and to identify forms of evidence that might resolve the conflict.

In this type of question, you will not be asked to decide which of the two scientists is correct. You will be required to identify points of agreement and disagreement. You may be asked to identify kinds of evidence that would tend to support or to deny either of the two viewpoints.

Here is a sample Conflicting Viewpoints passage, with a sample of possible questions at each of the three cognitive levels.

Passage

There has been a steady increase in the average temperature of the earth for the last 150 years. Since 1861, the average temperature, all over the world, has gone up one degree Fahrenheit. This may not seem like much, but if the trend continues, the result will be disastrous. The polar ice caps would melt, flooding all coastal areas and reducing the total land area of the earth by 30 percent. All climatic zones would change; farmland would turn to desert and forest would turn into prairie.

Scientist 1:

It has become increasingly clear that global warming is the result of the accumulation of the "greenhouse gases" in the atmosphere. These gases, chiefly carbon dioxide, act as a kind of blanket, preventing heat from escaping into outer space. As industry has advanced and automobiles fill our highways, the burning of coal, oil, gasoline, and natural gas has more than doubled the amount of carbon dioxide in the atmosphere. It is up to industry to find ways to reduce the amount of carbon dioxide coming out of smokestacks and exhaust pipes. Unless drastic steps are taken to deal with this problem, the world as we know it will disappear.

Scientist 2:

Before placing an enormously expensive burden on industry, we must be sure of our ground. While the greenhouse effect may well be a part of the reason for the warming of the earth, it cannot be the whole story. Most of the temperature increase occurred before 1940, but most of the carbon dioxide increase has happened since then. Something else is contributing to the warming of the earth. The temperature of the earth depends strongly on the level of sunspot activity on the sun. The sun heats up during high sunspot years. Solar activity goes through cycles. When activity is high, increased levels of ultraviolet radiation deplete the ozone layer of the upper atmosphere and the increased flow of charged particles from the sun affects the formation of clouds. All of these effects have complex and poorly understood effects on the earth's climate, and could easily result in long-range and cyclic climate changes.

1. The two scientists agree that

   F. sunspot activity affects the climate of the earth.
   G. there is a long-range trend to a warmer earth.
   H. the major cause of warming is carbon dioxide.
   J. something must be done to avert a catastrophe.

This is an *understanding* question. **F** is wrong because Scientist 1 does not address the question of sunspot activity at all. **H** is wrong because Scientist 2 thinks that sunspot activity may play the major role. **J** is wrong because Scientist 2's theory precludes the possibility of ameliorative action. The answer is **G**; both agree that the earth has gotten warmer.

2. In responding to Scientist 2, Scientist 1 might reply that

   A. the measured value of the increase in sunspot activity is far too small to account for the observed warming.
   B. it is widely known that it is the carbon dioxide in the atmosphere that produces the warming.
   C. the flow of charged particles from the sun actually decreases during periods of high sunspot activity.
   D. it is possible to cut down on the atmospheric carbon dioxide by promoting the growth of plants.

To answer this *analysis* question, you have to eliminate proffered answers that do not deal with issues discussed by either scientist, such as **D**. Appeals to authority, like **B**, are not acceptable scientific debate. **C** is an insult to Scientist 1, who surely knows the properties of an easily measurable phenomenon. The answer is **A**, because there is a strong element of judgment in making this decision, particularly since Scientist 2 admits that the phenomena are not well understood.

3. What course of action might be suggested by Scientist 2 and opposed by Scientist 1?

   F. Convene a committee of industry and government leaders to determine what steps can be taken to reduce carbon dioxide emission.
   G. Start a long-range research project to explore the possibility of neutralizing the flow of charged particles from the sun.
   H. Investigate the possibility that other greenhouse gases such as methane have an important effect on warming.
   J. Start a long-range research project to evaluate the relative importance of carbon dioxide and sunspot activity.

Now you must look for an appropriate *generalization*. **F** is wrong because Scientist 2 does not believe that carbon dioxide is at the heart of the problem. **G** is wrong; Scientist 2 has not committed himself to the idea that charged particles are the major culprit. **H** is wrong; neither scientist has suggested that other gases are involved. **J** is right; Scientist 2 feels that more information is needed, but Scientist 1 might object to a long-range project because the problem of carbon dioxide is too urgent.

Tactics

In approaching a question of this type, start by reading it quickly. This may be enough for you to apply the first important tactic: *Identify the basic disagreement.*

You can analyze the passage presented and any other like it, by asking yourself a series of questions about it. Only after you have answered them in your own mind are you in a position to look at the questions you will have to answer.

- **What is the basic question at issue?** You probably know the answer to this from your first, quick reading. In the given passage, the issue is what the main cause of global warming is.
- **What is the position of each of the scientists on the question?** Scientist 1 believes that greenhouse gases are adequate to account for global warming; Scientist 2 thinks sunspot activity may be as important.
- **What evidence does Scientist 1 bring to justify his position?** The temperature increase coincides with a massive increase in the amount of carbon dioxide in the atmosphere.
- **What evidence does Scientist 2 bring to support his position?** The temperature increase began long before most of the carbon dioxide was added to the air. Global temperature changes have occurred in the past, correlated with sunspot cycles.
- **What flaws did Scientist 1 find in the position of Scientist 2?** In this case, Scientist 1 did not offer any rebuttal to Scientist 2.
- **What flaws did Scientist 2 find in the position of Scientist 1?** Scientist 1 neglected to take into account the known effects of sunspot activity on the earth's climate.

As you read the questions, the first thing you should do is eliminate the obviously wrong answers. In many cases, this will be enough to determine the correct choice.

Try These

Using this approach, find the answers to the questions about the following passages. Write them down.

PRACTICE EXERCISES:
CONFLICTING VIEWPOINTS QUESTIONS

Passage 1

Frogs all over the world are in trouble. Populations are diminishing or disappearing, and many frogs are being born with deformities such as extra legs or limbs missing completely. Scientists are trying to find out why this is happening.

Scientist 1

Frogs are a sentinel species, like the canary that tells miners when their air is poisoned. The death and deformity of so many frogs is telling us that our environment is polluted.

A likely cause of the damage to frogs is that the growing tadpoles are being subjected to unusually high levels of ultraviolet radiation. Air pollution has significantly damaged the ozone layer of the atmosphere, allowing more of the damaging ultraviolet rays to reach the earth. In one experiment, when salamander eggs were subjected to normal levels of ultraviolet radiation, 85 percent died before hatching. It seems likely that this radiation is also damaging frogs.

Chemical pollution is another suspect. One pond in Minnesota was found to produce many deformed frogs. When frog embryos were laboratory-raised in water taken from that pond, three quarters of them grew with developmental deformities. One possible cause is methoprene in the water, a chemical that is widely used to control mosquitoes and fleas.

Meanwhile, we must surely take note of the fact that these deformed and dying frogs are giving us the message that pollutants produced by human activity are placing our worldwide biological system in jeopardy.

Scientist 2

There are serious flaws in the experiments that have attributed the frog crisis to pollution. The ultraviolet experiment was done with salamanders, not frogs. Frogs are different; they have an enzyme that repairs the damage caused by ultraviolet radiation. Methoprene is not a serious candidate, since it can do its damage only in concentrations hundreds of times greater than has ever been found in a pond.

It is probable that there is more than one frog problem. A dead embryo is not the same as a frog with a missing arm or with too many legs. A missing arm or leg might be the work of a heron or predatory fish that made a grab for the frog and managed to get only part of it. This surely happens, but no one knows how frequently; no studies have been done.

While there may be many reasons why frogs are deformed, only one reason has been thoroughly substantiated. The main, and perhaps the only, thing that makes a frog grow extra hind legs, is a parasitic worm, a type of trematode. These worms lay their eggs in tadpoles. Field studies on five different species of frogs in different parts of the country have found trematode parasites at the bases of the limbs of deformed frogs.

    While the case for pollutants has not been ruled out, parasitism is the only cause of developmental anomalies for which the detailed mechanism of the process is known. It is quite possible that parasites are responsible for other kinds of malformations.

1. The two scientists agree that:

    A. pollution is the main cause of abnormal development in frogs.
    B. there is a worldwide epidemic of death and malformation in frogs.
    C. the main cause of developmental anomaly is ultraviolet radiation.
    D. trematode parasitism causes a frog to form extra legs.

2. Scientist 2 challenges the evidence for methoprene as a cause because:

    F. the required dosages are not found in nature.
    G. methoprene has been shown to be safe.
    H. the necessary experiments were done on salamanders, not frogs.
    J. it has been shown that the cause of the deformities is parasites.

3. According to Scientist 2, an important fact that Scientist 1 has overlooked is that:

    A. it has been shown that ultraviolet radiation has no effect on salamanders.
    B. wherever frogs are dying, parasites are in the water.
    C. there has been no increase in the amount of ultraviolet radiation reaching the earth as the ozone layer becomes depleted.
    D. methoprene levels in ponds are too low to have an effect.

4. The position taken by Scientist 1 would be greatly strengthened by the discovery that:

    F. there are no parasites in certain ponds that produce deformed frogs.
    G. deformed frogs are not found in certain parts of the world.
    H. there is a common polluting chemical that causes deformation of frog embryos.
    J. parasites can be found in frogs that have not become deformed.

5. A serious limitation of the position of Scientist 2 is that:

    A. it accounts for only one kind of damage to frogs.
    B. it fails to explore the details of the process by which the damage is produced.
    C. it overlooks the damage produced by ultraviolet radiation.
    D. it overlooks the possibility that there may be many causes of deformity.

6. What is a likely response that Scientist 1 might make to the statement of Scientist 2?

    F. Scientist 2 is wrong because it is known that the developmental errors in frogs are the result of environmental pollution.
    G. Scientist 2 is damaging the international effort to deal with chemical pollution of the environment.
    H. Even if Scientist 2 is right, the world must still deal with the problem of chemical pollution.
    J. In the face of a worldwide pollution problem, it is a waste of time and money to investigate frog parasites.

Answers and Explanations

1. **(B)**

Both scientists are addressing the problem of the epidemic of deformed embryos in frogs. Scientist 2 challenges the evidence showing that ultraviolet radiation and chemical pollution are the cause, so **A** and **C** are wrong. **D** is wrong because Scientist 1 does not discuss the parasite problem.

2. **(F)**

Scientist 2 points out that it would take an enormous dose of methoprene to produce the observed deformities. There is no evidence as to the safety of methoprene, so **G** is wrong. **H** is wrong; that evidence applies to the ultraviolet problem, not methoprene. Scientist 2 agrees that there may be many causes in addition to parasites, so **J** is wrong.

3. **(D)**

This known fact was overlooked by Scientist 1. **A** is wrong because the effect of ultraviolet radiation on salamanders is not an issue. Scientist 1 does not address the problem of the level of ultraviolet radiation, so **C** is wrong. **B** is wrong because parasites cause deformities, not death of frogs.

4. **(H)**

Scientist 1's main thesis is that deformation is caused by environmental pollution, so the discovery of a pollutant that can be shown to cause deformation would greatly strengthen his position. **F** and **J** are wrong because Scientist 1 does not challenge the idea that some parasites may cause deformation in some frogs but not others. **G** is wrong because geographic data of this kind would not support the position of Scientist 1 unless correlation with pollution could be shown.

5. **(A)**

The trematode hypothesis accounts only for extra limbs, but not for missing limbs or early death. **B** is wrong because Scientist 2 specifically states the mechanism that interferes with development has been found. **C** is wrong; Scientist 2 specifically allows for other causes. **D** is wrong because Scientist 2 specifically makes the point that many other causes may be involved.

6. **(H)**

Scientist 1 sees the frog problem as only a part of the pollution of the earth. **F** is wrong because Scientist 2 has taken no position on pollution. **G** is wrong because Scientist 2 has said nothing to disparage the idea that pollution may be at fault. **J** is wrong; any scientist knows that many investigations are important even though they have no immediate application.

Passage 2

What is causing the loss of trees in the Appalachians? Two differing opinions are presented below. The forests of the high Appalachian Mountains are being destroyed. Millions of dead spruce and fir trees cover the peaks of the mountains, from Maine to Georgia. The new growth is low shrubbery, like blackberries, instead of trees.

Scientist 1

The forests are dying because of a combination of air pollution and unusual weather patterns. Recent years have shown a substantial increase in the concentration of ozone and of nitrogen and sulfur oxides in the air. The oxides come from the burning of fossil fuels. Rain, snow, and fog in the mountains pick up these oxides and turn acid. Ozone is produced by the action of ultraviolet light on hydrocarbons in the air, which are found in automobile exhaust and wastes from certain industrial processes. This pollution has been going on for decades, and the effect is cumulative. The last straw was added by the unusually high temperatures and drought of recent years. Unless serious steps are taken to reduce air pollution, there is a distinct danger that we will lose all our forests.

Scientist 2

While the air has surely become more polluted, there is no evidence that this is what is destroying the Appalachian trees. Trees in the high mountains are living precariously at best and are easily destroyed. The hot, dry summers and cold winters of recent years could easily account for the damage. Also, the spruce budworm and other insect pests are now unusually abundant and have done a great deal of damage to the trees. There have been other instances of massive die-off of trees at high elevations in years past, when the air was purer. If the chief source of damage were air pollution, we would expect that the damage would be worse at lower elevations, where the factories and automobiles that produce pollution are concentrated. Yet there is little evidence of damage to the commercial forests at lower elevations. This does not mean that we should ignore air pollution; it is clearly a threat, and we must learn more about it and develop ways to control it.

1. According to Scientist 2, what would be expected to happen to the forest in future years?

   A. Return of a permanent, self-sustaining forest in the high Appalachians
   B. Permanent conversion of the high mountains to low-growing shrubbery instead of trees
   C. Development of timber-producing commercial forest in the high mountains
   D. Regeneration of the forest, which will again be killed off from time to time

2. Without challenging any facts, what might Scientist 1 say to counter Scientist 2's argument about the effect of insect pests?

   F. Insects do not really do much damage.
   G. The insects have been able to proliferate so well because pollution has weakened the trees.
   H. Insect populations are being well controlled by birds.
   J. Insects are actually helpful because they cross-pollinate the trees.

3. What further development would weaken the case made by Scientist 2?

   A. Destruction of the blackberry bushes that are replacing the forests
   B. Evidence of damage to commercial forests at lower elevations
   C. Insect infestations of low-level forests
   D. Evidence that the mountain-top forests are showing signs of healthy regeneration

4. What is the opinion of Scientist 2 with respect to the problem of the effect of polluted air on the high forests?

   F. Polluted air does not damage forests, and no action is needed.
   G. The evidence is inadequate to prove that the damage in the high Appalachians is due to polluted air, but the problem needs to be studied further.
   H. Polluted air damages trees and may soon present a problem to commercial forests at lower levels.
   J. There is no substantial pollution in the air at high elevations, so it is not damaging the trees.

5. Suppose there were to appear a healthy new crop of spruce and fir trees on the mountain tops. Which of the following studies would NOT contribute to a resolution of the difference of opinion between the two scientists?

   A. A study to determine whether there has been any change in the ozone levels in the air
   B. A study of weather patterns over the preceding few years
   C. A study of changes in automobile exhausts due to new antipollution devices in cars
   D. A study of the conditions under which spruce seeds survive in the soil

6. What is a point on which both scientists agree?

   F. The air is being polluted by waste products of industry and transportation.
   G. The spruce budworm is a major cause of the destruction of forests.
   H. Stressful weather conditions alone can account for the destruction of the Appalachian forests.
   J. Low-elevation commercial forests are in imminent danger of destruction by polluted air.

7. To refute Scientist 2's opinion, Scientist 1 might:

   A. show that there is extensive damage to trees wherever in the world the air pollution levels are high.
   B. show that healthy spruce forests recover easily from damage by the spruce budworm.
   C. claim that spruce trees thrive at lower elevations, but are poorly adapted to the extremes of mountaintop weather.
   D. show that, because of atmospheric circulation patterns, the air at high elevations is not heavily polluted.

Answers and Explanations

1. **(D)**

Scientist 2 believes that from time to time unusual weather conditions kill off the high forest, even if there is no air pollution. Choice **A** is wrong because Scientist 2 does not believe that the forest can ever be permanent. **B** is wrong because he thinks that the forest can regenerate itself after it has been destroyed. **C** is wrong because he has never made any such suggestion.

2. **(G)**

Scientist 1 believes that pollution has damaged the trees, and might well suggest that this damage makes them subject to attack by insects. The other answers are wrong because they ignore the observable facts that the insects are rife and harmful.

3. **(B)**

One of the points that Scientist 2 makes is that pollution at low levels does not seem to be damaging the forests there. Choices **A** and **C** are irrelevant. **D** is wrong because regeneration of the high forest would support Scientist 2's contention that forest destruction occurs naturally from time to time.

4. **(G)**

Scientist 2 makes no claim that polluted air is innocent; but only that the evidence for its guilt is not conclusive. That is why **F** and **H** are wrong. He makes no claim that mountain air is unpolluted, so **J** is wrong.

5. **(D)**

Choices **A** and **C** are wrong because, if such studies showed a substantial decrease in pollution, Scientist 1's claim that pollution destroys the forest would be upheld. **B** is wrong because a correlation of weather patterns with forest regeneration would tend to support Scientist 2.

6. **(F)**

Both scientists recognize the existence of pollution, and both see that it is a problem. **G** is wrong because Scientist 1 might well think that the insects can damage only unhealthy trees. **H** is wrong because Scientist 1 thinks that the main cause of damage is pollution, and the weather is just a contributing factor. **J** is wrong because Scientist 2 has not found any damage to low-elevation trees, although he might agree that this could be a long-range problem.

7. **(A)**

This would strongly reinforce Scientist 1's opinion that the major cause of damage to trees is air pollution. **B** is wrong because Scientist 2 believes that forest destruction and recovery are common events. **C** is wrong because Scientist 2 thinks that mountaintop trees may be destroyed by extremes of weather alone. **D** is wrong because any such demonstration would undermine Scientist 1's claim that air pollution is the chief culprit.

SAMPLE SCIENCE REASONING TEST

Now that you have had practice on all three kinds of questions, here is a complete test, much like the one you will have to take. In trying it out, it is important that you time yourself. Allow only 35 minutes to complete the whole test. Remember these rules:

For each passage, study it carefully and answer the first question.

For the other questions, skip any that you cannot answer within a half minute or so.

When you have finished all those questions, go back and work on the ones you skipped. If you are not sure of an answer, make your best guess. If you still have any unanswered questions and there is only a minute left, enter answers at random.

Look at your clock and start NOW. Good luck!

Directions: This test consists of several distinct passages. Each passage is followed by a number of multiple-choice questions based on the passage. Study the passage, and then select the best answer to each question. You are allowed to reread the passage.

Passage 1

The graph below indicates the numbers of three different kinds of rare plants that were found in a grassy plot over a period of years.

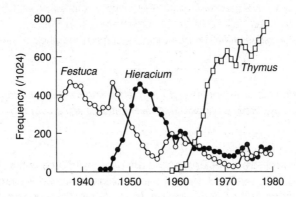

1. Which plants were present in approximately equal numbers in 1950?

   A. *Festuca* and *Thymus*
   B. *Festuca* and *Hieracium*
   C. *Hieracium* and *Thymus*
   D. *Hieracium*, *Festuca*, and *Thymus*

2. Which of the following statements correctly describes the situation in 1963?

   F. The densities of both *Festuca* and *Hieracium* were rapidly decreasing.
   G. The density of Thymus was much greater than that of either of the other two plants.
   H. All three plants had equal and unchanging densities.
   J. All three plants had equal densities, but one was increasing.

3. What was happening to the density of *Hieracium* in 1950?

   A. It was increasing at the rate of 20 units per year.
   B. It was increasing at the rate of 75 units per year.
   C. It did not change at all during that year.
   D. It was increasing at some undetermined rate.

4. Suppose a fourth species were introduced and found conditions there favorable for its growth. Based on experience with the species already there, what pattern might be expected for its density in the next ten years?

   F. It could not survive in competition with those already there.
   G. Its density might be expected to increase slightly for a couple of years and then level off.
   H. It might be expected to remain at low density for a few years and then increase rapidly.
   J. Its density might be expected to increase for a few years and then decrease rapidly.

5. Which of the following is NOT a possible explanation for the changes that took place after 1950?

    A. There was a period of drought.
    B. *Festuca* and *Hieracium* were unable to thrive in competition with Thymus.
    C. A newly arrived insect pest fed on some plants, but not others.
    D. A great increase in the shrubbery in the plot made the whole area more shady.

Passage 2

Three experiments are done to test the relative survivability of different mutant strains of fruit fly (Drosophila) when different strains are grown together.

Experiment 1

Three pure-bred strains of *Drosophila* are used: wild type, white-eye, and yellow-body. Fifty fertilized eggs of each strain are placed, separately, into standard culture bottles with a limited food supply. They go through larval stages, and then form pupae. The adults that hatch out of the pupa cases are counted:

    wild type: 42   white-eye: 36   yellow-body: 25

Experiment 2

Pairs of strains are grown together, with their larvae in the same culture bottle. Fifty eggs of each strain are placed in the bottle, and the number of adults of each kind that hatch out of the pupa cases are counted:

    Trial 1 wild type: 43, white-eye: 16
    Trial 2 wild type: 38, yellow-body: 22
    Trial 3 white-eye: 18, yellow-body: 27

Experiment 3

Fifty eggs of each of the three strains are placed in the same culture bottle, with the following numbers of adults produced:

    wild type: 33   white-eye: 8   yellow-body: 20

6. In Experiment 2 what was the purpose of growing two different strains of larvae in the same bottle?

    F. To find out how competition between strains affects survivability
    G. To test the effect of crowding of larvae in the culture bottles
    H. To determine the results of crossing two different strains
    J. To see whether the white-eye or yellow-body character can be transferred from one larva to another

7. What important variable was controlled by Experiment 1?

    A. Availability of food supply
    B. Survivability of each strain in the absence of competition
    C. Number of eggs to be used in the experiment
    D. Transformation of larvae to the pupa stage

8. Comparison of the results shows that competition:

    F. increases the survivability of the wild type.
    G. is most detrimental to the yellow-body.
    H. is most favorable to the yellow-body.
    J. is most detrimental to the white-eye.

9. What design factor in the experiments was crucial in establishing the existence of competition between strains?

    A. Keeping all culture bottles under the same conditions
    B. Supplying only enough food for about 60 larvae
    C. Testing strains in advance to be sure they were pure-bred
    D. Using no more than 3 different strains

10. What do these results imply about the structure of natural populations?

    F. About one fourth of all flies in nature are expected to be yellow-bodied.
    G. One reason why the wild type is most common in nature is that its larvae survive best in competition.
    H. There will be no white-eyed flies in natural populations.
    J. In the course of time, white-eyed and yellow-bodied flies will completely disappear in nature.

11. The evidence seems to show that yellow-bodied flies do not suffer in competition with the wild type. Why, then, are there so few yellow-bodied flies in nature?

    A. The evidence is misleading because the total number of flies in the experiment is so small.
    B. White-eyed flies promote the survivability of the yellow-bodied, and they are rare in nature.
    C. Under natural conditions, many factors other than competition determine survivability.
    D. When yellow-bodied flies mate with wild type, their offspring are wild type.

Passage 3

The cladogram below describes the evolutionary relationships of some reptiles. Each branching point represents the common ancestor of the branches. The more recent the common ancestor, the closer the relationship is considered to be. Dates, in millions of years, represent the time of transition from each era to the next. Base your answers only on the information in the diagram.

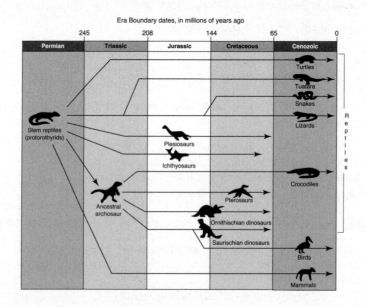

Era Boundary dates, in millions of years ago

12. The turtles are unique, of this group, in that:

    F. they are the only reptiles with a hard shell formed of ribs.
    G. they are not closely related to any other surviving reptile.
    H. they are not related to any other reptiles.
    J. they have existed unchanged for over 245 million years.

13. Of the following pairs, in which pair are the two forms most closely related?

    A. Ornithischian dinosaurs and lizards
    B. Birds and mammals
    C. Crocodiles and ichthyosaurs
    D. Birds and crocodiles

14. One major feature of the record is that:

    F. there was a mass extinction at the end of the Cretaceous.
    G. there are now far more reptiles than mammals or birds.
    H. about 200 million years ago there was a major radiation of reptiles into a variety of new forms.
    J. the snakes and lizards became distinct about 80 million years ago.

15. Of all the groups shown, only the birds and the mammals are known to be warm-blooded. How can this be interpreted?

    A. It is possible that the ancestral archosaur may also be warm-blooded.
    B. Warm-bloodedness is an ancestral character that has survived in these two lines.
    C. The diagram as given may be wrong, since the fact that these birds and mammals share this character indicates a close relationship.
    D. Warm-bloodedness is a useful property that may arise more than once, independently.

16. If a geologist reports finding a fossil feather in a rock layer 220 million years old, how might his colleagues initially react?

    F. Revise the cladogram to place the origin of the birds at an earlier date.
    G. Suggest a careful reexamination of the evidence for the date of the rock.
    H. Take this as proof that an early Saurischian dinosaur had feathers.
    J. Reject the report because it conflicts with known data of the origin of birds.

Passage 4

To find out how the electric current through various materials is controlled, a physicist applies various potential differences (voltages) to three different objects and measures the current produced in each case.
    A milliampere is a thousandth of an ampere.

Experiment 1: 10 meters of #30 copper wire

Potential difference (volts)	Current (milliamperes)
0	0
0.2	60
0.4	120
0.6	180
0.8	240
1.0	300

Experiment 2: 10 meters of #30 aluminum wire

Potential difference (volts)	Current (milliamperes)
0	0
0.2	40
0.4	80
0.6	120
0.8	160
1.0	200

Experiment 3: OC26 transistor

Potential difference (volts)	Current (milliamperes)
0	0
0.2	5
0.4	15
0.6	60
0.8	115
1.0	190

17. What scales on the voltmeter and ammeter would be most appropriate in making these measurements?

    A. 0-20 V, 0-20 A
    B. 0-5 V, 0-5 A
    C. 0-1 V, 0-10 A
    D. 0-1 V, 0-0.5 A

18. Why were wires of identical dimensions used in Experiments 1 and 2?

    F. To increase the variety of readings of the current
    G. To determine how the material of which the wire is made affects the current
    H. To determine how the dimensions of the wire affect the current
    J. To compare the properties of a wire with those of a transistor

19. Which readings serve as controls on the proper adjustment of the meters?

    A. The readings on the transistor
    B. All the zero readings
    C. All the readings at 1.0 volt
    D. The readings on the copper wire

20. When a 10-volt potential difference is applied to the aluminum wire, the ammeter records 1100 milliamperes. This indicates that:

    F. the proportionality between potential difference and current does not hold for large values.
    G. there is no usable rule relating potential difference to current.
    H. large potential differences reduce the current in the wire.
    J. aluminum wire reacts differently from copper wire.

21. Resistance is defined as the ratio of potential difference to current. Which of the following statements holds true over the range of values in the experiments?

    A. All three objects have the same resistance.
    B. The objects have different resistances, but the resistance is constant for each.
    C. None of the objects has constant resistance.
    D. The wires, but not the transistor, have constant resistance.

22. On the basis of these experiments, what hypothesis might be proposed?

    F. Transistors respond to applied potential differences in the same way as metal wires.

    G. In any circuit, a transistor will have more current than a wire.

    H. Transistors are too unreliable to be used in most electronic circuits.

    J. Transistors and wires can be used for different purposes in electronic circuits.

Passage 5

The Papuan aster has two distinct populations. Variety M grows in the high mountains, and variety V lives in the valleys at midlevel. Experiments are done to test the relative growth patterns of the two varieties under different conditions.

Experiment 1

One hundred seeds of each variety are planted in separate plots in the high mountains. After 3 months, the height of each of the surviving plants is measured and plotted on the bar graph below.

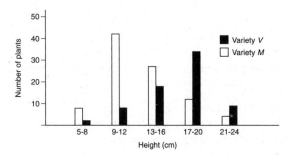

Experiment 2

One hundred seeds of each variety are planted in a midlevel valley, and their height is measured after 3 months and plotted:

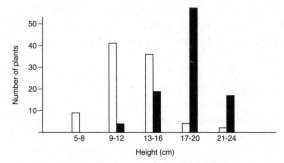

Experiment 3

One hundred seeds of each variety are planted in a dry lowland savannah; after 3 months:

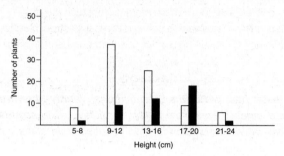

23. How many of the valley variety plants in the high mountains died in the first 3 months?

    A. 70
    B. 50
    C. 30
    D. 10

24. Which statement about the plants when in their normal environments is shown by the data?

    F. Valley plants are much taller than mountain plants.
    G. Valleys are a more favorable environment for this species.
    H. Valley plants are healthier than mountain plants.
    J. Plants in mountains are generally shorter than the ones that grow under more favorable conditions.

25. Which hypothesis is the most reasonable explanation for the results of Experiment 1?

    A. In the mountains, the V plants cannot survive in competition with the M plants.
    B. The V plants shade out the M plants, so they cannot grow to their full height.
    C. The lack of soil nutrients in the mountaintops keeps all the plants from reaching their full sizes.
    D. The V plants are programmed to grow tall, but they cannot reach their full height in the mountains.

26. What is the most likely explanation for the fact that the results of Experiment 3 are much like those of Experiment 1?

    F. The same kinds of seeds were planted in both places.
    G. In both high mountains and dry savannah, the amount of water is limited.
    H. In the savannah, the plants were irrigated with plenty of water.
    J. In both places, the plants were measured after the same length of growth period.

27. Which variety of the Papuan aster would be most suitable for use as a garden plant?

    A. It would depend on the individual taste of the gardener.
    B. The *M* variety because it is the hardiest and would be likely to survive best.
    C. Either one, depending on where it would be used in the garden.
    D. The *V* variety because it is a larger plant and would surely have nicer flowers.

Passage 6

A chemist performs a series of experiments to determine the relative chemical activities of three metals. Metal A is considered more active than metal B if metal A will replace metal B in a solution. Metal B will plate out on metal A.

Experiment 1

A piece of steel wool is placed into a solution of copper sulfate. Copper sulfate is blue because of the copper ions in it. The result of the experiment is that metallic copper forms on the steel wool and the blue solution turns colorless.

Experiment 2

A bundle of fine copper wire is placed into a solution of iron(II) sulfate, which is colorless. No change is observed.

Experiment 3

A fine spray of metallic mercury is inserted into a solution of copper sulfate. No change is observed.

Experiment 4

A bundle of fine copper wire is inserted into a solution of mercuric sulfate, which is colorless. The wire acquires a coating of the silvery color of mercury, and the solution acquires a bluish tint.

28. The results of Experiments 1 and 2 indicate that:

    F. copper is more active than iron.
    G. relative activity depends on how the experiment is done.
    H. iron is more active than copper.
    J. the two metals are probably equally active.

29. In Experiment 4, why did the solution become bluish?

    A. Some of the copper of the wire went into solution.
    B. Removal of the mercury revealed the true color of the solution.
    C. The silvery color of the deposited mercury reflects light and has a bluish cast.
    D. Some of the mercury in the solution changes to copper, which gives the solution a bluish color.

30. Why was there no reaction in Experiment 2?

    F. Copper is not soluble in water.
    G. The metal in the solution is the more active of the two.
    H. Metallic iron and metallic copper cannot mix.
    J. The iron sulfate solution was already saturated.

31. What would probably happen if steel wool were placed into a solution of mercuric sulfate?

    A. It is impossible to predict the result without experiment.
    B. Mercury would plate out on the steel wool.
    C. Nothing would happen.
    D. The solution would turn bluish.

32. Suppose fibers of metal X were placed into separate solutions of mercuric, copper, and iron sulfates. Copper and mercury deposit on the metal, but iron does not. Which of the following represents the order of activity of the four metals, from highest to lowest?

    F. Metal X mercury, copper, iron
    G. Mercury, copper, metal X, iron
    H. Copper, mercury, iron, metal X
    J. Iron, metal X, copper, mercury

33. An investigator hypothesizes that the relative activity of any metal depends only on the structure of its own atoms. Which of the following observations would support this view?

    A. In their reactions with sulfates, all the metals can be arranged in a linear sequence according to their activities.
    B. In any kind of reaction, there will always be some metals that are more active than others.
    C. If one metal is more active than another, it will be more active in any chemical reaction, not just with sulfates.
    D. In any reaction, it is always possible to compare two metals and find out which is more active.

Passage 7

Will future human evolution increase the number of twins in the population? Two scientists present opposing views.

Scientist 1

It is an established principle, the rule of Darwinian fitness, that natural selection favors the individuals who leave the largest number of viable and fertile offspring. It is also known that there is a genetic tendency that causes some women to produce more than one ovum at a time. These women will bear twins more often than other women. Since they have more offspring than other women, selection will favor them and the frequency of twin births will increase with time. This did not happen in the past because the conditions of life were so different. A woman in a hunter-gatherer society had to spend much of her time collecting plant food, while carrying her baby with her. She also had to be ready to run or otherwise protect herself from wild animals. Her chance of survival, avoiding both starvation and predation, was much worse if she was carrying two babies instead of only one. Thus, the genes that promote twinning carried an enormous liability, which more than offset the selective advantage of having twins. Under modern conditions, however, these negative features disappear and a woman who bears twins is likely to leave more offspring than one who does not. The frequency of the gene that promotes the release of more than one ovum at a time will increase in the population.

Scientist 2

You cannot think of evolutionary change in terms of a single feature. When many factors affect an outcome, it is necessary to consider how they interact to produce an optimum condition. Twins are often born prematurely, and their average birth weight is only 5.5 pounds. Single babies, on the average, come into the world weighing 7.5 pounds. Premature birth and low birth weight result in many kinds of medical problems. Twins' prospects for survival to a normal, healthy reproductive age are less than those for singly born babies. An evolutionary tendency to overcome this deficiency would call for mothers to produce twins weighing in at 7.5 pounds each. This would be an enormous strain on the mother, since she would have to gain more weight during pregnancy. The only way to neutralize this liability would be for women to be much bigger, weighing more than 200 pounds. This would, however, introduce another liability: strains on the skeleton and musculature. Evolution would have to produce a complete redesign of the body. The gain in selective value produced by twinning would be far outweighed by these disadvantages. Modern civilization has not changed the fact that single births are optimum for human women.

34. What is the basic question on which the two scientists disagree?

    F. Is human evolution a continuing, ongoing process?
    G. Do human twins start life at a disadvantage?
    H. Does natural selection favor genes that produce twins?
    J. Is the tendency to produce twins hereditary?

35. To refute Scientist 2's argument, Scientist 1 might point out that:

    A. modern medical science has greatly improved the survival rate of infants with low birth weights.

    B. many twins result from the division of a single fertilized egg, and this is not genetically controlled.

    C. evolutionary change is extremely slow, and there is no evidence that the human species has changed much in the last 100,000 years.

    D. large women have twins as frequently as small women do.

36. The arguments of both Scientist 1 and Scientist 2 would be invalidated if new evidence indicated that:

    F. the rate of twin births has not changed in the past century.

    G. genetics really makes very little difference in whether or not a woman produces twins.

    H. women in hunter-gatherer societies have twins more often than women in civilization.

    J. the genetic tendency to produce twins passes to women from their fathers, not their mothers.

37. What piece of statistical evidence would greatly strengthen Scientist 2's position?

    A. Twins born at 5.5 pounds have a poorer survival rate than babies born singly at 5.5 pounds.

    B. Twins born at 7 pounds have the same survival rate as babies born singly at 7 pounds.

    C. Twins born to large women have a better survival rate than twins born to small women.

    D. Twins born to small women have a better survival rate than twins born to large women.

38. Underlying the arguments of both scientists is the assumption that:

    F. production of twins is a desirable prospect for the human species.

    G. women who bear twins are healthier, on the average, than women who do not.

    H. the genetic composition of the father is irrelevant to the probability of a woman's bearing twins.

    J. natural selection acts on human beings in the same way as on other animals.

39. Which of the arguments of Scientist 1 was not refuted by Scientist 2?

    A. Modern medicine has no effect on the rate at which twins are born.

    B. In primitive conditions, natural selection will favor single births.

    C. Survival rate is a basic biological factor that is not influenced by external conditions.

    D. Large women are inherently capable of producing twins with large birth weights.

40. Scientist 2 claims that Scientist 1 has overlooked an important general principle of biological science. What is it?

    F. All biological factors interact with each other, and selective value depends on the optimal combination of values of many factors.

    G. Genetic factors influence all aspects of development, and must be considered in any long-term prediction.

    H. Genetic factors cannot be considered alone, but must be analyzed in terms of their interaction with external conditions.

    J. Evolution is the result of natural selection acting on the genetic composition of individuals.

Answer Key

1. B	11. C	21. D	31. B
2. J	12. G	22. J	32. J
3. B	13. D	23. C	33. C
4. H	14. F	24. F	34. H
5. B	15. D	25. D	35. A
6. F	16. G	26. G	36. G
7. B	17. D	27. C	37. C
8. J	18. G	28. H	38. J
9. B	19. B	29. A	39. B
10. G	20. F	30. G	40. F

Answer Explanations

1. **(B)**

The curves for *Festuca* and *Hieracium* cross in 1950, indicating that the density of both plants was the same. *Thymus* did not appear at all until 1960.

2. **(J)**

Since the three graphs all cross at this time, all three plants had equal densities; *Thymus* was increasing rapidly. The density of *Hieracium* had dropped, but remained nearly steady from 1963 to 1973. *Festuca* was dropping slowly.

3. **(B)**

The density increased from nearly 0 in 1946 to 450 in 1952, an increase of 450 units in six years. This rate of 75 units per year remained steady for the entire six-year period.

4. **(H)**

Both *Hieracium* and *Thymus* were newly introduced and followed the same pattern: low density for three or four years and then rapid increase for the next six years. This is the only evidence available.

5. **(B)**

Festuca began its decline in 1947 and *Hieracium* in 1952, but *Thymus* did not appear until 1959. *Thymus* might well be more tolerant of dry weather, shade, and that particular bug than the other two species.

6. **(F)**

With two different strains in competition, one or the other might prove to be better adapted. G is wrong because crowding could be tested, without introducing a different variable, by simply using more eggs of either strain. H is wrong because there is no mating in the larval stage. J is wrong because the experimental design does not allow for the testing of any such transfer, which is most unlikely in any event.

7. **(B)**

If the effect of competition is to be established, it is important to know how well each strain survives when there is no competition. None of the other choices represents a variable in the experiment.

8. **(J)**

The number of white-eyed adults that hatch is drastically less than the control number (Experiment 1) whenever one of the other strains is present.

9. **(B)**

Note that in Experiments 2 and 3 only about 60 larvae produced adults, even though there were 100 or 150 eggs. If there were no restriction on the food supply, it is possible that all the eggs could survive in the same numbers as in Experiment 1.

10. **(G)**

Whenever other strains are present with the wild type, it is the others that suffer, while the wild type maintains its predominance. F is wrong because there is no reason to believe that the numbers of eggs laid in nature are like those in the bottle. H and J are wrong because competition does not completely eliminate the white-eyed and yellow-bodied forms.

11. **(C)**

Do not confuse a culture bottle with nature. There is no evidence to support any of the other choices.

12. **(G)**

The turtles have no ancestor in common with all the other reptiles later than the earliest reptile of all. F is wrong because the cladogram gives no information about shells in reptiles. H is wrong because turtles descended from a reptilian ancestor in the long-distant past. J is wrong because the cladogram gives no information about the way the various reptiles have changed.

13. **(D)**

The common ancestor of the birds and crocodiles is an ancestral archosaur, about 220 million years ago. All of the other pairs have no common ancestor later than the stem reptiles, in the Permian.

14. **(F)**

Many of the lines in the diagram disappeared at the end of the Cretaceous. G is wrong because no information is given about the relative abundance of the different life forms. H is wrong because the major radiation took place long before 245 million years ago. J is wrong because snakes and lizards have been distinct for nearly 150 million years.

15. **(D)**

A and B are wrong because it would be most unlikely that a character would survive in two distantly related forms and not in any of the others. C is wrong because the cladogram depends on many characters, not just one. Independent evolution of a useful character is the most likely explanation.

16. **(G)**

This discovery cannot be rejected out of hand, but it suggests a really drastic revision of current theories, conflicting with much other evidence. It would have to be reviewed by others.

17. **(D)**

For best precision, you want the smallest scale that will incorporate the largest reading. The largest potential difference reading is 1 V, so a 1-volt scale will do very well. The largest current reading is 300 mA, or 0.3 A.

18. **(G)**

The dimensions are being controlled to eliminate them from consideration, so H is wrong. The only uncontrolled variable is the substance of the wire.

19. **(B)**

The meter must be zeroed; that is, it must be adjusted to make sure that it reads zero when there is no current or potential difference.

20. **(F)**

For all the readings in the table, the ratio between potential difference and current is constant at 200 mA/V. The ratio for the 10-V setting, however, is only 110 mA/V. G is wrong because there is surely a usable rule below 1 V, and further investigation might turn up a usable rule at higher potentials. H is wrong; the large potential difference increased the current; it was just not as much as might have been expected. J is wrong because there is no evidence about the behavior of copper wire at higher potential differences.

21. **(D)**

Checking the ratios at the smallest and largest values gives these results: copper wire, $0.20/60 = 0.0033$ and $1.00/300 = 0.0033$; aluminum wire, $0.20/40 = 0.0050$ and $1.0/200 = 0.0050$; transistor, $0.2/5 = 0.040$ and $1/190 = 0.0053$. The ratios are constant for the wires, but not for the transistor.

22. **(J)**

Since transistors and wires have different but reliable properties, they can be used for different purposes. F is wrong because the ratio of potential difference to current (for small currents) is constant for the wires, but not for the transistor. G is wrong because no information is given about the circuits. H is wrong because Experiment 3 gives no information about the reliability of transistors.

23. **(C)**

The sizes of the bars for valley plants in the mountains are $2 + 8 + 18 + 33 + 9 = 70$. Since only 70 of the 100 survived, 30 died.

24. **(F)**

Mountain plants are in their normal environment in Experiment 1, and their height is mainly in the 9 to 12 cm range. G is wrong because the mountain plants do very well in their normal environment. H is wrong because the data give no information about the health of the plants. J is wrong because this generalization (while true) cannot be assumed from data about one species.

25. **(D)**

Experiment 2 shows that when the V plants are in their normal environment, they grow tall. A and B are wrong because the conditions of the experiment indicate that the two kinds are grown in separate plots, so they cannot interfere with each other. C is wrong because the M plants are thriving in their normal environment.

26. **(G)**

F and J are wrong because these conditions are true of Experiment 2 also, and the results there were quite different. H is wrong because the purpose of the experiment was to find out how the plants grow under the dry savannah conditions. G is the only alternative.

27. **(C)**

Each variety is best suited for a particular environment; the M variety might do very well in a rock garden. C is wrong because a gardener must put the plant where it will do best, regardless of personal preference.

28. **(H)**

Copper has come out of solution in the form of copper metal. The loss of copper changes the color of the solution. Iron must have replaced copper in the solution, so iron is more active. This follows from the definition of a more active metal, given in the first paragraph of the passage.

29. **(A)**

The blue color indicates the presence of copper in solution. B is wrong because we have no reason to believe there is any such thing as the "true color" of the solution. C is wrong because we have no indication that the mercury coating is bluish. D is wrong because mercury cannot change into copper.

30. **(G)**

Since iron is more active than copper, copper cannot replace iron in the solution. F is wrong; in the blue solution, copper is dissolved. Nothing in the experiment points to either H or J.

31. **(B)**

Since iron is more active than copper (Experiment 1) and copper is more active than mercury (Experiment 4), it is reasonable to assume that iron is more active than mercury. Therefore, iron will replace mercury in solution, and the mercury will deposit on the steel wool.

32. **(J)**

We already know from the experiments that iron is more active than copper, and copper than mercury. Since metal X replaces copper and mercury from solution, it must be more active than either of them. It does not, however, replace iron.

33. **(C)**

The atomic structure of a metal atom is the same as it enters into any reaction. If atomic structure is what determines activity, then the relative activities of two metals do not depend on what the specific chemical reaction is. Choice A is wrong because a ranking with sulfates does not prove that the ranking would hold in other reactions. B and D prove only that there are different levels of activity in different reactions.

34. **(H)**

Both scientists agree that evolution continues and might involve changes in the frequency of genes producing twins, so F and J are wrong. Scientist 1 does not challenge the statement that twins have lower survival rates, so G is wrong. The only point at issue is whether the result of selection will be a higher frequency of twinning.

35. **(A)**

Scientist 2 argues that twinning has a negative selective value because twins are born small, but gains in medical science might nullify this disadvantage. None of the other choices is germane.

36. **(G)**

Both Scientist 1 and Scientist 2 assume that the tendency to produce twins is hereditary; they disagree only on how this will change the evolutionary trend. F is wrong because both might agree that a century is too short a time to show any effect. H is wrong because neither scientist makes any such claim. J is wrong because it would make no difference in the survival value of the gene.

37. **(C)**

Scientist 2 claims that large, healthy twins could be produced only by larger women, and statistics to this effect would support his case. B is wrong because this point is not at issue.

38. **(J)**

Both scientists base their arguments on natural selection of the most favorable combination of traits; they disagree on what that combination might be. F is wrong because neither scientist makes any value judgment. G is wrong because neither scientist makes any such claim. H is wrong because the arguments of neither scientist require any such assumption.

39. **(B)**

This claim is made by Scientist 1, and not addressed by Scientist 2. The others are wrong because Scientist 1 does not make any such claims.

40. **(F)**

This is the core of Scientist 2's rebuttal; Scientist 1 has not considered all the genetic interactions involved. G is wrong because both scientists agree that genetic factors are central to the issue. H is wrong because both scientists considered external conditions; they disagreed on which ones were important. J is wrong because they agreed on this point.

Preparing for the Writing Test

6

DESCRIPTION OF THE WRITING TEST

The optional ACT Writing Test, administered after the four multiple-choice sections of the ACT, consists of one essay to be written in 30 minutes.

Purpose of the Test

The score you earn on the test adds an important dimension to your college admissions profile. It tells admissions officials how well you write, especially how well you write under the pressure of time. More specifically, your score provides colleges with information about 1) the depth of your thinking, 2) your ability to organize ideas, 3) the way you express yourself, and 4) your mastery of standard written English.

Many colleges use the results of the ACT Writing Test as a criterion for admission. Some of these colleges weigh the scores as heavily as GPAs, class rank, and personal statements. Other colleges merely recommend that applicants take the test. Still others devise alternate means for assessing candidates' writing ability.

An Essay-Writing Strategy

An essay completed in half an hour is bound to be shorter than most essays required in high school or college courses. Yet, 30 minutes gives you plenty of time to prove that you have what it takes to write a substantial essay.

The question, or prompt, to which you must respond describes an issue or set of circumstances on which you must comment. Rest assured that the issue won't require specialized knowledge or training. It will be general and open-ended enough to elicit a response from virtually any high school student.

Although the prompt can't be predicted, you can depend on consistency in the instructions for writing the essay:

> *Please write an essay in response to the given topic. During the 30 minutes allowed, develop your thoughts clearly and effectively. Try to include relevant examples and specific evidence to support your point of view.*

A plain, natural style is best. The length is up to you, but quality should take precedence over quantity.
Be sure to write only on the assigned topic.

As ACT day draws near, review the above directions. Knowing exactly what to do when the essay assignment is given out will add to your peace of mind and allow you to set to work immediately, saving you precious time.

How the Essay Is Scored

Your essay will be evaluated on a scale of 6 (best) to 1 (worst). ACT readers, most of them experienced high school and college teachers, are trained to read essays quickly, or *holistically*. That is, they don't hunt down every little error but assign a grade based on their overall impression of your writing. Recognizing that ACT essays are written in less than half an hour, they won't hold minor mistakes against you and won't deduct a certain amount for every error. Naturally, an essay overrun with flaws will leave a less favorable impression than one that is mostly correct. Like all readers, they enjoy good writing and delight in lively, neatly phrased ideas. They abhor empty platitudes and know in an instant when a writer is "throwing the bull." Pretentiousness turns them off completely.

Readers try to evaluate essays fairly, rewarding students for what they have done well. During the evaluation, your essay won't be competing against some ideal essay written by a professional author. Rather, it will be compared to other students' essays written on the same topic at the same time.

Guidelines for Evaluation

Each essay is scored on a scale of 6 to 1.

Performance Categories	Score
Outstanding	6
Very Good	5
Good	4
Fair	3
Poor	2
Very Poor	1

Essays scored 4, 5, and 6 are considered average or above and attest to a level of writing skill appropriate for first-year college students. Essays rated 1, 2, or 3 are below average and suggest the writer's need for remediation.

SAMPLE STUDENT ESSAYS WITH EVALUATIONS

The essays on the following pages have been written by high school students in a testing situation. Each was composed in half an hour and appears exactly as written.

> **Prompt:** *Many high school history courses acquaint students with societies both past and present. English classes read and study many novels, stories, and plays that portray life in other times and places. Learning about other people and other eras, in fact, is an important part of an education and often inspires students to imagine what it might be like to live in another place and time.*
>
> *If you were somehow given the opportunity to lead your life in a place and time different from the here and now, would you take it? If so, write an essay that identifies your destination and cites the reasons for your choice. If not, write an essay explaining why you would decline the offer.*

Dan's Essay

If I could choose a place and time other than the here and now, I would pick the 1840s in the western parts of the United States, somewhere in the area we now call Colorado. Back then the region would have been perfect, a melange of adventure, exploration, and natural beauty.

I have been fortunate enough to travel to the West, and I was absolutely impressed by its beauty. At a glance I saw the deep gorge of the Rio Grande and the tremendous Rocky mountains. It was like nothing that I had seen before, and my only regret was that the vista was spoiled with cities and people and roads and malls. A hundred and seventy years ago civilization would have been far away and the land, air, and water would have been pure, making it a perfect paradise.

Another reason I view the old West as a perfect place to live is because of the people who were living there at that time. There were settlers and Native Americans. Unfortunately they didn't treat each other well, but if I was there, rather than attack or imprison the natives as my forefathers did, I would live at peace with them. I wouldn't take the view that the land was mine exclusively. I would share the land between me and all the other inhabitants. I would love to live the way the

Indians did. By living with them, I would learn how to make the most of the land, and also to fully appreciate it.

Living in the West, I could scale cliffs and sail down rivers whenever I felt like it. I could explore caves, canyons, and forests of old-growth timber that can take your breath away. In the wilderness, one can be totally free, and I would love to live my life with this freedom.

The Old West strikes me as a utopia because it was sort of dangerous. I am not foolish, but reasonable danger would be challenge because I love to go to new areas, and to try new things, and the West at that time period contained more challenges that I could ever imagine. I would never run out of opportunities for adventure.

The West in 1840 would satisfy every desire I have. I could live as one with the land. I could live a life of endless adventure. I could live a life completely seperated from civilization. Because of all this, I would choose the West in 1840 if I could live anywhere.

Comment to Dan: By using the memorable phrase "melange of adventure, exploration, and natural beauty" in your introduction, you promise the reader a well-structured essay that focuses on each of these three features in the order you have listed them. Too bad the promise is quickly broken. The next paragraph deals with the beauty of the land rather than with "adventure." In addition, the discussion is marred by the questionable statement that in Colorado one can see both the Rockies and the gorge of the Rio Grande. (Perhaps you meant another river; the Rio Grande is many hundreds of miles away.)

The paragraph that follows also diverges from the announced plan of the essay. It deals with how you would have taken up with the Indians and behaved more humanely than the original settlers—a noble sentiment, to be sure, but one unrelated to adventure, exploration, or beauty. The next two paragraphs consist of thoughts that refer generally to adventure and exploration.

Considering that the essay is short, the summary that ends the essay, while designed to wrap things up, seems a bit superfluous. What stands out about this essay is its sincerity. Your handling of words and syntax shows promise but to earn the highest score, the essay would have to be more consistent and coherent. Your essay is rated 5.

Lee-Ann's Essay

There are about thirty kids in this room writing an essay choosing a time and place to live other than the here and now. I'm sure that most of them will opt for some kind of tropical paradise in the distant past or a far-off imaginary place without the problems that face them and the world. As teenagers, they are mainly concerned about applying to college and choosing a profession and lifestyle. Then there is the daily threat of terrorism, environmental problems, social conditions that create extreme wealth and terrible poverty, diseases such as AIDS, drugs, and violence of all kinds of examples of man's inhumanity to man. Who could blame them for wanting to escape to a time and place where those problems don't exist.

It's hard for me to choose a different time and place in which I'd like to live. Not because I am content where I am now but more because I question the proverbial "grass is always greener" theory.

I saw a movie recently (I can't remember the name of it) taking place in the 70's, in which a character says "The 50's were boring, the 60's were dull, and the 70's are obviously the pits. With luck, the 80's will be radically different… they can't be any worse than today." But here we are today in the 2010's glorifying the 70's, the era of music, pot, and bell bottoms. The 70's remain a time period that many of us would love to have lived through, even though the people who actually experienced it didn't think of it as a glorious time. My parents, for example, were in high school then and remember how the country was torn apart by the war in Vietnam. They also remember Watergate and how it destroyed people's trust in government.

I could say that I'd love to live on an Indian reservation three centuries back or maybe move into an igloo with the Inuit people to live a basic existence. Occasionally, I have wanted to be a dog sledder in the Yukon Gold Rush and lived the rugged life of characters in Jack London's stories. I have also fantasized being part of the story of Robinson Crusoe, trapped on a deserted island. Many times I have wished to live anywhere but here, to find Paradise.

But I think there are no paradises, no Shangri Las, no Utopias, and I'm sure that if there were, we would find faults with them. To choose a different place to live would prove to be pointless in the end. One group of problems would merely replace another group, so if I spent as much time there as I have spent here I'm sure I'd want to find another place again. Living here and now is not my ideal but anyplace else would be a relief for only a short time. Then I'd want to move on. That's why I'll stay where I am. I've grown accustomed to it and don't think I could be more content anywhere else.

Comment to Lee-Ann: Your opening statement hooks the reader instantly. By speculating on what others may write, you raise the reader's curiosity to find out how your view will differ from theirs. Indeed, you reward the reader with a provocative thesis that is highlighted in the two-sentence paragraph that follows the introduction. Each paragraph that follows amplifies and explores the "grass is always greener" hypothesis. You cite specific examples, both from your own experience and from that of your parents, that have led you to the conviction that your present circumstances are good enough. Your sentences are varied, you make some colorful word choices, and write in a readable, natural style. The essay isn't perfect, but given the fact that it was written in 30 minutes, it creates a highly favorable impression of you as a writer. Your essay is rated 6.

Martin's Essay

This is a very interesting question to ask someone like me. The main reason is because I think about it all the time.

If I could pick a time frame to live in, it would be the 1800's in the midwest. When you look around you now, all you see are drugs and gangs. But back then all you would see, was pure and beutiful. The mid-west covered with green praries and freshwater streams and roaming buffalos. What better place to live in. There's no law man watching over you. No laws telling *you what to do and what not to do. Just the law of the land, and the wild. Their would be no use for money and no use of exploiting money. For that just like the buffalo, you can simply live off the land. And just like the hawk and buzzard wander through the fertile valleys. If life was like this there would be no need for fighting. There would be no land claims in the mid-west if man were responsible. The land is for the wild to share, and man is also part of the wild and land.*

Comment to Martin: Obviously, you feel oppressed by "drugs and gangs" and restrictive laws. Although no one can doubt that you abhor the society in which you find yourself, it would have been appropriate for you explain the source of your bitterness. With a vivid detail or two you might have shown exactly why you want to escape to another time and place. You have identified a destination, but frankly, "the 1800's in the midwest [sic]" covers an excessively broad expanse of time and territory. Think about the meaning of an entire century and the vast changes that can occur in 100 years. Also, your claim that the Midwest was covered with green prairies and roaming buffalo significantly distorts American geography.

Your essay contains some attempts at colorful imagery—"the hawk and buzzard wander through fertile valleys," for instance, but overall it creates an impression of incoherence because sentences skip quickly from one topic to another without being developed. Such disjointedness indicates a serious deficiency in writing competence and control. Your essay is rated 2.

THE CHALLENGE OF WRITING A 30-MINUTE ESSAY

When writing the ACT essay you must condense into a few minutes all the steps that other writers, enjoying the luxury of time, might stretch into hours or even into days. Chances are you've done it before. An essay test in social studies, for example, may have required you to quickly fill up a blank page with all you knew about the Depression or causes of the Civil War. The numerous in-class essays you've produced over the years have no doubt trained you for the kind of instant essay asked of you on the ACT. In your classes, of course, success was based partly on how closely your ideas resembled those that the teacher had in mind. That's not true on the ACT. The answer you write in response to the prompt is not predetermined. What you need to know is already lodged inside you. The task you face on test day is to organize your ideas and put them into readable form on paper. It is a measure of what you can do instead of what you know.

Making Every Second Count

No book can tell you just how much time to devote to each step in the process. What works for you may be different from what works for others. But the three best ways for anybody to prepare are 1) to practice, 2) to practice, and 3) to practice some more.

Pick sample essay topics found on pages 294–297. Following the instructions for ACT essays, write an essay a day for several days in a row, or until you get the feel of 30 minutes' writing time. Pace yourself. Keep a record of how much time you spend thinking about the topic, how many minutes you devote to composing the essay, and how long it takes you to proofread and edit. As you practice, adjust the following plan until you get the timing that suits you best and produces the results you want:

Prewriting: 5–6 minutes
　Reading and analyzing the prompt
　Picking and narrowing the topic
　Choosing a main idea
　Gathering and arranging supporting ideas
Composing the essay: 15–20 minutes
　Introducing the thesis
　Developing paragraphs
　Choosing the best words for meaning and effect
　Structuring sentences effectively
　Writing a conclusion
Editing and proofreading: 3–5 minutes
　Editing for clarity and coherence
　Editing to create interest
　Checking for standard usage and mechanical errors, including spelling, punctuation, and capitalization

To make every second count, don't waste time inventing an essay title (your essay doesn't need one). Don't count words and don't expect to recopy your first draft. Because readers understand that ACT essays are first drafts, feel free to cross out, insert words using carets (^), and move blocks of text—as though you were cutting and pasting—with neatly drawn arrows. If necessary, number the sentences to make clear the order in which they are to be read. You won't be penalized for a sloppy-looking paper. Just make sure that the essay is readable.

Because of the time limit, don't plan to write a long essay. Essays of more than 400 words are unnecessary. It doesn't take even that many words to demonstrate your writing ability. In fact, less can be more, for a shorter essay of, say, 250 to 300 words can focus sharply on a limited subject. It can also be written more quickly, leaving time for revising and polishing your work. But don't be satisfied with an abbreviated one-paragraph essay. That could suggest a case of airheadedness. Just remember that quantity counts less than quality.

The Essay-Writing Process

Because you won't have time to invent a process when you write the ACT essay, it pays to have one in mind ahead of time. In preparation for the test, try out various processes while writing practice essays. Then develop the one that enables you to work most rapidly and efficiently while producing the best results. In effect, make a plan for what to do during each stage of the writing process.

The first stage, often called *prewriting*, consists of everything that needs to be done before you actually start writing. During the second stage, *composing*, you choose the words and form the sentences that express your thoughts. And during the final stage, *revising and proofreading*, you polish and refine the text of your essay word by word, making it clear, correct, and graceful. The truth is that these three stages are not all discrete. They overlap and blend indiscriminately. For example, writers compose, revise, and proofread simultaneously, they jot down sentences during prewriting, and even late in the process sometimes weave new ideas into their text. In fact, no stage really ends until the final period of the last sentence is put in place—or until time is up and the test booklets are closed.

Regardless of the blurry boundaries between the stages, however, it's worth keeping the functions of each stage in mind as you familiarize yourself with several important principles of essay writing.

THIRTEEN PRINCIPLES OF ESSAY WRITING

As you write, keep these principles at your elbow. Refer to them time and again. Soon they'll become habitual, and you'll use them instinctively, not only during the ACT Writing Test, but any time you need to write an essay. They can be *that* useful!

PREWRITING
1. Analyze the topic carefully.
2. Narrow the topic.
3. Choose a main idea that matters.
4. Gather and arrange ideas purposefully.

COMPOSING

5. Write an appealing introduction.

6. Develop paragraphs fully.

7. Include transitions for coherence.

8. Use plain and precise words.

9. Vary the sentence structure.

10. End the essay with a distinct conclusion.

EDITING AND PROOFREADING

11. Edit for clarity.

12. Edit for interest.

13. Check for standard usage and mechanics.

If you've had plenty of writing experience, you probably recognize most, if not all, of these principles. But if any item on the list is new to you, refer to it often and practice it over and over. Let it help you evolve into a better writer.

Prewriting

1. Analyze the topic carefully.

At the risk of stating the obvious, begin by reading the assigned essay topic, or prompt, very carefully. Read it two or three times, or until you are certain what is being asked of you.

An ACT prompt may not turn you on right away, but once you begin to think about it you may begin bursting with ideas. School essay assignments often give you days, or even weeks, to prepare. Before writing a word you can ponder the topic, talk to others, search the Internet, psyche yourself, and do whatever you can to get ready. On the ACT, however, you have only a couple of minutes to prepare.

2. Narrow the topic.

Always favor a well-focused essay on a limited topic to an essay that tries to cover too much ground. That's why narrowing the topic is one of the crucial steps in planning an ACT essay. The sharper your focus, the better.

The good news is that the ACT gives you a gift. The essay prompt narrows the topic for you by asking a direct question something like one of these:

Do schools give too much homework?

Do teachers have the right to charge students they teach for tutoring in the evening or on weekends?

Should students be given the right to grade their teachers and to publish the results in the school newspaper?

Would you approve of an honor code in your school to reduce cheating?

By answering yes or no to any of these questions, you narrow the topic in the blink of an eye, and your argument is apt to fit nicely into an essay of roughly 250-300 words written in 30 minutes. (That is about the word count on a double-spaced typed page using 12-point type.) Even if your answer cannot be reduced to a simple yes or no, a position somewhere in-between is still likely to be narrow enough for you to write a convincing essay.

3. Choose a main idea that matters.

Although the prompt more or less hands you an essay topic, you are still obliged to make an important decision—which side of the issue to support. You are free to support either side, of course, or to present an altogether different point of view. Whatever position you take is the essay's *main idea*. Every piece of the essay from its opening sentence to the conclusion should contribute to its development. It lays out a well-defined path for the reader. Any material that wanders from the main idea should be discarded. It not only wastes words but detracts from the impact of your essay.

If the topic happened to relate to required dress codes in high school, a main idea might be any one of the following:

1. Yes, high schools should impose dress codes on students.
2. No, high schools should not impose dress codes on students.
3. High schools should impose dress codes on freshmen and sophomores but not on juniors and seniors.

Using one of these main ideas as your starting point, the essay would then go on to prove the validity of your opinion.

If possible, pick a main idea that matters to you personally, one that truly reflects your thinking. ACT readers won't fault you for stating opinions with which they disagree, so there's no good reason for choosing a main idea that makes you sound politically correct or one that you think will please or flatter the reader. If you give your readers only what you think they might want, you're being dishonest, posing as someone you are not. Likewise, because you don't want to sound pompous or pretentious, avoid picking a main idea solely to demonstrate your intellectual superiority. An essay that is truthful and comes from the heart will serve you best.

4. Gather and arrange ideas purposefully.

Unless you are blessed with a digital mind that can instantly process an issue and draw insightful conclusions, you could do yourself a favor by spending a few moments to gather and arrange ideas, arguments, anecdotes, examples—whatever you can think of to support and develop the thesis of your essay. Search your knowledge and experience. List your thoughts on paper as they occur to you—just a word or two for each idea. These jottings, in effect, will become the working outline of your essay. Once the flow of ideas has slowed to a trickle, sort through your notes by drawing circles around key words, connect related ideas with arrows, cross out the rejects, or just underline the thoughts you'll definitely use in your essay.

With materials assembled, put them in some kind of order. Decide what should come first. Second. Third. In most essays, the best order is the clearest, the order your reader can follow with the least effort. But, just as a highway map may show several routes from one place to another, there is no single way to get from the beginning to the end of an essay.

No plan is necessarily superior to another provided there's a valid reason for using it. The plan that fails is the aimless one, the one in which ideas are presented solely according to how they popped into your head. To guard against aimlessness, rank your ideas in order of importance. Then work toward your best point, not away from it. Giving away your *pièce de résistance* at the start is self-defeating. Therefore, if you have, say, three good ideas in support of your thesis, save the strongest for last. Launch the essay with your second best, and sandwich your least favorite between the other two. A solid opening draws readers into the essay and creates that all-important first impression, but a memorable ending is even more important. Coming last, it is what readers have fresh in their minds when they assign the essay a grade.

Although the following guideline may not apply to every ACT essay, a body consisting of three sections is just about right. Why three? Mainly because three is a number that works. When you can support your main idea with three pieces of solid evidence, you appear to know what you are talking about. One is insufficient and two only slightly better. But three indicates thoughtfulness. Psychologically, three also creates a sense of rhetorical wholeness, like "blood, sweat, and tears," and "of the people, by the people, and for the people."

It shouldn't be difficult to divide a main idea into three secondary ideas. A narrative essay, for instance, naturally breaks into a beginning, middle, and end. A process is likely to have at least three steps, some of which may be broken into sub-steps. In an essay of comparison and contrast, you should be able to find at least three similarities and differences to write about. A similar division into thirds applies to essays of cause-and-effect, definition, and description, and certainly to essays of argumentation.

Each of three ideas may not require an equal amount of emphasis, however. You might dispose of the weakest idea in just a couple of sentences, while each of the others gets a whole paragraph. But whatever you emphasize, be sure that each idea is separate and distinct. That is, the third idea mustn't simply rehash the first or second in the guise of something new.

Composing

5. Write an appealing introduction.

Introductions let readers know what they're in for. Don't make a formal announcement of your plan: "This discussion will show the significance of computers as an influence on the learning of children from age 3 to 12. Distinctions will be made between early childhood (age 3–7) and middle childhood (age 8–12)." Such announcements should be reserved for long expository essays or for subsections of monographs and textbooks. They may help keep readers focused on the purpose of the piece, but they would be out of place in an ACT essay.

Rather, just state your point. The reader will recognize the topic soon enough, even without a separate statement of your intention.

Jill B, for example, began an essay on the rights of high school students this way:

> On Monday morning, October 20th, I arrived in school to find every locker door in my corridor standing ajar. Over the weekend, school officials had searched through students' lockers for drugs and alcohol. I believe that this illegal action was a violation of both my civil rights and the civil rights of every other student in the school.

This opening sets the essay's boundaries. Jill can't include everything about students' rights or about the duties and responsibilities of school authorities. Instead, she'll concentrate on one issue raised by her personal experience on that Monday morning.

The best essays usually begin with something catchy, something to lure the reader into the piece. Think of the opening as a hook—a phrase, a sentence, or an idea that will make your audience want to keep reading. Hooks must be very simple and brief because time won't allow you to write a long introduction. Jill's hook is effective because it tells an informative anecdote that leads directly to the main subject of her essay.

Techniques for Hooking Readers

During the 30 minutes allotted for the ACT essay, you probably won't have time to write an elaborate opening. A statement that conveys the topic of your essay may be all you need to lure your readers into the essay. Use any of these five common techniques, each illustrated with an example from an essay by a high school student.

1. Start with a brief account of an incident—real or invented—that leads the reader into the essay:

   > By lunch period, Megan, a senior at Brookdale High School, had already traded text messages with her brother in college, with her dad at work, and with a friend who was absent from school that day.
   >
   > —Lisa

2. State a provocative idea in an ordinary way or an ordinary idea in a provocative way. Either one will ignite reader interest.

   > As any football hero will tell you, on the field brains count for more than brawn.
   >
   > —Ollie

3. Use a quotation—not necessarily a famous one—from Shakespeare, a popular song, or your grandmother. Whatever the source, its sentiment must relate to the essay's topic.

   > "You can take people out of the country but you can't take the country out of the people."
   >
   > —Gary

4. Refute a commonly held assumption or define a word in a new and surprising way.

   > Even though she's never written a rhyme or verse, my boss at Safeway is just as much a poet as Shelley or Keats.
   >
   > —Rebecca

5. Ask an interesting question or two that you will answer in your essay.

> *Why are stories of crime so fascinating?*
>
> *—Doug*

When writing your ACT essay, you're not obliged to write an opening for the ages. Remember your purpose: to demonstrate that you can think, organize ideas, and write correctly. Therefore, a direct, clearly worded statement of the essay's main idea should suffice. Work hard to get it right. Be thoughtful. Be clever if that's your style, but not overly cute, coarse, or shocking. And keep it short. An opening that comprises, say, more than a quarter of your essay reflects poorly on your sense of proportion.

6. Develop paragraphs fully.

Each paragraph of a well-written essay is, in effect, an essay in miniature. It has a purpose, an organizational plan, and a progression of ideas. You can scrutinize a paragraph just as you would scrutinize a complete essay. You can study its structure and development, identify its main idea and its purpose.

In an essay, most paragraphs play a primary role and one or more secondary roles. An *introductory paragraph,* for instance, launches the essay and makes the intent of the essay clear to the reader. The *concluding paragraph* leaves the reader with a thought to remember and provides a sense of closure. Most paragraphs, however, are *developmental.* That is, they are used to carry forward the main point of the essay. In one way or other, developmental paragraphs perform any number of functions, including

- adding new ideas to the preceding discussion
- continuing or explaining in more detail an idea presented earlier
- reiterating a previously stated idea
- citing an example of a previously stated idea
- evaluating an opinion stated earlier
- refuting previously stated ideas
- turning the essay in a new direction
- providing a new or contrasting point of view
- describing the relationship between ideas presented earlier
- providing background material
- raising a hypothetical or rhetorical question about the topic
- serving as a transition between sections of the essay
- summarizing an argument presented earlier

Whatever its functions, a paragraph should contribute to the essay's overall growth. A paragraph that fails to amplify the main idea of the essay should be revised or deleted. Similarly, any idea within a paragraph that doesn't contribute to the development of the paragraph's topic needs to be changed or eliminated.

Topic Sentences

Whether readers skim your paragraphs or slog doggedly through every word, they need to find sentences now and then that, like landmarks, help them to know where they are. Such guiding sentences differ from others because they define the paragraph's main topic; hence the name *topic sentence*.

Most, but not all, paragraphs contain topic sentences. The topic of some paragraphs is so obvious that to state it would be redundant. Then, too, groups of paragraphs can be so closely knit that one topic sentence states the most important idea for all of them.

What all topic sentences have in common is their helpfulness. Consider them landmarks that indicate turning points that tell readers the direction they'll be going for a while.

No rule governs every possible use of a topic sentence. A sense of what readers need in order to understand the essay must be your guide. Let topic sentences lead the way.

Developing Your Paragraphs

In terms of importance, the length of paragraphs takes a back seat to clear and purposeful organization. Like essays, paragraphs should have a discernable plan. Ideas can be arranged from general to specific, or vice versa. Chronological and spatial arrangements make sense in narrative and descriptive paragraphs. Clarity and intent should always govern sequence. Disjointed paragraphs consist of sentences in random order, but in coherent paragraphs, every sentence has a place and a function that contributes to its total effect.

7. Include transitions for coherence.

Picture your readers as naive tourists in a foreign country and your essay as a journey they must take from one place to another. Because you can't expect them to find their own way, you must, in effect, guide them.

In long essays readers need more guidance than in short ones. To keep readers informed, you needn't repeat what you've already written but rather, plant key ideas, slightly rephrased, as milestones along the way.

You can help readers along, too, by choosing transitional words that set up relationships between one thought and the next. This can be done with such words as *this*, which actually ties the sentence you are now reading to the previous one. The word *too* in the first sentence of this paragraph serves the same function; it acts as a link between this paragraph and the one before. Fortunately, the English language is brimming with transitional words and phrases that tie sentences and ideas together.

8. Use plain and precise words.

Plain Language

To write clearly, use plain words. Never use a complex word because it sounds good or makes you seem more sophisticated. The ACT Writing Test is not a place to flaunt your vocabulary. Use an elegant word only when it's the only word that will let you add something to the essay that you can't achieve in any other way. Why? Because an elegant word used merely to use an elegant word is bombastic… er… big-sounding and artificial.

Fortunately, English is loaded with simple words that can express the most profound ideas. A sign that says STOP! conveys its message more clearly than CEASE AND DESIST. When a dentist pokes at your teeth, it *hurts*, even if dentists call it "experiencing discomfort." Descartes, the famous French philosopher, said, "I think; therefore, I am," a statement that forever afterward shaped the way we think about existence. Descartes might have used more exotic words, of course, words more in keeping with the florid writing style of his time, but the very simplicity of his words endows his statement with great power. In fact, a sign of true intelligence is the ability to convey deep meetings with simple words.

For the ACT essay, a plain, conversational style will always be appropriate. The language should sound like you. Let your genuine voice ring out, although the way you speak is not necessarily the way you should write. Spoken language is often vague, clumsy, repetitive, confused, wordy. Consider writing as the everyday speech of someone who speaks exceedingly well. It's grammatically correct and free of pop expressions and clichés. Think of it as the kind of speech expected of you in a college interview or in serious conversation with the head of your school. Or maybe even the way this paragraph sounds. You could do a lot worse!

Precise Language

Precise words are memorable, while hazy, hard-to-grasp words fade as quickly as last night's dream. Tell your garage mechanic vaguely, "This car is a lemon," and he'll ask for more information. Say precisely, "My car won't start in freezing weather," and he'll raise the engine hood and go to work. If a patient in the E.R.

says, "I feel pain," a surgeon might at least like to know exactly where it hurts before pulling out her scalpels. In other words, precise language is more informative, more functional, and thus, more desirable.

Undoubtedly, vague, shadowy words are easier to think of. But they are often meant to cover up a lack of clear and rigorous thinking. It's a cinch to pass judgment on a book by calling it "good" or "interesting." But what readers want to know is precisely why you thought so. How simple it is to call someone an "old man" without bothering to show the reader a "stooped white-haired gentleman shuffling along the sidewalk." A writer who says her teacher is "ugly" sends a different image of ugliness to each reader. If the teacher is a "shifty-eyed tyrant who spits when she talks," then, by golly, say it. Or if the teacher's personality is ugly, show her ill temper, arrogance, and cruelty as she scolds her hapless students.

Good writers understand that their words must appeal to the readers' senses. To write precisely is to write with pictures, sounds, and actions that are as vivid on paper as they are in reality. Exact words leave distinct marks; abstract ones, blurry impressions.

Use Comparisons

Of course, it's not always easy to find just the right words. At such times, you can depend on figures of speech such as metaphors and similes to make your meaning clear.

Similes (Tim wrestles *like* a tiger) and metaphors (Tim *is* a tiger) point out likenesses between something familiar (tiger) and something unfamiliar (how Tim wrestles). To convey meaning, one side of a comparison must always be common and recognizable. Therefore, comparing the cry of the Arctic tern to the song of a tree toad won't enlighten a reader familiar with neither water birds nor tree toads. Because you can expect readers to know the sound of a fiddle, however, a more revealing comparison is *The cry of the Arctic tern sounds like a fiddler searching for a C-sharp.*

Make your comparisons fresh and original. Don't rely on old standbys such as "life is like a box of chocolates," or "like a bat out of hell," or "dead as a doornail." Our language is littered with countless comparisons that once may have been vibrant and fresh but have wilted from overuse. The fact is that every familiar combination of words, such as "I could care less" or "you've got to be kidding" or "what a bummer" was once new, cool, even poetic. But repetition has turned them into clichés.

9. Vary the sentence structure.

Sentence Patterns

Variety for its own sake is hardly preferable to assembly-line writing—writing in which every sentence has been cut from the same pattern. But variety that clarifies meaning or gives emphasis to a particular idea is something else.

Handy Phrases

One method of keeping readers interested is by varying sentence openings. For instance, start sentences with:

- A prepositional phrase: *From the start, In the first place, At the outset*
- Adverbs and adverbial phrases: *Originally, At first, Initially*
- Dependent clauses: *When you start with this, Because the opening is*
- Conjunctions: *And, But, Not only, Either, So, Yet*
- Adjectives and adjective phrases: *Fresh from, Introduced with, Headed by*
- Verbal infinitives: *To launch, To take the first step, To get going*
- Participles: *Leading off, Starting up, Commencing with*

It may be perilous, however, to scramble up sentence openings just to scramble up sentence openings, for you may end up with a mess on your hands. Be guided by what expresses your ideas most clearly and also seems varied enough to interest your readers.

Short and Long Sentences

Another technique for writing a readable essay is to vary the length of sentences.

Short sentences are easier to grasp—but not always. (Remember Descartes' famous five-word assertion: "I think; therefore, I am"?) But generally, a brief sentence makes its point quickly, sometimes with astonishing intensity, since all the words concentrate on a single point. Take, for example, the last sentence in this passage:

For three days, my parents and I sat in our S.U.V. and drove from college to college to college in search of the perfect place for me to spend the next four years. For seventy-two hours we lived as one person, sharing thoughts and dreams, stating opinions about each campus we visited, taking guided tours, interviewing students and admissions officials, asking directions a hundred times, eating together in town after town, and even sleeping in the same motel rooms. But mostly, we fought.

A terse closing sentence following a windy, 46-word sentence produces a mild jolt. Indeed, it has been planted in that spot deliberately to startle the reader. The technique is easily mastered but should be used sparingly. Overuse dilutes its impact. A balance of long and short sentences works best.

10. End the essay with a distinct conclusion.

At the end of your ACT essay you can lift your pen off the paper and be done with it. Or, if you have the time, you can present your readers with a little gift to remember you by—perhaps a surprising insight, a bit of wisdom, a catchy phrase—something likely to tease their brains, tickle their funny bones, or make them feel smart.

What follows are several techniques for writing conclusions:

1. Have a little fun with your conclusion; try to put a smile on your reader's face.
2. End with an apt quotation drawn from the essay itself, from the ACT prompt, or from another source.
3. Finish by clearly restating your essay's main point but using new words. If appropriate, add a short tag line, a brief sentence that creates a dramatic effect.
4. Bring your readers up to date or project them into the future. Say something about the months or years ahead.

Although an effective conclusion will add luster to an essay, don't feel obliged to add an ending just for the sake of form. ACT readers will have developed a fairly accurate sense of your writing ability before reaching your essay's last word. Rest assured that a good but incomplete piece of writing will be graded according to what you have done well instead of what you haven't done at all.

Editing and Proofreading

11. Edit for clarity.

Because many words have multiple meanings, check each word for clarity. Ask yourself whether any reader might misconstrue a word or find it ambiguous. Penny O wrote an essay about students who cut classes. One of her sentences read: "The last thing parents should do is talk to their kids." Coming upon that sentence, readers might wonder whether Penny means that parents should talk to their kids only as a last resort, or that, in a list of what parents ought to do, the final step is talking to their kids.

262 • Pass Key to the ACT

12. Edit for interest.

One of your goals on the ACT essay is to inject life into your prose. The most effective ways to do this are:

- Using *active* instead of *passive* verbs
- Writing *active* instead of *passive* sentences
- *Showing* instead of *telling*

Active Verbs

To an essay writer, it's important to know that *action* verbs differ from *being* verbs. Because active verbs describe or show movement, they create life. They perform, move around, and excel over all other words in pumping vitality into your prose. They add energy and variety to sentences, and as a bonus, promote economy by helping you trim needless words.

Active verbs are full of life; *being* verbs are not. Notice the lifelessness in the most common forms of the verb *to be*:

is	are	was
were	am	has been
had been	have been	will be

When used in sentences, each of these being verbs joins a subject to a predicate—and that's all. In fact, forms of the verb *to be* function much like an equal sign in an equation: "Five minus two *is* three" ($5 - 2 = 3$), or "Samantha *is* smart" (Samantha = smart), or "Your ACT score is going up" (That = good news!). Because being verbs (and equal signs) show little life, use active verbs whenever you can.

To be sure, it would be hard to get along in speech and writing without being verbs. Be stingy, however. Check over a few of your most recent essays. If more than, say, one-fourth of your sentences use a form of *to be* as the main verb, you may be relying too heavily on being verbs.

Active and Passive Sentences

To write lively prose, also keep in mind the distinction between *active* and *passive* sentences. A passive sentence—that is, a sentence structured in the *passive voice*—is one in which the performer of an action remains unnamed or receives less notice than either the receiver of the action or the action itself. Take the following examples.

1. Six weeks were spent preparing for the spring carnival.
   From this sentence it is impossible to tell who performed the action—that is, who prepared for the carnival.

2. A new painting was hung in the gallery.

Similarly, this sentence fails to identify the performer of the action—or who hung the painting. The following revisions clear up the uncertainty:

1. Six weeks were spent preparing for the spring carnival by the cheerleaders.
2. A new painting was hung in the gallery by Carmine.

These versions contain more information than the originals, but each emphasizes the action instead of the performer of the action. Sometimes the writer may want to do that, but more often than not, such passive sentence structure occurs when the writer ignores the advantages of sentences written in the *active voice*. When the performers of action become the grammatical subject, this is what you get:

1. The cheerleaders prepared for the spring carnival for six weeks.
2. Carmine hung a new painting in the gallery.

Cast in the active voice, these sentences give the performers of the action top billing. Essay writers should take advantage of readers' natural curiosity about others and strive to put the performer of the action into the grammatical subject of sentences. By doing so, they eliminate passive verbs and pep up the prose.

Showing vs. Telling

Remember the principle that a picture is worth a thousand words? Whether it is truly worth a thousand may be arguable, but the point is not. Words can help readers *see*. Therefore, *show* more than you *tell*! Instead of describing your uncle as "absent-minded," *show* him stepping into his morning shower dressed in his p.j.'s. Rather than telling the reader that your room is "a mess," *show* the pile of wrinkled clothes in the corner and the books and Snickers wrappers scattered on the floor next to your unmade futon. The same principle applies to smells: "Her breath was foul with the stench of stale whiskey." To sounds: "the growl of a chain saw in the distance." To touch: "the feel of cool linen bed sheets." And to tastes: "a cold, sweet drink of spring water on a scorching summer day." In short, showing recreates experience for the reader, ultimately making the prose more interesting.

13. Check for standard usage and mechanics.

Writing correctly and using standard English can take you far in college and beyond. Although potential for error exists with every word you write, familiarity with the basic grammatical rules governing the use of sentences, verbs, adjectives, adverbs, and pronouns can keep you from stumbling. The use of correct punctuation will help, too.

ESSAY-WRITING PRACTICE

At a time when your mind is fresh, set aside 30 minutes to write a practice essay. Do it today, or tomorrow, or next week, but do it, and do it often. Nothing can prepare you better for Test Day than to get into the habit of writing essays.

Ten Topics for Essay-Writing Practice

1. Increasingly, students are choosing to take time off between high school and college. Some use the year for public service or charity work. Others travel, find internships, or get paying jobs in a variety of fields.

   Advocates of postponing college claim that experiences away from the classroom contribute to personal growth and maturity. Those opposed say that students are bound to lose momentum and often fail to pick up where they left off in their education.

   Write an essay that states your views on the issue. Whatever you believe, be sure to include convincing reasons in support of your position.

2. Your local schoolboard is planning to raise high school graduation requirements by adding between 50 and 100 hours of community service for all seniors. Supporters of the change see great educational value in serving others. Those opposed assert that seniors belong in the classroom full time.

   Two related questions have come up: Should students be excused from their classes while performing their service? And should the requirement be waived for seniors already holding part-time jobs?

   The education editor of your local newspaper has asked students for their views on the issue of community service. In response, write a letter stating your position and supporting your views with persuasive reasons. (Concern yourself only with the content of the letter, not its format.)

3. Concerned about widespread cheating on tests, homework assignments, and research papers, the faculty of your school is promoting a student honor code. At the heart of the code is a provision that requires students to pledge that they will not cheat and will report instances of cheating that they observe. Violators of the pledge will be punished according to the seriousness of the offense.

   Predicting that the code will destroy morale and lead to distrust and animosity among students, the administration does not support the idea. Instead it is seeking other ways to discourage cheating but has no clear plan.

   What position do you take on the issue? Write a letter to the head of the faculty committee that proposed the honor code. Explain your view and cite convincing reasons in support of your opinion. (Concern yourself only with the content of the letter, not its format.)

4. Several parents of middle-school students in your district have petitioned the administration to reduce the amount of homework that teachers assign. Hoping to relieve pressure on their kids, they want homework limited to no more than half an hour per subject on weekdays and none on weekends. The teachers argue that homework is essential, not only for learning but to prepare students for standardized state and local examinations.

   As a former student of middle-school age, do you side with the parents or with the teachers? Please write a letter to the middle-school administration stating your views and explaining your reasoning. (Concern yourself only with the content of the letter, not its format.)

5. Graffiti is pervasive both inside and outside your school building. The principal has threatened to severely punish perpetrators and has promised a $100 reward for information leading to the apprehension of the guilty students.

   No students have submitted names, and the graffiti problem has grown worse. In response, the principal has cancelled dances and other evening events for the rest of the year, asserting that graffiti detracts from the school climate and interferes with the educational process.

   What is your opinion of the principal's action? Write a letter to the principal explaining your position and citing convincing reasons to support your views. (Concern yourself only with the content of the letter, not its format.)

6. A conversation overheard in the corridor near a bank of student lockers:

   Vickie: Why so depressed, Jake?

   Jake: Oh, just a problem with my parents.

   Vickie: What's up with them?

   Jake: They don't want me to drive to Newport this weekend. I planned to go and got tickets for me and two friends, and now they don't trust me to take my father's car. I can't figure them out. First they tell me I'm so mature for my age, and then they treat me like I'm a juvenile delinquent.

   Vickie: I know how you must feel. Something like that happened to me last summer, when my mother and stepfather wouldn't let me visit a friend in Virginia for a week when her parents were away. But I sat them down and talked about my sense of responsibility and finally convinced them that I could be trusted. I didn't pout or yell, just calmly talked to them until they said it was okay for me to go. Why don't you try the same thing?

Put yourself in Jake's shoes. Follow Vickie's advice and, in an essay, write a convincing argument that explains your idea of responsibility and how you hold yourself accountable for behaving responsibly. Cite examples that would persuade your readers to understand the depth and breadth of your trustworthiness.

7. In an effort to improve discipline, your school's administration plans to implement a student dress code that bans among other things, tank tops, ragged jeans, short shorts, and T-shirts with provocative or obscene imprints. Students wearing banned clothing will be sent home for the day; repeated violations will lead to harsher penalties. Also, Wednesdays will be dress-up day, when students must come dressed in a manner appropriate for such occasions as a job or college interview.

   Some parents and students object to this measure for improving discipline; others support it. How do you stand on the issue? Write an op-ed piece for your school newspaper that explains your point of view and cites convincing reasons for your position.

8. In the name of safety, your school's administration has begun to search lockers and backpacks at random for knives, guns, and other dangerous articles that students are forbidden to bring into the building. Some students say that the new procedure illegally violates their privacy. The principal and vice-principals, on the other hand, claim the right to carry out searches in order to keep students safe and improve the atmosphere in the school.

   How do you stand on the administration's policy? Write a letter to the school newspaper explaining your views and citing convincing reasons for your position.

9. In school students learn things they didn't know before, learn how to do things they couldn't do before, and start to think in ways they hadn't thought before.

   Obviously, much of this learning occurs in the classroom, but it also takes place through sports, clubs, performances, and other extracurricular activities. Wherever they occur, students frequently fail to realize the meaning of certain learning experiences at the time they are happening. Only with the passage of time does the significance become clear.

   Write an essay about a learning experience that you didn't appreciate at the time it occurred. Be sure to describe the experience explicitly and to show what it was and how you changed as a consequence. Also, explain why you couldn't appreciate it at the time and what caused you to realize its significance later on. Feel free to draw on your reading, the media, or on other people's experience if you can't think of something that happened specifically to you.

10. On occasion, each of us experiences sudden moments of insight into who we are or where our lives are going. Such insights may occur in school, on the playing field, or even while walking down the street. Such moments can be thrilling, frightening, emotionally charged. Sometimes these personal "epiphanies," as they are called, may later turn out to be minor events, not at all as significant as they seemed at first, but for a time they meant a great deal.

Write an essay that describes one of these epiphanies. Include specific details about the occurrence, the feelings that it evoked, and how it changed you. If you cannot think of an experience of your own, choose one that you know something about from your reading, studies, or observation.

7 | **Model Tests**

The purpose of the Model Tests is to help you evaluate your progress in preparing for the actual ACT. Take each exam under simulated testing conditions and within the time limits stated at the beginning of each test. Try to apply the test-taking tips recommended in this book. Detach the Answer Sheet and mark your answers on it.

After you finish each exam, check your answers against the Answer Keys and fill in the Analysis Charts. Rate your total scores by using the Performance Evaluation Chart on page 331. Read all of the Answer Explanations.

The Analysis Charts will indicate where you need further review. Go back to the "Preparing for . . ." sections to reinforce specific areas.

ANSWER SHEET—MODEL TEST A

Directions: Mark one answer only for each question. Make marks dark. Erase completely any mark made in error. (Additional or stray marks will be counted as mistakes.)

Test 1: English

1 Ⓐ Ⓑ Ⓒ Ⓓ	20 Ⓕ Ⓖ Ⓗ Ⓙ	39 Ⓐ Ⓑ Ⓒ Ⓓ	58 Ⓕ Ⓖ Ⓗ Ⓙ
2 Ⓕ Ⓖ Ⓗ Ⓙ	21 Ⓐ Ⓑ Ⓒ Ⓓ	40 Ⓕ Ⓖ Ⓗ Ⓙ	59 Ⓐ Ⓑ Ⓒ Ⓓ
3 Ⓐ Ⓑ Ⓒ Ⓓ	22 Ⓕ Ⓖ Ⓗ Ⓙ	41 Ⓐ Ⓑ Ⓒ Ⓓ	60 Ⓕ Ⓖ Ⓗ Ⓙ
4 Ⓕ Ⓖ Ⓗ Ⓙ	23 Ⓐ Ⓑ Ⓒ Ⓓ	42 Ⓕ Ⓖ Ⓗ Ⓙ	61 Ⓐ Ⓑ Ⓒ Ⓓ
5 Ⓐ Ⓑ Ⓒ Ⓓ	24 Ⓕ Ⓖ Ⓗ Ⓙ	43 Ⓐ Ⓑ Ⓒ Ⓓ	62 Ⓕ Ⓖ Ⓗ Ⓙ
6 Ⓕ Ⓖ Ⓗ Ⓙ	25 Ⓐ Ⓑ Ⓒ Ⓓ	44 Ⓕ Ⓖ Ⓗ Ⓙ	63 Ⓐ Ⓑ Ⓒ Ⓓ
7 Ⓐ Ⓑ Ⓒ Ⓓ	26 Ⓕ Ⓖ Ⓗ Ⓙ	45 Ⓐ Ⓑ Ⓒ Ⓓ	64 Ⓕ Ⓖ Ⓗ Ⓙ
8 Ⓕ Ⓖ Ⓗ Ⓙ	27 Ⓐ Ⓑ Ⓒ Ⓓ	46 Ⓕ Ⓖ Ⓗ Ⓙ	65 Ⓐ Ⓑ Ⓒ Ⓓ
9 Ⓐ Ⓑ Ⓒ Ⓓ	28 Ⓕ Ⓖ Ⓗ Ⓙ	47 Ⓐ Ⓑ Ⓒ Ⓓ	66 Ⓕ Ⓖ Ⓗ Ⓙ
10 Ⓕ Ⓖ Ⓗ Ⓙ	29 Ⓐ Ⓑ Ⓒ Ⓓ	48 Ⓕ Ⓖ Ⓗ Ⓙ	67 Ⓐ Ⓑ Ⓒ Ⓓ
11 Ⓐ Ⓑ Ⓒ Ⓓ	30 Ⓕ Ⓖ Ⓗ Ⓙ	49 Ⓐ Ⓑ Ⓒ Ⓓ	68 Ⓕ Ⓖ Ⓗ Ⓙ
12 Ⓕ Ⓖ Ⓗ Ⓙ	31 Ⓐ Ⓑ Ⓒ Ⓓ	50 Ⓕ Ⓖ Ⓗ Ⓙ	69 Ⓐ Ⓑ Ⓒ Ⓓ
13 Ⓐ Ⓑ Ⓒ Ⓓ	32 Ⓕ Ⓖ Ⓗ Ⓙ	51 Ⓐ Ⓑ Ⓒ Ⓓ	70 Ⓕ Ⓖ Ⓗ Ⓙ
14 Ⓕ Ⓖ Ⓗ Ⓙ	33 Ⓐ Ⓑ Ⓒ Ⓓ	52 Ⓕ Ⓖ Ⓗ Ⓙ	71 Ⓐ Ⓑ Ⓒ Ⓓ
15 Ⓐ Ⓑ Ⓒ Ⓓ	34 Ⓕ Ⓖ Ⓗ Ⓙ	53 Ⓐ Ⓑ Ⓒ Ⓓ	72 Ⓕ Ⓖ Ⓗ Ⓙ
16 Ⓕ Ⓖ Ⓗ Ⓙ	35 Ⓐ Ⓑ Ⓒ Ⓓ	54 Ⓕ Ⓖ Ⓗ Ⓙ	73 Ⓐ Ⓑ Ⓒ Ⓓ
17 Ⓐ Ⓑ Ⓒ Ⓓ	36 Ⓕ Ⓖ Ⓗ Ⓙ	55 Ⓐ Ⓑ Ⓒ Ⓓ	74 Ⓕ Ⓖ Ⓗ Ⓙ
18 Ⓕ Ⓖ Ⓗ Ⓙ	37 Ⓐ Ⓑ Ⓒ Ⓓ	56 Ⓕ Ⓖ Ⓗ Ⓙ	75 Ⓐ Ⓑ Ⓒ Ⓓ
19 Ⓐ Ⓑ Ⓒ Ⓓ	38 Ⓕ Ⓖ Ⓗ Ⓙ	57 Ⓐ Ⓑ Ⓒ Ⓓ	

Test 2: Mathematics

1 Ⓐ Ⓑ Ⓒ Ⓓ Ⓔ	16 Ⓕ Ⓖ Ⓗ Ⓙ Ⓚ	31 Ⓐ Ⓑ Ⓒ Ⓓ Ⓔ	46 Ⓕ Ⓖ Ⓗ Ⓙ Ⓚ
2 Ⓕ Ⓖ Ⓗ Ⓙ Ⓚ	17 Ⓐ Ⓑ Ⓒ Ⓓ Ⓔ	32 Ⓕ Ⓖ Ⓗ Ⓙ Ⓚ	47 Ⓐ Ⓑ Ⓒ Ⓓ Ⓔ
3 Ⓐ Ⓑ Ⓒ Ⓓ Ⓔ	18 Ⓕ Ⓖ Ⓗ Ⓙ Ⓚ	33 Ⓐ Ⓑ Ⓒ Ⓓ Ⓔ	48 Ⓕ Ⓖ Ⓗ Ⓙ Ⓚ
4 Ⓕ Ⓖ Ⓗ Ⓙ Ⓚ	19 Ⓐ Ⓑ Ⓒ Ⓓ Ⓔ	34 Ⓕ Ⓖ Ⓗ Ⓙ Ⓚ	49 Ⓐ Ⓑ Ⓒ Ⓓ Ⓔ
5 Ⓐ Ⓑ Ⓒ Ⓓ Ⓔ	20 Ⓕ Ⓖ Ⓗ Ⓙ Ⓚ	35 Ⓐ Ⓑ Ⓒ Ⓓ Ⓔ	50 Ⓕ Ⓖ Ⓗ Ⓙ Ⓚ
6 Ⓕ Ⓖ Ⓗ Ⓙ Ⓚ	21 Ⓐ Ⓑ Ⓒ Ⓓ Ⓔ	36 Ⓕ Ⓖ Ⓗ Ⓙ Ⓚ	51 Ⓐ Ⓑ Ⓒ Ⓓ Ⓔ
7 Ⓐ Ⓑ Ⓒ Ⓓ Ⓔ	22 Ⓕ Ⓖ Ⓗ Ⓙ Ⓚ	37 Ⓐ Ⓑ Ⓒ Ⓓ Ⓔ	52 Ⓕ Ⓖ Ⓗ Ⓙ Ⓚ
8 Ⓕ Ⓖ Ⓗ Ⓙ Ⓚ	23 Ⓐ Ⓑ Ⓒ Ⓓ Ⓔ	38 Ⓕ Ⓖ Ⓗ Ⓙ Ⓚ	53 Ⓐ Ⓑ Ⓒ Ⓓ Ⓔ
9 Ⓐ Ⓑ Ⓒ Ⓓ Ⓔ	24 Ⓕ Ⓖ Ⓗ Ⓙ Ⓚ	39 Ⓐ Ⓑ Ⓒ Ⓓ Ⓔ	54 Ⓕ Ⓖ Ⓗ Ⓙ Ⓚ
10 Ⓕ Ⓖ Ⓗ Ⓙ Ⓚ	25 Ⓐ Ⓑ Ⓒ Ⓓ Ⓔ	40 Ⓕ Ⓖ Ⓗ Ⓙ Ⓚ	55 Ⓐ Ⓑ Ⓒ Ⓓ Ⓔ
11 Ⓐ Ⓑ Ⓒ Ⓓ Ⓔ	26 Ⓕ Ⓖ Ⓗ Ⓙ Ⓚ	41 Ⓐ Ⓑ Ⓒ Ⓓ Ⓔ	56 Ⓕ Ⓖ Ⓗ Ⓙ Ⓚ
12 Ⓕ Ⓖ Ⓗ Ⓙ Ⓚ	27 Ⓐ Ⓑ Ⓒ Ⓓ Ⓔ	42 Ⓕ Ⓖ Ⓗ Ⓙ Ⓚ	57 Ⓐ Ⓑ Ⓒ Ⓓ Ⓔ
13 Ⓐ Ⓑ Ⓒ Ⓓ Ⓔ	28 Ⓕ Ⓖ Ⓗ Ⓙ Ⓚ	43 Ⓐ Ⓑ Ⓒ Ⓓ Ⓔ	58 Ⓕ Ⓖ Ⓗ Ⓙ Ⓚ
14 Ⓕ Ⓖ Ⓗ Ⓙ Ⓚ	29 Ⓐ Ⓑ Ⓒ Ⓓ Ⓔ	44 Ⓕ Ⓖ Ⓗ Ⓙ Ⓚ	59 Ⓐ Ⓑ Ⓒ Ⓓ Ⓔ
15 Ⓐ Ⓑ Ⓒ Ⓓ Ⓔ	30 Ⓕ Ⓖ Ⓗ Ⓙ Ⓚ	45 Ⓐ Ⓑ Ⓒ Ⓓ Ⓔ	60 Ⓕ Ⓖ Ⓗ Ⓙ Ⓚ

Test 3: Reading

1 Ⓐ Ⓑ Ⓒ Ⓓ   11 Ⓐ Ⓑ Ⓒ Ⓓ   21 Ⓐ Ⓑ Ⓒ Ⓓ   31 Ⓐ Ⓑ Ⓒ Ⓓ
2 Ⓕ Ⓖ Ⓗ Ⓙ   12 Ⓕ Ⓖ Ⓗ Ⓙ   22 Ⓕ Ⓖ Ⓗ Ⓙ   32 Ⓕ Ⓖ Ⓗ Ⓙ
3 Ⓐ Ⓑ Ⓒ Ⓓ   13 Ⓐ Ⓑ Ⓒ Ⓓ   23 Ⓐ Ⓑ Ⓒ Ⓓ   33 Ⓐ Ⓑ Ⓒ Ⓓ
4 Ⓕ Ⓖ Ⓗ Ⓙ   14 Ⓕ Ⓖ Ⓗ Ⓙ   24 Ⓕ Ⓖ Ⓗ Ⓙ   34 Ⓕ Ⓖ Ⓗ Ⓙ
5 Ⓐ Ⓑ Ⓒ Ⓓ   15 Ⓐ Ⓑ Ⓒ Ⓓ   25 Ⓐ Ⓑ Ⓒ Ⓓ   35 Ⓐ Ⓑ Ⓒ Ⓓ
6 Ⓕ Ⓖ Ⓗ Ⓙ   16 Ⓕ Ⓖ Ⓗ Ⓙ   26 Ⓕ Ⓖ Ⓗ Ⓙ   36 Ⓕ Ⓖ Ⓗ Ⓙ
7 Ⓐ Ⓑ Ⓒ Ⓓ   17 Ⓐ Ⓑ Ⓒ Ⓓ   27 Ⓐ Ⓑ Ⓒ Ⓓ   37 Ⓐ Ⓑ Ⓒ Ⓓ
8 Ⓕ Ⓖ Ⓗ Ⓙ   18 Ⓕ Ⓖ Ⓗ Ⓙ   28 Ⓕ Ⓖ Ⓗ Ⓙ   38 Ⓕ Ⓖ Ⓗ Ⓙ
9 Ⓐ Ⓑ Ⓒ Ⓓ   19 Ⓐ Ⓑ Ⓒ Ⓓ   29 Ⓐ Ⓑ Ⓒ Ⓓ   39 Ⓐ Ⓑ Ⓒ Ⓓ
10 Ⓕ Ⓖ Ⓗ Ⓙ   20 Ⓕ Ⓖ Ⓗ Ⓙ   30 Ⓕ Ⓖ Ⓗ Ⓙ   40 Ⓕ Ⓖ Ⓗ Ⓙ

Test 4: Science Reasoning

1 Ⓐ Ⓑ Ⓒ Ⓓ   11 Ⓐ Ⓑ Ⓒ Ⓓ   21 Ⓐ Ⓑ Ⓒ Ⓓ   31 Ⓐ Ⓑ Ⓒ Ⓓ
2 Ⓕ Ⓖ Ⓗ Ⓙ   12 Ⓕ Ⓖ Ⓗ Ⓙ   22 Ⓕ Ⓖ Ⓗ Ⓙ   32 Ⓕ Ⓖ Ⓗ Ⓙ
3 Ⓐ Ⓑ Ⓒ Ⓓ   13 Ⓐ Ⓑ Ⓒ Ⓓ   23 Ⓐ Ⓑ Ⓒ Ⓓ   33 Ⓐ Ⓑ Ⓒ Ⓓ
4 Ⓕ Ⓖ Ⓗ Ⓙ   14 Ⓕ Ⓖ Ⓗ Ⓙ   24 Ⓕ Ⓖ Ⓗ Ⓙ   34 Ⓕ Ⓖ Ⓗ Ⓙ
5 Ⓐ Ⓑ Ⓒ Ⓓ   15 Ⓐ Ⓑ Ⓒ Ⓓ   25 Ⓐ Ⓑ Ⓒ Ⓓ   35 Ⓐ Ⓑ Ⓒ Ⓓ
6 Ⓕ Ⓖ Ⓗ Ⓙ   16 Ⓕ Ⓖ Ⓗ Ⓙ   26 Ⓕ Ⓖ Ⓗ Ⓙ   36 Ⓕ Ⓖ Ⓗ Ⓙ
7 Ⓐ Ⓑ Ⓒ Ⓓ   17 Ⓐ Ⓑ Ⓒ Ⓓ   27 Ⓐ Ⓑ Ⓒ Ⓓ   37 Ⓐ Ⓑ Ⓒ Ⓓ
8 Ⓕ Ⓖ Ⓗ Ⓙ   18 Ⓕ Ⓖ Ⓗ Ⓙ   28 Ⓕ Ⓖ Ⓗ Ⓙ   38 Ⓕ Ⓖ Ⓗ Ⓙ
9 Ⓐ Ⓑ Ⓒ Ⓓ   19 Ⓐ Ⓑ Ⓒ Ⓓ   29 Ⓐ Ⓑ Ⓒ Ⓓ   39 Ⓐ Ⓑ Ⓒ Ⓓ
10 Ⓕ Ⓖ Ⓗ Ⓙ   20 Ⓕ Ⓖ Ⓗ Ⓙ   30 Ⓕ Ⓖ Ⓗ Ⓙ   40 Ⓕ Ⓖ Ⓗ Ⓙ

TEST 1: ENGLISH

Time—45 minutes
75 Questions

> **Directions:** The following test consists of 75 underlined words and phrases in context, or general questions about the passages. Most of the underlined sections contain errors and inappropriate expressions. You are asked to compare each with the answer choices. If you consider the original version best, choose letter A or F: NO CHANGE. For each question, blacken on the answer sheet the letter of the alternative you think best. Read each passage through before answering the questions based on it. (On the actual ACT, questions appear to the right of the underlined words and boxes. Here, however, questions follow the passage.)

Passage 1

(1)

Americans are living longer. The number of citizens sixty years or older totaled more than forty million in 1999, and one out of every nine Americans <u>were</u> sixty-five or older. Because advances in medical science
₁
and a more healthful lifestyle have lengthened the life spans of
<u>we Americans</u>, more and more of us are finding that the time comes when
₂
we either no longer want to<u>—or can—</u>live on our own.
₃

(2)

Unfortunately, in the past the words *retirement home* often brought to mind images of impersonal, lonely places. ☐4☐ However, conditions in retirement homes can vary, some homes earning awards for excellence in nursing care, and others earning citations for negligence. ☐5☐ Regulations regarding nursing homes are becoming <u>stricter than a research clinic</u>, and
₆
it is possible to find retirement conditions that are positive and comfortable. ☐7☐

(3)

But at the same time, the sad fact remains that, although most nursing homes are now licensed by the state, <u>unclean and unhealthy conditions can</u>
₈
<u>still be found</u>. Even if the homes follow the licensing procedures perfectly, the
₈
law does not guarantee a <u>warm friendly</u> staff or atmosphere. ☐10☐
₉

(4)

When looking at nursing homes, <u>qualities should be placed</u> in priority
₁₁
order. Family members should remember, as they look, that attitude toward
patients—the morale and personal contact—can be just as important as
new buildings, which, if they do not contain human warmth, can be little
better than prisons.

(5)

For these reasons, it <u>behooves us</u> to take the time to carefully check out
₁₂
the nursing homes the family is considering. If members of the family
cannot carry out all of the necessary steps, they should have a friend or
relative help with the evaluation.

(6)

Not everyone who is in a nursing home requires the 24-hour skilled care
offered there. Many residents are in homes because they can no longer
care for themselves at home, and have nowhere else to go. However,
alternatives to nursing homes do exist for people who need less care. [13]

(7)

Home care <u>services, which</u> allow a patient to stay in a familiar environment
₁₄
rather than being placed in a nursing home, are an option if the elderly
person needs only limited help, since home care causes far less disruption
to normal life. Such services are provided by a variety of public, voluntary,
and private agencies. [15]

1. **A.** NO CHANGE
   B. is
   C. have been
   D. was

2. **F.** NO CHANGE
   G. we, Americans,
   H. us Americans
   J. us, Americans,

3. **A.** NO CHANGE
   B. to or can live
   C. to, or can live
   D. to, or can, live

4. This idea (of "impersonal, lonely places") could best be illustrated in this passage by employing which of the following writing strategies?

    F. Explaining a process
    G. Persuasion
    H. Defining
    J. Description

5. Which of the following writing strategies would permit the writer to present details about both housing extremes?

    A. Classifying and dividing
    B. Narration
    C. Comparison and contrast
    D. Persuasion

6. **F.** NO CHANGE
    G. stricter
    H. stricter than clinics
    J. stricter than they once were

7. Suppose that at this point in the passage the writer wanted to add more information about the impact of government regulations on retirement home conditions. Which of the following additions would be most relevant to the passage as a whole?

    A. A description and brief history of the agencies regulating nursing homes
    B. A bibliography of government reports and summaries published by regulating agencies
    C. A separate paragraph summarizing briefly the recent activity and success of regulating agencies
    D. Inclusion of a typical case report on an existing nursing institution

8. **F.** NO CHANGE
    G. one can still find unclean and unhealthy conditions.
    H. conditions can be found of uncleanliness and unhealthiness.
    J. many of them are unclean and unhealthy.

9. **A.** NO CHANGE
    B. warm - friendly
    C. warm: friendly
    D. warm, friendly

10. The writer could most effectively strengthen this paragraph by adding:

    F. a list of retirement homes found to be substandard in cleanliness.
    G. an anecdote about a woman who has lived in a home for 20 years.
    H. details and examples that typify unclean and unhealthy conditions.
    J. details of the licensing procedure that homes are required to complete.

11. **A.** NO CHANGE
    B. interested parties should place qualities
    C. qualities are certainly to be placed
    D. the patient should place qualities

12. **F.** NO CHANGE
    G. best suits us
    H. is very important
    J. is not a bad idea

13. Which of the following means of discussing alternatives to 24-hour skilled nursing care would be most compatible with the methods employed so far in this passage?

    A. Detailed interviews with nursing home inmates who have experienced both forms of care
    B. Insertion of medical records of patients who have been moved from occasional care to 24-hour care
    C. A short paragraph mentioning several alternatives to 24-hour care
    D. Inclusion of a personal diary written by an elderly patient who made the change to permanent care

14. **F.** NO CHANGE
    G. services which
    H. services that
    J. services

15. Choose the sequence of paragraph numbers that make the structure of the passage most logical.

    A. NO CHANGE
    B. 7, 2, 3, 1, 5, 4, 6
    C. 1, 2, 3, 5, 4, 6, 7
    D. 1, 2, 7, 3, 4, 5, 6

Passage 2

Cultural activities form the loom on which the talents, skills, and dreams of individuals can sprout into something colorful and distinctive—a
                                    16   17
play, pageant, art center, music festival, museum, library, garden, park—to
  17
enrich community life. [18] Cultural activities are central to Rural Areas Development, a nationwide effort by rural people and those in public service and private endeavors who work with it to enrich the quality of life. [20]
                                                                    19
What may not be recognized by area leaders whose primary interest is in economic development is when cultural activities can be part of the steam
                                    21

that supplies the drive. The first heritage festival of Lawrence County in Arkansas illustrates how a cultural activity may emerge from a ferment of economic development and, in turn, engender still newer ideas for <u>farther</u>
₂₂
social and economic gain, as well as other cultural activities. Lawrence County, a mainly rural area in northeastern Arkansas, had a population of 17,000 in <u>nineteen-sixty.</u> Its eastern half is fertile. The Black River runs
₂₃
beneath the delta, planted to rice, soybeans, and cotton, and the hills, where the farms are in livestock and poultry. <u>Family-type farms</u> employ a
₂₄
third of the work force. ⬚25⬚

   Farmers <u>nevertheless</u> made up the largest occupational group in the
₂₆
Lawrence County Development Council when it was organized in 1962. Seventeen members of the Council were farmers—<u>nine in general farming,</u>
₂₇
<u>six livestock and poultry producers,</u> one a dairyman, another a ricegrower.
₂₇
Also on the Council were an industrial worker, two bankers, and several local businessmen and homemakers. <u>Addressing itself to the economic</u>
₂₈
<u>advancement of the county, the Council spent its first two years of</u>
₂₈
<u>existence.</u> It supported a one-mill tax to guarantee construction of an
₂₈
industrial building in Walnut Ridge, the county seat and the largest town. It was instrumental in getting a comprehensive manpower inventory and economic base study of the <u>area it</u> arranged for workshops in farm
₂₉
management. It helped leaders of Imboden to initiate a housing project for twenty elderly persons. ⬚30⬚

16. **F.** NO CHANGE
    G. can be woven
    H. can be sprouted
    J. can swell

17. **A.** NO CHANGE
    B. distinctive, a play, a pageant
    C. distinctive. A play, a pageant
    D. distinctive; a play, a pageant

18. Which of the following terms needs to be more carefully defined if the first paragraph is to carry substantial meaning?

    F. Pageant
    G. Cultural activities
    H. Loom
    J. Music festival

19. **A.** NO CHANGE
    B. they
    C. him
    D. them

20. Which of the following suggestions would improve the beginning of this passage?

    F. NO CHANGE
    G. OMIT the second paragraph.
    H. Combine the first and second paragraphs.
    J. Move the second paragraph to the end of the passage.

21. **A.** NO CHANGE
    B. is that
    C. is because
    D. is for

22. **F.** NO CHANGE
    G. even farther
    H. further
    J. furthermore

23. **A.** NO CHANGE
    B. nineteen-sixty a.d.
    C. 1960
    D. nineteen hundred and sixty

24. **F.** NO CHANGE
    G. Family type farms
    H. Family type-farms
    J. Family, type farms

25. This paragraph contains a major organizational problem. Which of the following critical statements best describes this problem?

    A. The paragraph does not contain enough specific details to support the main point.
    B. The first sentence of the paragraph presents an idea that is not developed in the body of the paragraph.
    C. No beginning thesis or topic is presented.
    D. There are many ideas in the paragraph, none of them developed.

26. **F.** NO CHANGE
    G. on the contrary
    H. however
    J. thus

27. **A.** NO CHANGE
    B. —nine in general farming, six in livestock and poultry production, one in dairy production, another in rice farming.
    C. —nine are general farmers, six as livestock and poultry producers, one a dairyman, another a ricegrower.
    D. —nine as general farmers, six livestock and poultry producers, one a dairyman, another a ricegrower.

28. **F.** NO CHANGE
    G. During its first two years, the Council addressed the economic advancement of the county.
    H. Addressing itself to the economic advancement of the county, the Council spent its first two years of existence.
    J. The Council spent its first two years of existence while addressing itself to the economic advancement of the county.

29. **A.** NO CHANGE
    B. area, it
    C. area. It
    D. area but it

30. Which of the following is a major flaw in the structure and sense of this passage?

    F. It omits all mention of children; children are certainly an important part of rural America.
    G. It fails to mention public works projects.
    H. The whole point of the passage is that cultural activities can "supply the drive" for social and economic development, but the passage does not address that issue at all.
    J. The passage does not list enough accomplishments of the Lawrence County Development Council.

Passage 3

Of all the musical instruments produced by human skill, the three of which are the most distinguished are the violin, the piano, and the pipe
<u>31</u>
organ. Of these, the violin still remains the instrument of the virtuoso. No method <u>to play it</u> has yet been <u>discovered</u> except by the slow and tedious
   <u>32</u>   <u>33</u>
process of learning it. It is the instrument of the <u>accomplish</u> musician. [35]
                                                       <u>34</u>
On the other hand, self-playing devices have been employed successfully with both the piano and the organ—but with this difference. Piano music derives some of its <u>essentialness</u> from the personality of the player. The
                                <u>36</u>
touch of human fingers has never been exactly reproduced by mechanical

devices. In some compositions, however, the mechanical piano player approaches the pianist, although not by any means in all. 38
37

The pipe organ consequently is made for automated playing. There is
39
virtually nothing the organist can do with his or her hands or feet that cannot be duplicated by mechanical devices. When an organ manual is touched, the resulting tone is the exact same, whether the touch be hard
40   41
or soft, slow or quick. The tone continues at the same volume until the key
42
is released. Brilliancy, variety, and other qualities are obtained by other sets of pipes, and these pipes are brought into play by pulling out stops. Such stops can be pulled by mechanical means just as effectively as by human fingers. If the organ music is correctly cut in the music roll, with all the stops, couplers, and swells operated at the proper places, the most
43
acutest ear cannot distinguish between the human organist and
43
the organist who is mechanical. 45
44

31. **A.** NO CHANGE
    B. that are most distinguished
    C. of those that are distinguished
    D. most distinguished

32. **F.** NO CHANGE
    G. playing at
    H. in playing it
    J. of playing it

33. **A.** NO CHANGE
    B. invented
    C. divined
    D. developed

34. **F.** NO CHANGE
    G. accomplishing
    H. accomplished
    J. more accomplished

35. Which of the following writing strategies would permit the writer to present details about all three types of instruments?

    A. Classifying and dividing
    B. Narration
    C. Comparison and contrast
    D. Persuasion

36. **F.** NO CHANGE
    G. pith
    H. quality
    J. life-blood

37. **A.** NO CHANGE
    B. approaches the sound of the pianist
    C. comes close to the piano
    D. typifies the piano

38. The writer could most effectively strengthen the passage at this point by adding:

    F. documentation and detail to support opinions delivered as facts.
    G. a review of all the orchestral instruments, including their musical ranges.
    H. a discussion of the great violin makers of the past.
    J. a detailed description of organ structure and mechanism.

39. **A.** NO CHANGE
    B. on the contrary
    C. to be sure
    D. similarly

40. **F.** NO CHANGE
    G. exact identical
    H. same
    J. equal

41. **A.** NO CHANGE
    B. is
    C. was
    D. has been

42. **F.** NO CHANGE
    G. soft, slow, or quick.
    H. soft: slow or quick.
    J. soft slow or quick.

43. **A.** NO CHANGE
    B. the acute ear
    C. the more acute ear
    D. the most acute ear

44. **F.** NO CHANGE
    G. the organist, who is mechanical.
    H. the mechanical organist.
    J. the organist who is a nonhuman.

45. The main purpose of this passage is to provide:

- **A.** a discussion of the virtues of the mechanical organ.
- **B.** a history of music.
- **C.** a comparison of the violin, piano, and organ.
- **D.** a general discussion of mechanized musical instruments.

Passage 4

Until his death, Charles Darwin complained that even many of his scientific critics failed to grasp the meaning of his theory of selection; it is not unlikely that if he were still alive the complaint would be
<u>46</u>
repeated. [47] Even where full comprehension of his theory of the causes of organic evolution has been reached, precise determination of the degree of its adequacy—for adequate in great measure it surely is—has not yet
<u>48</u>
been attained. The generalization that underlies it is so broad, the facts by which it must be verified or limited are always, it seems, accumulating, and the problems interrelated with it
<u>49</u>
are so intricate, that finality with regard to it must be indefinitely postponed. That must be left for the biology of the future.
<u>50</u>
Moreover, there need be little hesitation in expressing an estimate of
<u>51</u>
the great naturalist and his thought. They are obviously among the greatest intellectual forces of the early twentieth century, as they were of the nineteenth. Notwithstanding certain limitations, which Darwin himself unduly emphasizes, he was one of the greatest of men intellectually, and,
<u>52</u>
without qualification, one of the most attractive of personalities; this must
<u>53</u>
always remain true, whatever may be the ultimate verdict of science in regard to details of his hypotheses. Persons thus grandly molded have nothing to fear from the perspective of time. He was one cool cucumber at
<u>54</u>
one of history's junctures.
<u>54</u>
Darwin insisted that the principle of natural selection is only one of the causes of evolution of species, "the main but not the exclusive means of modification," and he was also profoundly aware of the evolutionary
<u>55</u>
importance of the underlying problems of variability, heredity, and isolating
<u>56</u>
that has occupied so absorbingly the attention of the post-Darwinians.
<u>57</u>
Naturalists, almost without exception, no longer doubt that natural selection, as expounded by him, is a cause of the evolution of species, and a most

important one, and <u>stood</u> as a general law that explains the causation of
58

organic evolution. <u>This view will be supported by the biology of the future, if</u>
59

<u>Darwin's place</u> in the history of science cannot be far below that of
59

Newton. ⌐60⌐

46. F. NO CHANGE
    G. it is not likely
    H. it is likely
    J. it is probable

47. When a passage mentions that a famous figure *complained* about a fact or situation, how might the reader be given greater understanding of the personality and character of that subject?

    A. By inclusion of a description of the occurrence
    B. By quoted examples of what he or she actually said
    C. By references to how other persons present at the time reported the conversation
    D. By a speculative commentary on what he or she meant

48. F. NO CHANGE
    G. adequacy; for
    H. adequacy, for
    J. adequacy for

49. A. NO CHANGE
    B. are so always accumulating
    C. are so constantly accumulating
    D. are accumulating

50. F. NO CHANGE
    G. This
    H. Those
    J. That judgment

51. A. NO CHANGE
    B. In addition
    C. In other words,
    D. However,

52. F. NO CHANGE
    G. emphasize
    H. emphasized
    J. had emphasized

53. **A.** NO CHANGE
    B. this assessment
    C. this alone
    D. this quality

54. **F.** NO CHANGE
    G. He has been one cool cucumber at one of history's junctures.
    H. He is one cool cucumber at one of history's junctures.
    J. OMIT this sentence.

55. **A.** NO CHANGE
    B. modification" and
    C. modification." And
    D. modification;" and

56. **F.** NO CHANGE
    G. isolatability
    H. isolation
    J. isolate

57. **A.** NO CHANGE
    B. had occupied
    C. has been occupied
    D. have occupied

58. **F.** NO CHANGE
    G. has stood
    H. stands
    J. will have stood

59. **A.** NO CHANGE
    B. If this view is supported by the biology of the future, Darwin's place
    C. This view will be supported by the biology of the future, although Darwin's place
    D. Nevertheless, this view is supported by the biology of the future, when Darwin's place

60. Readers are likely to regard the passage as best described by which of the following terms?

    F. Biographical
    G. Confessional
    H. Laudatory
    J. Inspirational

Passage 5

Almost everywhere <u>spread through</u> the British Isles are to be found
₆₁
antiquities. These are carefully marked on <u>governmental, and many private</u>
₆₂
maps <u>and historians describe them</u> in publicly available guides.
₆₃
Governmental agencies, the National Trust, and private landlords are
most accommodatingin permitting visits to these unattended sites,
<u>most of which are unsupervised yet immaculate.</u> [65]
₆₄

With interesting exceptions, the rock graphics of the British Isles are
a collection of pits, rings, and grooves, as well as <u>carefully-carved</u> symbols
₆₆
of Neolithic power (axheads, fertility symbols, etc.) and roughly sculpted
monoliths. The pit, ring, and groove sites usually are found on horizontal
surfaces, <u>because</u> many power symbols are found on vertical surfaces of
₆₇
menhirs (upright <u>monoliths</u>) lintels, and the walls of constructions. In the
₆₈
more than <u>five hundred</u> megalithic stone constructions, many have a
₆₉
number of menhirs whose natural shape has been abetted by human
enterprise into a variety of shapes. Stonehenge is the incorporating
universal structure <u>by which</u> one can discern many of the features found
₇₀
elsewhere. In Scotland <u>are found</u> a special series of menhirs that depict
₇₁
symbols, both pre-Christian and Christian, as well as human figures,
angels, and scenes. [72]

Surely one of the earliest stones to be erected is the one near
present-day Edinburgh in an area that came under Britannic control by
A.D. 480. [73] Christianity came to this region between the fifth and the
seventh centuries: St. Ninian founded the Candida Case monastery near
Whithorn on the Solway in A.D. 379–398; St. Oran established holy places in
Iona, Mull, and Tiree before A.D. 548. [74] The form of Christianity was the
monastic and hermitic type traditionally called Celtic, which demanded
poverty and obedience from its clergy, who were all monks. [75]

61. **A.** NO CHANGE
 B. widely dispersed through
 C. throughout
 D. all over, in nook and crook

62. **F.** NO CHANGE
    G. governmental; and many private
    H. governmental—and many private
    J. governmental and many private

63. **A.** NO CHANGE
    B. and described
    C. and describing
    D. and descriptively

64. **F.** NO CHANGE
    G. most of which are unsupervised although immaculate.
    H. most of which are immaculate.
    J. most of which are unsupervised.

65. Suppose this passage were written for an audience that was unfamiliar with antiquities and British history. The writer could most effectively strengthen the passage by:

    A. including a brief summary of the biographies of British monarchs.
    B. describing with detail and illustration just what an *antiquity* is.
    C. supplying a current map of England.
    D. defining in great detail the term *National Trust*.

66. **F.** NO CHANGE
    G. carefully, carved
    H. carefully carved
    J. carefully and carved

67. **A.** NO CHANGE
    B. while
    C. although
    D. yet

68. **F.** NO CHANGE
    G. monoliths),
    H. monoliths,)
    J. monoliths,

69. **A.** NO CHANGE
    B. 500
    C. 5 hundred
    D. five-hundred

70. **F.** NO CHANGE
    G. with which
    H. for which
    J. in which

71. A. NO CHANGE
    B. was found
    C. has always been found
    D. is found

72. Readers are likely to regard the passage as best described by which of the following terms?

    F. Fictional
    G. Scholarly
    H. Dramatic
    J. Persuasive

73. How can this paragraph be changed so that it will be more meaningful and understandable to a young reader?

    A. Include a chart of rock types, listing origins, scientific names, and descriptions.
    B. Provide a detailed description of many European prehistoric stoneworks.
    C. Describe more fully the one stone mentioned in the first sentence.
    D. Add a comparison of Easter Island monoliths with the Stonehenge monuments.

74. Look over the structure of this paragraph as it has unfolded so far. With which one of the following characterizations do you agree?

    F. It is surely and soundly organized, consisting of a general statement at the beginning that is supported throughout.
    G. It is not organized very well. It begins with a statement about monastic orders, but does not develop that idea.
    H. It is not organized very well. It begins with a statement about a stone, but then switches to the history of Christianity in the region.
    J. It is not organized very well. It begins with a brief history of Britannic rule, and then seems to shift to a history of Pict temples.

75. This paragraph would be strengthened by:

    A. supplying more details about the Christian leaders.
    B. beginning the paragraph with a general statement that encompasses the details presented in the body.
    C. including a short lesson on rock formation.
    D. defining the hermitic form of Christianity.

Answers to English Test begin on page 328.

TEST 2: MATHEMATICS

Time —60 minutes
60 Questions

> *Directions:* After solving each problem, darken the appropriate space on the answer sheet. Do not spend too much time on any one problem. Make a note of the ones that seem difficult, and return to them when you finish the others. Assume that the word *line* means "straight line," that geometric figures are not necessarily drawn to scale, and that all geometric figures lie in a plane.

1. Which of the following statements about the subsets of real numbers is true?

   A. Every integer is a whole number.
   B. All rational numbers are integers.
   C. 0 is not a real number.
   D. 3.14 is a rational number.
   E. All integers are negative.

2. Jane's score on her first test was 72. On her second test she received a score of 81. What percent increase did she have?

   F. 9%   G. $11\frac{1}{9}$%   H. 12.5%   J. $88\frac{8}{9}$%   K. 112.5%

3. $4^2 - 3 - 5 \cdot 8 - 2[(-3) - (-7)] = ?$

   A. 192   B. −7   C. −43   D. −33   E. −35

4. Four boxes, each one $2\frac{3}{8}$ feet high, are stacked in a room with a 10-foot ceiling. How much space is there between the top box and the ceiling?

   F. 2 feet   J. 1 inch
   G. 1 foot   K. None of these
   H. 6 inches

5. Which of the following inequalities corresponds to the graph?

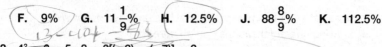

   A. $x \le 6$ D. $|x - 4| \le 2$
   B. $x \ge 2$ E. $|x - 6| = 2$
   C. $|x - 2| \le 6$

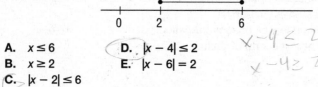

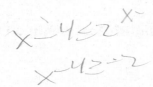

6. What is the lowest common denominator of the fractions $\dfrac{5}{4x^2y}$, $\dfrac{7}{6xy^2}$, and $\dfrac{-4}{15xy}$?

F. xy

G. $30xy$

H. $60xy$

J. $360x^2y^2$

K. $60x^2y^2$

7. What is the complete factorization of the polynomial $4x^3 - 24x^2 + 36x$?

A. $4x(x - 3)^2$

B. $x(2x - 6)^2$

C. $x(4x - 12)(x - 3)$

D. $x(4x^2 - 24x + 36)$

E. $4x(x^2 - 6x + 9)$

8. Which of the following numbers is composite?

F. 1   G. 43   H. $\dfrac{2}{3}$ J. 57   K. 83

9. If $a = -3$ and $b = 4$, then $ab^2 - (a - b) = ?$

A. 151   B. 55   C. -49   D. -47   E. -41

10. Which of the following is an inscribed angle in the diagram?

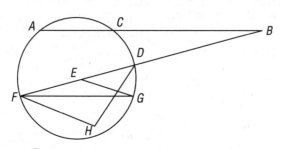

F. ∠ABF

G. ∠DFG

H. ∠FEG

J. ∠DEG

K. ∠FHD

11. Jon starts out on a trip at 40 mph. If $\frac{1}{2}$ hour later Joel starts out on the same route at 50 mph, which equation may be used to determine how long it will take Joel to overtake Jon?

A. $40\left(x + \frac{1}{2}\right) = 50x$

B. $40x + \frac{1}{2} = 50x$

C. $40x = 50\left(x + \frac{1}{2}\right)$

D. $4(x + 30) = 50x$

E. $40x = 50x + 30$

12. If lines l, m, and n are parallel, and $AB = 2$, $AC = 8$, and $EF = 5$, what is the length of $\overline{DE}$?

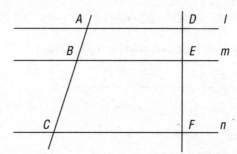

F.   15   G. $3\frac{1}{5}$ H. $1\frac{2}{3}$ J. $1\frac{1}{5}$ K. $\frac{3}{5}$

13. $5\frac{1}{8} - 3\frac{5}{6} = ?$

A. $1\frac{7}{24}$

B. $2\frac{17}{24}$

C. $1\frac{1}{2}$

D. $1\frac{1}{8}$

E. $2\frac{7}{24}$

14. In the diagram, the right angles are marked and $AB = BC = CD = DE = EF = 1$. What is the length of $\overline{AF}$?

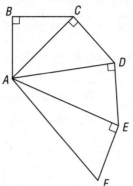

F. 2   **J.** $\sqrt{5}$

G. 3   **K.** $\sqrt{6}$

H. 5

15. What is the common decimal numeral for one hundred six and twenty-eight ten thousandths?

A. 106.00028   **D.** 106.28

B. 106.0028   **E.** 106,280,000

C. 106.028

16. What is the solution set for $3 - (x - 5) = 2x - 3(4 - x)$?

F. $\left\{-\dfrac{3}{2}\right\}$ **J.** ø

G. $\left\{\dfrac{3}{10}\right\}$ **K.** {5}

H. $\left\{\dfrac{10}{3}\right\}$

17. Which of the following is an arithmetic sequence?

A. $\dfrac{1}{2}, \dfrac{1}{4}, \dfrac{1}{6}, \dfrac{1}{8}, \ldots$

B. 2, 4, 8, 16, ...

C. 2, 5, 10, 17, ...

D. 5, 11, 17, 23, ...

E. −1, 3, −9, 27, ...

18. What is the value of i^{53}?

F. 1   **G.** i **H.** −1   **J.** $-i$ **K.** 0

19. The Science Club has ten members, and they want to form an election committee of four people. If everyone in the club is eligible to be on the committee, how many different committees can be formed?

    A. 1   B. 40   C. 210   D. 5040   E. 3,628,800

20. Which of the following trigonometric equations is false for all x?

    F. $\sin x = \dfrac{2}{\sqrt{5}}$

    G. $\tan x = -100$

    H. $\sec x = \dfrac{\sqrt{3}}{4}$

    J. $\cos^2 x + \sin^2 x = 1$

    K. $\cos x = -0.1439$

21. In the diagram, two chords of the circle intersect at point E. If AE = 3, DE = 5, and CE = 2, what is the length of $\overline{BE}$?

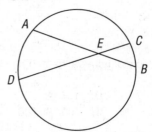

    A. $1\dfrac{1}{5}$ B. $3\dfrac{1}{3}$ C. 4   D. $7\dfrac{1}{2}$ E. $8\dfrac{1}{3}$

22. What is the probability of drawing a heart from a well-shuffled standard deck of playing cards?

    F. $\dfrac{1}{4}$ G. $\dfrac{1}{52}$ H. $\dfrac{1}{13}$ J. $\dfrac{4}{13}$ K. 1

23. Which expression is equal to $x - [3x - (1 - 2x)]$ when completely simplified?

    A. $-3x^2 + 2x - 1$
    B. $-4x + 1$
    C. 1

    D. -1
    E. $-4x - 1$

24. If $f(x) = 2x - 5$ and $g(x) = 1 + x^2$, then what is equal to $f(g(3))$?

    F. $2\sqrt{2} - 5$ G. 2   H. 10   J. 15   K. 16

25. If the length of a rectangle is 1 foot less than twice its width and its perimeter is 34 feet, what is the length of the rectangle in feet?

    A. 6   B. 11   C. $11\dfrac{2}{3}$ D. $22\dfrac{1}{3}$ E. None of these

26. If $2 \log_3 x - \frac{1}{2} \log_3 y + \log_3 z$ were written as a single logarithm, to what would it be equal?

F. $\log_3 \dfrac{x^2 z}{\sqrt{y}}$

G. $\log_3 \dfrac{x^2}{z\sqrt{y}}$

H. $\log_3 \dfrac{xz}{y}$

J. $\log_3 \dfrac{4xz}{y}$

K. $\log_3 \left(x^2 - \dfrac{y}{2} + z \right)$

27. Which expression would be appropriate to complete the following equation in order for the equation to illustrate the commutative property of addition: $5(3 + 0) = ?$

A. 5(3)   D. 5(3) + 5(0)
B. (3 + 0)5   E. 5(3) + 0
C. 5(0 + 3)

28. In a class of 27 students, $\frac{2}{3}$ are male. Five-sixths of the males in the class received a grade of C. How many male students received a grade of C?

F. 6   G. 12   H. 15   J. 18   K. 24

29. Which equation corresponds to the graph?

A. $\dfrac{x^2}{9} + \dfrac{y^2}{4} = 1$

B. $\dfrac{x^2}{9} - \dfrac{y^2}{4} = 1$

C. $\dfrac{x^2}{3} + \dfrac{y^2}{2} = 1$

D. $\dfrac{y^2}{4} - \dfrac{x^2}{9} = 1$

E. $(x - 3)^2 + (y - 2)^2 = 0$

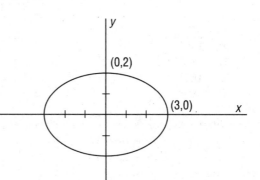

30. What is the solution set for the system of equations?

$$x \quad\quad = 2$$
$$y \quad\quad = -3$$
$$2z = 8$$

(handwritten: z = 4)

F. $\{(2, -3, 8)\}$
G. $\{(2, -3, 4)\}$
H. $\left\{\left(1, \dfrac{-3}{2}, 4\right)\right\}$
J. $\{(1, 1, 2)\}$
K. $\{\ \}$

31. What is the solution set of $\sqrt{x + 1} = x - 1$?

A. $\{0, 1\}$ B. $\{3\}$ C. $\{0\}$ D. $\{0, 3\}$ E. $\{-1, 1\}$

32. Which expression is equivalent to $\sqrt[3]{-12a^4b^2} \cdot \sqrt[3]{-6a^2b^2}$ in simplest radical form?

F. $\sqrt[3]{72a^6b^4}$
G. $-2a^2b\sqrt[3]{9b}$
H. $2a^2b\sqrt[3]{9b}$
J. $a^2b\sqrt[3]{72b}$
K. $2\sqrt[3]{9a^6b^4}$

(handwritten: $2a^3b\ 9b\ \sqrt[3]{72a^6b^4}$)

33. Given $\overline{CD}$ is tangent, m $\angle ABD = 62°$ and m $\angle BDC = 28°$, what is the measure of $\angle ADB$?

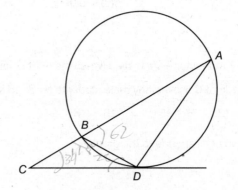

A. 90°
B. 100°
C. 118°
D. 152°
E. 180°

34. What is the solution set of the following system of equations?

$$\begin{pmatrix} 2x - 5y = 13 \\ 3x + 2y = 10 \end{pmatrix}$$

F. $\left\{\left(\dfrac{4}{19}, \dfrac{4}{19}\right)\right\}$
G. $\{(-3, -1)\}$
H. $\{(4, -1)\}$
J. $\{(-1, -3)\}$
K. None of these

(handwritten: $2x = 13 + 5y$; $x = \dfrac{13 + 5y}{2}$; $\dfrac{39}{2} + 15y = 20$)

35. What is the solution to this system of equations?

$$\begin{pmatrix} 2x + 3y = 12 \\ y = \dfrac{-2}{3}x + 5 \end{pmatrix}$$

A. {0}

B. {0, 0}

C. {(−3, 2}

D. {}

E. All points on the line.

36. If the measure of arc $ADC = 200°$ and $\overline{AB}$ and $\overline{BC}$ are tangent to circle O, what is the measure of $\angle OCA$?

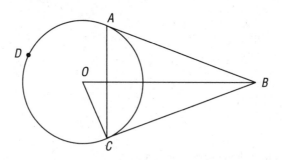

F. 40°   G. 20°   H. 10°   J. 8°   K. 5°

37. Suppose that a circular region (radius 2 cm) is cut from a square with sides 9 cm, leaving the shaded region shown in the diagram. What is the area of the shaded region?

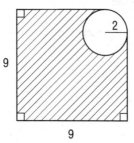

A. $81 - 4\pi$

B. $77 - 3\pi$

C. $78 - 4\pi$

D. $80 - 4\pi$

E. $81 - 3\pi$

38. Which statement is always true concerning an obtuse angle?

    F. It measures less than 90°.
    G. It measures greater than 180°.
    H. It is the supplement of another obtuse angle.
    J. There can be only one in a triangle.
    K. There cannot be one in a quadrilateral.

39. What is the simplified form of the complex fraction

$$\frac{\dfrac{x}{y} - \dfrac{y}{x}}{\dfrac{1}{x} - \dfrac{1}{y}}?$$

    A. $x + y$
    B. $x - y$
    C. $-x - y$
    D. $\dfrac{x^2 - y^2}{y - x}$
    E. $\dfrac{x^2 - y^2}{x - y}$

40. Which of the following statements is false?

    F. All isoceles triangles are similar.
    G. If two lines are cut by a transversal, the alternate interior angles are equal.
    H. All circles are congruent.
    J. The angles of a triangle are supplementary.
    K. All four of the above are false.

41. Which of the following is the graph of the solution set of the inequality $|x - 3| > 2$?

    A.
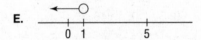

    B.
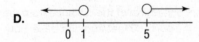

    C.
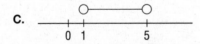

    D.
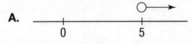

    E.
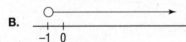

42. If $\overline{AC} \perp \overline{BD}$, $DE = 2$, $BE = 1$, $EC = \frac{1}{2}$, what is the length of $\overline{AB}$?

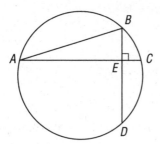

 F. $\sqrt{17}$ G. 4   H. $\sqrt{5}$ J. 3   K. 2

43. In the diagram, lines m and n in a plane are cut by transversal ℓ. Which statement would allow the conclusion that $m \parallel n$?

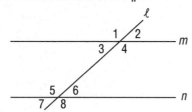

 A. $m\angle 1 = m\angle 4$
 B. $\angle 3$ and $\angle 4$ are supplementary
 C. $m\angle 3 = m\angle 8$
 D. $m\angle 3 = m\angle 6$
 E. $\angle 1$ and $\angle 6$ are complementary

44. How many terms does the complete expansion of $(x + 2y)^9$ have?

 F. 8   G. 9   H. 10   J. 18   K. 81

45. Which of the following is NOT a rational number?

 A. 0.5   B. $0.\overline{5}$ C. $\sqrt{48}$ D. $\sqrt{49}$ E. 15%

46. What is the period of the following function:

$$y = 2 \tan \left(3x - \frac{\pi}{2} \right)?$$

 F. 1   G. π H. $\frac{\pi}{3}$ J. $\frac{\pi}{2}$ K. $\frac{2\pi}{3}$

47. In a windstorm a tower was bent at a point one fourth of the distance from the bottom. If the top of the tower now rests at a point 60 feet from the base, how tall, in feet, was the tower?

 A. 100   B. 80   C. $60\sqrt{2}$ D. $60\sqrt{3}$ E. $240\sqrt{2}$

48. Which of the following is NOT the equation of a conic section?

    F. $2x^2 + 5y^2 - 2x + 7y - 8 = 0$

    G. $y = 3x^2 + 7x - 3$

    H. $y = 2^x + 5$

    J. $\dfrac{x^2}{9} - \dfrac{(y - 3)^2}{16} = 1$

    K. $(x - 2)^2 + (y + 3)^2 = 25$

49. If $\cos \theta = \dfrac{-1}{2}$ and θ is in quadrant III, what is the value of $\sin 2\theta$?

    A. $\dfrac{1}{2}$ **B.** $\dfrac{-1}{2}$ **C.** $\dfrac{\sqrt{3}}{2}$ **D.** $\dfrac{-\sqrt{3}}{2}$ **E.** -1

50. Given quadrilateral $ABCD$, which statement would allow the conclusion that $ABCD$ is a parallelogram?

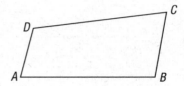

    F. $m \angle A = m \angle C$

    G. $AD = BC$

    H. $m \angle A + m \angle D = 180°$

    J. $AD \parallel BC$

    K. None of these

51. What is the standard form of the equation of the line perpendicular to the graph of $2x + 3y = 7$ at point $(2, 1)$?

    A. $x = 2$ **D.** $3x + 2y = 8$

    B. $2x - 3y = 1$ **E.** $y = 1$

    C. $3x - 2y = 4$

52. Which of the following is NOT a real number?

    F. $\dfrac{0}{5}$ **G.** $3 - 9$ **H.** $\sqrt{25}$ **J.** $-\sqrt{7}$ **K.** $\sqrt{-4}$

53. What is the degree of the polynomial $2^2x^2yz - 2^3x^3yz - 3$?

    A. 0   **B.** 4   **C.** 5   **D.** 6   **E.** 8

54. Tangent line $\overleftrightarrow{AD}$ and chord $\overline{AC}$ intersect at point A. If the measure of arc $ABC = 220°$, what is the measure of $\angle CAD$?

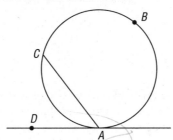

F. 220°   **G.** 110°   **H.** 140°   **J.** 70°   **K.** 35°

55. Which of the following is NOT equal to the others?

A. 0.015

B. 1.5×10^{-2}

C. 1.5%

D. $\dfrac{3}{200}$

E. (0.3)(0.005)

56. What is the simplified form of $\dfrac{6}{4 - \sqrt{2}}$?

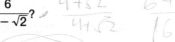

F. $12 + 3\sqrt{2}$

G. $\dfrac{3\sqrt{2}}{2\sqrt{2} - 1}$

H. $\dfrac{4 + \sqrt{2}}{3}$

J. $\dfrac{12 + 3\sqrt{2}}{7}$

K. $\dfrac{24 + 6\sqrt{2}}{14}$

57. Which of the following is equivalent to $|x - 5| > 2$?

A. $x > 7$

B. $x + 5 > 2$

C. $x < 3$

D. $x > 7$ or $x < 3$

E. $3 < x < 7$

58. In $\triangle ABC$ ($\angle C$ is the right angle), $\overline{CD}$ is drawn perpendicular to $\overline{AB}$. If $AD = 3$ and $BD = 12$, what is the length of $\overline{DC}$?

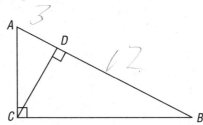

F. 6   **G.** $3\sqrt{5}$ **H.** $7\dfrac{1}{2}$ **J.** 9   **K.** $4\dfrac{1}{2}$

59. Which of the following expressions is NOT equal to cos (−512°)?

    A. cos 208°
    B. −cos 28°
    C. sin (−62°)
    D. sin 152°
    E. cos 152°

60. The gravitational attraction between two bodies varies inversely as the square of the distance between them. If the force of attraction is 64 pounds when the distance between the bodies is 9 feet, what is the force, in pounds, when they are 24 feet apart?

    F. 5184
    G. 729
    H. 216
    J. 24
    K. 9

Answers to Mathematics Test begin on page 329.

TEST 3: READING

Time —35 minutes
40 Questions

Directions: This test consists of four passages, each followed by ten multiple-choice questions. Read each passage and then pick the best answer for each question. Fill in the spaces on your answer sheet that correspond to your choices. Refer to the passage as often as you wish while answering the questions.

Passage 1

PROSE FICTION: *This passage, taken from the short story "Gaspar Ruiz: A Romantic Tale" by Joseph Conrad, takes place after Gaspar, a rebel soldier, has been accused of fighting for the Royalists.*

Gaspar Ruiz, condemned to death as a deserter, was not thinking either of his native place or of his parents, to whom he had been a good son on account of the mildness of his character and the great strength of his limbs. The practical advantage of this last was made still more valuable to his
(5) father by his obedient disposition. Gaspar Ruiz had an acquiescent soul.

But it was stirred now to a sort of dim revolt by his dislike to die the death of a traitor. He was not a traitor. He said again to the sergeant: "You know I did not desert, Esteban. You know I remained behind amongst the trees with three others to keep the enemy back while the detachment was running away!"

(10) Lieutenant Santierra, little more than a boy at the time, and unused as yet to the sanguinary imbecilities of a state of war, had lingered nearby, as if fascinated by the sight of these men who were to be shot presently—"for an example"—as the *Commandante* had said.

The sergeant, without deigning to look at the prisoner, addressed himself
(15) to the young officer with a superior smile.

"Ten Men would not have been enough to make him a prisoner, *mi tenente*. Moreover, the other three rejoined the detachment after dark. Why should he, unwounded and the strongest of them all, have failed to do so?"

"My strength is as nothing against a mounted man with a lasso," Gaspar
(20) Ruiz protested eagerly. "He dragged me behind his horse for half a mile."

At this excellent reason the sergeant only laughed contemptuously. The young officer hurried away after the *Commandante*.

Presently the adjutant of the castle came by. The sergeant learned from him that the condemned men would not be shot till sunset. He begged then
(25) to know what he was to do with them in the meantime.

The adjutant looked savagely round the courtyard and, pointing to the door of a small dungeon-like guardroom, receiving light and air through one heavily barred window, said: "Drive the scoundrels in there."

(30) The sergeant, tightening his grip upon the stick he carried by virtue of his rank, executed this order with alacrity and zeal. He hit Gaspar Ruiz, whose movements were slow, over his head and shoulders. Gaspar Ruiz stood still for a moment, biting his lip thoughtfully—then followed the others without haste. The door was locked, and the adjutant carried off the key.

(35) By noon the heat of that vaulted place had become unbearable. The prisoners crowded towards the window, begging their guards for a drop of water; but the soldiers remained lying in indolent attitudes wherever there was a little shade under a wall, while the sentry sat with his back against the door smoking a cigarette. Gaspar Ruiz had pushed his way to the window. His capacious chest needed more air than the others; his big face pressed

(40) close to the bars seemed to support the other faces crowding up for breath. From moaned entreaties they had passed to desperate cries. The tumultuous howling of those thirsty young men obliged a young officer just then crossing the courtyard to shout, "Why don't you give some water to these prisoners?"

The sergeant, with an air of surprised innocence, excused himself by the

(45) remark that all those men were condemned to die in a very few hours.

Lieutenant Santierra stamped his foot. "They are condemned to death, not to torture," he shouted. "Give them some water at once."

Impressed by this appearance of anger, the soldiers bestirred themselves, and the sentry, snatching up his musket, stood to attention.

(50) But when a couple of buckets were found and filled from the well, it was discovered that they could not be passed through the bars, which were set too close. The soldiers were not equipped with canteens. A small tin cup was found, but its approach to the opening caused such a commotion, such yells of rage and pain in the vague mass of limbs behind the straining faces

(55) at the window, that Lieutenant Santierra cried out hurriedly, "No, no—you must open the door, sergeant."

The sergeant, shrugging his shoulders, explained that he had no right to open the door even if had the key. But he had not the key. The adjutant of the garrison kept the key. Those men were giving much unnecessary

(60) trouble, since they had to die at sunset in any case. Why they had not been shot early in the morning he could not understand.

Lieutenant Santierra kept his back studiously to the window. It was at his earnest solicitations that the *Commandante* had delayed the execution. This favor had been granted to him in consideration of his distinguished family

(65) and of his father's high position amongst the chiefs of the Republican party. Lieutenant Santierra believed that the commanding General would visit the fort sometime in the afternoon, and he ingenuously hoped that his naive intercession would induce that severe man to pardon some, at least, of those criminals. In the revulsion of his feeling his interference stood revealed

(70) now as guilty and futile meddling.

1. Based on information in the passage, Gaspar Ruiz is alleged to have committed treason because he:

   A. ran away at the height of a battle.
   B. stayed up all night.
   C. got separated from his detachment.
   D. lassoed a soldier riding on a horse.

2. The narrator's assertion that Gaspar had been a "good son" (line 2) is based on which of Gaspar's characteristics?

   F. His willingness to work hard
   G. A strong desire to help others
   H. An agreeable nature
   J. His ambition to be a success in life

3. Considering the events in the entire passage, Sergeant Esteban's attitude toward Lieutenant Santierra can best be described as a combination of:

   A. discretion and prudence.
   B. admiration and respect.
   C. cynicism and contempt.
   D. antagonism and insolence.

4. That Gaspar and the other men are to be shot "for an example" (lines 12–13) suggests which of the following about the *Commandante*?

   F. He wants to raise the morale of his troops.
   G. He is concerned that other soldiers may try to desert.
   H. He is uncertain about Gaspar's guilt.
   J. He thinks that Gaspar and the others need to be taught a lesson.

5. The *Commandante* delays the executions at the behest of Lieutenant Santierra because:

   A. of Santierra's connections.
   B. Santierra made a strong and convincing argument.
   C. he is not convinced that the men are guilty.
   D. he wanted to impress the commanding general.

6. All of the following characters are represented as harsh, brutal military men EXCEPT:

   F. Esteban.
   G. Lieutenant Santierra.
   H. the adjutant.
   J. the *Commandante*.

7. Based on the passage, it is reasonable to infer that the guards assigned to watch the prisoners were:

   A. fearful of the men locked up in the guardhouse.
   B. indifferent to the suffering of the men.
   C. confident that Gaspar and the other men were guilty.
   D. anxious to release the men as soon as they were given the order to do so.

8. The details and events in the passage suggest that Lieutenant Santierra:

   F. has quickly grown accustomed to military life.
   G. has won the respect of his commanding officer.
   H. will soon receive a promotion.
   J. has values that differ from those of the other men in his detachment.

9. It can be reasonably be inferred that Santierra feels "guilty" (line 70) because:

   A. his interference in the case caused the prisoners to suffer needlessly.
   B. he has failed to win a pardon for the condemned men.
   C. he lost his temper in ordering water for the men locked inside the guardhouse.
   D. of his inadequacy as an officer and a leader of men.

10. Which of the following events does the passage suggest is the immediate result of Santierra's hurrying away (lines 21–22)?

    F. The sergeant laughs contemptuously.
    G. The adjutant informs the sergeant that the prisoners will die at sunset.
    H. The adjutant utters, "Drive the scoundrels in there."
    J. The sergeant hits Gaspar on the head and shoulders with a stick.

Passage 2

SOCIAL STUDIES: *This passage is adapted from an article published by the Naval Historical Center, an agency affiliated with the U.S. Department of the Navy.*

Though it now seems merely a folk-memory, the Influenza epidemic of 1918 was the third greatest plague in the history of mankind. The most devastating epidemic since the Middle Ages, it took over 21 million lives and affected over half the world's population. Logically, one would think that an epidemic of this
(5) proportion would have left an indelible imprint on the American people. In the United States alone, 550,000 died within the 16-week period from October 1918 to February 1919. Yet, it never inspired awe, not in 1918 and not since.

As one searches for explanation as to why Americans took little notice of the epidemic and then quickly forgot what they did notice, a mystery and a
(10) paradox emerge. The mystery was the complacency the American people displayed as a group toward the epidemic. The paradox was the common individual's clear acknowledgment that the epidemic was the most influential experience of his life.

(15) To understand this lack of attention, one must look at the years preceding the outbreak. Lethal epidemics were not as unexpected and therefore not as impressive as they might be in the more technologically advanced surroundings of today. The terror of typhoid, yellow fever, diphtheria, and cholera were well within living memory. Most Americans had lived through the typhoid and small pox epidemics of 1876 and 1890.

(20) Beyond this complacent acceptance of epidemics as a part of life, one must rely almost entirely on speculation in finding further answers.

If the "Spanish Influenza" had settled down as a permanent source of misery in the country, then possibly Americans might have granted this variety of the flu the notoriety it deserved. But the devastation came,
(25) scooped up its victims, and all but disappeared within a few short months. If the flu had been a disease that evoked a memory of terror, Americans might have panicked. This complete absence of fear, which until 1918 had inflicted no more than a few uncomfortable days of cold-like symptoms, is reflected in a statement by A.J. McLaughlin of the U.S. Public Health
(30) Service: " It is remarkable to see the placidity by which the people have generally taken the almost sudden loss of thousands of lives."

The nature of the disease and its contagiousness encouraged forgetfulness. The swiftness of its spread and its ability to flourish then disappear before it had any real effect on the economy made it easier for
(35) people to accept, despite killing 3 percent of the nation's population.

World War I perhaps best explained the relative indifference to the pandemic. The 5 Nov 1918 issue of the *New York Times* suggested that "war had taught the people to think in terms other than individual interest and safety, and death itself had become so familiar as to lose its grimness."
(40) Such an explanation may seem quite naive, but most of those who died were young adults of the same age as those lost in combat. The obituary columns of influenza victims became one and the same blur with the war casualty list.

Influenza seemed unimportant compared with the news on the front pages
(45) of the city's newspapers. Suffragette agitation was rising as the Senate vote on the rights for women drew near, and Eugene V. Debs was on his way to jail for allegedly violating the Espionage Act. On the last day of August 1918, Babe Ruth made the headlines as he pitched a three-hitter and banged out a long double to win the American League pennant for the Boston Red Sox.
(50) It was apparently of no consequence that on the same day the first cases of flu were recognized among Navy personnel in Boston and 26 sailors died.

The interweaving of the war and pandemic seems almost to resemble a pattern of insanity. On 11 Sept 1918 Washington officials disclosed that the Spanish Influenza had arrived in the city. On the next day 13 million men,
(55) precisely the age most likely to die of the flu, lined up all over the United States and crammed into city halls, post offices, and schools to register for the draft. "It was a gala flag-waving affair everywhere including Boston where 96,000 registered then sneezed and coughed on one another.

(60) The epidemic did not kill the ranks of the famous and powerful. Perhaps if Woodrow Wilson or someone of like stature had died, the world might have remembered. It killed the daughter of General Edwards of the 26th Division of the American Expeditionary Forces, but not the general. It killed the daughter of Samuel Gompers, president of the American Federation of Labor, but left America's most powerful labor leaders alive.

(65) On the level of organizations and institutions, the Spanish Influenza had little impact. It did spur great activity among medical scientists and their institutions, but this was the single great exception. It did not lead to great changes in government, armies, and corporations. It had little influence on the course of political and military events because it affected all sides

(70) equally.

Carla R. Morrisey, RN, BSN

11. It can reasonably be inferred that the primary function of the first sentence (lines 1–2) is to:

   A. suggest that folklore is a second-rate medium for recording significant historical events.
   B. emphasize the author's surprise about the place in history of the influenza epidemic of 1918.
   C. establish that the author believes that the seriousness of the 1918 influenza epidemic has been overrated.
   D. caution the reader that the account of the influenza epidemic in the rest of the passage is not altogether factual.

12. When the author asserts that the influenza epidemic of 1918 "never inspired awe" (line 7), she most likely means that:

   F. due to poor communication, specific facts about the intensity of the epidemic was unavailable.
   G. Americans lacked the ability to grasp the seriousness of the epidemic.
   H. Americans somehow remained relatively insensitive to the gravity of the epidemic.
   J. the death toll in America paled next to the number of deaths abroad.

13. The main function of the second paragraph (lines 8–13) in relation to the passage as a whole is to:

   A. contrast the epidemic's effect on Americans with its effects on citizens of other countries.
   B. shift the passage to a discussion of the mysterious causes of the epidemic.
   C. criticize America's indifference toward the catastrophic epidemic.
   D. provide a framework for comprehending the people's response to the epidemic.

14. Based on the passage, which of the following statements best explains the mystery of America's "complacency" (line 10) toward the epidemic?

    F. In 1918, people were generally accustomed to periods of large-scale sickness and death.

    G. America was spared the worst of the epidemic; many more people died in other parts of the world.

    H. Compared to other epidemics, the 1918 influenza was relatively mild.

    J. Few Americans were personally affected by the epidemic.

15. By using the phrase "technologically advanced" (line 16), the author expresses her belief that:

    A. America is better prepared today to battle a deadly flu epidemic than it was in 1918.

    B. technology played almost no part in the lives of Americans in 1918.

    C. the advent of technology has reduced the likelihood of a deadly flu epidemic in today's America.

    D. advanced technology could have prevented, or at least diluted, the effects of the influenza outbreak in 1918.

16. Which of the following does NOT reasonably reflect the function of the fourth paragraph (lines 20–21) in relation to the passage as a whole?

    F. To alert the reader that the discussion is about to shift from factual to hypothetical.

    G. To summarize briefly the main point of the previous three paragraphs.

    H. To concede that it is difficult to pinpoint the specific reason for America's reaction to the 1918 epidemic.

    J. To provide evidence that contradicts an important point made earlier in the passage.

17. The tone of the passage suggests that the author's personal view of America's attitude toward the influenza epidemic of 1918 is that of:

    A. admiration that the people did not panic or overreact to the crisis.

    B. astonishment over America's apathy.

    C. puzzlement that the epidemic failed to evoke a more robust response.

    D. disgust over Americans' indifference toward a terrible calamity.

18. Based on the passage, which of the following best describes the spread of influenza across the United States during 1918–1919?

    F. It swept across the land from east to west.

    G. It progressed much like the 19th century epidemics of typhoid, cholera, and other diseases.

    H. The symptoms of infection came and went relatively quickly.

    J. The victims of the disease were mostly children and old people.

19. According to the passage, the single greatest benefit that emerged from the 1918 influenza epidemic was:

   A. a flurry of medical research.
   B. an increase of enlistments into the armed forces.
   C. more enthusiasm for the United States to enter World War I.
   D. the recognition of America's ability to endure great hardship.

20. The primary purpose of the last two paragraphs of the passage (lines 59–70) is to make the point that the influenza epidemic:

   F. had no effect on celebrities or people in power.
   G. took its greatest toll on ordinary people.
   H. victimized people at random.
   J. preyed mostly on people serving in the military.

Passage 3

HUMANITIES: *This passage is excerpted from "The Parisian Stage," an essay written for a London newspaper late in the nineteenth century by the American author Henry James.*

It is impossible to spend many weeks in Paris without observing that the theater plays a very important part in French civilization; and it is impossible to go much to the theater without finding it a copious source of instruction as to French ideas, manners, and philosophy. I supposed that I had a certain
(5) acquaintance with these complex phenomena, but during the last couple of months I have occupied a great many orchestra chairs, and in the merciless glare of the footlights I have read a great many of my old convictions with a new distinctness. I have had at the same time one of the greatest attainable pleasures; for, surely, among the pleasures that one deliberately seeks and
(10) pays for, none beguiles the heavy human consciousness so totally as a first-rate evening at the *Théâtre Français*. It was the poet Gray, I believe, who said that his idea of heaven was to lie all day on a sofa and read novels. He, poor man, spoke while *Clarissa Harlowe* was still the fashion, and a novel was synonymous with an eternity. A much better heaven, I think, would be
(15) to sit all night on a theater seat (if they were only a little better stuffed) listening to Delaunay, watching Got, or falling in love with Mademoiselle Desclée.
   An acted play is a novel intensified; it realizes what the novel suggests, and, by paying a liberal tribute to the senses, anticipates your possible complaint
(20) that your entertainment is of the meager sort styled "intellectual." The stage throws into relief the best gifts of the French mind, and the *Théâtre Français* is not only the most amiable but the most characteristic of French institutions. I often think of the inevitable first sensations there of the "cultivated foreigner," let him be as stuffed with hostile prejudices as you
(25) please. He leaves the theater crying, Ah, France is the civilized nation *par*

excellence. Such art, such finish, such grace, such taste, such a marvelous exhibition of applied science, are the mark of a chosen people, and these delightful talents imply the existence of every virtue. His enthusiasm may be short and make few converts; but certainly during his stay in Paris, whatever
(30) may be his mind in the intervals, he never listens to the traditional *toc-toc-toc* which sounds up the curtains in the Rue Richelieu's theaters, without murmuring, as he squares himself in his chair and grasps his opera glasses, that, after all, the French are prodigiously great!

I shall never forget a certain evening in the early summer when, after a
(35) busy, dusty, weary day in the streets, staring at charred ruins and finding in all things a vague aftertaste of gunpowder, I repaired to the *Théâtre Français* to listen to Molière's *Mariage Forcé* and Alfred de Musset's *Il ne Faut Jurer de Rien*. The entertainment seemed to my travel-tired brain what a perfumed bath is to one's weary limbs, and I sat in a sort of languid ecstasy of
(40) contemplation and wonder—wonder that the tender flower of poetry and art should bloom again so bravely over blood-stained pavements and fresh made-up graves.

Molière is played at the *Théâtre Français* as he deserves to be—one can hardly say more—with the most ungrudging breadth, exuberance and verve,
(45) and yet with a kind of academic harmony and solemnity. Molière, if he ever drops a kindly glance on Monsieur Got and Monsieur Coquelin, must be the happiest of immortals. To be read two hundred years after your death is something; but to be acted is better, at least when your name does not happen to be Shakespeare and your interpreter the great American (or,
(50) indeed, the great British) tragedian. Such powerful, natural, wholesome comedy as that of Molière certainly never was conceived, and the actors I have just named give it its utmost force. I have often wondered that, in the keen and lucid atmosphere which Molière casts about him, some of the effusions of his modern successors should live for an hour. Alfred de Musset,
(55) however, need fear no neighborhood, and his *Il ne Faut Jurer*, after Molière's tremendous farce, was like fine sherry after strong ale. Got plays in it a small part, which he makes a great one, and Delaunay, the silver-tongued, the ever-young, and that plain robust person and admirable artist, Madame Nathalie, and that divinely ingenuous ingénue, Mademoiselle Reichemberg. It would
(60) be a poor compliment to the performance to say that it might have been mistaken for real life. If real life were a tithe as charming it would be a merry world.

21. Which of the following descriptions most accurately and completely represents this passage?

   A. The author's fond recollections of his experience in Paris
   B. An evocative and affectionate appreciation of French theater
   C. A detailed and objective critique of the *Théâtre Français*
   D. An abstract and scholarly appraisal of Molière's plays

22. All of the following are clearly identified in the passage as actors EXCEPT:

    F. Delaunay.
    G. Got.
    H. de Musset.
    J. Reichemberg.

23. Which of the following quotations best expresses the main point of the passage?

    A. " . . . in the merciless glare of the footlights I have read a great many of my old convictions with a new distinctness."
    B. "An acted play is a novel intensified."
    C. "The stage throws into relief the best gifts of the French mind."
    D. "Such powerful, natural, wholesome comedy as that of Molière certainly was never conceived."

24. As it is used in line 13, the word *poor* most nearly means:

    F. deprived.
    G. poverty-stricken.
    H. ill.
    J. lazy.

25. It can be most reasonably concluded from the author's allusions to conditions in Paris (lines 34–42) that:

    A. it was difficult for him to get around in the city.
    B. the city was undergoing a construction boom.
    C. the city suffered from the aftereffects of war.
    D. a major fire had destroyed most of the city.

26. Given the information in the passage, one can infer all of the following about Molière EXCEPT that:

    F. his works serve as a model for other playwrights.
    G. his plays were meant to provoke laughter.
    H. as a playwright, he was not as great as Shakespeare.
    J. he was a founder of the *Théâtre Français*.

27. It can be inferred from the passage that the author most highly valued which of the following about the theater?

    A. Intellectual stimulation
    B. Escaping from the dirty, crowded streets of Paris
    C. Sitting in a comfortable seat
    D. Learning about French culture

28. During his evening at the theater to see a play by Molière and a play by de Musset, which of the following features of the performances does the author observe?

    F. The superiority of Molière's play
    G. The beauty of the language
    H. The realism of the performances
    J. The audience's appreciation

29. By asserting that Molière "deserves" (line 43) to be played at the *Théâtre Français*, the author implies that:

    A. the best of French plays should be performed in the best of French theaters.
    B. Molière's plays should be performed only in large halls like the *Théâtre Français*.
    C. the tradition of performing Molière at the *Théâtre Français* should continue.
    D. Molière expected his plays to be performed at the *Théâtre Français* after his death.

30. Which of the following best describes the reactions of a hypothetical "cultivated foreigner" (line 24) who sees a play at the *Théâtre Français* for the first time?

    F. France must be envied by cultured people everywhere.
    G. To attend a play in Paris is extraordinarily eye-opening.
    H. France epitomizes refinement in art and culture.
    J. The French theater causes people to lose their prejudices.

Passage 4

NATURAL SCIENCE: *This passage, from a publication titled "The Health Effects of Caffeine," discusses the complexities of governing the use of caffeine in food and beverages.*

The use of beverages that contain caffeine has been debated for centuries. In almost every part of the world where coffee and tea have been available, religious or government leaders have tried to ban or restrict its use. All such attempts, until the present time, lacked scientific credibility.

(5)   New studies linking caffeine use to central nervous system problems and birth defects in test animals have prompted scientists and policy makers in the U.S. to reconsider caffeine's regulatory status. This is a complex task, however, because caffeine is regulated under three different sections of the Federal Food, Drug, and Cosmetic Act. It is a natural ingredient in coffee and

(10)   tea, a food additive in soft drinks, and an added ingredient in over-the-counter drugs.

    Foods containing any poisonous or hazardous substance are defined as adulterated and prohibited by the Food and Drug Act. However, foods which naturally contain harmful substances may be permitted if the amount of the

(15) substance does not ordinarily injure health. Thus, foods containing caffeine, like coffee and tea, are approved despite caffeine's adverse health effects at high dose levels.

As a food additive, caffeine is regulated as a "generally recognized as safe" (GRAS) substance. Because of this regulatory status, food processors are not
(20) required to prove caffeine's safety before adding it to their products. Instead, caffeine's long and widespread history of use is considered sufficient proof of safety. The Food and Drug Administration (FDA) has published rules which limit the amount of caffeine that can be added to foods.

Caffeine is also an ingredient in many over-the-counter drug preparations.
(25) The Food and Drug Act specifies that all drug ingredients must be safe and effective for their intended use. Caffeine is an effective stimulant which is why it is added to pain relievers and cold remedies. When used as directed in these medicines, caffeine is safe and presents no health hazards to the vast majority of consumers.

(30) Recently, a committee of the Federation of American Societies for Experimental Biology reviewed all the scientific evidence on caffeine. Based on caffeine's stimulant properties, this advisory group recommended to the FDA that caffeine be removed from the so-called GRAS list of food chemicals. As a result of this and petitions from other groups, the FDA proposed new
(35) regulations for caffeine use. If these proposals are adopted, caffeine will be removed from the GRAS list. The FDA will also amend the current rule which governs the mandatory use of caffeine in certain soft drinks.

Removing caffeine from the GRAS list would have little immediate impact on consumers. This action would require food processors to gather
(40) additional scientific evidence to prove caffeine is safe. During the time needed to conduct proper studies, caffeine would still be available for use. However, if food processors fail to provide this required information, or find additional evidence that caffeine is harmful, the FDA could take action to ban the use of caffeine as a food additive.

(45) Current regulations state that caffeine must be an ingredient in "cola" and "pepper" flavored soft drinks. About 10 percent of the caffeine in these products is obtained naturally from cola nuts, the chief flavoring agent. The remaining 90 percent is added caffeine.

Current rules do not require added caffeine other than that naturally
(50) present in cola nuts. Added caffeine is an optional ingredient which must be listed on the product label. The caffeine derived from cola nuts does not have to be listed among the product ingredients.

Under the new FDA proposal, both natural and added caffeine would become optional ingredients in cola and pepper soft drinks. Thus, manufacturers could
(55) make an essentially caffeine-free product by decaffeinating cola nuts and avoiding added caffeine. The new proposal would also require that any caffeine, whether added or natural, be listed on the ingredient label.

These proposed regulations would not affect the use of caffeine in non-cola soft drinks or in over-the-counter drugs.

American Council on Science and Health, "The Health Effects of Caffeine"

31. Based on information in the passage, the main function of the Food and Drug Administration is to:

   A. make the rules governing the use of caffeine in food products.
   B. force soft-drink manufacturers to keep caffeine in colas and pepper-flavored drinks to a minimum.
   C. make laws that must be followed by food manufacturers.
   D. control caffeine in food products and in over-the-counter drugs.

32. As used in line 13, the word *adulterated* means:

   F. prohibited.
   G. unlawful.
   H. lethal.
   J. dangerous.

33. Despite its apparent hazards, caffeine has not been banned from food products because:

   A. it has a long and honorable history of use.
   B. consumers can avoid caffeine by reading ingredient labels.
   C. small quantities have never been proved harmful.
   D. food manufacturers claim that the caffeine controversy has been exaggerated.

34. "Generally recognized as safe" (line 18) is:

   F. a description of caffeine used by manufacturers of food products.
   G. an official government designation applied to any number of food products.
   H. a phrase called "misleading" by the Federation of American Societies for Experimental Biology.
   J. the FDA's stamp of approval that appears on pain relievers and cold remedies containing caffeine.

35. According to the passage, which of the following is most likely to occur if caffeine is taken off the GRAS list?

   A. All soft drinks will be caffeine-free.
   B. Manufacturers will stop adding caffeine to food products.
   C. All food products containing caffeine will be labeled with a warning to consumers.
   D. Manufacturers of food products will be required to prove that caffeine is harmless.

36. Based on the passage, when changes are planned in federal food and drug laws, the government must consider the interests of all of the following groups EXCEPT:

    F. pharmacists who dispense over-the-counter drugs.
    G. manufacturers of food products.
    H. consumer groups.
    J. scientists and other researchers.

37. Soft drink manufacturers prefer to use the natural caffeine found in cola nuts in their products because:

    A. caffeine makes drinks more flavorful.
    B. consumers enjoy the lift they get from caffeine.
    C. caffeine helps to keep the drink from spoiling.
    D. it is one of the least expensive food additives.

38. According to the passage, past attempts to ban drinks containing caffeine have failed because:

    F. people refused to change their habits.
    G. the tea, coffee, and soft drink industries were too strong.
    H. opponents of caffeine lacked scientific data to back up their objections.
    J. lawmakers could not agree on how to enforce anti-caffeine regulations.

39. Which of the following properties of caffeine is not indicated by information in the passage?

    A. It is addictive.
    B. It has been shown to be hazardous to laboratory animals.
    C. It is found in nature.
    D. It makes sick people feel better.

40. The author of the passage seems primarily concerned with:

    F. procedures for amending the Federal Food, Drug, and Cosmetic Act.
    G. the future of caffeine in foods.
    H. warning readers about the hazards of caffeine.
    J. the need for more scientific investigation of the effects of caffeine.

Answers to Reading Test begin on page 330.

TEST 1: SCIENCE REASONING

Time —35 minutes
40 Questions

> **_Directions:_** This test consists of several distinct passages. Each passage is fol-
> lowed by a number of multiple-choice questions based on the passage.
> Study the passage, and then select the best answer to each question. You
> are allowed to reread the passage. Record your answer by blackening the
> appropriate space on the Answer Sheet.

Passage 1

The charts below show the composition of the average American diet as it exists
(dark bar) and as recommended by the National Research Council (light bar) in
1987. (These recommendations have since been challenged, but their validity has
not been decisively disproved.) Chart I gives the total intake in grams per day of
each nutrient class. Chart II gives the energy distribution among the nutrients, the
fraction of total kilocalories in each nutrient. Chart III gives the fraction of each
nutrient by weight.

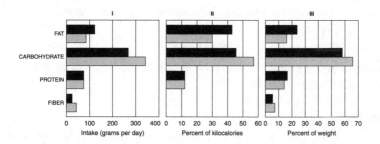

1. If the recommendations of the National Research Council were followed, people
   would eat:

   A. more protein and less fiber.
   B. more protein and less fat.
   C. more carbohydrate and less fat.
   D. more fiber and less protein.

2. Comparison of the charts shows that:

   F. most of our food energy comes from proteins.
   G. we now get much more of our energy from carbohydrates than from fats.
   H. we cannot increase our energy intake by eating more fiber.
   J. the quantities of fats and carbohydrates in our present diet are
      approximately equal.

3. According to these recommendations, what comment can be made about the present American diet?

   A. It is overloaded with carbohydrates.
   B. It has too much fiber.
   C. It does not have enough fat.
   D. It contains the proper amounts of proteins.

4. If the recommendations for a changed diet were followed, our diet would have about:

   F. four times as much carbohydrate as fat.
   G. two and a half times as much carbohydrate as fat.
   H. equal amounts of carbohydrate and fat.
   J. nearly twice as much carbohydrate as fat.

5. Comparison of the percent by weight of the different nutrients in the diet and the percent of energy each supplies shows that:

   A. 1 gram of fat supplies more energy than 1 gram of carbohydrate.
   B. 1 gram of carbohydrate supplies more energy than 1 gram of protein.
   C. 1 gram of protein supplies about three times as much energy as 1 gram of fiber.
   D. 1 gram of carbohydrate supplies more energy than 1 gram of fat.

Passage 2

A bacteriologist is investigating the use of glucose by a type of bacterium as a source of energy in spore formation.

Experiment 1

The bacteria are grown in a nutrient solution containing a supply of glucose. When the glucose has been largely depleted, the contents of each cell shrink away from the cell wall and form a spore, which is highly resistant to environmental damage of all kinds.

Experiment 2

A culture of the bacteria is grown in a medium containing little glucose. The bacteria use the glucose as they grow, but do not form spores when the glucose has been depleted.

Experiment 3

A culture is grown in a medium containing ample glucose, but the cells are removed while there is still plenty of glucose in the medium. They are placed in distilled water, and form spores in about 13 hours.

Experiment 4

As in Experiment 3, cells are transferred from a glucose-rich medium to distilled water. If glucose is added to the water 5 hours later, the cells never form spores. If glucose is added 10 hours after the transfer, spores form 3 hours later.

6. Comparison of Experiments 1 and 2 shows that:

    F. glucose is necessary for the bacteria to grow.

    G. the process of spore formation needs a good supply of glucose.

    H. bacteria can protect themselves against unfavorable conditions by forming spores.

    J. spore formation is inhibited by large concentrations of glucose.

7. A reasonable hypothesis from Experiment 3 is that:

    A. distilled water promotes the formation of spores.

    B. distilled water retards the formation of spores, but does not prevent it.

    C. bacterial cells store enough glucose to form spores.

    D. bacterial cells are able to form spores without any source of glucose.

8. Experiment 1 indicates that spore formation is stimulated by deprivation of glucose. Considering the results of Experiment 4, how long must this deprivation continue?

    F. Less than 5 hours

    G. Somewhere between 5 and 10 hours

    H. More than 10 hours

    J. At least 13 hours

9. The results of Experiments 3 and 4 show that withholding glucose for 10 hours:

    A. causes spores to form 3 hours later.

    B. delays the formation of spores for 3 hours.

    C. speeds up the formation of spores by 5 hours.

    D. has no effect at all on the formation of spores.

10. Which of the following experiments would NOT be useful in efforts to learn more about the way bacteria use sugars in spore formation?

    F. Repeat Experiment 4 adding glucose to the water at various times after transferring the bacteria to distilled water.

    G. Repeat Experiments 3 and 4 using bread molds instead of bacteria as the spore-forming organism.

    H. Repeat Experiments 1 and 2 using other kinds of sugar than glucose as energy sources.

    J. Repeat Experiment 2 using different concentrations of glucose.

11. According to these experiments, what condition must be met in order for this type of bacterium to form spores?

    A. A good supply of glucose in the medium, followed by a period in which there is little glucose
    B. A steady supply of glucose in high concentration
    C. A prolonged period of glucose deprivation
    D. A sudden increase in the concentration of glucose in the medium

Passage 3

The graph below represents the number of boys born per thousand girls in the United States for a period of years (= males; = females).

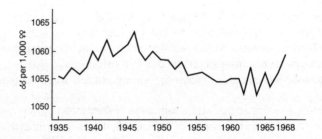

The following graph represents the sex ratio at birth as a function of the ages of the parents. (Sex ratio is the fraction of all newborn babies that are male.)

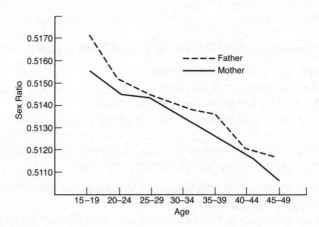

12. The sex ratio in 1946 was:

    F. 1063/2063
    G. 1063/2000
    H. 1063/2
    J. 1063/1052

13. Which general statement is true?

   A. There has been a steady decline in the proportion of male births.
   B. At all times, more boys than girls are born.
   C. The total number of male births decreases with the age of the parents.
   D. Younger parents have more children than older ones.

14. A couple in their early twenties decide that they would like to have a girl. Would it be a good idea for them to wait five years?

   F. No. The probability of having a boy goes up substantially in those years.
   G. Yes. The probability of having a girl goes up substantially during those years.
   H. No. The increased probability of having a girl is too small to make much difference.
   J. Yes. The probability of having a boy goes down substantially during those years.

15. The sex ratio increased during the war years 1940 to 1946, and started to rise again during the Vietnam War in 1967. This increase has been noticed during war years in other countries and during other wars. A possible explanation is that:

   A. many men are killed in wars, so the number of male babies increases to compensate.
   B. as younger men die in the war, more babies are fathered by older men.
   C. prolonged periods of sexual abstinence favor the production of the kinds of sperm that produce male babies.
   D. this may be merely a statistical accident with no real significance.

16. Is it the age of the mother or of the father that is most significant in determining the sex ratio?

   F. The father, since the line for the father lies always above the line for the mother.
   G. The mother, since the line for the mother lies always below that for the father.
   H. They affect the result equally, since both follow the same pattern of decrease with age.
   J. It is impossible to tell from the graphs because people generally tend to marry spouses of about their own age.

Passage 4

The chart below gives the number of diagnosed cases of diabetes in the United States from the years 1958 to 1995, and projections for total cases in 2000 and 2025.

The Diabetes Explosion

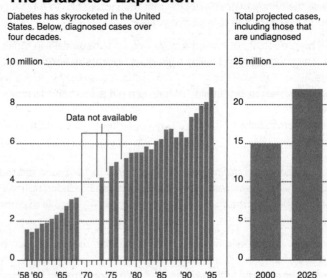

Diabetes has skyrocketed in the United States. Below, diagnosed cases over four decades.

Total projected cases, including those that are undiagnosed

17. Between 1960 and 1975, the number of diagnosed cases of diabetes in the United States increased by:

    A. 1 million.   C. 3 million.
    B. 2 million.   D. 6 million.

18. The biggest observed annual increase in the number of diagnosed cases occurred in:

    F. 1994.   H. 1986.
    G. 1991.   J. 1973.

19. It was projected that the number of undiagnosed cases in the year 2000 would be about:

    A. 15 million.   C. 10 million.
    B. 13 million.   D. 5 million.

20. An important possible source of error in any conclusion reached from the graphs is that:

    F. data from several years are unavailable.
    G. methods of diagnosis may have improved over the years.
    H. some years show very little increase, while in others, the increase is large.
    J. there is no clue as to the reason for the increase.

21. One assumption made in preparing this chart is that:

A. there is some increasing factor in the American lifestyle that promotes the development of diabetes.

B. the trend to increase the incidence of diabetes in the American population will continue for some years.

C. the health of Americans is increasingly at risk from diabetes.

D. undiagnosed cases of diabetes are on the increase.

Passage 5

The ideal gas law is a rule for determining approximately the relationship between volume, pressure, and temperature of a gas. Experiments were done to determine how closely real gases obey this law. These are the gases that were tested, with their respective molecular weights:

Gas	Formula	Molecular weight
helium	H_e	4
nitrogen	N_2	28
carbon dioxide	CO_2	44
xenon	X_e	54
sulfur dioxide	SO_2	64

Experiment 1

A 1-liter steel cylinder is equipped with a pressure gauge and a thermometer. The cylinder is filled with various gases, in turn, at a temperature of 200 K (−73.2°C). The gases are heated and the pressure is measured at various temperatures. The chart on the next page shows the pressure as calculated from the ideal gas law, and the actual pressures measured at various temperatures.

Temperature (kelvins)	Pressure (atmospheres)					
	Ideal	H_e	N_2	CO_2	Xe	SO_2
200	1.00	1.00	1.00	1.00	1.00	1.00
500	2.50	2.50	2.51	2.52	2.52	2.54
800	4.00	4.00	4.02	4.04	4.05	4.08
1100	5.50	5.50	5.53	5.56	5.57	5.62
1400	7.00	7.00	7.03	7.07	7.09	7.16
1700	8.50	8.50	8.54	8.59	8.62	8.70
2000	10.00	10.00	10.05	10.11	10.14	10.24

Experiment 2

The same gases are inserted, in turn, into a 1-liter cylinder fitted with a piston that can be pushed in to decrease the volume of the gas, thus increasing the pressure. The cylinder is kept in a water bath that keeps the temperature constant. The pressure is measured at various volumes. As before, the value calculated from the ideal gas law is also listed in the table.

Volume (cm³)	Pressure (atmospheres)					
	Ideal	He	N_2	CO_2	Xe	SO_2
1000	1.00	1.00	1.00	1.00	1.00	1.00
500	2.00	2.00	2.12	1.98	1.97	1.96
250	4.00	4.02	4.25	3.93	3.85	3.82
100	10.00	10.12	12.32	9.01	8.86	8.55
50	20.00	20.52	25.84	15.87	15.28	13.87

22. The cylinder in Experiment 2 was equipped with a piston. Why was none used in Experiment 1?

   F. It was not needed because the temperature was allowed to vary.
   G. It could not be installed because a thermometer and a pressure gauge were needed.
   H. In Experiment 1, volume was kept constant.
   J. It would interfere with the pressure gauge readings.

23. Of the gases measured, which behaves LEAST like an ideal gas?

   A. Helium, always
   B. Nitrogen, always
   C. Sulfur dioxide always
   D. It depends on the nature of the experiment

24. What is the most probable explanation of the fact that no deviation from the ideal gas pressure was found when the volume of helium was reduced from 1000 cm3 to 500 cm3?

   F. Helium maintains its pressure until its volume is reduced more substantially.
   G. There was an unpredicted drop in the temperature during the experiment.
   H. Measurements were made only to the nearest hundredth of an atmosphere.
   J. Helium is an ideal gas at moderate pressures.

25. As the volume is decreased at constant temperature, what would result from using the ideal gas law to predict the pressure?

   A. Constant minor overestimation.
   B. Either overestimation or underestimation depending on the gas being studied.
   C. Constant underestimation.
   D. Unpredictably, either overestimation or underestimation.

26. Why does the first row of the data for both experiments show a value of 1.00 atmosphere regardless of which gas was used?

    F. Every experiment was started arbitrarily at ordinary atmospheric pressure.
    G. At low pressure, all gases obey the ideal gas law.
    H. Deviations from the ideal gas law are very small at low pressure, and were not detected.
    J. This is pure coincidence; that value might be different if other gases were tried.

27. Which of the following hypotheses is suggested by the data?

    A. The ideal gas law gives the most accurate predictions at high temperatures and pressures.
    B. The ideal gas law always gives a good approximation of pressure.
    C. As a gas is compressed at constant temperature, its pressure is inversely proportional to its volume.
    D. At constant volume, gases with the smallest molecules obey the ideal gas law most closely.

Passage 6

If the highest possible pile is made of a quantity of loose material, the sides of the pile form an angle with the horizontal called the *angle of repose*. This is the largest angle at which the material can remain without having some of it slide down.

The angles of repose of various materials were measured with the apparatus shown in the sketch below. The material, such as sand, is placed in a hopper and then allowed to flow through an opening until it piles up below. The angle of the side of the pile is then measured.

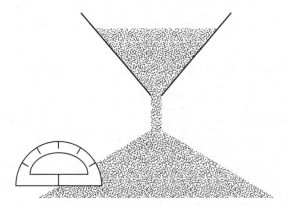

Experiment 1

Smooth, dry, quartz sand, of water-abraded, rounded grains, is sieved and sorted according to size. Each size, separately, is fed into the hopper, and the angle of repose is measured for each.

Grain size (mm)	Angle of repose (degrees)
0.1	18
0.5	20
1.0	23
1.5	25
2.0	28
2.5	30

Experiment 2

Crushed marble, made of dry, sharp-angled fragments of many sizes, is sieved and sorted by size. Each size is then fed separately into the hopper.

Grain size (mm)	Angle of repose (degrees)
1.0	28
1.5	30
2.0	33
2.5	35
3.0	36
3.5	37
4.0	37

Experiment 3

Using the same method, the angles of repose of various other kinds of materials are measured:

Substance	Angle of repose
Crushed marble, unsorted, mixed 1.0–4.0 mm	37
Crushed marble, 3.0 mm, mixed 3 parts to 1 part water	12
Water-abraded sand, 3.0 mm, mixed 3 parts to 1 part water	12
Garden soil, dry	27
Garden soil, slightly moist	46
Garden soil, saturated with water	14

28. The angle of repose depends on:

    F. the size of the particles only.
    G. the particle shape and water content of the material only.
    H. the particle size and shape and the water content of the material.
    J. the particle size and water content of the material only.

29. The experimenter compares the results of Experiments 1 and 2, and concludes that the angle of repose is larger for sharp-angled than for rounded particles. This conclusion might be challenged because:

    A. there was no control of the chemical composition of the material.
    B. no experiments were done with rounded particles larger than 2.5 mm.
    C. no experiments were done with angled particles smaller than 1.0 mm.
    D. all angles of repose were measured as accurate to only the nearest whole degree.

30. What is a reasonable hypothesis based on the trials in Experiments 2 and 3?

    F. Wet sand will pile up in taller piles than an equal quantity of dry sand.
    G. As a pile of water-saturated garden soil dries out, it will slump to form a lower, wider pile.
    H. Natural abrasion of sand, mixed with water, causes its angle of repose to decrease.
    J. In a dry sample of mixed sizes, the angle of repose depends on the size of the largest fragments in the mixture.

31. In hilly or mountainous regions, landslides occur during the rainy season. According to the results of these experiments, why is this so?

    A. Water flowing downhill carries soil along with it.
    B. When materials are mixed with water, the angle of repose becomes smaller.
    C. Water abrades the soil particles and makes them smooth and round.
    D. The slope of the hillsides is less than the angle of repose in the dry season.

32. The results of Experiment 2 suggest a relationship between angle of repose and particle size of angled fragments of marble. What additional kind of material might be used to test this hypothesis?

    F. Crushed feldspar, sorted at 3.0 mm
    G. Marble particles 3.0 mm wide, abraded to produce rounding
    H. Sharp-angled marble fragments 5.0 mm wide
    J. Rounded marble particles 3.0 mm wide

33. A company in the business of supplying building and paving materials keeps various kinds of sand and gravel piled up in storage. For equal amounts of material, which of the following materials would use the largest amount of land space?

    A. Beach sand, consisting of rounded grains
    B. Builders' sand, consisting of sharp-angled grains
    C. Crushed stone, consisting of sharp-angled particles
    D. River gravel, consisting of well-rounded particles

Passage 7

It has been found that a chemical called acrylamide is found in many foods and that it is produced when starch is heated to high temperatures, as in baking or especially in frying foods. Two scientists differ as to the appropriate course of action for dealing with this.

Scientist 1

The recent discovery that acrylamide is widespread in the foods we eat poses a major threat to the health of the community. Acrylamide is known to produce cancer in dogs, and is suspected of doing the same in humans. The chemical is widespread in water, and the U.S. Environmental Protection agency has set a standard of tolerance of 0.12 micrograms in a glass of drinking water.

While there is no acrylamide in a boiled potato, a serving of french fries can have over 80 micrograms of it. Breakfast cereals are prepared at high temperatures, and have substantial amounts of acrylamide. Even a slice of bread, baked in the normal way, has more acrylamide than the flour that went into it. Frying uses higher temperatures than baking, and accordingly fried foods have the highest levels.

The danger posed by acrylamide has been brought to the courts. In California, some fast-food outlets are being sued for violation of the state law that requires manufacturers to warn consumers of toxic chemicals in their food. Plaintiffs will argue that most chemical carcinogenics in dogs also promote the formation of cancer in humans. This would put acrylamide into the dangerous chemical category.

Tests are underway to determine what levels of acrylamide pose a serious threat to people, but it is extremely difficult to get reliable data. While these studies are being made it is prudent to eat less fried food, and particularly to eat no foods that are deep fried or burned. Meanwhile, research chemists are studying the production of acrylamide in food, perhaps leading to a method of preventing its formation in the cooking of our favorite foods.

Scientist 2

Acrylamide is a systemic poison, but the lethal dose is thousands of times higher than any that might be gotten in our food. True, it produces cancer in dogs when fed to them in extraordinarily high doses, but it has not been linked to cancer in humans.

Eating is never completely risk-free. Acrylamide is one of many substances in our food that may be detrimental to our health. We are constantly exposed to many kinds of chemicals in our food. Most are natural substances, intrinsic parts of the metabolism of the animals and plants that make up our diet. Plants of the nightshade family, including potatoes, tomatoes, and eggplant, contain solanine, the same deadly poison as in nightshade and loco weed. Other substances have been added to our food by our agricultural and processing practices. Just about any of them could be poisonous, and many carcinogenic, if the dose is high enough.

The crucial question about any of these substances is whether the concentration is high enough to cause concern. In the case of acrylamide, there is no real information about the dosage level in food that might be dangerous. Even the level of acrylamide considered acceptable by the Environmental Protection Agency is based on educated guesswork, not hard data. There is really no reason to single it out for special attention; it is just one of a multitude of trace chemicals in our food whose danger level is unknown. The best advice is to eat a balanced, varied diet, with no special concentration on any one food. French fries, in moderation, can be included.

34. Both scientists agree that:

    F. our foods contain many dangerous substances.
    G. many of our foods contain acrylamide.
    H. the standard of the Environmental Protection Agency is too low.
    J. there is too much acrylamide in our food.

35. The chief point of disagreement between the two scientists is whether:

    A. acrylamide is naturally present in the food or is introduced artificially.
    B. acrylamide has been shown to cause cancer in dogs.
    C. acrylamide is present in larger amounts in fried foods.
    D. we should modify our diets to take account of the presence of acrylamide in the food.

36. Scientist 1 might respond to Scientist 2 by saying:

    F. the levels of acrylamide in fried foods are very high.
    G. while the evidence is not in, it is a good idea to err on the side of caution.
    H. since acrylamide is a known carcinogen, it should be kept out of all food we eat.
    J. the amount of acrylamide in our food is too small to present a danger.

37. What additional information would be needed to resolve the differences between the two scientists?

    A. What level of acrylamide in the food constitutes a danger of causing cancer?
    B. What foods contain large amounts of acrylamide?
    C. What other chemicals found in food are carcinogenic?
    D. How much fried food does the average person eat?

38. Scientist 2 points out that tomatoes and potatoes:

    F. naturally contain acrylamide in small quantities.
    G. should be labeled with a warning of their poison content.
    H. are examples of foods containing negligible amounts of poison.
    J. like fried foods, should be eaten in small quantities only.

39. If called as an expert witness in a hearing to determine whether foods should be labeled with acrylamide content, what would Scientist 2 be most likely to say?

    A. The levels of acrylamide in food are too low to constitute a danger.
    B. In the present state of our knowledge, there is no more reason to label acrylamide content than many other chemicals.
    C. To be conservative about the issue, foods should be labeled with acrylamide content.
    D. The issue cannot be decided until more information is available.

40. When this disagreement becomes public knowledge, an important outcome might be:

    F. a ban on the sale of fried foods.
    G. reexamination of the laws requiring labeling of foods containing hazardous substances.
    H. public disgrace of one or the other of the scientists.
    J. a law requiring that foods containing acrylamide be labeled as such.

Answers to Science Reasoning Test begin on page 330.

MODEL WRITING TEST (Optional)

Time —30 minutes

<u>Directions:</u> Please write an essay in response to the topic below. During the 30 minutes allowed, develop your thoughts clearly and effectively. Try to include relevant examples and specific evidence to support your point of view. A plain, natural style is best. The length of your essay is up to you, but quality should take precedence over quantity. Be sure to write only on the assigned topic.

TOPIC: The senior class in your school traditionally picks the graduation speaker. This year's seniors chose Mr. Gans, a highly controversial community figure who habitually finds fault with the high school's curriculum and staff.

In spite of the seniors' vote, the principal has forbidden Gans to speak. For one thing, Gans's presence threatens to spoil the occasion. Also, at a school board meeting last year Gans got into a fistfight with an assistant principal and was permanently barred from the school campus.

Terry F., senior class president, opposes the principal's decision and vows to organize a boycott of graduation unless the principal changes his mind. Most seniors don't really care whether Gans speaks or not, but Terry is a very close friend of yours and asks you to support him. To complicate the issue, your family considers your graduation a major milestone and has invited out-of-town relatives to come and see you get your diploma.

What will you do? On lined paper, write an essay that explains your decision.

ANSWER KEYS AND ANALYSIS CHARTS

Test 1: English

1. D	20. H	39. B	58. H
2. H	21. B	40. H	59. B
3. A	22. H	41. A	60. H
4. J	23. C	42. F	61. C
5. C	24. F	43. D	62. J
6. J	25. B	44. H	63. B
7. C	26. J	45. A	64. H
8. J	27. B	46. F	65. B
9. D	28. G	47. B	66. H
10. H	29. C	48. F	67. B
11. B	30. H	49. C	68. G
12. H	31. D	50. J	69. A
13. C	32. J	51. D	70. J
14. F	33. D	52. H	71. D
15. C	34. H	53. B	72. G
16. G	35. A	54. J	73. C
17. A	36. H	55. A	74. H
18. G	37. B	56. H	75. B
19. D	38. F	57. D	

ANSWER ANALYSIS CHART			
Skills	Questions	Possible Score	Your Score
Usage/Mechanics			
Punctuation	3, 9, 14, 17, 24, 48, 55, 62, 66, 68	10	
Basic Grammar and Usage	1, 2, 6, 19, 21, 23, 34, 50, 53, 69, 70, 71	12	
Sentence Structure	8, 11, 26, 29, 31, 39, 41, 43, 44, 49, 51, 52, 56, 57, 58, 59, 63, 67	18	
Rhetorical Skills			
Strategy	4, 5, 10, 13, 18, 30, 35, 38, 47, 65, 72, 73	12	
Organization	7, 15, 20, 25, 27, 28, 42, 45, 64, 74, 75	11	
Style	12, 16, 22, 32, 33, 36, 37, 40, 46, 54, 60, 61	12	

Total: 75

Number Correct: _____

Test 2: Mathematics

1. D	16. H	31. B	46. H
2. H	17. D	32. H	47. C
3. E	18. G	33. A	48. H
4. H	19. C	34. H	49. C
5. D	20. H	35. D	50. K
6. K	21. B	36. H	51. C
7. A	22. F	37. B	52. K
8. J	23. B	38. J	53. C
9. E	24. J	39. C	54. J
10. G	25. B	40. K	55. E
11. A	26. F	41. D	56. J
12. H	27. C	42. F	57. D
13. A	28. H	43. D	58. F
14. J	29. A	44. H	59. D
15. B	30. G	45. C	60. K

ANSWER ANALYSIS CHART					
Content Area	**Skill Level**			**Possible Score**	**Your Score**
	Basic Skills	**Application**	**Analysis**		
Pre-Algebra Algebra	1, 8, 15, 27, 45, 52, 53, 55	2, 3, 6, 9, 13, 16, 23, 31, 34, 35, 37, 39	4, 11, 25, 28	24	
Intermediate Algebra Coordinate Geometry	17, 29, 30, 44, 48, 51, 56	5, 7, 22, 24, 26, 32, 57	18, 19, 41, 47, 60	19	
Geometry	10, 38, 40, 43, 50	12, 14, 21, 33, 36, 42, 54, 58		13	
Trigonometry	20, 46	49, 59		4	

Total: 60

Number Correct: _____

Test 3: Reading

1. C	9. A	17. C	25. C	33. H
2. H	10. G	18. H	26. J	34. G
3. C	11. B	19. A	27. D	35. D
4. G	12. H	20. H	28. G	36. F
5. A	13. D	21. B	29. A	37. A
6. G	14. F	22. H	30. H	38. H
7. B	15. C	23. C	31. C	39. A
8. J	16. J	24. F	32. D	40. G

ANSWER ANALYSIS CHART				
Passage Type	Referring	Reasoning	Possible Score	Your Score
Prose Fiction	1, 2, 5, 6	3, 4, 7, 8, 9, 10	10	
Social Studies	15, 18, 19	11, 12, 13, 14, 16, 17, 20	10	
Humanities	22, 28, 30	21, 23, 24, 25, 26, 27, 29	10	
Natural Science	32, 33, 38, 39	31, 34, 35, 36, 37, 40	10	

Total: 40

Number Correct: _____

Test 4: Science Reasoning

1. C	11. A	21. B	31. B
2. H	12. F	22. H	32. H
3. D	13. B	23. C	33. A
4. F	14. H	24. H	34. G
5. A	15. C	25. B	35. D
6. G	16. J	26. F	36. G
7. C	17. C	27. D	37. A
8. G	18. G	28. H	38. H
9. D	19. D	29. A	39. B
10. G	20. G	30. J	40. G

ANSWER ANALYSIS CHART					
Kind of Question	Skill Level			Possible Score	Your Score
	Understanding	Analysis	Generalization		
Data Representation	1, 12, 13, 17, 18	2, 3, 16, 19, 20	4, 5, 14, 15, 21	15	
Research Summaries	6, 22, 23, 26, 28	7, 8, 9, 24, 25, 29	10, 11, 27, 30, 31, 32, 33	18	
Conflicting Viewpoints	34, 35, 36	37, 39	38, 40	7	

Total: 40

Number Correct: _____

DETERMINING YOUR COMPOSITE SCORE

To calculate your composite score (not including the Writing Test) follow these directions:
1. On the form below fill in the first column of blanks with the number of correct answers on each test.
2. Multiply each number by 36 and divide the product by the number of questions on each test. The results are your scale scores.
3. Add up your scale scores and divide by 4. The result should be rounded to the nearest whole number to determine your composite score.

	Number of correct answers			Scale score
English	_____ $\times$ 36 =	_____ $\div$ 75 =		_____
Math	_____ $\times$ 36 =	_____ $\div$ 60 =		_____
Reading	_____ $\times$ 36 =	_____ $\div$ 40 =		_____
Science	_____ $\times$ 36 =	_____ $\div$ 40 =		_____

Total _____ $\div$ 4 = _____

Composite Score

PERFORMANCE EVALUATION CHART				
Rating	English	Mathematics	Reading	Science Reasoning
Excellent	66–75	54–60	35–40	36–40
Very good	54–65	44–53	29–34	29–35
Above average	45–53	30–43	24–28	20–28
Below average	36–44	21–29	19–23	14–19
Weak	25–35	14–20	14–18	9–13
Poor	0–24	0–13	0–13	0–8

No test can give you a totally precise measurement of your academic achievement. Rather, think of your composite score as the mid-point in a range of scores that can vary one or more points in either direction. A composite score of 27, for example, means that you scored somewhere between 25 and 29.

Answer Explanations

Test 1: English

1. **(D)**

The singular subject *one* requires a singular verb, so A and C are wrong. Choice B is incorrect because both the verb *totaled* in the same sentence and the verb in question refer to the year 1999, which is in the past.

2. **(H)**

An objective-case pronoun is required after the preposition *of;* hence choices F and G are wrong. The comma in G and J is unnecessary.

3. **(A)**

The dash is appropriately employed here to dramatize the pathos of *or can.*

4. **(J)**

The first sentence of the paragraph mentions *images*, and therefore calls for description.

5. **(C)**

To present an orderly and economical review of both nursing home extremes, with details characteristic of each type, the best choice of those given is the comparison/contrast strategy.

6. **(J)**

The adverbial clause *than they once were* helps maintain the sequence of tenses in this paragraph.

7. **(C)**

This passage is characterized by quick summaries and sparse detail. It would not be consistent with the rest of the passage to include detailed material.

8. **(J)**

The clause *many of them are unclean and unhealthy* is the best choice because the pronoun them refers to the existing *nursing homes*; the other choices introduce a new subject.

9. **(D)**

Parallel adjectives occurring before a noun must be separated by commas.

10. **(H)**

The paragraph is about conditions within nursing homes; the other options touch on related but basically irrelevant subject matter.

11. **(B)**

If the noun *qualities* is used as the subject (A and C), the introductory phrase becomes a dangling participle. *Interested parties* is a better choice of subject than *the patient* (D) because, as the passage makes clear, choosing a home is usually a family undertaking.

12. **(H)**

The phrase *behooves us* (F) is archaic; *best suits us* (G) and *is not a bad idea* (J) depart from the serious tone of the passage.

13. **(C)**

This article is almost journalistic in style, given to quick summary and unembellished detail. Only a sparse summary paragraph would be appropriate in this context.

14. **(F)**

The relative pronoun *which,* preceded by a comma, is needed to introduce a nonrestrictive clause.

15. **(C)**

Paragraph 5 begins with the phrase *For these reasons.* With a quick scanning of the passage, it is clear that the reasons referred to are given at the end of paragraph 3, and that paragraph 5 should follow.

16. **(G)**

The metaphor in this sentence is that of a loom; the verb *can be woven* maintains the metaphor.

17. **(A)**

The dash correctly sets off examples.

18. **(G)**

The term *cultural activities* is the focus of this passage, and yet it is not clearly defined.

19. **(D)**

The antecedent of the pronoun in question is *rural people*.

20. **(H)**

Paragraphs 1 and 2 both deal with the concept *cultural activities* and belong together.

21. **(B)**

The word that is needed before the last clause to make it a noun clause. The conjunction *when* (A), *because* (C), or *for* (D) cannot introduce a clause used as a predicate nominative.

22. **(H)**

Farther is used to refer to a measurable distance or space. *Further* means "greater in measure, time, and degree."

23. **(C)**

Use digits for dates; years are almost never spelled out.

24. **(F)**

Hyphenate a compound adjective that precedes the noun it modifies.

25. **(B)**

The first sentence suggests that a heritage festival may begin economic development, but the paragraph as it stands does not pick up that idea.

26. **(J)**

The preceding sentence makes the point that farms in this area employ a third of the work force. Here the conjunction should be *thus* for that reason. The other options suggest contrast, which is meaningless at this point.

27. **(B)**

The repetition of the preposition *in* and the noun *farming* or *production* results in parallelism.

28. **(G)**

The three awkward options employ the phrase *spent its years of existence* in various versions, all of them unnatural sounding. The correct choice is a strong, clear statement.

29. **(C)**

The pattern in this paragraph has been to give each accomplishment of the Council its own sentence. Also, choices A and B are run-on sentences.

30. **(H)**

The paragraph does describe economic development, but does not explain how cultural activities "supplied the drive" for such development.

31. **(D)**

All choices but *most distinguished* are either awkward or unnecessarily wordy.

32. **(J)**

The most familiar idiom using these words is *method of playing*.

33. **(D)**

Fine shades of meaning separate these words, but the only sound one to use here is *developed*.

34. **(H)**

The participle *accomplished* modifies *musician* and is the most sensible choice. *More accomplished* compares *two musicians*.

35. **(A)**

Classifying and dividing is the strategy that permits a writer full scope in exploring three or more subjects in one passage.

36. **(H)**

The only meaningful choice is *quality*.

37. **(B)**

Only the correct phrase conveys meaning that relates to the point being made in the paragraph—the difference in sound between the human and the mechanical piano player.

38. **(F)**

The statements listing the three most distinguished musical instruments and comparing a player piano with a concert pianist are very opinionated; the passage would be more substantial if some hard data accompanied the opinions.

39. **(B)**

The statement about the organ is in contrast to those made about other instruments, so a transitional word that indicates contrast is required.

40. **(H)**

The other options are either redundant (F and G) or inferior (J).

41. **(A)**

The word *whether* signals the need for the subjunctive mood at this point.

42. **(F)**

Two characteristics are being considered in the sentence; *pressure* ("hard or soft") and speed ("slow or quick"), so each pair should remain intact, the pairs separated by a comma.

43. **(D)**

Most acutest (A) is a double superlative, *more acute* (C) incorrectly suggests that there are only two listeners, and *acute* (B) lacks the force of the superlative and is therefore misleading.

44. **(H)**

All the other options are awkward and wordy, and are not parallel to *the human organist*.

45. **(A)**

The point of the passage is to persuade potential buyers to consider an organ.

46. **(F)**

This phrase, not a common one in popular English, is appropriate to the deliberate, reflective tone of this passage.

47. **(B)**

Quoted material, when available, is one of the most effective means of representing a person's thought and personality.

48. **(F)**

The dash is appropriately used here to punctuate a parenthetical aside.

49. **(C)**

This sentence consists of three clauses ending with predicate adjectives— *broad*, (*constantly*) *accumulating*, and *intricate*—each adjective (or adverb) modified by the adverb *so*. The only choice that maintains this parallel structure is C.

50. **(J)**

The pronoun *that* does not have a clear antecedent here, so a noun should be supplied.

51. **(D)**

This sentence is in contrast to the ideas expressed in the preceding paragraph.

52. **(H)**

The past tense is appropriate here. The historical present is usually reserved for discussions of what a writer says or thinks in a particular work of literature.

53. **(B)**

The pronoun *this* almost never is adequate by itself; a noun is required here for clarity.

54. **(J)**

This sentence is incompatible in style and content with the rest of the passage.

55. **(A)**

Coordinate sentences, that is, two independent clauses joined by a coordinate conjunction, must be separated by a comma.

56. **(H)**

Three parallel prepositional phrases modify the noun *problems* in this sentence: problems *of variability, (of) heredity, and (of) isolation.* The object of the preposition is always a noun.

57. **(D)**

The pronoun *that* refers to the plural *problems*, and the verb must agree. The tense must be the present perfect (*have occupied*) since the reference is to the immediate past.

58. **(H)**

The present tense is required because natural selection still stands as a general law today.

59. **(B)**

The statement regarding Darwin's place in history *depends upon* how his theories are regarded in the future—thus the need for the *if* clause at the beginning of the sentence.

60. **(H)**

If nothing else, this passage praises Darwin.

61. **(C)**

The use of *throughout* is clear and direct; the other options are awkward or wordy.

62. **(J)**

There is no need for any punctuation between the parallel adjectives *governmental* and *(many) private.*

63. **(B)**

The verb *described* completes the parallel pair of passive verbs *are ... marked* and *(are) described.*

64. **(H)**

The word *unattended* in the preceding clause renders the word *unsupervised* redundant.

65. **(B)**

An understanding of the word *antiquities* is essential to an understanding of the passage.

66. **(H)**

Word combinations containing an *-ly* word should not be hyphenated. The adverb *carefully* modifies the adjective *carved,* and there should be no hyphen between them.

67. **(B)**

Instead of a subordinating conjunction indicating *cause,* what is required here is a conjunction signaling *contrast* (*vertical* versus *horizontal*).

68. **(G)**

The comma separating items in a series must come after the parenthesis.

69. **(A)**

Spell out an occasional number that can be expressed in one or two words; with the exception of numbers from twenty-one through ninety-nine, which are always hyphenated, compound numbers are not hyphenated.

70. **(J)**

In which is the only prepositional phrase that draws focus to the structure itself.

71. **(D)**

The subject of this sentence is the singular *series.*

72. **(G)**

This passage has all the characteristics of a scholarly paper, including assumption of some sophistication on the part of the reader, close attention to detail, and esoteric language.

73. **(C)**

The paragraph begins with a bare statement about a significant prehistoric stone, one of the earliest erected. A younger reader would require more detail to understand the significance of such early monoliths.

74. **(H)**

This paragraph seems to have two main ideas needing development: the stone first mentioned, and the development of Christianity in the region. With two main ideas, the structure is deeply flawed.

75. **(B)**

The paragraph needs either to be restructured or to be introduced by a general statement that could accommodate both of the ideas present in the paragraph.

Answer Explanations

Test 2: Mathematics

1. **(D)**

Although 3.14 is frequently used as an approximate for π, it is rational since it represents $3\frac{14}{100}$ or $\frac{314}{100}$.

2. **(H)**

Jane's score increased 9 points. The question is "9 is what percent of 72?" $A = 9$, P is unknown, and $B = 72$.

$$\frac{P}{100} = \frac{9}{72}\left(=\frac{1}{8}\right)$$
$$8P = 100$$
$$P = 12.5$$

3. **(E)**

$4^2 - 3 - 5 \cdot 8 - 2[(-3) - (-7)]$
$= 4^2 - 3 - 5 \cdot 8 - 2[(-3) + 7]$
$= 4^2 - 3 - 5 \cdot 8 - 2[4] = 16 - 3 - 5 \cdot 8 - 2[4]$
$= 16 - 3 - 40 - 8 = 13 - 40 - 8 = -27 - 8$
$= -35$

4. **(H)**

The space at the top is found by multiplying 4 times $2\frac{3}{8}$ and then subtracting the product from 10.

$$10 - 4\left(2\frac{3}{8}\right) = 10 - 4\left(\frac{19}{8}\right) = 10 - \frac{19}{2}$$

$$= 10 - 9\frac{1}{2}$$

$$= \frac{1}{2}$$

(This means $\frac{1}{2}$ of a foot.)

$\frac{1}{2}$ (12 inches) = 6 inches

5. **(D)**

The inequality $|x - 4| \le 2$ is easily translated to
$$-2 \le x - 4 \le 2$$
$$2 \le x \le 6$$
The solution set of this inequality is the set of numbers between 2 and 6 inclusive. These are the numbers shown on the graph.

6. **(K)**

The lowest common denominator is the least common multiple of the denominators.
$4x^2y = 2 \cdot 2x^2y$
$6xy^2 = 2 \cdot 3xy^2$
$15xy = 3 \cdot 5xy$
   To find the lowest common denominator, use each factor the greatest number of times it appears in any of the factorizations.
$$LCD = 2 \cdot 2 \cdot 3 \cdot 5x^2y^2 = 60x^2y^2$$

7. **(A)**

The greatest common factor must be factored out first.
$4x^3 - 24x^2 + 36x$
$= 4x(x^2 - 6x + 9)$
   (a perfect square trinomial)
$= 4x(x - 3)^2$

8. **(J)**

Composite numbers are whole numbers, greater than 1, that are not prime. The numbers 1 and $\frac{2}{3}$ are not greater than 1, and 43 and 83 are prime, but $57 = (3)(19)$.

9. **(E)**

$$\begin{aligned} ab^2 - (a - b) &= (-3)4^2 - [(-3) - 4] \\ &= (-3)4^2 - [(-3) + (-4)] \\ &= (-3)4^2 - (-7) \\ &= (-3)\,16 - (-7) \\ &= -48 - (-7) \\ &= -48 + 7 = -41 \end{aligned}$$

10. **(G)**

Among the choices only $\angle DFG$ has its vertex on the circle.

11. **(A)**

$D =$		$r \cdot$	t
Jon	$40\left(x + \frac{1}{2}\right)$	40	$x + \frac{1}{2}$
Joel	$50x$	50	x

The distances are equal, so the equation is
$$40\left(x + \frac{1}{2}\right) = 50x$$

12. **(H)**

Three or more parallel lines cut transversals in the same proportion, so

$$\frac{AB}{BC} = \frac{DE}{EF}$$

$$\frac{2}{6} = \frac{DE}{5}$$

$$6(DE) = 10$$

$$DE = \frac{5}{3} = 1\frac{2}{3}$$

13. **(A)**

$$5\frac{1}{8} \qquad 5\frac{3}{24}$$

$$-3\frac{5}{6} \qquad -3\frac{20}{24}$$

The LCD is 24.

$$4\frac{27}{24}$$

Borrow $\frac{24}{24}$ from the 5

$$-3\frac{20}{24}$$

and add to $\frac{3}{24}$.

$$1\frac{7}{24}$$

14. **(J)**

Use the Pythagorean Theorem to first find the length of $\overline{AC}$.

$$(AC)^2 = 1^2 + 1^2$$
$$AC = \sqrt{2}$$

Then $\overline{AC}$ is a leg of $\triangle ACD$. Another application of the Pythagorean Theorem yields

$$(AC)^2 + (CD)^2 = (AD)^2$$
$$(\sqrt{2})^2 + 1^2 = (AD)^2$$
$$2 + 1 = (AD)^2$$
$$AD = \sqrt{3}$$

Repeating this process two more times gives $AF = \sqrt{5}$.

15. **(B)**

The last digit must be in the ten thousandths position.

16. **(H)**

$$3 - (x - 5) = 2x - 3(4 - x)$$
$$3 - x + 5 = 2x - 12 + 3x$$
$$8 - x = 5x - 12$$
$$8 = 6x - 12$$
$$20 = 6x$$
$$x = \frac{20}{6} = \frac{10}{3}$$

17. **(D)**

An arithmetic sequence is one whose successive terms differ by a constant. Only in D is there a constant difference between terms.

18. **(G)**

If the exponent on i is a multiple of 4, the result is 1. But if there is a remainder when the exponent is divided by 4, then it has the following values:

rem	in
1	i
2	-1
3	$-i$
0	1

$53 \div 4 = 13$ rem 1, so $i^{53} = i$.

19. **(C)**

This is a combination problem. The number of combinations of n things taken r at a time is given by the formula:

$$_nC_r = \frac{n!}{(n - r)!r!}$$

The number of 4-person committees is

$$_{10}C_4 = \frac{10!}{(10-4)!4!}$$

$$= \frac{10!}{6!4!}$$

$$= \frac{10 \cdot 9 \cdot 8 \cdot 7 \cdot 6!}{6! \cdot 4 \cdot 3 \cdot 2 \cdot 1}$$

$$= \frac{10 \cdot 3 \cdot 7}{1} = 210$$

20. **(H)**

Since $\dfrac{\sqrt{3}}{4} < 1$ and the range of the secant function is $\{x \mid x > 1 \text{ or } x < -1\}$,

there are no angles for which $\sec x = \dfrac{\sqrt{3}}{4}$.

21. **(B)**

If two chords intersect in a circle, the product of the segments of one chord equals the product of the lengths of the segments of the other.

$$3x = (5)(2)$$
$$= 10$$
$$x = 3\dfrac{1}{3}$$

22. **(F)**

The sample space consists of all 52 cards in the deck. The event "drawing a heart" can be satisfied by any one of the 13 hearts.

$$P(\text{Heart}) = \dfrac{13}{52} = \dfrac{1}{4}.$$

23. **(B)**

$$
\begin{aligned}
x - [3x - (1 - 2x)] &= x - [3x - 1 + 2x] \\
&= x - 3x + 1 - 2x \\
&= -4x + 1
\end{aligned}
$$

24. **(J)**

If $g(x) = 1 + x^2$, then
$g(3) = 1 + 3^2 = 1 + 9 = 10$. So
$f(g(3)) = f(10) = 2(10) - 5 = 20 - 5 = 15$

25. **(B)**

Let x = width of the rectangle.
Then $2x - 1$ = length.
 The perimeter of a rectangle is found by the formula $P = 2w + 2\ell$.
The equation is
$34 = 2x + 2(2x - 1)$
$34 = 2x + 4x - 2$
$34 = 6x - 2$
$36 = 6x$
$x = 6$

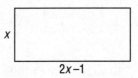

x

$2x-1$

 But $x = 6$ is the width. The question is "What is the length?"
$$2x - 1 = 2(6) - 1 = 12 - 1 = 11$$

26. **(F)**

$$2 \log_3 x - \frac{1}{2} \log_3 y + \log_3 z$$

$$= \log_3 x^2 - \log_3 \sqrt{y} + \log_3 z$$

$$= \log_3 \frac{x^2 z}{\sqrt{y}}$$

27. **(C)**

By the commutative property of addition
$$5(3 + 0) = 5(0 + 3)$$

28. **(H)**

The number of male students receiving a grade of C is $\frac{5}{6}$ of

$\frac{2}{3}$ of 27.

$$\frac{5}{6} \cdot \frac{2}{3} \cdot 27 = \frac{5}{6} \cdot 18$$
$$= 15$$

29. **(A)**

An equation of an ellipse with center at the origin, x-intercepts 3 and -3, and y-intercepts 2 and -2 is

$$\frac{x^2}{9} + \frac{y^2}{4} = 1$$

30. **(G)**

Divide both sides of the bottom equation by 2.
So the solution set is $\{(2, -3, 4)\}$.

31. **(B)**

Square both sides of the radical equation.

$$(\sqrt{x+1})^2 = (x-1)^2$$
$$x + 1 = x^2 - 2x + 1$$
$$x^2 - 3x = 0$$
$$x(x - 3) = 0$$
$$x = 0 \quad x - 3 = 0$$
$$x = 3$$

Both potential solutions must be checked in the original equation.
Check 0: $\sqrt{0+1} \overset{?}{=} 0 - 1$
$1 \neq -1$
0 is not in the solution set.
Check 3: $\sqrt{3+1} \overset{?}{=} 3 - 1$
$\sqrt{4} \overset{?}{=} 2$
$2 = 2$ The solution set is $\{3\}$.

32. **(H)**

$$\sqrt[3]{-12a^4b^2} \ \sqrt[3]{-6a^4b^2} = \sqrt[3]{72a^6b^4}$$

Now separate the radicand into cube and noncube factors.

$$= \sqrt[3]{8a^6b^3 \cdot 9b}$$
$$= 2a^2b \sqrt[3]{9b}$$

33. **(A)**

If m $\angle ABD = 62°$, then the measure of arc $AD = 124°$. If m $\angle BDC = 28°$, then the measure of arc $BD = 56°$. So the measure of arc $ADB = (56 + 124)° = 180°$, and the measure of an angle inscribed in a semicircle $= 90°$.

34. (H)

Multiply the top equation by 2 and the bottom equation by 5.

$$2(2x - 5y) = 13(2)$$
$$5(3x + 2y) = 10(5)$$

This gives

$$4x - 10y = 26$$
$$\underline{15x + 10y = 50}$$
$$19x = 76$$
$$x = 4$$

Substituting $x = 4$ into either equation gives $y = -1$. The solution is $\{(4, -1)\}$.

35. (D)

Use the substitution method

$$\left(\begin{array}{c} 2x + 3y = 12 \\ y = \dfrac{-2}{3}x + 5 \end{array} \right)$$

Substitute for y in the first equation

$$2x + 3\left(\frac{-2}{3}x + 5\right) = 12$$

$$2x - 2x + 15 = 12$$

$$15 = 12$$

False. The solution is empty, { }.

36. (H)

The measure of $\angle ABC = \frac{1}{2}(200 - 160)° = 20°$.

$\triangle ABC$ is an isosceles triangle, so m$\angle ACB = 80°$. Since a radius is perpendicular to a tangent at the point of tangency, m$\angle OCA = (90 - 80)°$.

37. (B)

In reality the shaded portion represents the big square minus $\frac{3}{4}$ of the circle minus a small 2×2 square.

$$9^2 - \frac{3}{4}(\pi 2^2) - 2^2 = 81 - 3\pi - 4$$
$$= 77 - 3\pi$$

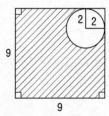

38. **(J)**

There can be only one obtuse angle in a triangle.

39. **(C)**

Multiply the numerator and denominator by xy:

$$\frac{xy\left(\dfrac{x}{y} - \dfrac{y}{x}\right)}{xy\left(\dfrac{1}{x} - \dfrac{1}{y}\right)} = \frac{x^2 - y^2}{y - x}$$

$$= \frac{(x - y)(x + y)}{y - x}$$

$$= -(x + y) \text{ because } y - x$$
$$\text{and } x - y \text{ are opposites.}$$

40. **(K)**

All four statements are false.

41. **(D)**

$|x - 3| > 2$ is equivalent to

$$x - 3 > 2 \text{ or } x - 3 < -2$$
$$x > 5 \text{ or } x < 1$$

42. **(F)**

First find AE.

$$(BE)(ED) = (AE)(EC)$$

$$(1)(2) = AE\left(\frac{1}{2}\right)$$

$$AE = 4$$

Then use the Pythagorean Theorem.

$$4^2 + 1^2 = (AB)^2$$
$$16 + 1 = (AB)^2$$
$$AB = \sqrt{17}$$

43. **(D)**

If two lines are cut by a transversal in such a way that a pair of alternate interior angles are equal, the lines are parallel.

44. (H)

The binomial expansion of $(a + b)^n$ has $n + 1$ terms.

45. (C)

The only one of these numbers that cannot be written as a fraction is $\sqrt{48}$. Note that $0.\overline{5} = 0.5555 \ldots$ is a nonterminating repeating decimal, which is rational.

46. (H)

The period of the function $y = a \tan b(x - c)$ is $\dfrac{\pi}{|b|}$. So the period of the given function is $\dfrac{\pi}{3}$ since this function can be rewritten as $y = 2 \tan 3(x - \dfrac{\pi}{6})$.

47. (C)

Let x = height of the tower. Then the distance from the ground to the bend is $\dfrac{x}{4}$, and the slanted part is $\dfrac{3x}{4}$. Use the Pythagorean Theorem:

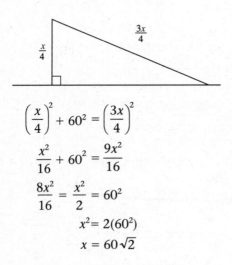

$$\left(\frac{x}{4}\right)^2 + 60^2 = \left(\frac{3x}{4}\right)^2$$

$$\frac{x^2}{16} + 60^2 = \frac{9x^2}{16}$$

$$\frac{8x^2}{16} = \frac{x^2}{2} = 60^2$$

$$x^2 = 2(60^2)$$

$$x = 60\sqrt{2}$$

48. (H)

Exponential functions do not represent conic sections.

49. **(C)**

If $\cos \theta = \dfrac{-1}{2}$ and θ is in quadrant III, then

$$\sin \theta = -\sqrt{1 - \cos^2 \theta}$$

$$= -\sqrt{1 - \left(\dfrac{-1}{2}\right)^2} = -\sqrt{1 - \dfrac{1}{4}}$$

$$= -\sqrt{\dfrac{3}{4}} = -\dfrac{\sqrt{3}}{2}$$

$$\sin 2\theta = 2 \sin \theta \cos \theta$$

$$= 2\left(\dfrac{-\sqrt{3}}{2}\right)\left(\dfrac{-1}{2}\right)$$

$$= \dfrac{\sqrt{3}}{2}$$

50. **(K)**

None of these choices is enough to prove that *ABCD* is a parallelogram.

51. **(C)**

The slope of the given line can be found from the slope-intercept form:

$$y = \dfrac{-2}{3}x + \dfrac{7}{3}$$

Since the slope is $\dfrac{-2}{3}$, the slope of the line perpendicular to it is $\dfrac{3}{2}$. Using the point-slope form of the equation of the line, we have

$$y - 1 = \dfrac{3}{2}(x - 2)$$

$$2y - 2 = 3x - 6$$

$$3x - 2y = 4$$

52. **(K)**

Square roots of negative numbers are imaginary.

53. **(C)**

Degree concerns itself only with the exponents on the *variables*. The degree of a polynomial is the greatest of the degrees of its terms. The degree of the first term is 4; of the second term, 5; and of the third, 0.

54. **(J)**

The measure of arc $AC = (360 - 220)° = 140°$. The angle formed by a chord and a tangent line is measured by half of the intercepted arc. The measure of $\angle CAD = 70°$.

55. **(E)**

0.015
$1.5 \times 10^{-2} = 0.015$
$1.5\% = 0.015$
$\dfrac{3}{200} = 0.015$
$(0.3)(0.005) = 0.0015$

56. **(J)**

Multiply the numerator and denominator by the conjugate of the denominator.

$$\frac{6(4 + \sqrt{2})}{(4 - \sqrt{2})(4 + \sqrt{2})} = \frac{6(4 + \sqrt{2})}{16 - 2} = \frac{6(4 + \sqrt{2})}{14}$$

$$= \frac{3(4 + \sqrt{2})}{7} = \frac{12 + 3\sqrt{2}}{7}$$

57. **(D)**

$|x - 5| > 2$ is equivalent to

$$x - 5 > 2 \quad \text{or} \quad x - 5 < -2$$
$$x > 7 \quad \text{or} \quad x < 3$$

58. **(F)**

The altitude to the hypotenuse of a right triangle is the mean proportional between the two segments of the hypotenuse.

$$\frac{AD}{DC} = \frac{DC}{BD}$$

$$\frac{3}{DC} = \frac{DC}{12}$$

$$(DC)^2 = 36$$

$$DC = 6$$

59. **(D)**

$\cos(-512°) = \cos(208°)$

Add 2(360°) to the angle. The reference angle is (208 − 108)°. Cofunctions of complementary angles are equal. −62° is in Quadrant IV, where the sine is negative.

60. **(K)**

$$g = \frac{k}{d^2}$$

$$64 = \frac{k}{9^2}$$

$$k = 64(81)$$

$$g = \frac{64(81)}{24^2}$$

$$= \frac{8 \cdot 8(9 \cdot 9)}{(8 \cdot 3)(8 \cdot 3)}$$

$$= 9 \qquad \text{This can be obtained easily by canceling.}$$

Answer Explanations

Test 3: Reading

1. **(C)**

Gaspar explains to the sergeant that he had "remained behind . . . to keep the enemy back while the detachment was running away." The sergeant later alludes to Gaspar's failure to rejoin the detachment after dark (lines 16–18). Nothing in the passage suggests that Gaspar ran away (A) or stayed up all night (B). Choice D states the opposite of what actually occurred; it was Gaspar who was lassoed by a mounted soldier.

2. **(H)**

The first paragraph lists Gaspar's agreeable qualities, including "mildness of character," and an "acquiescent soul." He may well have possessed the traits listed by the other choices, but they they are not mentioned in the passage.

3. **(C)**

Line 15 finds the sergeant addressing Lieutenant Santierra with "a superior smile." Later, given the order to provide water to the prisoners, the sergeant questions the need (lines 44–45). Still later he sneers at the decision to keep the prisoners alive, and D overstates the sergeant's antipathy.

4. **(G)**

It's safe to infer that the *Commandante* orders the soldiers' execution to deter other troops from deserting. Choice F cannot be correct because the troops' morale is likely to suffer as a consequence of an execution of one of their fellow soldiers. H is an equally poor choice. If anything, the Commandante's uncertainty would be more likely to save Gaspar and the others from execution instead of condemning them to death. G is totally illogical. What lesson can you teach men by killing them?

5. **(A)**

According to lines 63–65, the favor had been granted in consideration of the high position of Santierra's father and the lieutenant's distinguished family. If any of the other choices (B, C, or D) influenced the *Commandante*, they are not mentioned in the passage.

6. **(G)**

In line 10, Santierra is described as "little more than a boy." Later, he wishes to give the prisoners a drink of water. We learn at the end of the passage that he tried to gain pardons for some of the condemned men. On the other hand, Esteban, the sergeant, hits Gaspar with a stick and herds the prisoners into the guardhouse "with alacrity and zeal" (line 30). The adjutant looks "savagely" around the courtyard and orders the prisoners, whom he calls "scoundrels," to be locked up in a stifling cell. In condemning the prisoners to death "for an example" (lines 12–13), the *Commandante* shows his lack of human decency.

7. **(B)**

The text of lines 36–38 shows the guards lying around in the shade unconcerned about the welfare of the prisoners. Choice A is not mentioned in the passage. Both C and D may be true but neither is discussed in the passage.

8. **(J)**

If anything, Santierra is a misfit. Unlike the other men in his unit, he shows compassion for Gaspar and the other prisoners. Furthermore, he is still not used to "sanguinary imbecilities of a state of war" (line 11). In other words, he has not yet grown accustomed to war's bloody insanity. Rule out F because of Santierra's aversion to the inhumane treatment of the prisoners. Eliminate G because the *Commandante* respects only Santierra's prestigious family, not the lieutenant himself. H is irrelevant to the passage.

9. **(A)**

Realizing that his meddling was "futile" (line 70), Santierra regrets having pro-longed the men's agony. Had he not interfered, they would have been shot early in the day and avoided their incarceration in the guardhouse. B may seem like the answer, but Santierra does next to nothing to win a pardon for the prisoners. His loss of temper (C) appears not to bother him, and, if he feels inadequate (D), the passage neither says nor implies it.

10. **(G)**

As we learn only at the end of the passage, Santierra hurried after the *Commandante* in order to ask for the execution to be delayed. Eliminate F because the sergeant laughs out loud *before* Santierra leaves. H and J occur subsequent to Santierra's departure but are not the immediate result of the lieutenant's talk with the *Commandante*.

11. **(B)**

The sentence expresses the author's wonderment that history's third most serious worldwide plague is hardly remembered today. It has been reduced to a "folk-memory."

12. **(H)**

In context, the phrase suggests that Americans took in stride the tragic consequences of the epidemic. Many thousands died, but the country's overall reaction was dispassionate. The remainder of the passage explores the reasons why.

13. **(D)**

In the second paragraph the author begins to analyze America's tepid response to the epidemic. She describes the response as a "mystery" and as a "paradox."

14. **(F)**

Through much of the passage, the author speculates on the reasons for America's complacency: the war, the brevity of the illness that preceded death, the social and political scene at the time of the epidemic, and so forth. Only the "acceptance of epidemics as part of life" (line 20) is cited as a certainty.

15. **(C)**

The author claims that a lethal epidemic would have a significant impact on contemporary Americans because technological advances have made epidemics a rarity today.

16. **(J)**

The fourth paragraph consists of a single transitional sentence that reinforces the idea that America's ho-hum response can be partially explained by the people's fatalistic acceptance of the epidemic. The sentence further states that additional explanations are speculative rather than factual. Overall, the sentence suggests that the author is groping for answers rather than declaring outright that she knows exactly why America responded as it did. (J) is the best answer because there is nothing in the sentence that contradicts earlier material.

17. **(C)**

At one point in the passage, the author comments that Americans failed to grant the epidemic "the notoriety it deserved" (line 24), suggesting that America's reaction ought to have been more forceful. In addition, lines 44–49 hint that the author doesn't quite understand how Americans could have been more consumed by daily headlines, including the results of a baseball game, than by the deadly consequences of the flu epidemic. Then, too, the author calls the enlistment of millions of men into the armed forces after the flu arrived in Washington a "pattern of insanity."

18. **(H)**

The author makes the point in lines 33–35 that the disease spread and disappeared swiftly—usually within a few months, according to line 25. Choices F and G are not valid because the passage does not discuss the manner in which the disease spread, nor its resemblance to previous epidemics. As for the age of victims, the passage indicates that most deaths occurred in the early adult population, mostly 18–21 year olds.

19. **(A)**

The last paragraph states that the epidemic spurred "great activity among medical scientists and their institutions." Although the epidemic inspired enlistments into the armed forces, the author makes no claim that the increase of military volunteers was beneficial in any way. On the contrary, she describes an event in Boston where 96,000 new registrants "sneezed and coughed on one another" (line 58).

20. **(H)**

In terms of the entire passage the two final paragraphs argue that the epidemic left a lackluster legacy because it killed almost no famous or powerful people. Also, "it affected all sides equally" (lines 69–70). To put it another way, had well-known people succumbed, or if it had appeared to single out a specific group or nationality, the epidemic might have become more memorable. Its randomness, in short, doomed it to near oblivion.

21. **(B)**

The author devotes virtually the entire passage to an adulation of various aspects of the French theater. Choice A is too broad; the author is fond of Paris but writes only about the theater. Eliminate C; in this passage James is neither detailed nor objective. Reject D; although James is clearly a fan of Molière's plays, he doesn't analyze them.

22. **(H)**

Because the author *listened* to Delauney and *watched* Got (see line 16), both must be performers. Likewise, Reichemberg is described in line 59 as a "divinely ingenuous ingénue." Only de Musset (see lines 54–56) is not an actor but, as the creator of *Il ne Faut Jurer*, a playwright.

23. **(C)**

To one degree or another, all the other choices merely support the idea that French theater exemplifies the best of French thought and culture, but only C conveys the substance of the passage.

24. **(F)**

The epithet "poor man" is applied to the poet Gray because he never had the opportunity to sit in the theater and enjoy performances by Delauney, Got, and others. Instead, he was stuck reading novels such as *Clarissa Harlowe*.

25. **(C)**

The phrase "charred ruins" suggests a recent fire (D), but other phrases such as "aftertaste of gunpowder" and "blood-stained pavements" indicate that the city had been ravaged by war. Neither A nor B is supported by evidence in the passage.

26. **(J)**

There is no indication in the passage that Molière founded the *Théâtre Français*. Choice F is incorrect because de Musset's play is based on Molière's farce (lines 55–56). Because Molière wrote comedies and farces, G is wrong. Nor is H a good answer because lines 47–50 suggest that Molière, although he's very, very good, is not Shakespeare's equal.

27. **(D)**

What attracted James to the theater is "finding it a copious source of instruction as to French ideas, manners, and philosophy" (line 4). It's true that B is appealing, but the theater was a refuge from the busy and dusty streets only one "certain evening in early summer" (lines 34–35). Choice A is wrong because the author enjoys the sensual rewards of a play (lines 19–20), and C is contradicted by the observation that the seats ought to be "better stuffed" (line 15).

28. **(G)**

In lines 40–41, the author admires the "tender flower of poetry." Choice F is contradicted by the author's assertion in lines 54–55 that Musset "need fear no neighborhood," suggesting that his work stacks up quite favorably against that of Molière. H is also invalid in light of the author's statement in lines 60–61 that the actors' performance could not be "mistaken for real life." J is not a good choice because the author, ignoring the rest of the audience, writes solely about his own reactions.

29. **(A)**

Earlier in the passage (lines 21–23) the author calls the *Théâtre Français* "not only the most amiable but the most characteristic of French institutions." Molière, the premier French playwright, therefore, "deserves" to be performed there. There is no evidence in the passage to support the other choices.

30. **(H)**

The author envisions the foreigner leaving the theater saying "Ah, France is the civilized nation *par excellence*" (lines 25–26). Choice F may be valid to some extent, but there is nothing about international envy in the passage. G describes the foreigner's experience but not his reaction. Likewise, J sums up what happened to the foreigner but fails to describe his reaction.

31. **(C)**

The FDA's legal powers are implied throughout the passage. Choice A states one of the agency's functions, but making rules governing caffeine is by no means its main function. Likewise, B and D fail to identify the FDA's primary function.

32. **(D)**

Adulterated usually means impure. In the context of the third paragraph, however, the use of such words as "poisonous" and "hazardous" suggests that a stronger meaning is intended, but not as strong as C, "lethal."

33. **(H)**

According to lines 13–15, caffeine in small amounts poses no threat to health. Adverse effects come only from high doses. F is a weak answer because 21st century food regulations cannot be based on obsolete data from the past. G is wrong because the FDA is supposed to protect consumers, not advise them to read ingredient labels in order to assess the safety of a product. J is not mentioned in the passage.

34. **(G)**

In line 19, the GRAS is identified as a "regulatory" designation. It comes from FDA policy via the Federal Food, Drug, and Cosmetic Act, a measure that regulates the ingredients of all processed food. The other choices—F, H, and J—misrepresent the purpose and meaning of GRAS.

35. **(D)**

Lines 39–40 state that this action "would require food processors to gather additional scientific evidence to prove caffeine is safe." Choices A, B, and C do not name an effect that would follow if caffeine were removed from the GRAS list.

36. **(F)**

The concerns and interests of pharmacists are not mentioned in the passage. Choice G is not a good choice because lines 38–45 and 53–57 deal with the impact of FDA decisions on manufacturers. H is discussed briefly in lines 38–39, and J is covered by lines 39–41.

37. **(A)**

Lines 46–57 make the point that caffeine found naturally in cola nuts is the "chief flavoring agent," of soft drinks. Choices B, C, and D are accurate descriptions of caffeine but are not discussed in the passage.

38. **(H)**

Line 4 say that previous attempts to ban or restrict the use of beverages containing caffeine "lacked scientific credibility." The issues raised by the other choices are not discussed in the passage.

39. **(A)**

The addictive quality of caffeine is not stated anywhere in the passage. That caffeine can be harmful to animals is stated in lines 5–7. That it is found in nature is suggested by its presence in coffee and tea (lines 9–10), and its presence in pain killers and cold remedies (lines 26–27) implies its salutary effects.

40. **(G)**

The passage concentrates on what will happen if regulations governing the use of caffeine are changed. The matters mentioned by choices F, H, and J play little or no part in the passage.

Answer Explanations

Test 4: Science Reasoning

1. **(C)**

The intake chart shows that the recommended carbohydrate is more than the carbohydrate consumed, and the recommended fat is less than the fat consumed. The other choices are wrong because there is no recommendation for a change in the protein.

2. **(H)**

The energy chart (II) shows that fiber supplies no energy at all. F is wrong because the energy chart shows much less energy from protein than from carbohydrates or fats. Since the chart shows about equal amounts of energy now obtained from fats and carbohydrates, G is wrong. J deals with quantity, not energy, and the intake chart (I) shows that the quantity of carbohydrates is far greater than the amount of fat.

3. **(D)**

In all these charts the two bars match perfectly for protein intake. A is wrong because the bar for recommended carbohydrate is longer than that for actual intake. Similarly, more, not less, fiber is recommended, so B is wrong. C is wrong because the recommended diet is reduced in fat.

4. **(F)**

The bars for recommended intake (chart I) show about 80 g of fat and 330 g of carbohydrate.

5. **(A)**

When the values for present diet are used, fats are about 23% of our diet by weight, and supply 43% of our energy; carbohydrates constitute 58% of our food, but give us only 45% of our energy. B is wrong because the ratio of percent by weight to energy for carbohydrates (58%/45%) is about the same as the ratio for proteins (16%/13%). C is wrong because fiber supplies no energy at all, and 3 times 0 is 0. D is the opposite of A.

6. **(G)**

In Experiment 2, where there was little glucose, the bacteria were unable to form spores. F is wrong because no data about growth were presented. H is wrong because Experiments 1 and 2 have nothing to do with the usefulness of spores. J is wrong because Experiment 1 shows that glucose actually promotes spore formation.

7. **(C)**

Since Experiment 1 shows that glucose is needed, and there is none in distilled water, it is quite likely that the bacterial cells stored glucose when it was available. A and D are wrong because Experiment 1 shows that the bacteria need glucose to form spores. B is wrong because we have no data indicating how long it took to form spores when there is plenty of glucose.

8. **(G)**

Experiment 4 shows that if glucose is added in less than 5 hours spore formation is prevented, but if it is added after 10 hours spores form anyway.

9. **(D)**

In Experiment 3, spores formed 13 hours after the cells were put into distilled water; in Experiment 4, the same thing happened, even though glucose was added after 10 hours.

10. **(G)**

Bread mold spores are entirely different from bacterial spores, and there is no reason to believe that any similarity exists in the way they are formed.

11. **(A)**

In both Experiment 1 and Experiment 3, spores were formed when a period of growth in an ample supply of glucose was followed by glucose deprivation. B is wrong because no spores are formed as long as there is plenty of glucose in the medium. Experiment 2 shows that no spores can be formed unless there is first an ample supply of glucose, so C is wrong. There is no evidence anywhere to support D.

12. **(F)**

Adding male births (1063) and female births (1000) gives a total of 2063; males are 1063 of this total.

13. **(B)**

Although the sex ratio went down, it then went up, and was always more than 0.5, which would indicate equal numbers of boys and girls. No information was given about total numbers.

14. **(H)**

While parents are in their twenties, the sex ratio decreases by only about 1 or 2 parts per thousand, not enough to take into account.

15. **(C)**

A is wrong because it is not an explanation, since it fails to suggest a mechanism by which the result is brought about. B is wrong because the second graph indicates that older men produce a smaller fraction of boys, not a larger one. D is wrong; you are told that this effect has been noticed in many wars and many countries, so it is unlikely that this result is coincidental. By elimination, C is the only feasible answer of those offered.

16. **(J)**

Since spouses are generally only a little different in age, there is no way that the graphs can distinguish the effect of the mother's age from that of the father's.

17. **(C)**

In 1960 it was about 1.5 million; in 1975, about 4.5 million.

18. **(G)**

The difference between the 1990 bar and the 1991 bar is more than one million, larger than any of the other yearly jumps. The 1973 bar is longer than the 1968 bar by the same amount, but the intervening years are missing.

19. **(D)**

If the present trend continued for another 5 years, the number of diagnosed cases would be about 10 million in the year 2000. Since the total for that year was expected to be 15 million, 5 million will be undiagnosed.

20. **(G)**

It is possible that part, or even all, of the increase is simply because more cases are being found. F is wrong; the steady increase is apparent even without those years. H is wrong because the minor fluctuations do not negate the overall trend. J is wrong because the only function of the graph is to show the trend, without ascribing any cause.

21. **(B)**

The chart predicts 22 million cases by 2025, but only 15 million in 2000. A is wrong because the chart makes no statement as to the cause of the increase. C is a valid conclusion from the chart, not an assumption. D is wrong because there is nothing in the yearly data that gives any indication of the number of undiagnosed cases.

22. **(H)**

The rigid cylinder keeps the volume of the gas constant, so that the only two variables were pressure and temperature.

23. **(C)**

Of all the gases, sulfur dioxide shows the largest difference from the ideal value in both experiments.

24. **(H)**

It is probable that the pressure rose to, say, 20.001 atmospheres, which would not have been detected at the level of accuracy to which the experiment was done. F is wrong because the pressure actually doubled when the volume dropped to half. Don't insult the experimenter by answering G. It is never safe to conclude that additional accuracy would not reveal something different, so J is wrong.

25. **(B)**

At all volumes, helium and nitrogen had higher pressures than predicted; and carbon dioxide, xenon, and sulfur dioxide had lower pressures. The result can be predicted once you know which gas is being studied.

26. **(F)**

You have to start the experiment with some gas in the cylinder, and the experimenter decides how much and at what pressure and temperature. Why bother to use anything but what is already there?

27. **(D)**

The pressure-temperature chart shows no detectable deviation for the smallest molecules (helium) and successively more for each of the larger molecules. Deviations from the ideal gas law get larger, not smaller, as the pressure goes up. C expresses the ideal gas law; the whole burden of this experiment is to test deviations from this law.

28. **(H)**

Experiments 1 and 2 show that the angle of repose increases with grain size. Comparison of these two experiments shows that sharp-angled fragments have a larger angle of repose than rounded ones. The soil samples of Experiment 3 show that water content is also involved.

29. **(A)**

The two experimental materials differ in both shape and composition of the particles, and no effort was made to distinguish between these two possible causes of the difference found. B and C are wrong because the evidence from particles from 1.0 to 2.5 mm, in both experiments, provides a clear contrast. D is wrong because the differences are of several degrees and are consistent, so accuracy of 1 degree is sufficient to produce an answer.

30. **(J)**

The angle of repose for the mixed sample of crushed marble is the same as for the largest size of the screened samples. F is wrong because the angle of repose is smaller for wet than for dry sand, so the pile of wet sand will be lower than the pile of dry. G is wrong because the angle of repose is smaller for the saturated soil; the pile becomes more stable as it dries out. H is wrong because no information is available to compare sand grains of various sizes if they are mixed with water.

31. **(B)**

The soil is piled up, possibly to its angle of repose when dry. When it gets wet, the angle of repose decreases, so the angle of the hill is larger than the new angle of repose. A is wrong because the experiments do not deal with the effects of running water. C is wrong because the particles are not abraded as they rest during the dry season. D is surely true, but it says nothing about the effect of rain.

32. **(H)**

The hypothesis must be that the angle of repose does not increase for particles beyond 3.5 mm, and this can be tested by trying larger particles.

33. **(A)**

The experiments show that small, rounded particles have the smallest angle of repose. They will form lower, flatter piles and thus will spread out more on the ground.

34. **(G)**

Both scientists agree that there is acrylamide in our food, but J is wrong because they differ on whether the amount represents a danger. F is wrong because Scientist 1 does not discuss the presence of other dangerous substances in our food. H is wrong because neither scientist discusses the EPA standard.

35. **(D)**

Scientist 2 believes that the current state of knowledge does not justify taking any action with our diet. The other points are made by Scientist 1, but Scientist 2 does not dispute any of them.

36. **(G)**

This is the recommendation made by Scientist 1. The other choices are wrong because Scientist 2 says we do not know what constitutes a dangerous level of acrylamide in the diet.

37. **(A)**

This is the main crux of Scientist 1's argument. B is wrong because this information is already available. C is wrong because information about other chemicals is not pertinent. D is wrong because any conclusions must apply to everyone, not just to the average person.

38. **(H)**

Scientist 2 cites these foods as examples of natural poisons in food in negligible quantities. A is wrong because the poison in these foods is not acrylamide. B and J are wrong because Scientist 2 believes that the amount of these substances in food is negligibly small.

39. **(B)**

The other choices are wrong because Scientist 2 believes that there is not enough information to ban acrylamide, any- more than many other substances as well.

40. **(G)**

As a result of the hearings, some legislators might feel that the topic deserves further study. F and J are wrong because none of them is likely to take such drastic action until there is more information available. H is wrong; there is no shame for a scientist to hold a contrary opinion.

Answer Explanations

Test 5: Writing (Optional)

To evaluate your essay, complete the following checklist. Focus on both the strengths and weaknesses of your essay.

	Yes!	Mostly	Hardly	No
Does the essay address the ACT prompt?	___	___	___	___
Is the topic sufficiently narrowed?	___	___	___	___
Is the essay's main idea clear?	___	___	___	___
Have you written an appealing introduction?	___	___	___	___
Does the essay sound natural?	___	___	___	___
Have you used plain words?	___	___	___	___
Have you used precise language?	___	___	___	___
Does your essay have a clear focus?	___	___	___	___
Do all parts fit together coherently?	___	___	___	___
Is each sentence accurately worded?	___	___	___	___
Have you trimmed needless words?	___	___	___	___
Do you show more than tell?	___	___	___	___
Have you used active verbs?	___	___	___	___
Is the language fresh?	___	___	___	___
Do you include verbal surprises?	___	___	___	___
Are the sentences varied?	___	___	___	___
Is sentence length balanced?	___	___	___	___
Does the essay have a distinct conclusion?	___	___	___	___
Is the essay mostly error-free?	___	___	___	___

Identify the three greatest strengths of your essay:

1. _____

2. _____

3. _____

Name three specific things that you could do to improve your essay:

1. _____

2. _____

3. _____

Circle the score your essay deserves: 6   5   4   3   2   1

ANSWER SHEET—MODEL TEST B

Directions: Mark one answer only for each question. Make marks dark. Erase completely any mark made in error. (Additional or stray marks will be counted as mistakes.)

Test 1: English

1 Ⓐ Ⓑ Ⓒ Ⓓ	26 Ⓕ Ⓖ Ⓗ Ⓙ	51 Ⓐ Ⓑ Ⓒ Ⓓ
2 Ⓕ Ⓖ Ⓗ Ⓙ	27 Ⓐ Ⓑ Ⓒ Ⓓ	52 Ⓕ Ⓖ Ⓗ Ⓙ
3 Ⓐ Ⓑ Ⓒ Ⓓ	28 Ⓕ Ⓖ Ⓗ Ⓙ	53 Ⓐ Ⓑ Ⓒ Ⓓ
4 Ⓕ Ⓖ Ⓗ Ⓙ	29 Ⓐ Ⓑ Ⓒ Ⓓ	54 Ⓕ Ⓖ Ⓗ Ⓙ
5 Ⓐ Ⓑ Ⓒ Ⓓ	30 Ⓕ Ⓖ Ⓗ Ⓙ	55 Ⓐ Ⓑ Ⓒ Ⓓ
6 Ⓕ Ⓖ Ⓗ Ⓙ	31 Ⓐ Ⓑ Ⓒ Ⓓ	56 Ⓕ Ⓖ Ⓗ Ⓙ
7 Ⓐ Ⓑ Ⓒ Ⓓ	32 Ⓕ Ⓖ Ⓗ Ⓙ	57 Ⓐ Ⓑ Ⓒ Ⓓ
8 Ⓕ Ⓖ Ⓗ Ⓙ	33 Ⓐ Ⓑ Ⓒ Ⓓ	58 Ⓕ Ⓖ Ⓗ Ⓙ
9 Ⓐ Ⓑ Ⓒ Ⓓ	34 Ⓕ Ⓖ Ⓗ Ⓙ	59 Ⓐ Ⓑ Ⓒ Ⓓ
10 Ⓕ Ⓖ Ⓗ Ⓙ	35 Ⓐ Ⓑ Ⓒ Ⓓ	60 Ⓕ Ⓖ Ⓗ Ⓙ
11 Ⓐ Ⓑ Ⓒ Ⓓ	36 Ⓕ Ⓖ Ⓗ Ⓙ	61 Ⓐ Ⓑ Ⓒ Ⓓ
12 Ⓕ Ⓖ Ⓗ Ⓙ	37 Ⓐ Ⓑ Ⓒ Ⓓ	62 Ⓕ Ⓖ Ⓗ Ⓙ
13 Ⓐ Ⓑ Ⓒ Ⓓ	38 Ⓕ Ⓖ Ⓗ Ⓙ	63 Ⓐ Ⓑ Ⓒ Ⓓ
14 Ⓕ Ⓖ Ⓗ Ⓙ	39 Ⓐ Ⓑ Ⓒ Ⓓ	64 Ⓕ Ⓖ Ⓗ Ⓙ
15 Ⓐ Ⓑ Ⓒ Ⓓ	40 Ⓕ Ⓖ Ⓗ Ⓙ	65 Ⓐ Ⓑ Ⓒ Ⓓ
16 Ⓕ Ⓖ Ⓗ Ⓙ	41 Ⓐ Ⓑ Ⓒ Ⓓ	66 Ⓕ Ⓖ Ⓗ Ⓙ
17 Ⓐ Ⓑ Ⓒ Ⓓ	42 Ⓕ Ⓖ Ⓗ Ⓙ	67 Ⓐ Ⓑ Ⓒ Ⓓ
18 Ⓕ Ⓖ Ⓗ Ⓙ	43 Ⓐ Ⓑ Ⓒ Ⓓ	68 Ⓕ Ⓖ Ⓗ Ⓙ
19 Ⓐ Ⓑ Ⓒ Ⓓ	44 Ⓕ Ⓖ Ⓗ Ⓙ	69 Ⓐ Ⓑ Ⓒ Ⓓ
20 Ⓕ Ⓖ Ⓗ Ⓙ	45 Ⓐ Ⓑ Ⓒ Ⓓ	70 Ⓕ Ⓖ Ⓗ Ⓙ
21 Ⓐ Ⓑ Ⓒ Ⓓ	46 Ⓕ Ⓖ Ⓗ Ⓙ	71 Ⓐ Ⓑ Ⓒ Ⓓ
22 Ⓕ Ⓖ Ⓗ Ⓙ	47 Ⓐ Ⓑ Ⓒ Ⓓ	72 Ⓕ Ⓖ Ⓗ Ⓙ
23 Ⓐ Ⓑ Ⓒ Ⓓ	48 Ⓕ Ⓖ Ⓗ Ⓙ	73 Ⓐ Ⓑ Ⓒ Ⓓ
24 Ⓕ Ⓖ Ⓗ Ⓙ	49 Ⓐ Ⓑ Ⓒ Ⓓ	74 Ⓕ Ⓖ Ⓗ Ⓙ
25 Ⓐ Ⓑ Ⓒ Ⓓ	50 Ⓕ Ⓖ Ⓗ Ⓙ	75 Ⓐ Ⓑ Ⓒ Ⓓ

Test 2: Mathematics

1 Ⓐ Ⓑ Ⓒ Ⓓ Ⓔ	21 Ⓐ Ⓑ Ⓒ Ⓓ Ⓔ	41 Ⓐ Ⓑ Ⓒ Ⓓ Ⓔ
2 Ⓕ Ⓖ Ⓗ Ⓙ Ⓚ	22 Ⓕ Ⓖ Ⓗ Ⓙ Ⓚ	42 Ⓕ Ⓖ Ⓗ Ⓙ Ⓚ
3 Ⓐ Ⓑ Ⓒ Ⓓ Ⓔ	23 Ⓐ Ⓑ Ⓒ Ⓓ Ⓔ	43 Ⓐ Ⓑ Ⓒ Ⓓ Ⓔ
4 Ⓕ Ⓖ Ⓗ Ⓙ Ⓚ	24 Ⓕ Ⓖ Ⓗ Ⓙ Ⓚ	44 Ⓕ Ⓖ Ⓗ Ⓙ Ⓚ
5 Ⓐ Ⓑ Ⓒ Ⓓ Ⓔ	25 Ⓐ Ⓑ Ⓒ Ⓓ Ⓔ	45 Ⓐ Ⓑ Ⓒ Ⓓ Ⓔ
6 Ⓕ Ⓖ Ⓗ Ⓙ Ⓚ	26 Ⓕ Ⓖ Ⓗ Ⓙ Ⓚ	46 Ⓕ Ⓖ Ⓗ Ⓙ Ⓚ
7 Ⓐ Ⓑ Ⓒ Ⓓ Ⓔ	27 Ⓐ Ⓑ Ⓒ Ⓓ Ⓔ	47 Ⓐ Ⓑ Ⓒ Ⓓ Ⓔ
8 Ⓕ Ⓖ Ⓗ Ⓙ Ⓚ	28 Ⓕ Ⓖ Ⓗ Ⓙ Ⓚ	48 Ⓕ Ⓖ Ⓗ Ⓙ Ⓚ
9 Ⓐ Ⓑ Ⓒ Ⓓ Ⓔ	29 Ⓐ Ⓑ Ⓒ Ⓓ Ⓔ	49 Ⓐ Ⓑ Ⓒ Ⓓ Ⓔ
10 Ⓕ Ⓖ Ⓗ Ⓙ Ⓚ	30 Ⓕ Ⓖ Ⓗ Ⓙ Ⓚ	50 Ⓕ Ⓖ Ⓗ Ⓙ Ⓚ
11 Ⓐ Ⓑ Ⓒ Ⓓ Ⓔ	31 Ⓐ Ⓑ Ⓒ Ⓓ Ⓔ	51 Ⓐ Ⓑ Ⓒ Ⓓ Ⓔ
12 Ⓕ Ⓖ Ⓗ Ⓙ Ⓚ	32 Ⓕ Ⓖ Ⓗ Ⓙ Ⓚ	52 Ⓕ Ⓖ Ⓗ Ⓙ Ⓚ
13 Ⓐ Ⓑ Ⓒ Ⓓ Ⓔ	33 Ⓐ Ⓑ Ⓒ Ⓓ Ⓔ	53 Ⓐ Ⓑ Ⓒ Ⓓ Ⓔ
14 Ⓕ Ⓖ Ⓗ Ⓙ Ⓚ	34 Ⓕ Ⓖ Ⓗ Ⓙ Ⓚ	54 Ⓕ Ⓖ Ⓗ Ⓙ Ⓚ
15 Ⓐ Ⓑ Ⓒ Ⓓ Ⓔ	35 Ⓐ Ⓑ Ⓒ Ⓓ Ⓔ	55 Ⓐ Ⓑ Ⓒ Ⓓ Ⓔ
16 Ⓕ Ⓖ Ⓗ Ⓙ Ⓚ	36 Ⓕ Ⓖ Ⓗ Ⓙ Ⓚ	56 Ⓕ Ⓖ Ⓗ Ⓙ Ⓚ
17 Ⓐ Ⓑ Ⓒ Ⓓ Ⓔ	37 Ⓐ Ⓑ Ⓒ Ⓓ Ⓔ	57 Ⓐ Ⓑ Ⓒ Ⓓ Ⓔ
18 Ⓕ Ⓖ Ⓗ Ⓙ Ⓚ	38 Ⓕ Ⓖ Ⓗ Ⓙ Ⓚ	58 Ⓕ Ⓖ Ⓗ Ⓙ Ⓚ
19 Ⓐ Ⓑ Ⓒ Ⓓ Ⓔ	39 Ⓐ Ⓑ Ⓒ Ⓓ Ⓔ	59 Ⓐ Ⓑ Ⓒ Ⓓ Ⓔ
20 Ⓕ Ⓖ Ⓗ Ⓙ Ⓚ	40 Ⓕ Ⓖ Ⓗ Ⓙ Ⓚ	60 Ⓕ Ⓖ Ⓗ Ⓙ Ⓚ

Test 3: Reading

1 Ⓐ Ⓑ Ⓒ Ⓓ	15 Ⓐ Ⓑ Ⓒ Ⓓ	29 Ⓐ Ⓑ Ⓒ Ⓓ
2 Ⓕ Ⓖ Ⓗ Ⓙ	16 Ⓕ Ⓖ Ⓗ Ⓙ	30 Ⓕ Ⓖ Ⓗ Ⓙ
3 Ⓐ Ⓑ Ⓒ Ⓓ	17 Ⓐ Ⓑ Ⓒ Ⓓ	31 Ⓐ Ⓑ Ⓒ Ⓓ
4 Ⓕ Ⓖ Ⓗ Ⓙ	18 Ⓕ Ⓖ Ⓗ Ⓙ	32 Ⓕ Ⓖ Ⓗ Ⓙ
5 Ⓐ Ⓑ Ⓒ Ⓓ	19 Ⓐ Ⓑ Ⓒ Ⓓ	33 Ⓐ Ⓑ Ⓒ Ⓓ
6 Ⓕ Ⓖ Ⓗ Ⓙ	20 Ⓕ Ⓖ Ⓗ Ⓙ	34 Ⓕ Ⓖ Ⓗ Ⓙ
7 Ⓐ Ⓑ Ⓒ Ⓓ	21 Ⓐ Ⓑ Ⓒ Ⓓ	35 Ⓐ Ⓑ Ⓒ Ⓓ
8 Ⓕ Ⓖ Ⓗ Ⓙ	22 Ⓕ Ⓖ Ⓗ Ⓙ	36 Ⓕ Ⓖ Ⓗ Ⓙ
9 Ⓐ Ⓑ Ⓒ Ⓓ	23 Ⓐ Ⓑ Ⓒ Ⓓ	37 Ⓐ Ⓑ Ⓒ Ⓓ
10 Ⓕ Ⓖ Ⓗ Ⓙ	24 Ⓕ Ⓖ Ⓗ Ⓙ	38 Ⓕ Ⓖ Ⓗ Ⓙ
11 Ⓐ Ⓑ Ⓒ Ⓓ	25 Ⓐ Ⓑ Ⓒ Ⓓ	39 Ⓐ Ⓑ Ⓒ Ⓓ
12 Ⓕ Ⓖ Ⓗ Ⓙ	26 Ⓕ Ⓖ Ⓗ Ⓙ	40 Ⓕ Ⓖ Ⓗ Ⓙ
13 Ⓐ Ⓑ Ⓒ Ⓓ	27 Ⓐ Ⓑ Ⓒ Ⓓ	
14 Ⓕ Ⓖ Ⓗ Ⓙ	28 Ⓕ Ⓖ Ⓗ Ⓙ	

Test 4: Science Reasoning

1 Ⓐ Ⓑ Ⓒ Ⓓ   15 Ⓐ Ⓑ Ⓒ Ⓓ   29 Ⓐ Ⓑ Ⓒ Ⓓ
2 Ⓕ Ⓖ Ⓗ Ⓙ   16 Ⓕ Ⓖ Ⓗ Ⓙ   30 Ⓕ Ⓖ Ⓗ Ⓙ
3 Ⓐ Ⓑ Ⓒ Ⓓ   17 Ⓐ Ⓑ Ⓒ Ⓓ   31 Ⓐ Ⓑ Ⓒ Ⓓ
4 Ⓕ Ⓖ Ⓗ Ⓙ   18 Ⓕ Ⓖ Ⓗ Ⓙ   32 Ⓕ Ⓖ Ⓗ Ⓙ
5 Ⓐ Ⓑ Ⓒ Ⓓ   19 Ⓐ Ⓑ Ⓒ Ⓓ   33 Ⓐ Ⓑ Ⓒ Ⓓ
6 Ⓕ Ⓖ Ⓗ Ⓙ   20 Ⓕ Ⓖ Ⓗ Ⓙ   34 Ⓕ Ⓖ Ⓗ Ⓙ
7 Ⓐ Ⓑ Ⓒ Ⓓ   21 Ⓐ Ⓑ Ⓒ Ⓓ   35 Ⓐ Ⓑ Ⓒ Ⓓ
8 Ⓕ Ⓖ Ⓗ Ⓙ   22 Ⓕ Ⓖ Ⓗ Ⓙ   36 Ⓕ Ⓖ Ⓗ Ⓙ
9 Ⓐ Ⓑ Ⓒ Ⓓ   23 Ⓐ Ⓑ Ⓒ Ⓓ   37 Ⓐ Ⓑ Ⓒ Ⓓ
10 Ⓕ Ⓖ Ⓗ Ⓙ   24 Ⓕ Ⓖ Ⓗ Ⓙ   38 Ⓕ Ⓖ Ⓗ Ⓙ
11 Ⓐ Ⓑ Ⓒ Ⓓ   25 Ⓐ Ⓑ Ⓒ Ⓓ   39 Ⓐ Ⓑ Ⓒ Ⓓ
12 Ⓕ Ⓖ Ⓗ Ⓙ   26 Ⓕ Ⓖ Ⓗ Ⓙ   40 Ⓕ Ⓖ Ⓗ Ⓙ
13 Ⓐ Ⓑ Ⓒ Ⓓ   27 Ⓐ Ⓑ Ⓒ Ⓓ
14 Ⓕ Ⓖ Ⓗ Ⓙ   28 Ⓕ Ⓖ Ⓗ Ⓙ

TEST 1: ENGLISH

Time —45 minutes
75 Questions

Directions: The following test consists of 75 underlined words and phrases in context, or general questions about the passages. Most of the underlined sections contain errors and inappropriate expressions. You are asked to compare each with the four answer choices. If you consider the original version best, choose letter A or F: NO CHANGE. For each question, blacken on the answer sheet the letter of the alternative you think best. Read each passage through before answering the questions based on it. (On the actual ACT, questions appear to the right of the underlined words and boxes. Here, however, questions follow the passage.)

Passage 1

(1)

Abraham Lincoln has been quoted as advising a new lawyer, "Young man, it's more important to know what cases not to take than it is to know the law." New attorneys soon learn to recognize what cases will probably be unprofitable, or they quickly end up looking for new jobs <u>in the newspaper</u>
₁
<u>because of lack of funds.</u> [2]
₁

(2)

During the initial interview with the client, the lawyer discovers whether or not a case is meritorious. Examples of cases without merit include an argument with neighbors over a pesky dog or an accident that results from the victim's own negligence, such as someone falling in a local supermarket because <u>they were drunk.</u> This <u>questionable and dubious</u>
₃   ₄
type of case can be easily seen as lacking merit, because each of the elements of a tort (a civil wrongdoing) was not present, and thus no law was broken. <u>We must all try to behave as adults as we wend our way</u>
₅
<u>through this troubled interval.</u>
₅

(3)

Finally, there is the type of case in which the prospective client has been represented in the matter by another attorney. Accepting such a case can be risky, <u>although</u> multiple lawyers are evidence of a worthless <u>case an</u>
₆   ₇

uncooperative client, or a client who does not pay his or her bill. Even if the reason for the <u>client's</u> changing attorneys is a good <u>one—let's say</u> a
₈ ₉
personality clash between the client and the prior attorney—it makes the new lawyer's task of reaching a fair settlement with the other party strategically difficult.

(4)

There are some cases that seem to have merit but are economically unfeasible for a new attorney to handle. Such cases are easy to spot once a <u>full, adequate enough disclosure</u> of the facts has been obtained from the
₁₀
client during the initial interview. One type of unprofitable case is the "hurt feelings" case stemming from an incident where the defendant has <u>been guilty of caddish behavior—but what young man in springtime has</u>
₁₁
<u>been able to resist the pull of the heart?</u>—but where the victim cannot
₁₁
prove he or she has been specifically damaged, or where damages are nominal. For instance, in an action for slander, not only is it difficult to prove <u>slander but also</u> the monetary damage to the victim resulting from
₁₂
the slanderous action may be small or even nonexistent. In these kinds of cases, a prospective client may be so righteously angered as to say that he or she does not care about the money, that it is the principle that <u>matters, that may</u> be true for the prospective client, but the attorney
₁₃
cannot pay his secretary's salary, his office rent, or his malpractice insurance <u>premium will not be reduced</u> with a client's "principle." 15
₁₄

1. **A.** NO CHANGE
   B. because of lack of funds.
   C. in the newspaper.
   D. OMIT the underlined portion.

2. Is the quotation from Abraham Lincoln an appropriate way to begin this passage?

   F. Yes, because quotations are always better than straight prose as attention-getters.
   G. No, because it misleads the reader, suggesting that Lincoln is the topic of the passage.
   H. No, because it is too short a quotation to add any meaning.
   J. Yes, because Abraham Lincoln is an authority figure, often quoted because of the truth and simplicity of his statements.

3. A. NO CHANGE
    B. he or she was drunk.
    C. they had been drinking.
    D. they were considerably under the influence.

4. F. NO CHANGE
    G. OMIT the underlined portion.
    H. questionable
    J. dubious

5. A. NO CHANGE
    B. We must all try to be mature.
    C. We must all do our best.
    D. OMIT the underlined portion.

6. F. NO CHANGE
    G. when
    H. because
    J. similarly

7. A. NO CHANGE
    B. case. An
    C. case, an
    D. case: an

8. F. NO CHANGE
    G. clients
    H. client
    J. clients'

9. A. NO CHANGE
    B. one, let's say
    C. one let's say
    D. one let's say,

10. F. NO CHANGE
    G. full, adequate disclosure
    H. full, adequate, complete disclosure
    J. full disclosure

11. A. NO CHANGE
    B. been guilty of caddish behavior—but sometimes that happens to young
        people—
    C. been guilty of wrongful behavior,
    D. OMIT the underlined portion.

12. **F.** NO CHANGE
    G. slander, but also
    H. slander. But also
    J. slander; but also

13. **A.** NO CHANGE
    B. matters that
    C. matters. That
    D. matters: that

14. **F.** NO CHANGE
    G. premium reduction
    H. premium reduced
    J. premium

15. Choose the sequence of paragraph numbers that makes the structure of the passage most logical.

    A. NO CHANGE
    B. 1, 4, 2, 3
    C. 1, 3, 2, 4
    D. 1, 2, 4, 3

Passage 2

(1)

Of all the many differences between people, there is one that goes more deeper than any other or than all combined, and that is whether the
₁₆
person are parents or not. Variations in cultural background, religion,
₁₇
politics, or education do not come close to parent versus nonparent differences. 18

(2)

Conversely, few if any knickknacks remain whole in a home with small children, the only plants left are those hanging, brown and wilted, from a
₁₉
very high ceiling. Instead, toys strewn carelessly about the various living
₂₀
areas. The somewhat disheveled rooms usually look slightly askew, since
₂₁
little ones delight in moving furniture around and are especially prone to do so unless a guest or two are expected. Walls are usually smudged
₂₂   ₂₃
with the prints of tiny hands and feet (yes, feet—don't ask me how) and decorated with children's artwork, which also adorns the refrigerator, kitchen cabinets, message center, and any other available blank space.

To a parent, there is no such thing as a sparkling clean mirror or window. <u>A handy way to clean windows and mirrors is by using crushed</u> <u>newsprint</u>. Children simply cannot keep from touching—with their hands,
24

noses, mouths, whatever—clean mirrors and windows. It has something to do with marking one's territory, I believe. 25

(3)

The very way a house is decorated proclaims the owner's status. My childless friends have plants, expensive accessories, and elegant knickknacks placed strategically about their <u>finely-furnished</u> homes.
26

Framed prints hang on their spotlessly white walls, while their mirrors and windows sparkle. 27

(4)

Another <u>distinguishing</u> great difference between people without children and
28

people with them is their attitude toward life. Before my daughter came along five years ago, I was a competent legal secretary, a faithful wife, and a person who enjoyed a quiet lifestyle interspersed with an occasional party or outing. I was <u>well-adjusted but ill-prepared</u> for chaotic living, and, I see now,
29

quite naive. 30

16. **F.** NO CHANGE
    G. deeper
    H. deep
    J. deepest

17. **A.** NO CHANGE
    B. is a parent or not.
    C. is parents or not.
    D. are a parent or not.

18. This passage was probably written for readers who:

    F. are experts in child development.
    G. are expecting a child.
    H. are general readers.
    J. are childless.

19. **A.** NO CHANGE
    B. children the only
    C. children: the only
    D. children. The

20. **F.** NO CHANGE
    G. toys strew
    H. toys were strewn
    J. toys are strewn

21. **A.** NO CHANGE
    B. disheveled rooms
    C. rooms
    D. somewhat, disheveled rooms

22. **F.** NO CHANGE
    G. after
    H. as
    J. when

23. **A.** NO CHANGE
    B. are expecting.
    C. is expected.
    D. will be expected.

24. **F.** NO CHANGE
    G. OMIT the underlined portion.
    H. Clean windows with newsprint.
    J. A handy way to clean windows is with newsprint.

25. Which of the phrases below demonstrates the intent of the writer to be whimsical and humorous?

    A. toys strewn carelessly
    B. marking one's territory
    C. sparkling clean mirror
    D. available blank space

26. **F.** NO CHANGE
    G. finely furnished
    H. finely, furnished
    J. furnished

27. Examination of paragraphs 2 and 3 reveals that the author of this passage wants to emphasize:

    A. fine art in American homes.
    B. styles and decor in contemporary homes.
    C. the impact of children on a home.
    D. indoor plant styles in contemporary American homes.

28. F. NO CHANGE
    G. OMIT this word
    H. discriminating
    J. differentiating

29. A. NO CHANGE
    B. well adjusted but ill-prepared
    C. well adjusted but ill prepared
    D. well-adjusted but ill prepared

30. Choose the sequence of paragraph numbers that makes the structure of the passage most logical.

    F. NO CHANGE
    G. 1, 3, 2, 4
    H. 1, 3, 4, 2
    J. 1, 4, 2, 3

Passage 3

(1)

By the late 1900s, the climate <u>were growing</u> slowly better for
31
incarcerated women, and the improvement in their treatment could be
directly traced to the women's rights movement. Some changes were
significant. Women reformers had argued not only that women should
<u>supervised</u> by women but also that reform could not be carried out in a jail
32
cell. By the late 19th century, women prepared for release were placed in
programs centered on development of domestic <u>roles some</u> settings were
33
cottages rather than cells. Although these conditions existed in some
prisons, the vast majority of women were placed in attics or storage space
outside of the regular prison. The effect was that women were deprived of
basic (albeit limited) resources that the male prisoners had.

Today, there are many more minority women (along with their male
counterparts) in prison. Much of this imbalance can be explained by
America's war on drugs. It is not hard to remember the crack epidemic of
the mid-1980s to the early 1990s. Media were reporting <u>it,</u> and it was
34
everywhere, on television, in *Time* magazine articles, in the newspapers,
and at local high schools. However, when one looks at the New York State
Department of Correctional Services Report (written by Clarice Feinman) on
new court commitments, one must pause, consider the figures, and realize

the awful facts of what is happening to these addicts. Consider the commitments that occurred between 1988 and 1991:

- There was a 123 percent increase in woman commitments, from 1,014 to 2,264.
- The proportion of females committed for drug offenses <u>had risen</u>
  ₃₅
  from 53 percent to 72 percent.
- Black commitments increased 166 percent, 68 percent drug-related.
- Hispanic commitments increased 1,224 percent, 87 percent drug-related.
- White commitments increased 25 percent, 44 percent drug-related. 36

(2)

Throughout history, if one wished to have a glimpse of the deprived class, a quick trip to a prison <u>is</u> the easiest solution. Today is no different:
₃₇
Prisons still house the poor and uneducated. In books and movies, rarely does one see the face of a woman prisoner. Rather, a person is more likely to see a barbarous and depraved man who, many would agree, belongs where he is. But, truthfully, prisons do not always house the barbarous and depraved: In fact, prisons usually house the weak and unfortunate. And our system of justice does not just incarcerate men: Today, there are tens of thousands of women <u>stuffing</u> into overcrowded prisons.
₃₈
The city of London established the first workhouse in an abandoned royal palace named Bridewell. The supposed function was to "care for and discipline" the "riffraff," who <u>are considered</u> a danger to the rest of society.
₃₉
England did not always throw its "riffraff" into prison; many times, the royal courts would exile them to places like Australia or the New World.

(3)

The cause of these arrest figures is debatable. While some people suggest that minorities of lower socioeconomic status might use drugs to escape the realities of unemployment and racism, some conclude that the fault is actually in how the police work in minority neighborhoods: <u>It is observed</u> that
₄₀
there is more police surveillance in minority communities, and since black and Hispanic populations are more youthful and more likely to be out in the

streets for recreation, they are more likely to be picked up for acts that might also occur in private in white, middle-class neighborhoods. Whatever the case, life in minority neighborhoods can be very dangerous and stressful, especially for young black males and females. Consider the statistics: A male black has a 1 in 2 chance of being murdered in his lifetime, and a male white, a 1 in 131 chance. A black female has a 1 in 124 chance of being murdered, while a white female has a 1 in 606 chance. And, regardless of how these young people are arrested, the real hurdles for them begin in court.

When minority defendants appear in court for the first time, one of the most important issues <u>he faces</u> is whether they will be held for trial or
₄₁
released until their next court date. As history has shown, minorities usually find themselves still in custody or facing a bail amount they cannot afford. This circumstance can be explained by, among other facts, a judge's behavior. A judge might deny bail so he or she can maintain a "positive political image" or set bail so high that the defendant cannot afford to bail out. Many times, minorities find themselves being represented by young or incompetent court-appointed counsel. Currently, it is estimated that more than 60 percent of accused felons are represented by public defenders. And just imagine what a minority defendant thinks when he or she is not on trial in front of his or her own peers. Minority women, compared with their white counterparts, "are more likely to be single, poor, and responsible for dependent children" (Feinman). Such a profile can be a disaster for a minority defendant on trial in a death penalty case. ⬚42

(4)

<u>The death penalty has a long and sordid history in the United States.</u> In the
₄₃
years between 1608 and 1993, 12,438 people were executed in the United <u>States, 287</u> of those were women. The first known woman, Jane Champion
₄₄
of Virginia, was executed in 1632. Throughout the years, many black slave women were lynched and hanged. Many times, a slave woman would be hanged for some crime because her husband had already been lynched or because he was suspected of doing something for which he would have been lynched. Clearly, the United States needs to take a long, hard look at the way we treat minorities in the prison system, as well as the guidelines for the death penalty. ⬚45

31. A. NO CHANGE
    B. are growing
    C. had grown
    D. were growing

32. F. NO CHANGE
    G. supervision
    H. be supervision
    J. be supervised

33. A. NO CHANGE
    B. roles; some
    C. roles—some
    D. roles. Some

34. F. NO CHANGE
    G. them
    H. many
    J. those judged guilty

35. A. NO CHANGE
    B. raised
    C. rises
    D. rose

36. Is the first sentence of the second paragraph in this section necessary?

    F. No. The author seems to be unfairly referring to minority women.
    G. No. The author is linking drugs with minorities.
    H. No, because the article refers only to those women who are in jail.
    J. Yes, because the facts listed in the bulleted list at the end of the paragraph argue strongly the point that there is imbalance in the numbers of minorities being imprisoned.

37. A. NO CHANGE
    B. would be
    C. would have been
    D. will have been

38. F. NO CHANGE
    G. being stuffed
    H. are being stuffed
    J. were being stuffed

39. A. NO CHANGE
    B. were considered
    C. is considered
    D. had been considered

40. F. NO CHANGE
    G. were considered
    H. is considered
    J. they observe

41. A. NO CHANGE
    B. they face
    C. he is facing
    D. he will be faced

42. Is the reference to jurors meaningful at this place in the passage?

    F. No, because it virtually changes the subject.
    G. No, because the whole passage is about minority defendants.
    H. No, because it is about the problems of jurors, not the defendants.
    J. Yes, because it is a specific example of a "hurdle" minority defendants face in court.

43. How do you regard the supporting material that follows this statement?

    A. It is not effective because it calls up negative images about women.
    B. It is effective because it hammers home the point of the long and sordid history of the death penalty as it pertains to women minorities.
    C. Not effective or pertinent to the subject at hand.
    D. It is effective because it gives statistics.

44. F. NO CHANGE
    G. States; 287
    H. States: 287
    J. States 287

45. Choose the sequence of paragraph numbers that makes the structure of the passage most logical.

    A. NO CHANGE
    B. 2, 1, 3, 4
    C. 1, 4, 3, 2
    D. 4, 1, 3, 2

Passage 4

(1)

My Ántonia depicts life on the Nebraska prairie during the early 1900s, mirroring Willa Cather's own experiences as a girl living on the "Great Divide," as that part of Nebraska <u>had been called</u>. The protagonist
46
of the novel<u>, Antonia Shimerda</u> was modeled on Annie Sadilek, an
47
<u>actual living</u> Bohemian girl hired by one of Willa Cather's neighbors in the
48
town of Red Cloud. $\boxed{49}$

(2)

A close friend of Willa Cather, the author of *My Ántonia*, has written, "Willa forever preferred rural life, although she was never quite so inartistic as to announce that 'the country is preferable to the <u>city</u>'." Certainly,
50
My Ántonia, Willa Cather's third prairie novel, is a joyous song of praise for "the virtues of a settled agricultural existence" as opposed to life in the cities. Her belief that the ideal civilization is to be found in the country, <u>albeit</u> a country tempered with such desirable urban qualities as cultural
51
refinement and order, is developed by the use of <u>multi-level</u> contrasts and
52
comparisons, both obvious and symbolic. $\boxed{53}$ $\boxed{54}$

(3)

A richly creative novel, *My Ántonia* has been analyzed through a number of critical approaches. John H. Randall's criticism <u>dealt</u> with broad
55
thematic questions regarding Cather's arguments for certain values and ideas, such as the urban versus the bucolic life, using the mythic or archetypal school of criticism to explain many of the symbols <u>employed</u> by
56
the author to show her beliefs. James E. Miller explains the symbolism of the three different cycles used by Cather in the novel: the seasons of the year, the phases of Antonia's life, and, most important to this essay, <u>the people</u>
57
<u>move westward in cycles</u> to America's frontiers. Wallace Stegner, a novelist
57
in his own right, wrote an essay about <u>*My Ántonia*. In which</u> he used
58
archetypal criticism in relation to Antonia's identification with the land, and the psychological approach to show how Cather's life and character were crucial to the novel's central theme of country versus city values. $\boxed{59}$ $\boxed{60}$

46. F. NO CHANGE
    G. was called
    H. is called
    J. called

47. A. NO CHANGE
    B. , Antonia Shimerda,
    C. Antonia Shimerda
    D. novel Antonia Shimerda,

48. F. NO CHANGE
    G. actual, living
    H. living
    J. actual

49. This paragraph serves as a summary of the novel being discussed in this passage. How might it be strengthened?

    A. NO CHANGE
    B. It should describe the Great Plains setting more fully.
    C. It should give us the entire plot of the story, not part of it.
    D. It should supply more details regarding the family background of the Shimerdas.

50. F. NO CHANGE
    G. city' ".
    H. city.' "
    J. city."

51. A. NO CHANGE
    B. nevertheless
    C. and
    D. yet

52. F. NO CHANGE
    G. multi level
    H. multilevel
    J. many level

53. This paragraph begins with a quotation from a close friend of Willa Cather. Is the use of the quotation relevant to the passage?

    A. No, it is irrelevant and has no bearing on the passage or paragraph.
    B. No, it is misleading, dealing with Willa Cather's life, rather than the substance of the passage.
    C. Yes, it is a valuable insight from a reliable source; in addition, it is relevant to the paragraph and passage.
    D. Yes, it is a humorous touch that does no harm.

54. This passage was probably written for readers who:

    F. are beginning readers in a youngsters' educational program.
    G. are mature students of literature who are interested in critical analysis.
    H. are middle-westerners who want to learn more about their heritage.
    J. are authors themselves.

55. A. NO CHANGE
    B. had dealt
    C. deals
    D. has been dealing

56. F. NO CHANGE
    G. being employed
    H. employing
    J. employ

57. A. NO CHANGE
    B. the people moved westward in cycles
    C. the cycles in the movement of people westward
    D. the people were frequently moving westward in cycles

58. F. NO CHANGE
    G. *My Ántonia*, in which
    H. *My Ántonia*; in which
    J. *My Ántonia*—in which

59. This paragraph begins with the general statement: ". . . *My Ántonia* has been analyzed through a number of critical approaches." In what ways does the rest of the paragraph support or fail to support this statement?

    A. It supplies the names of several critical approaches and defines them in detail.
    B. It avoids the mention of critical approaches, but names three critics and discusses their ideas.
    C. It names three critics, but says little about critical approaches.
    D. It names three critics and their specific critical approaches to the novel, identifying the critical schools employed by two of them.

60. Choose the sequence of paragraph numbers that makes the structure of the passage most logical.

    F. NO CHANGE
    G. 2, 3, 1
    H. 3, 2, 1
    J. 3, 1, 2

Passage 5

(1)

Simone de Beauvoir, in *The Second Sex*, makes much of the "antique traditions" that were keeping women tied to the home and marriage. We can still often see the "antique traditions" today in America; for example, there has been no female President, or even a candidate in the past, and there are <u>relatively female firefighters</u>, police officers, or even taxi
<u>61</u>
drivers. <u>Still, in America, men are rapidly becoming almost equal.</u>
<u>62</u>
However, in my country, Japan, even though the situation has been getting a little better because of the change in company policies or laws, we can still see the "antique traditions" operating very often.

Strangely, most Japanese know America's first lady's name and face: Laura Bush is known in Japanese society because she is often featured on television programs or in newspapers. But, the wife of the Japanese Prime Minister is completely unknown. The mass media never pays attention to her, so we do not know her face or even her name. There is a relic notion that women should support their husbands secretly. ▢63▢

In addition, women members of the Diet are still quite rare, especially the Secretaries. This year, the disaster-prevention measures received a lot of media attention because the Secretary of the Ministry of Construction was a woman, <u>because</u> her measures were distinguished. People paid
<u>64</u>
attention, not to the disaster-prevention measures she <u>did</u> but to how she
<u>65</u>
would perform in front of the world-wide mass media. One of the reporters said ironically, "She is doing a good job, isn't she?" Nobody makes those kinds of statements about men. He implies that she is doing well although she is a woman!

(2)

<u>These</u> demonstrate the manner in which women are treated by Japanese
<u>66</u>
society. Let me tell you exactly how women are prevented from growing due to the "antique traditions" that are their heritage. Mainly, in my culture, the traditions are disrupting women's emergence from the ways of the old world. Even now, women are encouraged to stay home and do housework and take care of children, not work in careers outside of the home. When

women marry firstborn sons, they usually live in their husband's home with his parents. These women have to take care of the parents. Even though the wives do not want to be so controlled, it is part of their age-old custom and very difficult to avoid. At the same time, the psychological burden of living with another's family is excruciatingly difficult, because, regardless of everything, these women are living in someone else's home: the wives have to keep silent at night, for example, or they may hesitate to go out with their friends or have visitors, or it is simply impossible to know if one can engage in such a simple task as use the kitchen. There is no doubt that this affects their jobs as well as their lives. We Japanese often say, not too jokingly, "I will never marry a firstborn son." The situation causes women to have difficulties in their work and <u>families, as a result,</u> there are
                                                                                      67
more and more single women in Japan. They choose their jobs rather than marriage because marriage usually means the end of their careers. I have misgivings about the fact that only women have to suffer from these problems. It is quite unfair.

(3)

Such problems occur regularly, not only in marriage or the family, <u>and also</u>
                                                                              68
in the workplace; companies discriminate against women which prevent women's professional growth. Last spring, my good friend landed a job at a large enterprise. She was happy because she secured a good job in spite of the depression. However, at her entrance ceremony, a man came up to her and said, <u>"I am sorry, but I decided not to employ you."</u> She was so
                                                     69
depressed, of course. At the same time, she became very angry. It was not because she was denied the company's offer, or that she was denied the job at the entrance ceremony; it was because she was denied the job due to her gender. That is never understandable or forgivable. ⌐70⌐

   <u>To be sure, the situation of women in Japan is getting better</u>
                                                          71
<u>compared to the past, but still there are many women who are suffering</u>
                                              71
<u>from such "antique traditions."</u> I believe traditions to be very important and
                 71
valuable, but those traditions that prevent <u>women's</u> growth should be taken
                                              72
away. I believe old people's stultified thoughts and actions about women's rights must not be allowed to prevent the rise of women anywhere. <u>For</u>
                                                                              73
<u>example, the law guarantees the same employment opportunities; yet,</u>
                                              73

<u>actually, they do not work, as in my friend's case.</u> To improve this situation,
^73
we women have to attempt to change this discrimination by never relenting
and by being aware of it, just as, for example, women achieving women's
suffrage in the past. We cannot accomplish the victory without a lot of
effort. I believe we can do it by being ever vigilant. [74] [75]

61. A. NO CHANGE
    B. relatively firefighters,
    C. woefully low numbers of female firefighters,
    D. relatively few firefighters,

62. F. NO CHANGE
    G. Still, relatively, men and women are rapidly becoming almost equal.
    H. Still, additionally, men and women are rapidly becoming almost equal.
    J. Still, to me, American men and women are rapidly becoming almost equal.

63. The writer could most effectively strengthen this passage by adding which of
    the following?

    A. A list of countries that have clearly visible and effective administrators.
    B. Mentioning a few other women who are shortchanged by the refusal of
       Japanese society to recognize them and their accomplishments.
    C. A list of publications that have reporters so prejudiced.
    D. A list of companies and governmental offices that have female workers.

64. F. NO CHANGE
    G. indeed because
    H. not because
    J. that

65. A. NO CHANGE
    B. instituted
    C. worked on
    D. popularized

66. F. NO CHANGE
    G. This
    H. These things
    J. These two examples

67. A. NO CHANGE
    B. families and
    C. families; as a result,
    D. families, but

68. F. NO CHANGE
    G. but
    H. if
    J. besides

69. A. NO CHANGE
    B. "We aren't going to hire you."
    C. "We have decided not to employ any women this year because of the depression."
    D. "We refuse to hire you."

70. Readers are likely to regard the passage thus far as best described by which of the following terms?

    F. Concerned
    G. Conciliatory
    H. Apologetic
    J. Confessional

71. This sentence alone indicates that the intention of the author is to be:

    A. dominating
    B. understanding
    C. underhanded
    D. superior

72. F. NO CHANGE
    G. womens
    H. womens'
    J. Womans

73. A. NO CHANGE
    B. For example, the law guarantees all jobs to men and women; yet, they have no jobs.
    C. For example, the law guarantees women the same employment opportunities that men have; yet women are given very few jobs.
    D. For example, all women are guaranteed the jobs that men are given; they do not get the jobs.

74. The word "change" in the third sentence from the end takes the position that women have to adopt two stances. What are they?

    F. To never relent and to be ever aware of discrimination
    G. To improve the situation and attempt to change it
    H. To be aware of discrimination and to achieve suffrage as in the past
    J. To improve this situation and to achieve suffrage as in the past

75. Choose the sequence of sections that makes the structure of the essay most logical.

    A. NO CHANGE
    B. 3, 1, 2
    C. 3, 2, 1
    D. 1, 3, 2

Answers to English Test begin on page 427.

TEST 2: MATHEMATICS

Time —60 minutes
60 Questions

> **_Directions:_** After solving each problem, darken the appropriate space on the answer sheet. Do not spend too much time on any one problem. Make a note of the ones that seem difficult, and return to them when you finish the others. Assume that the word *line* means "straight line," that geometric figures are not necessarily drawn to scale, and that all geometric figures lie in a plane.

1. The following expression $\dfrac{a}{b} - \dfrac{c}{d} = ?$

   A. $\dfrac{a-b}{cd}$

   B. $\dfrac{a}{d} - \dfrac{c}{b}$

   C. $\dfrac{ad - bc}{bd}$

   D. $\dfrac{a-c}{bd}$

   E. $\dfrac{a-d}{bc}$

2. If $x \neq 0$, which of the following is equal to $\dfrac{2x^4 + x^3}{x^6}$?

   F. $\dfrac{3}{x^3}$

   G. $\dfrac{x+1}{x^2}$

   H. $2x^2 + x^3$

   J. $\dfrac{2x+1}{x^3}$

   K. $\dfrac{2x+1}{x}$

3. A certain city has 1600 public telephones. Three-fourths of the phones have dials. If one-third of the dial phones are replaced by push-button phones, how many dial phones remain?

   A. 800   B. 750   C. 700   D. 600   E. 400

4. If x and y are both positive integers, which of the following is NOT necessarily an integer?

   F. $x + y$

   G. $x - y$

   H. xy

   J. x^y

   K. $\dfrac{x}{y}$

5. If a negative number is subtracted from a positive number, which of the following will always be the result?

   A. Zero
   B. A positive number
   C. A negative number
   D. A number having the sign of the number with the larger absolute value
   E. A number having the sign of the number with the smaller absolute value

6. What is the solution set of the equation $\dfrac{5}{4x-3} = 5$?

   F. {7}   G. {4}   H. {2}   J. {1.5}   K. {1}

7. If t represents the tens digit of a two-digit number, and u represents the units digit, which of the following expressions represents the number?

   A. $t + u$ B. $10t + u$ C. $10u + t$ D. $10(t + u)$ E. tu

8. What is the simplified form of the product of the two polynomials $(x - 1)(x^2 + x + 1)$?

   F. $x^3 + 1$ J. $x^3 + x^2 + x$
   G. $x^3 - 1$ K. $x^3 + 2x^2 + 2x + 1$
   H. $x^3 - x - 1$

9.

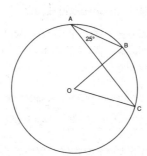

   In circle with center O, $m(\angle BAC) = 25°$. What is the measure of $\angle BOC$?

   A. 25°   D. 75°
   B. 50°   E. None of these.
   C. 90°

10. Which of the following numbers is unequal to the others?

   F. 2.5%   G. $\dfrac{1}{40}$ H. $2.5(10^{-2})$ J. $\dfrac{75}{30}$ K. 0.025

11. If apples are 35 cents or 3 for $1.00, how much is saved on each apple by buying them 3 at a time?

    A. 5 cents   **D.** $1\frac{2}{3}$ cents

    B. $1.05

    C. $\frac{3}{5}$ cents   **E.** $11\frac{2}{3}$ cents

12. If Joan can run 1 mile in a minutes, how much of a mile has she run after b minutes if she runs at a constant rate?

    F. $\frac{a}{b}$ **G.** $\frac{b}{a}$ **H.** $\frac{1}{ab}$ **J.** ab **K.** $\frac{a+b}{a}$

13. Which of the following is NOT a real number?

    A. $\sqrt[5]{0}$ **B.** 50   **C.** 05   **D.** $0 \cdot 5$ **E.** $\frac{5}{0}$

14. $3\frac{3}{5} \times 4\frac{1}{6} = ?$

    F. 15   **G.** $7\frac{23}{30}$ **H.** $\frac{108}{125}$ **J.** $\frac{17}{30}$ **K.** $\frac{1}{15}$

15. Yvette has 5 more nickels than dimes. If the value of her money is $1.30, how many coins of each kind does she have?

    A. 12 dimes and 7 nickels   **D.** 7 dimes and 12 nickels
    B. 5 dimes and 16 nickels   **E.** 3 dimes and 20 nickels
    C. 5 dimes and 10 nickels

16. What is the tenth term of the arithmetic sequence 3, 8, 13, . . . ?

    F. 18   **G.** 43   **H.** 48   **J.** 53   **K.** None of these

17. What is the solution set of the equation $0.2(100 - x) + 0.05x = 0.1(100)$?

    A. $\left\{-33\frac{1}{3}\right\}$ **D.** $\left\{66\frac{2}{3}\right\}$

    B. $\{10\}$ **E.** $\left\{95\frac{95}{399}\right\}$

    C. $\{40\}$

18. Which of the following statements is false?

    F. A regular triangle is equilateral.
    G. A regular quadrilateral is a square.
    H. An interior angle of a regular pentagon has a measure of 108°.
    J. A regular polygon of seven sides does not exist.
    K. All of these statements are true.

19. What is the simplest form of the radical $\sqrt[3]{54x^4y^6}$? (Assume that x and y are nonnegative.)

A. $3xy^2\sqrt[3]{2x}$

D. $3x^2\sqrt[3]{6y^6}$

B. $3x^2y^3\sqrt[3]{6}$

E. $3xy^2\sqrt[3]{6x}$

C. $3y^3\sqrt[3]{2x^4}$

20. Which of the following is NOT an equation of a conic section?

F. $y = 5x^2 - 3x + 2$

G. $x^2 + y^2 - 5x + 2y - 7 = 0$

H. $2x^2 - 5y^2 = 7$

J. $y = x^3$

K. $\dfrac{(x + 2)^2}{25} + \dfrac{(y - 3)^2}{16} = 1$

21. What is the degree of $-5x^2y + 3xy^3 + 2xy + 6$?

A. 9 B. 5 C. 4 D. 3 E. 2

22. What is the solution set of the following system of equations?

$$\begin{pmatrix} 2x - y = 5 \\ x + y = 1 \end{pmatrix}$$

F. $\{(2, 1)\}$ G. $\{2\}$ H. $\{(3, 1)\}$ J. $\{(4, -3)\}$ K. $\{(2, -1)\}$

23. A number from the set $\{1, 2, 3, \ldots, 20\}$ is chosen at random. What is the probability that the number is even and less than 10?

A. $\dfrac{1}{2}$ B. $\dfrac{9}{20}$ C. $\dfrac{1}{5}$ D. $\dfrac{9}{40}$ E. $\dfrac{1}{4}$

24. If $x \neq 0$ and $y \neq 0$, what is the simplified form of the complex fraction $\dfrac{x + y}{\dfrac{1}{x} + \dfrac{1}{y}}$?

F. $\dfrac{x + y}{xy}$

J. $2 + \dfrac{x}{y} + \dfrac{y}{x}$

G. $\dfrac{xy}{x + y}$

K. xy

H. $(x + y)^2$

25. If $m \angle ABC = 70°$, then $m \angle ADC = ?$

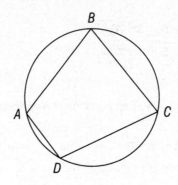

A. 35° **B.** 70° **C.** 90° **D.** 110° **E.** 140°

26. If $a > b$, then $|a - b| + |b - a|$ is equal to what expression?

F. 0 **G.** $2a$ **H.** $2b$ **J.** $2a + 2b$ **K.** $2a - 2b$

27. What is the value of -3^{-2}?

A. 6 **B.** 9 **C.** -9 **D.** $\dfrac{-1}{9}$ **E.** $\dfrac{1}{9}$

28. What is the center of the ellipse with the equation $x^2 + 4y^2 - 4x + 24y + 36 = 0$?

F. (2, 1) **G.** (1, 2) **H.** (2, −3) **J.** (−2, 3) **K.** (1, 4)

29. Nick can do a certain job in 2 hours less time than it takes Bonnie to do the same job. If they can complete the job together in 7 hours, what equation could be used to determine how long it would take Bonnie to do the job alone?

A. $7(x - 2) = 7x$　　**D.** $\dfrac{7}{x - 2} + \dfrac{7}{x} = 1$

B. $\dfrac{7}{x - 2} = \dfrac{7}{x}$　　**E.** None of these

C. $7(x - 2) + 7x = 1$

30. Which of the following is the graph of a one-to-one function?

F. 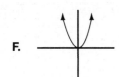   J.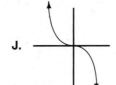

G.    K.

H.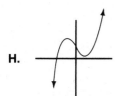

31. Which of the following numbers could NOT be the base of an exponential function?

A. $\dfrac{1}{2}$ **B.** 1   **C.** 2   **D.** 3   **E.** $\sqrt{5}$

32. What is the simplified form of the expression $(5x - 3y^2)^2$?

F. $25x^2 + 9y^4$ J. $25x^2 - 15xy^2 + 9y^4$
G. $25x^2 - 9y^4$ K. $25x^2 - 30xy^2 + 9y^4$
H. $25x^2 - 30xy + 9y^2$

33. What is the reciprocal of i?

A. 1   **B.** −1   **C.** i **D.** −i **E.** None of these

34. What is the simplified form of the expression $\dfrac{a^{-3}bc^2}{a^{-4}b^2c^{-3}}$?
(Assume that the variables are not equal to zero. Write without negative exponents.)

F. $\dfrac{c^5}{a^7b}$ J. $\dfrac{c}{ab}$

G. $\dfrac{ac^5}{b}$ K. $\dfrac{a^7}{bc^5}$

H. $\dfrac{a^7c^5}{b}$

35. In right triangle ABC, m $\angle A = 30°$, m $\angle B = 60°$, and $AC = 6$. What is the length of $\overline{AB}$?

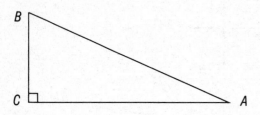

   A. $3\sqrt{2}$ **B.** $6\sqrt{3}$ **C.** $4\sqrt{2}$ **D.** $3\sqrt{3}$ **E.** $4\sqrt{3}$

36. Which of the following is identically equal to sin 2A?

   F. $1 - \cos^2 2A$ **J.** $2 \sin A$

   G. $2 \sin A \cos A$ **K.** None of these

   H. $\dfrac{1}{\sec 2a}$

37. What is the solution set of $3x^2 - 4x - 6 = 0$?

   A. $\left\{\dfrac{-2}{3}, 3\right\}$ **D.** $\left\{\dfrac{4 + i\sqrt{66}}{6}, \dfrac{4 - i\sqrt{66}}{6}\right\}$

   B. $\left\{\dfrac{2 + 2\sqrt{22}}{3}, \dfrac{2 - 2\sqrt{22}}{3}\right\}$ **E.** $\left\{\dfrac{2 + \sqrt{22}}{3}, \dfrac{2 - \sqrt{22}}{3}\right\}$

   C. $\left\{\dfrac{4 + \sqrt{22}}{3}, \dfrac{4 - \sqrt{22}}{3}\right\}$

38. What is the simplified form of the radical expression $3\sqrt{3} - \sqrt{48} + 3\sqrt{\dfrac{1}{3}}$?

   F. 0 **J.** $3\sqrt{3} - 2\sqrt{12} + \sqrt{3}$

   G. $\sqrt{3}$ **K.** It is already in simplest form.

   H. $4\sqrt{3} \div 2\sqrt{12}$

39. Which of the following equations does NOT define a function?

   A. $y = x + 2$ **B.** $x = y + 2$ **C.** $y = 2^x$ **D.** $y = x^2$ **E.** $x = y^2$

40. If tangent $\overline{CD}$ is 6 cm long and $BC = 4$, what is the length of $\overline{AB}$?

F. $2\frac{2}{3}$

G. 3

H. 4

J. 5

K. 6

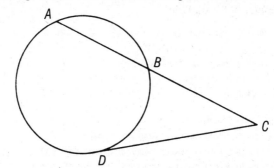

41. Diane averages 12 miles per hour riding her bike to work. Averaging 36 miles per hour on the way home by car takes her $\frac{1}{2}$ hour less time. What equation could be used to determine how far she travels to work?

A. $12x + 36x = 30$

B. $\dfrac{x}{12} = \dfrac{x}{36} - \dfrac{1}{2}$

C. $\dfrac{x}{12} + \dfrac{x}{36} = 30$

D. $\dfrac{x}{36} = \dfrac{x}{12} - \dfrac{1}{2}$

E. $\dfrac{36}{x} = \dfrac{12}{x} + \dfrac{1}{2}$

42. What are the coordinates of the midpoint of a segment with endpoints $A(3, 7)$ and $B(-5, -6)$?

F. $(0, 0)$

G. $\left(1, \dfrac{-1}{2}\right)$

H. $\left(-1, \dfrac{1}{2}\right)$

J. $(-2, 1)$

K. $(8, 13)$

43. What is the solution set of the radical equation $\sqrt{2x - 3} = -5$?

A. $\{-1\}$ B. $\{4\}$ C. $\{7\}$ D. $\{14\}$ E. ø

44. Which of the following statements is false?

F. Every whole number is an integer.

G. Some rational numbers are natural numbers.

H. The set of integers is a subset of the set of real numbers.

J. $\sqrt{49}$ is a rational number.

K. None of these statements is false.

45. If an equilateral triangle is inscribed in a circle of radius 8 cm, what is the perimeter of the triangle?

A. $24\sqrt{3}$ B. $8\sqrt{3}$ C. $4\sqrt{3}$ D. 12   E. 24

46. What is the domain of the function
$$f(x) = \frac{x+3}{x^2 - 2x - 3}?$$

F. All real numbers
G. $\{x \mid x$ is a real number and $x \neq -3\}$
H. $\{x \mid x$ is a real number and $x \neq 3$ and $x \neq -1\}$
J. $\{x \mid x$ is a real number and $x \neq 3$, $x \neq -1$, and $x \neq -3\}$
K. $\{x \mid x \neq 0\}$

47. Circles A and B are tangent to each other. $\overline{CD}$ is a common tangent to the two circles. If the radius of circle A is 5 and the radius of circle B is 3, what is the length of $\overline{CD}$?

A. 4
B. 8
C. $\sqrt{34}$
D. $2\sqrt{15}$
E. $2\sqrt{17}$

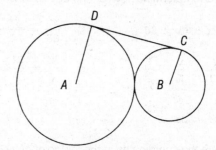

48. If $\overline{AD}$ is a diameter and $m \angle C = 125°$, what is the measure of $\angle A$?

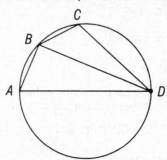

F. 35°   G. 55°   H. 62.5°   J. 90°   K. 125°

49. If $AC = 8$ and $BD = 6$, then what is the length of $\overline{BC}$?

A. 1
B. 5
C. $7\frac{1}{2}$
D. 15
E. There is not enough information.

50. If $A(-3, 4)$ lies on the terminal side of angle θ, what is the value of $\sec \theta$?

    F. $\dfrac{-3}{5}$ G. $\dfrac{4}{5}$ H. $\dfrac{-5}{3}$ J. $\dfrac{-4}{3}$ K. $\dfrac{5}{4}$

51. What is the value of $\displaystyle\sum_{k=1}^{5} 2k^2$?

    A. 2 B. 50 C. 52 D. 110 E. None of these

52. In which quadrant must θ lie if $\cos \theta > 0$ and $\cot \theta < 0$?

    F. I G. II H. III J. IV K. No such angle exists.

53. Let A and B be any two sets. Which of the following statements is always true?

    A. $(A \cup B) \subseteq A$ D. $B \subseteq (A \cap B)$
    B. $(A \cap B) \subseteq B$ E. $(A \cup B) = (A \cap B)$
    C. $(A \cup B) \cup (A \cap B)$

54. The length of the diagonal of a rectangular piece of wood is $\sqrt{145}$ feet. If one side is 1 foot longer than the other, what are the lengths of the sides?

    F. 8 feet and -9 feet   J. 5 feet and 6 feet
    G. 8 feet and 9 feet   K. 2 feet and 36 feet
    H. 12 feet and 13 feet

55. What is the value of $\sin\left(\cos^{-1}\dfrac{2}{3}\right)$?

    A. $\dfrac{2}{3}$ B. $\dfrac{\sqrt{5}}{3}$ C. $\dfrac{-\sqrt{5}}{3}$ D. $\dfrac{\pm\sqrt{5}}{3}$ E. $\dfrac{\sqrt{13}}{3}$

56. Jon scored 75, 84, and 80 on his first three tests. What score must he get on his fourth test so that his average will be at least 80?

    F. 81
    G. Greater than 81
    H. Less than 81
    J. Greater than or equal to 81
    K. Less than or equal to 81

57. What is the measure of an exterior angle of a regular octagon?

    A. $45°$ B. $60°$ C. $72°$ D. $120°$ E. $135°$

58. If the lengths of the diagonals of a rhombus are 6 and 8 meters, what is the perimeter, in meters, of the rhombus?

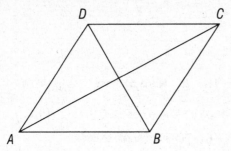

    F. 5 **G.** 14 **H.** 20 **J.** 28 **K.** 40

59. Which of the following statements is true?

    A. Complements of complementary angles are equal.
    B. A line segment has only one bisector.
    C. A line perpendicular to a segment also bisects the segment.
    D. An isosceles triangle may also be scalene.
    E. None of these statements is true.

60. In $\triangle ABC$, $\overline{AB} \perp \overline{BC}$ and $\overline{BD} \perp \overline{AC}$. If $BD = 4$ and $AC = 10$, what is the length of $\overline{AD}$ (the shorter portion of the hypotenuse)?

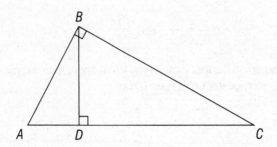

    F. 2 **G.** 3 **H.** 4 **J.** 6 **K.** 8

Answers to Mathematics Test begin on page 428.

TEST 3: READING

Time —35 minutes
40 Questions

> **_Directions:_** This test consists of four passages, each followed by ten multiple-choice questions. Read each passage and then pick the best answer for each question. Fill in the spaces on your answer sheet that correspond to your choices. Refer to the passage as often as you wish while answering the questions.

Passage 1

PROSE FICTION: *This passage is an excerpt from "The Egg," a short story by Sherwood Anderson. In it the narrator recounts his family's vain efforts to run a chicken farm.*

My father was, I am sure, intended by nature to be a cheerful, kindly man. Until he was thirty-four years old he worked as a farm hand for a man named Thomas Butterworth whose place lay near the town of Bidwell, Ohio. He had then a horse of his own and on Saturday evenings drove into town to spend a
(5)   few hours in social intercourse with other farm hands.... At ten o'clock Father drove home along a lonely country road, made his horse comfortable for the night and himself went to bed, quite happy in his position in life. He had at that time no notion of trying to rise in the world.

It was in the spring of his thirty-fifth year that Father married my mother, then
(10)   a country schoolteacher, and in the following spring I came wriggling and crying into the world. Something happened to the two people. They became ambitious. The American passion for getting up in the world took possession of them.

It may have been that Mother was responsible. Being a schoolteacher she
(15)   had no doubt read books and magazines. She had, I presume, read of how Garfield, Lincoln and other Americans rose from poverty to fame and greatness and as I lay beside her—in the days of her lying-in—she may have dreamed that I would some day rule men and cities. At any rate, she induced Father to give up his place as a farm hand, sell his horse and embark on an independent
(20)   enterprise of his own....

The first venture into which the two people went turned out badly. They rented ten acres of poor stony land on Grigg's Road, eight miles from Bidwell, and launched into chicken raising. I grew into boyhood on the place and got my first impressions of life there. From the beginning they were impressions of
(25)   disaster and if, in my turn, I am a gloomy man inclined to see the darker side of life, I attribute it to the fact that what should have been for me the happy joyous days of childhood were spent on a chicken farm.

One unversed in such matters can have no notion of the many and tragic things that can happen to a chicken. It is born out of an egg, lives for a few
(30)   weeks as a tiny fluffy thing such as you will see pictured on Easter cards, then

becomes hideously naked, eats quantities of corn and meal bought by the sweat of your father's brow, gets diseases called pip, cholera and other names, stands looking with stupid eyes at the sun, becomes sick and dies. A few hens and now and then a rooster, intended to serve God's mysterious ends, struggle

(35) through to maturity. The hens lay eggs out of which come other chickens and the dreadful cycle is thus made complete. It is all unbelievably complex. Most philosophers must have been raised on chicken farms. One hopes for so much from a chicken and is so dreadfully disillusioned. Small chickens just setting out on the journey of life, look so bright and alert and they are in fact so

(40) dreadfully stupid. They are so much like people they mix one up in one's judgments of life. If disease does not kill them they wait until your expectations are thoroughly aroused and then walk under the wheels of a wagon.... In later life I have seen how a literature has been built up on the subject of fortunes to be made out of the raising of chickens. . . . Do not be led astray by it. It was not

(45) written for you. Go hunt for gold on the frozen hills of Alaska, put your faith in the honesty of a politician, believe if you will that the world is daily growing better and that good will triumph over evil, but do not read and believe the literature that is written concerning the hen. . . .

I, however, digress. My tale does not primarily concern itself with the hen.

(50) If correctly told it will center on the egg. For ten years my father and mother struggled to make our chicken farm pay and then they gave up that struggle and began another. They moved into the town of Bidwell, Ohio, and embarked in the restaurant business. After ten years of worry, ...we threw all aside and packing our belongings on a wagon drove down Grigg's Road toward Bidwell,

(55) a tiny caravan of hope looking for a new place from which to start on our upward journey through life.

Sherwood Anderson, "The Egg"

1. The narrator of the story views life pessimistically because:

    A. he grew up on a chicken farm.
    B. his parents never succeeded at anything they did.
    C. his life has been all work and no play.
    D. he and his family were always in debt.

2. The books and magazines mentioned in line 18:

    F. aided Mother in her work as a schoolteacher.
    G. indicate that Mother was a scholar and an intellect.
    H. gave Mother ideas about how one ought to conduct one's life.
    J. were given to Mother in the hospital.

3. When he abandoned chicken farming, Father was about:

    A. 35 years old.
    B. 40 years old.
    C. 45 years old.
    D. 50 years old.

4. Which of these changes did NOT take place after Father got married?

    F. Father gave up his job at Butterworth's.
    G. Father became an ambitious person.
    H. Father stopped his Saturday-night socializing with the boys.
    J. Father wanted to stop working on a farm.

5. According to the narrator, in which way do chickens resemble human beings?

    A. Chickens, like people, appear to be brighter than they really are.
    B. Chickens, like children, are expensive to bring up.
    C. Chickens, as well as humans, are dirty, diseased, and smelly.
    D. Tragedies befall both chickens and humans.

6. According to the narrator, one of the few pleasures in raising chickens is that:

    F. you have the chance to witness the life cycle.
    G. the creatures are cute when they are chicks.
    H. if you are lucky, you can become rich.
    J. you'll never run out of eggs.

7. The narrator's opinion of books and articles written about chicken farming is that they are:

    A. all a pack of lies.
    B. not written for anyone who is serious about raising chickens.
    C. likely to exaggerate the rewards of chicken farming.
    D. meant only for people with nothing to lose.

8. Mother's ambition for her family's success led to all EXCEPT which of the following consequences?

    F. Father's cheerful and kindly disposition was changed.
    G. Mother and Father became poverty-stricken.
    H. Mother and Father were forced to work very hard.
    J. Mother and Father thought that they were failures.

9. Which pair of adjectives most accurately conveys the narrator's feelings about his childhood?

    A. resentful/bitter
    B. detached/unemotional
    C. satirical/humorous
    D. sentimental/sad

10. "Most philosophers must have been raised on chicken farms" (fifth paragraph) means that chicken farming:

    F.   gives you a philosophical outlook on life.
    G.   exposes you to profound issues like good and evil, life and death.
    H.   allows you time to think.
    J.   is so complex that only a philosopher can comprehend it.

Passage 2

SOCIAL STUDIES: *This passage is from a governmental report on domestic violence titled "Characteristics of the Abusive Situation." It discusses several problems faced by abused and battered spouses.*

Abusive husbands systematically isolate their wives from family and friends. Even women who seek legal, medical or emotional help view themselves as unable to succeed against their all-powerful husbands who, they fear, will "pay witnesses to lie in court," "kill my family if I testify," "get custody of the

(5) children," and "refuse to give me a divorce." Physical and emotional abuse of women is an exercise of power and control in which the weight of society has been traditionally on the side of the oppressor. Thus, battered women who feel powerless to alter their circumstances are reacting realistically to what they have experienced. They are trapped, and their descriptions of the responses of

(10) police, prosecutors and judges are not paranoid delusions.

Many victims have been beaten repeatedly and their attackers have not been apprehended and punished. Assault is a crime. Legally it makes no difference if the victim and her attacker are strangers or are married to each other. Yet police officers often refuse to arrest husbands (or live-in companions) who

(15) beat their wives. Police, prosecutors, judges and society in general share the prejudice that women provoke men by constant nagging, overspending or questioning their virility. Verbal provocation, even assuming it exists, however, is not justification for violence.

The absence of negative sanctions gives the abusive family member license

(20) to continue his threats and violence. The lack of societal restraints on the husband's violence, the emphasis on defendant's rights in the courts, the long court delays, the opportunity for intimidation, the husband's promises of reform and the woman's fear of economic privation contribute to the drop out rate of 50 percent by battered-wife complainants in the criminal courts and in

(25) the Family Court.

Civil actions for support, separation or divorce are also subject to delays which make it virtually impossible to get emergency relief. Judges frequently refuse to "throw a man out of his home," so it is the woman and children who must leave. Crowded court calendars make the legal process work in favor of

(30) the person who controls the family income and assets. Getting temporary alimony or maintenance and child support can take months, sometimes as

long as a divorce itself. Unless there is a refuge for battered women, the abused wife may be forced to live with her husband during a divorce action.

(35) Equitable distribution of property may also be problematic for the financially dependent spouse because the litigation to define, evaluate and divide the property can continue for years and is very costly. The ultimate irony is that, even when the battered wife gets an award for alimony and child support, the amount of support is usually inadequate for her to maintain herself and the children. Moreover, often it is not paid at all.

(40) Because the separated or divorced wife cannot rely on payment of court-ordered support, many battered wives stay with their husbands. Professor Richard J. Gelles, a sociologist who studied battered wives, found that the wives who hold a job are better able to obtain assistance and leave the abusive situation… Viewing the difficult situation in which legal, economic and

(45) social realities place the battered woman, one should ask: where does this woman get the stamina to survive the attacks and the courage to leave? Part of the work of the helping professionals is to convince the battered woman that she must use the enormous strength she has for self-preservation, not just for self-sacrifice.

(50) The legal system requires that an injured adult initiate and follow through with the steps necessary to obtain protection, child custody, financial support, divorce or money damages. Usually the injured person bears the expense of engaging an attorney to represent her in a civil case. The legal process is complex and confusing so that referral to a sympathetic and

(55) competent lawyer is important. Other helping professionals must understand the laws concerning family violence if they are to provide effective support. Accompanying a client to court helps develop a first-hand sense of the obstacles that the client faces.

The victim of domestic violence is in the best position to decide if legal action

(60) will be the most effective way to stop the violence or psychological abuse. Her decision on this matter must be respected. If just moving away (and getting a divorce if necessary) will work, then there is no reason to get entangled in a complicated legal process in which control is given to an unknown judge. But there are situations in which police assistance and court protection are

(65) essential.

Governor's Commission on Domestic Violence,
"Characteristics of the Abusive Situation"

11. According to the first paragraph, the main reason that abused women often feel helpless is that:

A. they don't know where to get help.
B. society customarily takes the man's side.
C. they can't afford to seek assistance.
D. witnesses to incidents of abuse are hard to find.

12. In lines 9–10 the assertion that "their descriptions… are not paranoid delusions…" implies that battered women:

    F. often cannot separate fantasy from reality.
    G. tend to exaggerate incidents of abuse.
    H. feel maltreated by those whose help they seek.
    J. frequently need psychological help.

13. It can be reasonably inferred from the second paragraph that officials often think that incidents of wife abuse:

    A. should be settled within the family itself, if possible.
    B. are less serious than conflicts between strangers.
    C. should be blamed equally on the husband and the wife.
    D. have most likely been provoked by the wife.

14. The passage indicates that half the lawsuits brought against abusive husbands remain incomplete because of all the following reasons EXCEPT that the:

    F. husband and wife are reconciled.
    G. wife feels threatened by loss of financial support.
    H. courts take too long to hear cases.
    J. husband pledges to stop abusing his wife.

15. The passage suggests that, in an emergency, an abused wife should:

    A. call a neighbor.
    B. immediately report her husband to the police.
    C. try to go to a shelter for battered women.
    D. contact a social worker.

16. Which of the following statements most accurately summarizes the author's view on how to solve the problems of abused wives?

    F. Change the legal system to give abused wives special consideration.
    G. Help abused women overcome feelings of hopelessness.
    H. Strictly enforce the laws governing alimony payments.
    J. Educate society about the problems of abused wives.

17. A primary purpose of the passage is to:

    A. argue for new laws to protect abused women.
    B. convince readers that abusive behavior is never justified.
    C. point out the injustices faced by abused women.
    D. advise abused women of their rights.

18. The passage implies that the severest hardships of abused women pertain to:

    F.   fears of bodily harm.

    G. lack of financial support.

    H. psychological trauma.

    J.   the well-being of their children.

19. According to the passage, an abused wife may invoke all of the following legal remedies EXCEPT:

    A. filing for an official separation from her husband.

    B. maintaining custody of the children.

    C. forcing the husband to continue financial support.

    D. requiring the husband to pay her attorney's fees.

20. The passage suggests that, to stop domestic violence, an abused woman should turn to the courts only when:

    F.   there is no alternative.

    G. she suffers psychological trauma.

    H. her husband would be charged with criminal behavior.

    J.   she can get help from an understanding lawyer.

Passage 3

HUMANITIES: *This passage is from an essay about the unusual effects that a famous radio program had on its listeners.*

On October 30, 1938, the night before Halloween, the Mercury Theater radio program broadcast a dramatization of *The War of the Worlds*, by British writer H. G. Wells. The program began as if it were a musical evening with Ramon Raquello's orchestra in a New York hotel, when news bulletins
(5) interrupted to report that a strange meteorite had struck New Jersey. A few minutes later, the music was replaced by eyewitness observations of the object itself, an immense, yellowish-white cylinder that had blasted a crater in a nearby farm. Soon, war machines emerged from it and began annihilating the United States Army. The public was relatively unfamiliar with
(10) science fiction stories at that point in history, and many took the realistic drama for actual news reports. Many thousands of people were frightened by the program, and some panicked.

    A group of sociologists, including Hadley Cantril, had been working on a major study of the effect of radio, funded by the Rockefeller Foundation.
(15) Quickly securing supplementary grants, they were able to launch a sudden research study. Cantril's team interviewed 135 people who had been frightened, collected newspaper stories, administered surveys, and analyzed polls conducted by other organizations. An estimated 6,000,000 people heard the broadcast; 1,700,000 of them thought it was factual news,
(20) and 1,200,000 were frightened or disturbed. It did not take many of these

people to flood the telephone switchboards of police and radio stations with worried calls.

Among the factors that encouraged listeners to believe that Martians were actually attacking the earth were the realism of the program itself, the fact that
(25) radio had become a standard medium for important announcements, the apparent prestige of the speakers who included expert astronomers, the ease of visualizing specific incidents, the realistically baffled behavior of radio characters themselves, and the unified quality of the total experience. Many listeners tuned in late, and others tuned in only because friends who were
(30) worried by the broadcast telephoned them. These people missed the beginning of the program when it was clearly labeled fiction drama.

Questionnaires and interviews allowed Cantril to investigate how listeners had tried to verify the impressions they got from the program. Some checked internal evidence from the broadcast against things they already knew. For
(35) example, a few had read the first science fiction magazine, *Amazing Stories*, and recognized the style. Or they noticed that events in the story were moving unrealistically fast. Some others checked external evidence, for example, turning to other stations on the radio or checking the program listing in the newspaper. A number of listeners tried to check external evidence but failed
(40) for some reason. One person looked out the window and saw a strange greenish glow on the horizon. Failure to reach parents on the telephone was taken as evidence that they had been destroyed. A street full of cars was seen as proof that people were fleeing, and an empty street was seen as evidence the way had been blocked so they could not flee. Other listeners were so
(45) confused they didn't even try to check the truth of the invasion report.

People who failed to verify the report tended to be more frightened than those who did so. Listeners with less education and relatively poor people were more likely to panic and less likely to use effective means for testing the veracity of the report. Cantril argued that some people have more critical ability
(50) than others, whereas some are especially suggestible or anxious. If two or more people listened to the program together, or if friends called each other on the phone, one person's reaction would be influenced by those of the others. Some listeners perceived themselves to be relatively safe for the time being, for example, those distant from the supposed invasion point in New Jersey.
(55) The Martian invasion panic was greatly stimulated by the fact that the world really was in great danger at that point in history. Hitler had taken Austria and was in the process of seizing Czechoslovakia. Less than a year later, the Second World War would break out in Europe, and most people already sensed it coming. A decade into the Great Depression, many people had good
(60) reason to be terrified about their economic futures, and it seemed that the social norms were disintegrating around them. Listeners had become used to hearing alarming news reports on the radio, and it seemed plausible that a new horror could erupt at any moment.

William Sims Bainbridge, *Sociology*, Barron's (1997)

21. The passage suggests that the producers of the Mercury Theater radio program created a sense of realism by:

    A. urging listeners not to call the police or radio stations.
    B. broadcasting realistic sound effects in the background.
    C. canceling commercials for one evening.
    D. employing "experts" to comment on the attack.

22. Which of the following facts was NOT included in the report of the landing of the meteorite?

    F. American soldiers had been killed.
    G. While descending, the meteorite had been brightly illuminated.
    H. It crashed into a rural area of New Jersey.
    J. Its landing had been observed by eyewitnesses.

23. According to the passage, many listeners thought that the report of the landing in New Jersey was true because:

    A. they hadn't realized it was Halloween eve.
    B. they had never before heard a radio program interrupted by a news bulletin.
    C. the report was made to sound authentic.
    D. they had vivid imaginations.

24. It is reasonable to infer that many people were genuinely alarmed by the radio program because:

    F. Hadley Cantril and other sociologists studied their reactions.
    G. phone calls to emergency services increased during the broadcast.
    H. friends quickly gathered to share their fears and worries.
    J. people turned off their radios to keep their families from being frightened.

25. The passage suggests that in October 1938 the genre of science fiction:

    A. was still in its infancy.
    B. had not yet been invented.
    C. was dominated by British writers.
    D. held little interest to Americans.

26. The passage implies that some listeners were convinced of the truth of the attack when they:

    F. discerned similarities between the broadcast and material in *Amazing Stories*.
    G. jumped to conclusions about what they observed.
    H. noticed that the pace of events in the broadcast matched the pace of other crises.
    J. listened to the broadcast alone.

27. Information in lines 32–39 in the fourth paragraph suggests that:

    A. some listeners were skeptical of the program's authenticity.
    B. only very gullible people believed that the attack occurred.
    C. people who had read a certain science fiction magazine immediately recognized the program as a hoax.
    D. most of the radio audience hoped that the attack had not actually occurred.

28. The implications of Cantril's findings on the effect of the broadcast are best summed up by which of the following statements?

    F. All listeners to the program were shaken up to some degree or other.
    G. The program made lasting impressions on poor, uneducated listeners.
    H. Apprehensive, impressionable listeners were more upset by the program than discerning, incisive listeners.
    J. The program left the least impact on listeners located farthest from New Jersey.

29. The "great danger" referred to in line 56 can best be described as:

    A. various political and economic crises.
    B. the threat of mob violence brought about uncontrollable fear.
    C. the daily troubles faced by impoverished Americans.
    D. listeners' lack of self-confidence.

30. The passage states that the public's reaction to the broadcast was influenced by:

    F. the popularity of H. G. Wells' *War of the Worlds*.
    G. the introduction of *Amazing Stories*, a sci-fi periodical.
    H. recent reports of unexplained lights on the horizon.
    J. events taking place overseas.

Passage 4

NATURAL SCIENCE: *This passage is adapted from a report prepared by the National Aeronautical and Space Administration (NASA) on the problems associated with establishing settlements in outer space.*

Solar sails are a way of moving things around in space, from one orbit to another. They are beginning to look like the best means of transportation in an area as big as space. And space is big! It would take as many Earths to fill the solar system (500,000,000,000,000,000) as elephants to fill the sea (an
(5) unpleasant prospect). The Earth's orbit around the Sun is 23,000 times the Earth's circumference. Driving to the Moon (1/400 of the distance to the Sun) would take six months, at 55 mph. Driving to the nearest star would take 50,000,000 years, and so on. Space is Big. To get anywhere you have to go fast.

(10)   But, you say, since there is no air resistance in space, perhaps a patient
traveler (or load of freight) could start out slowly and simply take whatever time
was needed, drifting along. But, alas, gravity is in control. If left to themselves,
objects in space don't really go anywhere; they simply go around in orbits.
Unless you kick something so hard that it stops completely, in which case it
(15)   falls into whatever it was orbiting, or kick it so hard in the other direction that it
can fly away, despite gravity, never to return, the object will simply grunt at the
kick, and shift its orbit somewhat. To get from one orbit to another generally
takes two perfectly measured pushes from a rocket.
         But rockets have limits because of the weight of fuel they must carry. A
(20)   rocket can reach the same velocity as its exhaust fairly easily; not much fuel is
needed to reach a few kilometers per second. The problem is that fuel has
mass, just like a payload. Let's say you have a rocket with enough fuel to reach
1 km/sec, and to take a ton of payload with it. How much fuel would you need
to reach 2 km/sec? Enough fuel to take the ton of payload to 1 km/sec, and
(25)   also enough fuel to take the fuel needed for the second km/sec to 1 km/sec.
The total fuel mass needed turns out to increase exponentially with the velocity
reached, just as population has been increasing exponentially with time. Both
increases can gobble up more resources than you can afford to provide. Using
the Saturn V moon rocket as a first stage, and piling up rockets from there, we
(30)   could have reached 30 km/sec with enough payload to drop one haunch off an
elephant into the Sun (an unpleasant prospect).
         Rockets burning chemical fuels run out of ability fast when measured against
the solar system, although they were decent for getting us as far as the Moon.
The exponential curve that gets rockets into trouble can be made less steep,
(35)   however, if more energy can be put into the exhaust. This is the principle of the
electric rocket; by soaking up solar energy in space and using it to throw small
amounts of mass away, payloads may be pushed around the solar system in a
reasonable way. The main problem is the cost and mass of the solar power
plant. To use it efficiently accelerations must be low and trips long. Costs are
(40)   also low: freight rates from Earth orbit to Mars orbit might be as little as
$.20 per pound.
         That brings us to solar sails. For decades people have looked at the problem
of stuffing about a square mile of folded reflecting surface into the nose of a
rocket, of launching it, and of making it unfold and stretch into a reasonably
(45)   flat surface in space. A design for a kite-like sail, with thin, aluminized plastic
film for the reflecting surface, has reached an advanced planning stage at the
Jet Propulsion Laboratory in Pasadena, California. Their design can accelerate
at about 1/7,000 of gravity, which is actually fairly good: the sail can reach 1
km/sec in about eight days. This lets you get around, and because it needs no
(50)   fuel, and no fuel to help carry fuel, and so on, it doesn't peter out at high
velocities like a rocket. But 1/7,000 of Earth's gravity isn't spectacular, and
solar electric rockets, mentioned above, still look good by comparison.
         Can solar sails be made better? The answer seems to be yes, if you forget
about folding them up and launching them from the ground. Instead, they can
(55)   be made in space, not as aluminized plastic sheets, but as aluminized nothing,

which weighs far less. Designs now worked out on paper use aluminum foil as the reflecting surface, but foil 1/1000 the thickness of the kitchen kind. These sails are over 40 times as light, and therefore over 40 times as fast, as previous designs. This is spectacular.

(60) If I had to draw a sail today, it would be a hexagon about six miles across, and weighing 20 tons. This is somewhere between the size of Manhattan and San Francisco, but the metal of the sail could be wadded up to the size of a Volkswagen bug.

31. The main point of the first paragraph is that:

    A. compared to the sun, Earth is tiny.
    B. it is impossible to drive to the nearest star.
    C. solar sails are the best means of transportation in space.
    D. high speed is needed to cover the vast distances of space.

32. The passage states that orbiting objects in space:

    F. drift along at a relatively slow rate of speed.
    G. are subject to the force of gravity.
    H. can remain aloft indefinitely.
    J. require occasional adjustments by rockets.

33. According to the passage, one of the main shortcomings of electric rockets is that:

    A. the electricity they need is expensive to generate in space.
    B. they are efficient only on voyages beyond the solar system.
    C. they tend to be too fragile to withstand the rigors of being shot into orbit.
    D. they require larger amounts of chemical fuel than conventional rockets.

34. The passage asserts that solar sails are a promising alternative to rockets for all of the following reasons EXCEPT:

    F. they are cheaper.
    G. they hold more fuel.
    H. their source of power is found in space.
    J. they weigh less.

35. The passage suggests that ordinary rockets have limited use in long-distance space travel because:

    A. their technology is growing increasingly obsolete.
    B. they accelerate too slowly.
    C. they require too much fuel.
    D. their orbits change frequently.

36. The passage states that increasing a rocket's speed from one kilometer per second to *two* kilometers per second requires:

    F. multiplying the number of engines on the rocket.
    G. twice the amount of fuel needed to reach one kilometer per second.
    H. reducing the total payload by half.
    J. many times the amount of fuel needed to reach one kilometer per second.

37. In which of the following ways is an electric rocket superior to a chemically fueled rocket of the same size and weight?

    A. It is more resistant to the pull of gravity.
    B. It carries less fuel.
    C. Its thrust exceeds the thrust of a chemical rocket.
    D. It can accelerate faster.

38. It can reasonably be inferred from the third paragraph (lines 19–31) that the velocity of the rocket's exhaust:

    F. increases in proportion to the rocket's altitude.
    G. depends on the distance the rocket is programmed to travel.
    H. is a factor in determining the speed of the vehicle.
    J. can easily be measured.

39. The author suggests that the successful use of solar sails depends on finding solutions to all of the following problems EXCEPT:

    A. reducing the weight of the sails.
    B. determining the best shape for the sails.
    C. speeding up the acceleration rate of the sails.
    D. deploying folded up sails in space.

40. The phrase "aluminized nothing" (line 55) describes a solar sail that:

    F. can float in the air.
    G. is hypothetical.
    H. can be rolled up like aluminum foil.
    J. is made of plastic.

Answers to Reading Test begin on page 429.

TEST 4: SCIENCE REASONING

Time — 35 minutes
40 Questions

Directions: This test consists of several distinct passages. Each passage is followed by a number of multiple-choice questions based on the passage. Study the passage, and then select the best answer to each question. You are allowed to reread the passage. Record your answer by blackening the appropriate space on the answer sheet.

Passage 1

Chart I below shows the total areas planted in genetically modified (GM) and unmodified crops in 2002. Chart II breaks down the GM crops into the type of modification: 1) insect resistance to protect the crop against insect damage, and 2) weed-killer tolerance to allow chemical weed-killers to be used without damage to the crop.

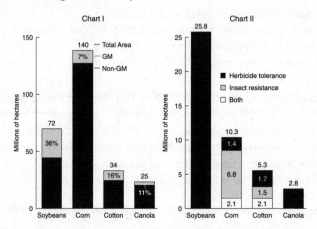

1. How much area was planted in soybeans that had not been genetically modified?

    A. 12 million hectares
    B. 26 million hectares
    C. 43 million hectares
    D. 70 million hectares

2. Which of the four crops has the largest area using genetically modified plants?

    F. Soybeans
    G. Corn
    H. Cotton
    J. Canola

3. One feature of the use of genetically modified crops is that:

   A. the chief result of the program is protection against insect damage.
   B. most corn in cultivation has been protected against insect damage.
   C. canola is grown less widely than the other three crops.
   D. soybeans have not been protected against insect damage.

4. A major outcome of the genetic modification program is the decreased need for insect killers in

   F. chiefly, soybean fields.
   G. all four crops.
   H. soybean fields and cornfields.
   J. cornfields and cotton fields.

5. In 2002, the total area GM protected against insect damage was

   A. 8.3 million hectares
   B. 12.5 million hectares
   C. 15.6 million hectares
   D. 18.4 million hectares

Passage 2

In the sterilizing process, instruments and cultures are exposed to high temperatures for a definite length of time. The diagram below displays the combinations of temperature and time required to kill various kinds of microorganisms. The six graph areas represent the living stages of bacteria, yeasts, and molds, and the spore stages of these kinds of organisms.

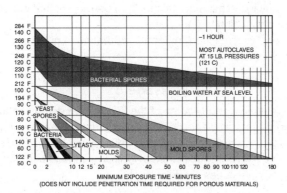

6. The kind of microorganism that is most difficult to kill is:

   F. mold spores.
   G. bacterial spores.
   H. yeasts.
   J. yeast spores.

7. If a laboratory technician keeps instruments in boiling water for 3 hours, the result of the procedure is to kill:

   A. mold spores
   B. bacterial spores.
   C. all spores.
   D. all organisms.

8. What procedure could be used to kill off mold spores in a culture, but leave the yeast spores still viable?

   F. Hold the culture at 80°C for 20 minutes.
   G. Keep the culture at 90°C for 8 minutes and then at 85°C for another 5 minutes.
   H. Keep the culture at 70°C for 10 minutes.
   J. No combination of time and temperature can do this.

9. The chart suggests that, by controlling time and temperature, a technician might be able to:

   A. kill off bacterial spores while leaving live bacteria viable.
   B. kill all bacterial spores without destroying all the mold spores.
   C. kill off certain kinds of bacterial spores and leave other kinds still viable.
   D. destroy all living molds without killing off the living bacteria.

10. What general biological rule might be suggested by the contents of this graph?

    F. Microorganisms form spores to enable them to survive all kinds of unfavorable conditions.
    G. Molds are more sensitive than bacteria to high temperature.
    H. Spore formation in microorganisms is a mechanism that protects the species against high temperatures.
    J. Spores are a vital mechanism for the reproduction of certain microorganisms.

Passage 3

Experiments are done to study some of the factors that determine the rate of a reaction. When sulfuric acid acts on potassium iodate, elemental iodine is released and its concentration increases gradually. In a test vessel, starch is included because it reacts with elemental iodine by turning blue when the iodine concentration reaches a critical level.

Experiment 1

A test solution is made of sulfuric acid and soluble starch in water. If potassium iodate is added, iodine accumulates at some definite rate. When the iodine reaches a certain concentration, the solution suddenly turns blue. Various concentrations of potassium iodate solution are used, and the time required for the mixture to turn blue is measured. The temperature was 20°C.

Potassium iodate concentration (%)	Time (seconds)
10	18
9	20
8	22
7	24
6	26
5	29
4	32

Experiment 2

To determine the effect of temperature on reaction rate, a 5% solution of potassium iodate is added to the test solution at various temperatures.

Temperature (° C)	Time (seconds)
5	36
15	31
25	27
35	24
45	22

11. Starch was added to the solution because:

   A. it speeds the reaction that produces iodine.
   B. it provides a test for the presence of elemental iodine.
   C. it slows down the reaction so that the time becomes easily measurable.
   D. it prevents the sulfuric acid from destroying the potassium iodate.

12. Experiment 1 shows that:

   F. elemental iodine turns starch blue.
   G. at higher iodate concentration, iodine is liberated more quickly.
   H. the rate of the reaction depends on the concentration of sulfuric acid used.
   J. the release of elemental iodine occurs suddenly.

13. Experiment 2 is an example of a general rule that:
   A. higher concentrations speed reactions.
   B. higher concentrations slow down reactions.
   C. higher temperatures speed reactions.
   D. higher temperatures slow down reactions.

14. Experiment 1 was done at a temperature of about:

    F. 10°C   **H.** 30°C
    G. 20°C   **J.** 40°C

15. By studying the results of this experiment, what can be concluded as to the time the reaction would take at a temperature of −15°C?

    A. It would take about 48 seconds.
    B. It would take longer than 36 seconds, but it is impossible to predict how long.
    C. It is not possible to make any prediction because the results of the experiment are too scattered.
    D. It might take a long time, or the whole thing might freeze and stop the reaction.

16. About how long would it take for the starch to turn blue if a 10% solution of potassium iodate was used at 45°C?

    F. 15 seconds   **H.** 22 seconds
    G. 18 seconds   **J.** 29 seconds

Passage 4

The graphs below represent the percentages of fat and of water in the human body, by age and sex.

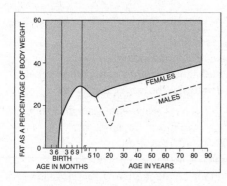 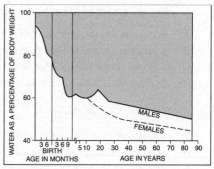

17. During the adolescent years, the most notable change is:

    A. a decrease in fat percentage for boys.
    B. an increase in fat percentage for girls.
    C. a decrease in water percentage for boys.
    D. an increase in water percentage for girls.

18. The percent of fat in the body increases most rapidly during:

    F. middle age.   **H.** babyhood.
    G. adolescence. **J.** the prenatal period.

19. At age 60, the amount of water in the body of a 150-pound man is:

    A. the same as that in a 150-pound woman.
    B. twice as much as that in a 150-pound woman.
    C. about the same as that in a 140-pound woman.
    D. about the same as that in a 160-pound woman.

20. As people get older after the age of 40:

    F. men and women become more and more different in the fat content of their bodies.
    G. men and women become more and more different in the water content of their bodies.
    H. both the water and the fat contents of the bodies of men and women become increasingly different.
    J. the difference of both fat and water contents of the bodies of the two genders does not change.

21. What hypothesis about the role of sex hormones during adolescence might be advanced from the graphs?

    A. Both male and female sex hormones cause an increase in the percent of fat in the body.
    B. Male hormones cause a reduction in the percent of fat and an increase in the percent of water.
    C. Female hormones have a much greater influence than male hormones on the percent of water.
    D. Male hormones cause the growth of male secondary sex characteristics.

Passage 5

Seeds are tested for their ability to produce substances that kill microorganisms. Each seed is placed on cultures of two bacteria (*Staphylococcus* and *Escherichia*) and two molds. Seeds are classified on a scale of 0 (no effect) to 5 (strong effect), according to the amount of microorganism-free space that develops around the seed.

Experiment 1

Seeds of two members of the Lily family are tested against four different microorganisms:

	Lily Family	
Microorganism	Garlic	Daylily
Staphylococcus	4	0
Escherichia	5	4
Bread mold	2	2
Penicillium mold	3	0

Experiment 2

The same experiment is repeated using seeds of two members of the Composite family:

	Composite Family	
Microorganism	Dandelion	Thistle
Staphylococcus	5	5
Escherichia	4	5
Bread mold	4	3
Penicillium mold	2	2

Experiment 3

The experiment is then done with two members of the Legume family:

	Legume Family	
Microorganism	Soybean	Alfalfa
Staphylococcus	0	0
Escherichia	4	2
Bread mold	2	3
Penicillium mold	3	4

22. Which of the microorganisms is most susceptible to attacks by the chemicals produced by seeds?

   F. *Staphylococcus*
   G. *Escherichia*
   H. Bread mold
   J. *Penicillium* mold

23. Of the following, which kind of seed is more effective against molds than against bacteria?

   A. Alfalfa
   B. Daylily
   C. Thistle
   D. Garlic

24. To find an antibiotic that will protect oranges against *Penicillium* mold, a scientist would concentrate on:

   F. seeds of the thistle and its close relatives.
   G. a variety of members of the Composite family.
   H. members of the Legume family.
   J. seeds of the daylily and its relatives.

25. What conclusion can be reached about bread mold?

   A. It can survive by attacking seeds.
   B. It is highly resistant to chemical poisoning.
   C. It cannot be destroyed by seeds of the Composite family.
   D. It is moderately susceptible to attack by many kinds of seeds.

26. What hint might a scientist trying to find an antibiotic to control *Staphylococcus* infections get from these experiments?

    F. Looking for seeds that produce such an antibiotic would be a waste of effort.
    G. It would be inadvisable to concentrate on seeds of the Legume family.
    H. It would be wise to concentrate on *Penicillium* mold and its close relatives.
    J. The scientist should not waste time trying the bread mold and its close relatives.

27. Which of the following ecological hypotheses is supported by the evidence of these experiments?

    A. Molds are better able to survive than bacteria wherever the two kinds of microorganisms compete.
    B. The Legume family produces valuable fodder crops because its seeds have a high survival rate.
    C. The bacteria *Escherichia* and *Staphylococcus* may be highly damaging to leguminous crops.
    D. The Composite family has so many successful sturdy weeds because its seeds destroy microorganisms.

Passage 6

Experiments are done to test the optical properties of lenses immersed in media having different indices of refraction.

Experiment 1

A lens made of flint glass, index of refraction 1.720, is tested.
A beam of parallel light rays is sent into the lens, and the distance from the lens to the point of convergence of the beam is measured. This is the focal length of the lens. This focal length is measured with the lens immersed in media of various indices of refraction.

Medium	Index of refraction	Focal length (cm)
Air	1.00	8
Folinol	1.24	13
Water	1.33	20
11% Sugar solution	1.50	39
Carbon disulfide	1.62	95
Methylene iodide	1.74	*

*Rays do not converge at all.

Experiment 2

Another lens is tested. It is made of the same kind of glass as in Experiment 1, but this lens is thicker, more strongly curved.

Medium	Index of refraction	Focal length (cm)
Air	1.00	5
Folinol	1.24	8
Water	1.33	12
11% Sugar solution	1.50	24
Carbon disulfide	1.62	60
Methylene iodide	1.74	*

Experiment 3

A lens made of a new plastic is then tested. This lens is identical in size and shape to the glass lens in Experiment 2.

Medium	Index of refraction	Focal length (cm)
Air	1.00	13
Folinol	1.24	34
Water	1.33	360
11% Sugar solution	1.50	*
Carbon disulfide	1.62	*
Methylene iodide	1.74	*

28. The index of refraction column is the same in all three experiments because:

   F. all three lenses have the same basic properties.
   G. the same liquids are used in all three experiments.
   H. the temperatures at which the experiments are performed are carefully controlled.
   J. the color of the light source is not allowed to change from one experiment to another.

29. As the index of refraction of the medium increases, what happens to the rays of light emerging from the lens?

   A. They converge more strongly in all cases.
   B. They converge more strongly on leaving the glass lenses, but not the plastic lens.
   C. They converge less strongly in all cases.
   D. They converge less strongly on leaving the plastic lens, but not the glass lens.

30. Making a lens thicker and more strongly curved:

    F. shortens the focal length.
    G. increases the focal length.
    H. increases the index of refraction.
    J. decreases the index of refraction.

31. A reasonable hypothesis that can be derived from Experiments 1 and 2 is that:

    A. a lens will not focus light if its index of refraction is lower than that of the medium it is in.
    B. methylene iodide tends to spread light out so that it does not come to a focus.
    C. the focal length of a lens depends entirely on the index of refraction of the medium it is in.
    D. the thicker a lens, the less the convergence it produces on the light that passes through it.

32. Measurements of the kind made in these experiments would NOT be useful in efforts to find:

    F. the index of refraction of a liquid.
    G. the way a prism in a fluid would bend light rays.
    H. the concentration of a sugar solution.
    J. the transparency of a newly developed plastic.

33. The index of refraction of the plastic lens in Experiment 3 must be:

    A. less than 1.33.   **C.** more than 1.33.
    B. between 1.33 and 1.50.   **D.** more than 1.50.

Passage 7

Two scientists disagree on the question of the origin of petroleum.

Scientist 1

There have been many theories suggesting a non-organic origin of petroleum, but none of them have been successful. It is now accepted almost universally by geologists that petroleum comes from the decay of living things. Petroleum formation occurs in enclosed oceanic basins, such as the Black Sea. There must be an extremely large and continuous supply of marine organisms, adding their corpses to an accumulation at the bottom of the sea. They are quickly buried in sediment, so quickly that they do not have time to decay. In the enclosed basin, there is little circulation, so there is no supply of fresh, oxygenated water. In the absence of oxygen, there is little decay. The organic matter of the corpses degenerates into hydrocarbons, which accumulate as oil and gas. Since oil is lighter than water, it rises. As the deposits are covered with more sediments, the oil and gas rise into them and accumulate there. Petroleum geologists know that oil is often found in salt domes, formed by the evaporation of seawater.

Scientist 2

The current theory about the origin of petroleum postulates a very unlikely combination of circumstances. It needs an enclosed basin, exceptionally rich in marine life, with sediments pouring rapidly into it from the surrounding countryside. Although this combination might occur occasionally, it is too rare to account for the enormous earth areas underlain by petroleum. In my opinion, oil has been present deep in the earth since its origin. Meteorites, comets, and satellites are rich in hydrocarbons. The earth formed by agglomeration of these kinds of objects. After the earth formed, the hydrocarbons seeped upward, accumulating in porous sedimentary rocks. However, oil and gas are sometimes found seeping out of igneous rocks, which have no fossils at all, if these rocks have been thoroughly fractured by deep earthquakes. Oil wells now drill down to only about 15,000 feet. A recent explorational drilling found an oily sludge at 20,000 feet. If we could get to 30,000 feet, we would find an enormous pool of oil underlying the whole crust of the earth.

34. Both scientists agree that petroleum:

    F. forms at the bottom of the sea.
    G. seeps upward into sedimentary rocks.
    H. is present in great quantities below 30,000 feet.
    J. has always been present on earth.

35. Which of the following discoveries would greatly weaken the argument of Scientist 2?

    A. A vast oil deposit is found in sedimentary strata 20,000 feet deep.
    B. A meteorite is analyzed and found to contain few hydrocarbons.
    C. The sludge discovered at 20,000 feet turns out to be contamination from drilling oil.
    D. A large accumulation of oil is found in highly fractured igneous rock.

36. According to Scientist 2, what strategy would be most likely to increase world supplies of petroleum?

    F. Drill wells to greater depths.
    G. Increase exploration of offshore sedimentary strata.
    H. Drill wells in igneous rocks.
    J. Develop techniques of extraction from meteorites.

37. Exploration of the Persian Gulf reveals that it is an enclosed body of water rich in marine life. According to the hypothesis of Scientist 1, what additional condition would be necessary in order for petroleum deposits to develop?

    A. Vertical circulation to carry oxygen downward
    B. High concentration of salt in the water
    C. An accumulation of meteorites
    D. Rapid deposition of sediments

38. Scientist 2 considers that oil seepage from igneous rocks is damaging to Scientist 1's theory because igneous rocks:

    F. are easily fractured by earthquakes.
    G. never contain fossils.
    H. are always located deep in the crust.
    J. contain many meteorites.

39. What evidence given by Scientist 1 was not refuted by Scientist 2?

    A. There have been many theories of a nonorganic origin of petroleum, and all of them have failed.
    B. Petroleum is very often found associated with salt domes.
    C. All petroleum deposits are in porous sedimentary rock.
    D. Meterorites come to earth in the ocean just as often as on land.

40. The chief objection that Scientist 2 has to the theory of Scientist 1 is that it:

    F. postulates the formation of petroleum in a highly unusual set of conditions.
    G. cannot account for the accumulation of petroleum in sedimentary rocks.
    H. arbitrarily rejects the theory of nonorganic origin.
    J. places a limit on the amount of petroleum that can be extracted from the earth.

Answers to Science Reasoning Test begin on page 430.

Model Writing Test (Optional)   30 minutes

Time —30 minutes

> <u>*Directions:*</u> Please write an essay in response to the topic below. During the 30 minutes allowed, develop your thoughts clearly and effectively. Try to include relevant examples and specific evidence to support your point of view.
>
> A plain, natural style is best. The length of your essay is up to you, but quality should take precedence over quantity.
>
> Be sure to write only on the assigned topic.

TOPIC: J. D., a senior, boasts a sterling academic record, is a top athlete, and has the respect of the faculty and her classmates. In the fall, she plans to go to Cornell University on a full scholarship. Mr. M., a new social studies teacher, however, has made a startling discovery: J. D. has regularly been submitting work copied from Internet web sites and from books and periodicals.

After confronting J. D., who insisted on her innocence, Mr. M. reported his findings to the principal. To avoid a scandal and preserve J. D.'s reputation, the principal did nothing except tell J. D. not to do it any more. He also ordered Mr. M. not to penalize J. D. in any way. Mr. M was outraged that J. D. had cheated all year long and gotten away with it. Frustrated, he wrote a letter to Cornell about J. D.'s plagiarism. When the principal found out, he fired Mr. M. on the spot for being insubordinate. Now the school and community are in an uproar, some supporting the principal, some supporting Mr. M., still others offering compromise solutions to the problem.

Knowing these facts, where do you stand on the issue? On lined paper, write an essay that explains your position and cites reasons for your views.

ANSWER KEYS AND ANALYSIS CHARTS

Test 1: English

1. D	16. G	31. C	46. H	61. C
2. J	17. B	32. J	47. B	62. J
3. B	18. H	33. B	48. J	63. B
4. G	19. D	34. F	49. C	64. H
5. D	20. J	35. D	50. H	65. B
6. H	21. C	36. J	51. A	66. J
7. C	22. J	37. B	52. H	67. C
8. F	23. A	38. G	53. C	68. G
9. A	24. G	39. B	54. G	69. C
10. J	25. B	40. J	55. C	70. F
11. C	26. G	41. B	56. F	71. B
12. G	27. C	42. J	57. C	72. F
13. C	28. G	43. B	58. G	73. C
14. J	29. C	44. H	59. D	74. F
15. D	30. G	45. B	60. G	75. A

ANSWER ANALYSIS CHART			
Skills	**Questions**	**Possible Score**	**Your Score**
Usage/Mechanics			
Punctuation	7, 9, 12, 26, 29, 33, 44, 47, 50, 72	10	
Basic Grammar and Usage	3, 8, 23, 31, 34, 35, 37, 38, 39, 40, 41, 66	12	
Sentence Structure	6, 13, 14, 16, 17, 19, 20, 22, 32, 46, 55, 56, 57, 58, 62, 64, 67, 68	18	
Rhetorical Skills			
Strategy	2, 18, 25, 27, 36, 42, 43, 49, 53, 54, 70, 71	12	
Organization	5, 15, 24, 30, 45, 59, 60, 63, 73, 74, 75	11	
Style	1, 4, 10, 11, 21, 28, 48, 51, 52, 61, 65, 69	12	

Total: 75

Number Correct: _____

Test 2: Mathematics

1. C	16. H	31. B	46. H
2. J	17. D	32. K	47. D
3. A	18. J	33. D	48. G
4. K	19. A	34. G	49. E
5. B	20. J	35. E	50. H
6. K	21. C	36. G	51. D
7. B	22. K	37. E	52. J
8. G	23. C	38. F	53. B
9. B	24. K	39. E	54. G
10. J	25. D	40. J	55. B
11. D	26. K	41. D	56. J
12. G	27. D	42. H	57. A
13. E	28. H	43. E	58. H
14. F	29. D	44. K	59. E
15. D	30. J	45. A	60. F

ANSWER ANALYSIS CHART					
Content Area	Skill Level			Possible Score	Your Score
	Basic Skills	Application	Analysis		
Pre-Algebra Algebra	1, 4, 5, 9, 10, 14, 21, 44	2, 6, 7, 17, 22, 24, 27, 32, 34, 37, 38, 43	3, 11, 12, 15	24	
Intermediate Algebra Coordinate Geometry	13, 20, 30, 31, 39, 46, 53	8, 16, 19, 23, 26, 28, 33	29, 41, 54, 56	18	
Geometry	18, 35, 42, 49, 51, 57, 59	25, 40, 45, 47, 48, 58, 60		14	
Trigonometry	36, 50	52, 55		4	

Total: 60

Number Correct: _____

Test 3: Reading

1. A	11. B	21. D	31. C
2. H	12. H	22. G	32. G
3. C	13. D	23. C	33. A
4. J	14. F	24. G	34. G
5. A	15. C	25. A	35. C
6. G	16. G	26. G	36. J
7. C	17. C	27. A	37. B
8. J	18. G	28. H	38. H
9. C	19. D	29. A	39. B
10. F	20. F	30. J	40. G

ANSWER ANALYSIS CHART

Passage Type	Referring	Reasoning	Possible Score	Your Score
Prose Fiction	1, 2, 4, 6	3, 5, 7, 8, 9, 10	10	
Social Studies	11, 14, 19	12, 13, 15, 16, 17, 18, 20	10	
Humanities	22, 23, 30	21, 24, 25, 26, 27, 28, 29	10	
Natural Science	32, 33, 34, 36	31, 35, 37, 38, 39, 40	10	

Total: 40

Number Correct: _____

Test 4: Science Reasoning

1. C	6. G	11. B	16. F	21. B	26. G	31. A	36. F
2. F	7. D	12. G	17. A	22. G	27. D	32. J	37. D
3. D	8. J	13. C	18. J	23. A	28. G	33. B	38. G
4. J	9. C	14. G	19. D	24. H	29. C	34. G	39. B
5. B	10. H	15. D	20. J	25. D	30. F	35. C	40. F

ANSWER ANALYSIS CHART					
	Skill Level				
Kind of Question	Understanding	Analysis	Generalization	Possible Score	Your Score
Data Representation	1, 2, 3, 6, 17, 18	4, 7, 8, 9, 19, 20	5, 10, 21	15	
Research Summaries	11, 12, 22, 23, 28, 29	14, 24, 25, 30, 31, 33	13, 15, 16, 26, 27, 32,	18	
Conflicting Viewpoints	34, 35, 38	36, 37, 39	40	7	

Total: 40

Number Correct: _____

DETERMINING YOUR COMPOSITE SCORE

To calculate your composite score (not including the Writing Test) follow these directions:

1. On the form below fill in the first column of blanks with the number of correct answers on each test.
2. Multiply each number by 36 and divide the product by the number of questions on each test. The results are your scale scores.
3. Add up your scale scores and divide by 4. The result should be rounded to the nearest whole number to determine your composite score.

	Number of correct answers			Scale score
English	_____ × 36 =	_____	÷ 75 =	_____
Math	_____ × 36 =	_____	÷ 60 =	_____
Reading	_____ × 36 =	_____	÷ 40 =	_____
Science	_____ × 36 =	_____	÷ 40 =	_____

Total _____ ÷ 4 = _____

Composite Score

PERFORMANCE EVALUATION CHART

Rating	English	Mathematics	Reading	Science Reasoning
Excellent	66–75	54–60	35–40	36–40
Very good	54–65	44–53	29–34	29–35
Above average	45–53	30–43	24–28	20–28
Below average	36–44	21–29	19–23	14–19
Weak	25–35	14–20	14–18	9–13
Poor	0–24	0–13	0–13	0–8

No test can give you a totally precise measurement of your academic achievement. Rather, think of your composite score as the mid-point in a range of scores that can vary one or more points in either direction. A composite score of 27, for example, means that you scored somewhere between 25 and 29.

Answer Explanations

Test 1: English

1. **(D)**

All meanings carried by the underlined portion are implicit in the words preceding it. The entire portion is redundant.

2. **(J)**

The quotation is pertinent, short, and authoritative. As such, it is a sound way to begin the passage.

3. **(B)**

The antecedent of the pronoun in question is the singular *someone*.

4. **(G)**

The phrase *lacking merit* at the end of the clause is adequate characterization of the type of case under discussion.

5. **(D)**

As idealistic as the thought is, it is off the topic and has no place in this passage.

6. **(H)**

The logic of this sentence requires that a transitional word indicating *cause* be employed in this spot.

7. **(C)**

Three or more items in a series must be set off by commas.

8. **(F)**

The phrase *changing attorneys* is a gerund phrase, that is, a *noun* phrase. Since it is an activity of the noun *client*, that noun requires the possessive apostrophe and final *s*.

9. **(A)**

Dashes are appropriate marks to set off a parenthetical phrase, especially if one intends to emphasize the phrase.

10. **(J)**

All other options are wordy or redundant.

11. **(C)**

Colloquial and whimsical language is not in keeping with the matter-of-fact tone of the passage.

12. **(G)**

Coordinate clauses must be separated by a comma.

13. **(C)**

A new sentence begins at this point.

14. **(J)**

At this spot a third noun—namely, *premium*—should parallel the objects *salary* and *rent*.

15. **(D)**

Paragraph 3 begins with a clear signal that it should follow paragraph 4 rather than precede it, specifically the word *Finally*.

16. **(G)**

The adverb *more* and the comparative adverb ending *-er* are equivalent, and cannot be used together. The result is a double comparison.

17. **(B)**

The subject of this clause is the singular *person*.

18. **(H)**

There is no suggestion or clue to suggest that the passage is intended for any one group.

19. **(D)**

As it stands, the text contains a comma splice at this point; of the options, only the period break is correct.

20. **(J)**

The present-tense, passive-voice verb is appropriate because the focus is on the toys, and the passage is written in the present tense. As it stands, this is a sentence fragment.

21. **(C)**

The fact that the sentence later mentions that the rooms are "slightly askew" is reason enough to avoid the modifiers of the word *rooms*.

22. **(J)**

The logic of this sentence requires that a conjunction indicating time be used at this transition; *when* is the only choice that makes sense.

23. **(A)**

The verb agrees with the nearer subject (two) and is in the present tense.

24. **(G)**

As interesting as the information may be, this sentence is wholly off the topic, and must be removed.

25. **(B)**

The notion of children marking their territory with smudges and smears is humorous and whimsical. The other options do not suggest humor.

26. **(G)**

A compound adjective preceding the noun it modifies is hyphenated, but the two words before *homes* do not comprise a compound adjective; one, *finely*, is an adverb modifying the adjective *furnished*.

27. **(C)**

The enormous difference in the size of these paragraphs, as well as the amount of data they contain, shows the writer's bias.

28. **(G)**

The noun *difference* clearly indicates that two kinds of people are being compared; *distinguishing* is not needed.

29. **(C)**

A compound adjective that *precedes* the noun is hyphenated; one that *follows* the noun usually is not.

30. **(G)**

The word *Conversely* is a clue that paragraph 2 must occur after paragraph 3; the words *another great difference* at the outset of paragraph 4 place it after paragraph 2.

31. **(C)**

The verb *had grown* agrees with the subject *climate* and with the tense of the rest of the sentence and paragraph.

32. **(J)**

The sentence calls for the passive verb *be supervised* (by women). The other choices either are not verbs at all or are verbs that do not make sense in the context.

33. **(B)**

The best choice here is *roles; some* to introduce a new clause. The clause is very close to and a derivative of the first clause of the sentence, so the semicolon is more appropriate than the period.

34. **(F)**

It is a pronoun whose antecedent is a substantive in the previous sentence, *crack epidemic*. The other noun choices miss entirely the relationship between the two.

35. **(D)**

Rose has as its subject the noun *proportion*; the simple past tense is in agreement with the tense of the upper paragraph as well as all the bulleted sentences at its close.

36. **(J)**

The answer is *yes* because of the facts one garners in the bulleted list at the end of the paragraph.

37. **(B)**

The sentence is cast in the subjunctive mood and is in the simple past tense, while all other choices are written in incompatible tenses.

38. **(G)**

The subject *tens of thousands* calls for the present passive progressive tense *being stuffed*. All other choices are in the wrong tense or voice.

39. **(B)**

The past passive tense *were considered* is the only choice for this verb of the subject "riffraff"; all other choices have incompatible tenses or voices.

40. **(J)**

Some people, near the beginning of the paragraph, is the subject of the sentence. It is far enough removed from its original source to require the use of *they* as the subject of the verb *observe*. Other choices present incompatible subjects or sentences left without a subject.

41. **(B)**

The noun *defendants* appears in the introductory clause; the pronoun that is the antecedent to that noun must be plural, as it is in *they face*. No other choices have an appropriate antecedent or an appropriate verb.

42. **(J)**

This choice is the only correct choice because it has as its purpose delineating the "hurdles" always faced by minority defendants.

43. **(B)**

This choice clearly makes clear many facts about the sordid history of the death penalty in the United States. The other sentences address nonpertinent matters.

44. **(H)**

Between the word *States* and the number 287 occurs a break between sentences. The division using a *colon* is the most appropriate because the second sentence is closely related to and is derived from the first. The other choices either are not signaling the close relationship or are run-on sentences.

45. **(B)**

The second division, [Section (2)], introduces readers to the whole topic of the essay, prisons and prisoners, and its reference to early times of London clearly indicate that it belongs in the first position. Section (1) begins by the late 1900s; in addition, the fact that woman have increased as inmates fits nicely in a position just after section (2). Section (3) begins with the point "the cause of these arrest figures is debatable," clearly referring to the data at the end of Section (1). The description of the death penalty history is most understandable here and is a good conclusion to the whole selection.

46. **(H)**

This verb must be in the present tense to express what is still true.

47. **(B)**

The name *Antonia Shimerda* is in apposition with *protagonist* and is properly set off with two commas.

48. **(J)**

The adjective *actual* is the only choice that indicates what is intended, that the girl was a genuine Bohemian girl. The other choices are either redundant or misleading.

49. **(C)**

This "summary" is inconclusive; it should include more information about the story.

50. **(H)**

Commas and periods are *always* placed *inside* quotation marks, even when there are single and double quotation marks because the sentence contains a quote within a quote.

51. **(A)**

The word *albeit* means literally "although it be," a meaning that is required for the sense of the clause to remain intact, and which is not repeated in the other options.

52. **(H)**

The prefix *multi* is most often incorporated with another word as a unit.

53. **(C)**

Since the paragraph deals with Cather's preference in the novel to the country over the city, and since the entire passage is about the novel *My Antonia*, the quotation is clearly meaningful.

54. **(G)**

This passage represents a relatively concentrated discussion of other critical works, and is likely to interest only readers who are knowledgeable about and interested in critical essays.

55. **(C)**

The passage is written in the present tense, and employs the historical present whenever necessary.

56. **(F)**

Employed in this sentence is a participle modifying the noun *symbols*.

57. **(C)**

To be parallel with the phrases naming the first two cycles, this one must begin with the noun *cycle*, rather than a clause describing it.

58. **(G)**

Only the comma, introducing a nonrestrictive clause, is correct. Choice F results in a sentence fragment beginning with *In which*, and neither the semicolon (H) or the dash (J) is appropriate.

59. **(D)**

The body of the paragraph does a comprehensive job of developing the beginning generalization.

60. **(G)**

Paragraph 2 begins with broad, general statements about the novel, and spells out what the passage will be about. Accordingly, it is the introductory paragraph, and is logically followed by paragraph 3, which develops the critical analysis begun at the end of paragraph 2. The summary paragraph logically follows.

61. **(C)**

This choice is the only complete choice; all other choices leave the sentence without an essential part of the syntax or gender description.

62. **(J)**

The writer makes clear that she is in America with this choice. All other choices present the reader with confusing adverbs or genders.

63. **(B)**

The entire passage is about women in Japan; of the choices, this is the only one to give emphasis to that essential point being made by the author. The other choices are not nearly so specific.

64. **(H)**

This choice is the only one that makes clear the point that the Secretary of the Ministry of Construction received attention from the local press because she was a woman, and not because her work was so distinguished.

65. **(B)**

Instituted is the proper verb to represent the Secretary's official actions. All other choices are off in meaning and nuance.

66. **(J)**

The sentence must refer to two specific oblique compliments of faint praise made by a reporter and by people in general to have any point in the present sentence. No other choices come as close to that reference as J.

67. **(C)**

The sentence must be divided by a semicolon in order to set up the following point for the cause-result sentence. None of the other choices provides the cause-effect conclusion.

68. **(G)**

The sentence begins with a well-known phrase, "not only...but also...." F is the only choice that completes this phrase satisfactorily.

69. **(C)**

The whole sentence is about women receiving faint, insincere phrases and polite dismissals. This gentle choice is compatible with the tone of the rest of the essay.

70. **(F)**

The woman who wrote this essay is concerned about the way women are being treated in her native Japan. The other choices miss her intentions by quite a margin.

71. **(B)**

The writer is understanding of the slow progress of women's rights. At the same time, she tacitly admits to a need for recognizing the old world and its traditions. No other choice describes her attitude as well.

72. **(F)**

This choice is the only correct one. All other choices are ungrammatical.

73. **(C)**

This choice states clearly the point of the author. All other choices come close but are slightly maligned or are grammatically incorrect.

74. **(F)**

This choice repeats exactly the two changes that the author set down. The other choices, while close, are not correct.

75. **(A)**

The sequence is correct as it stands. The first section introduces Simon de Beauvoir, her work, *The Second Sex*, and the problems with women's rights in Japan. The second section begins with direct reference to a point made in the first section, namely, the two examples of faint praise made toward the Secretary of the Ministry of Construction. Similarly, the third section makes direct reference to the problems discussed at the end of the second section using the words "such problems...."

Answer Explanations

Test 2: Mathematics

1. **(C)**

$$\frac{a}{b} - \frac{c}{d} = \frac{ad}{bd} - \frac{bc}{bd}$$

$$= \frac{ad - bc}{bd}$$

2. **(J)**

First factor the numerator

$$\frac{2x^4 + x^3}{x^6} = \frac{x^3(2x + 1)}{x^6} \quad \text{Cancel } x^3.$$

$$= \frac{2x + 1}{x^3}$$

3. **(A)**

$\dfrac{3}{4}$ (1600) = 1200 phones have dials.

$\dfrac{1}{3}$ (1200) = 400 dial phones are replaced by push-button phones.

1200 − 400 = 800 dial phones remain.

4. **(K)**

$\dfrac{x}{y}$ is not necessarily an integer.

5. **(B)**

For example: 5 − (−7) = 12, which is positive.

6. **(K)**

Multiply both sides by $4x - 3$.
($\dfrac{3}{4}$ is a restricted value.)

$$\frac{4}{4x-3}(4x-3) = 5(4x-3)$$
$$5 = 5(4x-3) = 20x - 15$$
$$20 = 20x$$
$$x = 1$$

7. **(B)**

Ten times the tens digit plus the units digit: $10t + u$.

8. **(G)**

Multiply each term of the first polynomial times each term of the second polynomial.

$(x - 1)(x^2 + x + 1)$
$= x^3 + x^2 + x - x^2 - x - 1$
$= x^3 - 1$

9. **(B)**

Inscribed $\angle BAC$ is half the measure of the intercepted arc $\overset{\frown}{BC}$. So m $(\overset{\frown}{BC})$ = 50°. The central angle BOC has the same measure as its intercepted arc.

10. **(J)**

$$2.5\% = 0.025$$

$$\frac{1}{40} = 0.025$$

$$2.5(10^{-2}) = 0.025$$

$$\frac{75}{30} = 2.5$$

11. **(D)**

Each apple costs $\frac{100}{3} = 33\frac{1}{3}$ in the 3 for $1.00 deal. The difference between

35 cents and $33\frac{1}{3}$ is $1\frac{2}{3}$ cents.

12. **(G)**

In 1 minute Joan can run $\frac{1}{a}$ part of a mile. After b minutes,

she has run $b\left(\frac{1}{a}\right) = \frac{b}{a}$.

13. **(E)**

Division by 0 is never allowed.

14. **(F)**

$$3\frac{3}{5} \cdot 4\frac{1}{6} = \frac{18}{5} \cdot \frac{25}{6}$$

$$= \frac{3}{1} \cdot \frac{5}{1} \quad \text{Cancel.}$$

$$= 15$$

15. **(D)**

Write two equations with two variables, n and d.

$$n = d + 5$$

$$5n + 10d = 130 \quad \text{Then substitute for } n.$$

$$5(d + 5) + 10d = 130$$

$$5d + 25 + 10d = 130$$

$$15d + 25 = 130$$

$$15d = 105$$

$$d = 7$$

Then $n = 12$.

16. **(H)**

In an arithmetic sequence, the nth term is given by
$$a_n = a_1 + (n - 1)d$$
in which a_1 is the first term, n is the number of the term, and d is the common difference between terms. In the given sequence the tenth term is sought and the common difference is 5.
$$a_{10} = 3 + (10 - 1)5 = 3 + 45$$

17. **(D)**

First multiply by 100 to get rid of the decimals.
$$100[0.2(100 - x) + 0.05x] = 100[0.1(100)]$$
$$20(100 - x) + 5x = 10(100)$$
$$2000 - 20x + 5x = 1000$$
$$-15x = -1000$$
$$x = 66\frac{2}{3}$$

18. **(J)**

There certainly is a regular polygon of seven sides.

19. **(A)**

$\sqrt[3]{54x^4y^6} = \sqrt[3]{27x^3y^6} \cdot 2x$ Separate the radicand into cube and noncube parts.
$= 3xy^2\sqrt[3]{2x}$

20. **(J)**

Conic sections are second-degree (or less) curves only. The equation $y = x^3$ is not of degree 2.

21. **(C)**

The degree of a polynomial is the greatest of the degrees of its terms. The degrees of the terms of the given polynomial are 3, 4, 2, and 0. The greatest degree is 4.

22. **(K)**

Add.

$$2x - y = 5$$
$$x + y = 1$$
$$\overline{3x = 6}$$
$$x = 2$$

Substitute $x = 2$ into either equation (say the second one).

$2 + y = 1$

$y = -1$

23. **(C)**

The numbers 2, 4, 6, and 8 satisfy the conditions of being even and less than 10. $P(A) = \dfrac{4}{20} = \dfrac{1}{5}$.

24. **(K)**

Multiply the numerator and denominator by the LCD, which is xy.

$$\frac{xy(x + y)}{xy\left(\dfrac{1}{x} + \dfrac{1}{y}\right)} = \frac{xy(x + y)}{y + x}$$

$$= xy$$

25. **(D)**

Inscribed angle ABC intercepts an arc that is twice the measure of the angle, so arc ADC measures 140° and the measure of arc ABC is $(360 - 140)° = 220°$. The measure of inscribed angle ADC is half the measure of its intercepted arc: 110°. (Opposite angles of an inscribed quadrilateral are supplementary.)

26. **(K)**

Since $a > b$, then $a - b > 0$ and $b - a < 0$. The absolute value of a positive number is equal to that number, but the absolute value of a negative number is the opposite of the number.

$|a - b| = a - b$ and $|b - a|$

$= -(b - a) = a - b$.

$|a - b| + |b - a| = (a - b) + (a - b) = 2a - 2b$.

27. **(D)**

The expression -3^{-2} is properly read as "the opposite of 3 to the -2 power." Follow the rules for the order of operations:

$$-3^{-2} = -(3^{-2}) = -\left(\frac{1}{3^2}\right) = -\left(\frac{1}{9}\right)$$

28. **(H)**

To put this equation into standard form, complete the square in both variables.

$$(x^2 - 4x \quad) + 4(y^2 + 6y \quad) = -36$$
$$(x^2 - 4x + 4) + 4(y^2 + 6y + 9) = -36 + 4 + 36$$
$$(x - 2)^2 + 4(y + 3)^2 = 4$$
$$\frac{(x - 2)^2}{4} + \frac{(y + 3)^2}{1} = 1$$

The center is $(2, -3)$.

29. **(D)**

This is a work-type word problem, for which the formula $w = rt$ applies. Let Bonnie's time to complete the job be x hours, then Nick's time is $x - 2$ hours.

Her rate of work is $\frac{1}{x}$ part of the job per hour. His rate is $\frac{1}{x - 2}$.

	w	$=$	r	t
Nick	$\frac{7}{x - 2}$		$\frac{1}{x - 2}$	7
Bonie	$\frac{7}{x}$		$\frac{1}{x}$	7

The sum of the work column is equal to 1 (one completed job). The equation is

$$\frac{7}{x - 2} + \frac{7}{x} = 1.$$

30. **(J)**

A function is one-to-one if all of the ordered pairs in the function not only have different first components but also have different second components. This means that the graph must pass both the vertical line test and the horizontal line test. If a vertical line crosses the graph once at most, then it is a function. If a horizontal line crosses the graph once at most, then the function is one-to-one (and thus it has an inverse). Only J satisfies both tests.

31. **(B)**

An exponential function is any function of the type:

$$f(x) = a^x, \text{ for } a > 0, a \neq 1.$$

32. **(K)**

$(5x - 3y^2)^2 = 25x^2 - 30xy^2 + 9y^4.$

33. **(D)**

The reciprocal of i is $\dfrac{1}{i}$. Multiply both numerator and denominator by the conjugate of the denominator $-i$: $\dfrac{-i(1)}{-i(i)}$.

$$\frac{-i}{1} = -i$$

34. **(G)**

$$\frac{a^{-3}bc^2}{a^{-4}b^2c^{-3}} = a^{-3-(-4)}b^{1-2}c^{2-(-3)}$$
$$= a^1b^{-1}c^5$$
$$= \frac{ac^5}{b}$$

35. **(E)**

The length of the longer leg of a 30-60-90 triangle is equal to $\sqrt{3}$ times the length of the shorter leg, and the length of the hypotenuse is twice the length of the shorter leg. The length of the longer leg is given, so to find the length of the shorter leg divide by $\sqrt{3}$.

$$BC = \frac{6}{\sqrt{3}} = 2\sqrt{3}$$

Therefore $AB = 2(2\sqrt{3}) = 4\sqrt{3}$

36. **(G)**

The identity is $\sin 2A = 2 \sin A \cos A$.

37. **(E)**

Use the quadratic formula:

$$x = \frac{-b \pm \sqrt{b^2 - 4ac}}{2a}$$

Here

$$x = \frac{4 \pm \sqrt{16 - (-72)}}{6}$$

$$= \frac{4 \pm \sqrt{88}}{6} = \frac{4 \pm 2\sqrt{22}}{6} = \frac{2 \pm \sqrt{22}}{3}$$

38. **(F)**

$$3\sqrt{3} - \sqrt{48} + 3\sqrt{\frac{1}{3}} = 3\sqrt{3} - 4\sqrt{3} + \sqrt{3}$$
$$= 0$$

39. **(E)**

The two ordered pairs (4, 2) and (4, −2) both satisfy the equation $x = y^2$, and so it does not define a function.

40. **(J)**

The length of a tangent is the mean proportional between the length of a secant from a common external point and the length of the secant's external segment.

$$\frac{x + 4}{6} = \frac{6}{4}$$
$$4x + 16 = 36$$
$$4x = 20$$
$$x = 5$$

41. **(D)**

This is a uniform motion-type word problem, for which the formula $d = rt$ applies.

	D	=	r	t
Bike	x		12	$\frac{x}{12}$
Car	x		36	$\frac{x}{36}$

The time for the car trip is $\frac{1}{2}$ hour less than the time for the bike trip. The equation is:

$$\frac{x}{36} = \frac{x}{12} - \frac{1}{2}$$

42. **(H)**

The midpoint formula is $\left(\dfrac{x_1 + x_2}{2}, \dfrac{y_1 + y_2}{2} \right)$

Here

$$\left(\frac{3 + (-5)}{2}, \frac{7 + (-6)}{2} \right) = \left(-1, \frac{1}{2} \right)$$

43. **(E)**

A square root radical by definition is positive. The solution set is empty.

44. **(K)**

All these statements are true.

45. **(A)**

The diagram shows a 30-60-90 triangle with the hypotenuse equal in length to the radius of the circle, the length of the shorter leg half the length of the hypotenuse, and the length of the longer leg $\sqrt{3}$ times the length of the shorter leg. The perimeter of the triangle is equal to 6 times the length of the longer leg of the triangle.

$$6(4\sqrt{3}) = 24\sqrt{3}$$

46. **(H)**

The domain contains all real numbers except those for which the denominator is zero. Set the denominator equal to zero and solve.

$$x^2 - 2x - 3 = 0$$
$$(x - 3)(x + 1) = 0$$
$$x - 3 = 0 \quad x + 1 = 0$$
$$x = 3 \quad\quad x = -1$$

47. **(D)**

Draw the line of centers and a line parallel to $\overline{CD}$ through $B(\overline{BE}\|\overline{CD})$. The length of $\overline{AB}$ is the sum of the lengths of the radii of the circles. A radius of a circle is perpendicular to a tangent at the point of tangency. Therefore $BCDE$ is a rectangle.

$BC = 3$, so $DE = 3$.
$AD = 5$, so $AE = 2$.
Apply the Pythagorean Theorem to right triangle ABE.

$$(BE)^2 + 2^2 = 8^2$$
$$(BE)^2 + 4 = 64$$
$$(BE)^2 = 60$$
$$BE = \sqrt{60} = 2\sqrt{15}$$

And $BE = CD = 2\sqrt{15}$.

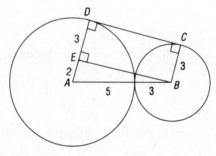

48. **(G)**

The measure of inscribed angle C is half the measure of its intercepted arc BAD.

$$m \angle C = \frac{1}{2}(180 + m \text{ arc } AB)$$

$$125 = \frac{1}{2}(180 + m \text{ arc } AB)$$

$$250 = 180 + m \text{ arc } AB$$

$$m \text{ arc } AB = 70$$

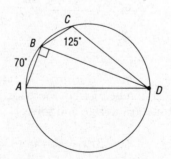

Therefore arc $BCD = 180 - 70 = 110$. The measure of inscribed angle A is half the measure of its intercepted arc.

$$m \angle A = \frac{1}{2} (110) = 55.$$

49. (E)

There is not enough information to answer this question uniquely.

50. (H)

The distance from the origin to A is $r = \sqrt{(-3)^2 + 4^2} = 5$.

The definition of $\sec \theta$ is $\dfrac{r}{x}$, so $\sec \theta = \dfrac{5}{-3}$

51. (D)

$$\sum_{k=1}^{5} 2k^2 = 2 \cdot 1^2 + 2 \cdot 2^2 + 2 \cdot 3^2 + 2 \cdot 4^2 + 2 \cdot 5^2$$
$$= 2 + 8 + 18 + 32 + 50 = 110$$

52. (J)

Cosine is positive in quadrants I and IV; cotangent is negative in quadrants II and IV. There is an angle in quadrant IV that satisfies the given conditions.

53. (B)

A Venn diagram (see below) will help clarify these statements. The statement in B, $(A \cap B) \subseteq B$, is true. Every element in the intersection of sets A and B is contained in B.

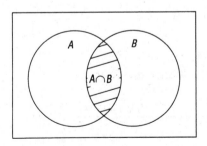

54. (G)

Let one side be x; then the other side is $x + 1$. Use the Pythagorean Theorem:

$$x^2 + (x + 1)^2 = (\sqrt{145})^2$$
$$x^2 + x^2 + 2x + 1 = 145$$
$$2x^2 + 2x - 144 = 0$$
$$x^2 + x - 72 = 0$$
$$(x + 9)(x - 8) = 0$$

$$x + 9 = 0 \qquad\qquad x - 8 = 0$$
$$x = -9 \text{ (extraneous)} \qquad x = 8$$
$$\text{Then } x + 1 = 8 + 1 = 9.$$

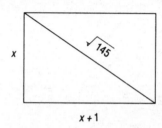

55. (B)

Think of $\cos^{-1}\frac{2}{3}$ as an angle, θ. Then the question asks for $\sin\theta$, where θ is the angle whose cosine is $\frac{2}{3}$. This angle is in quadrant I.

$$\sin\theta = +\sqrt{1 - \cos^2\theta}$$
$$= \sqrt{1 - \left(\frac{2}{3}\right)^2} = \sqrt{1 - \frac{4}{9}}$$
$$= \sqrt{\frac{5}{9}} = \frac{\sqrt{5}}{3}$$

56. (J)

Let x be the score on the fourth test. Then

$$\frac{75 + 84 + 80 + x}{4} \geq 80$$
$$239 + x \geq 320$$
$$x \geq 81$$

57. (A)

The sum of the exterior angles of any polygon is 360°. In a regular polygon the angles have the same measure, so one exterior angle of a regular octagon is $\frac{360°}{8} = 45°$.

58. **(H)**

The diagonals of a rhombus are perpendicular bisectors of each other. Therefore in right triangle ABE, $AE = 4$ and $BE = 3$. Use the Pythagorean Theorem.

$$(AB)^2 = 4^2 + 3^2 = 14 + 9 = 25$$
$$AB = 5$$

The perimeter of the rhombus is $4(5) = 20$.

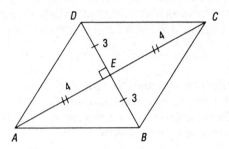

59. **(E)**

All these statements are false.

60. **(F)**

The length of the altitude of a right triangle is the mean proportional between the lengths of the two segments of the hypotenuse.

$$\frac{x}{4} = \frac{4}{10 - x}$$
$$x(10 - x) = 16$$
$$10x - x^2 = 16$$
$$0 = x^2 - 10x + 16$$
$$(x - 8)(x - 2) = 0$$

$$x - 8 = 0 \qquad\qquad x - 2 = 0$$
$$x = 8 \text{ (extraneous)} \quad x = 2$$

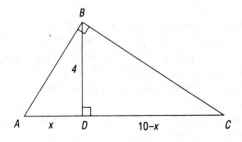

Answer Explanations

Test 3: Reading

1. **(A)**

In lines 24–27, the narrator attributes his gloomy nature to a childhood spent on a chicken farm. B is incorrect because Father, once a happy contented farmhand, and Mother, an ex-schoolteacher, had both experienced success in former years. C sounds as though it could have shaped the narrator's state of mind, but it is not mentioned in the passage. D may border on the truth, but the passage, while mentioning that the family struggled to make the farm pay, doesn't imply that constant debt molded the narrator's view of life.

2. **(H)**

In lines 14–20, the narrator presumes that Mother's reading was responsible for her ambition. F is a tempting answer, but there is no hint that Mother's reading influenced her teaching. G overstates Mother's devotion to reading and studying. J is not mentioned in the passage.

3. **(C)**

Father married at 34 (in "his thirty-fifth year"), according to the third paragraph, and a year later he launched a 10-year period as a chicken farmer.

4. **(J)**

Father continued to work on a farm, not as a hired farmhand, however, but as an owner. Choices F, G, and H are postmarital changes that occurred in Father's life.

5. **(A)**

The narrator comments in lines 38–40 that chickens look so bright and alert but are stupid—much like people. Choices B, C, and D seem like reasonable similarities between people and chickens, but the narrator fails to mention them.

6. **(G)**

In line 30, the narrator describes a chick as "a tiny fluffy thing such as you will see pictured on Easter cards." F is not a good answer because the narrator views the brief life cycle of a chicken as "tragic" (line 28). H may reflect the experience of some folks who have raised chickens but not the experience of this family, which found few pleasures in chicken farming. J is true but irrelevant to the passage.

7. **(C)**

According to lines 42–44, literature on raising chickens leads unsuspecting people astray by holding out the unrealistic prospects of making a fortune. Choice A overstates the narrator's opinion by saying that everything in these books and articles deliberately misrepresents the truth. B does not apply to the passage. D may be inferred from the circumstances spelled out in the narrative but is not in keeping with the point of the passage.

8. **(J)**

Mother and Father never considered themselves failures. In spite of setbacks they continued on their "upward journey through life," according to line 56. All the other choices—F, G, and H—represent events that took place in the narrative.

9. **(C)**

The narrator gently pokes fun at life on the chicken farm of his youth. Choices A and B are not at all reflected in the tone of the passage. D is only half right; there are distressing elements to the tale, but in dealing with them the narrator adopts a humorous tone.

10. **(F)**

The narrator believes that if chicken farmers were not calm and hopeful (i.e., *philosophical* by nature), they'd grow too frustrated to continue doing their work. Choices G and J express weighty thoughts that don't apply to this relatively light and witty tale. H is not discussed in the passage.

11. **(B)**

Choice A is supported in part by the statement that battered women feel "trapped" (line 9), but choice B is a better answer because the question asks you to identify the *most important* reason behind women's helplessness. The answer is found in lines 6–7, which state outright that the "weight of society has been traditionally on the side of the oppressor," namely, the male. There's no doubt that C also contributes to women's sense of powerlessness, but lack of funds is not discussed until much later in the passage. D is incorrect because the passage ignores the role of witnesses.

12. **(H)**

The assertion clearly implies that police, prosecutors, and sometimes even judges contribute to the victim's feelings of helplessness. Choice F is not discussed or suggested by the passage. G is a generalization not supported by evidence in the passage. J certainly applies to some victims of abuse, but the passage doesn't deal with issues of women's psychology.

13. **(D)**

Lines 15–18 suggest that police and others believe that abused women often provoke violent behavior in men. Choice A seems a reasonable but temporary solution to abuse problems, but later the passage says that without outside intervention abuse is apt to continue. B is not discussed, and C contradicts the assertion that police officers are predisposed to hold wives responsible for their own abuse.

14. **(F)**

Reconciliation is not mentioned anywhere in the passage as an explanation for aborted lawsuits. The financial implications (G) are discussed fully throughout the passage, especially in paragraphs 3–6. H, the duration of court cases, is discussed in the third paragraph, and J, the husband's vow to shape up, in lines 22–23.

15. **(C)**

Line 39 suggests that, if possible, the wife should seek refuge in a shelter for battered women. Choices A and D seem like reasonable actions, but they are not a quick remedy nor are they suggested by the passage. B may take care of the emergency, but as the first two paragraphs indicate, calling the police won't provide a long-term solution to the problem.

16. **(G)**

Lines 46–49 state that with professional assistance battered women recognize and employ their own enormous powers of self-preservation. The other choices spell out steps that would no doubt help solve abuse problems, but the passage takes the position that women should be helped to take control of their own lives.

17. **(C)**

Most of the passage in one way or another focuses on problems that confront abused women. Choices A, B, and D are details that support the main purpose of the passage.

18. **(G)**

The heart of the passage (paragraphs 3–6) emphasizes the financial hardships faced by abused women. Choices F, H, and J are hardships that the passage briefly alludes to.

19. **(D)**

Because the passage says nothing about requiring husbands to pay for their wives' legal expenses, D is the best answer. Choice A is cited as a course of action—although an ineffective one—in line 26. B and C are discussed in the fifth paragraph (lines 34–39).

20. **(F)**

Lines 61–65 imply that an abused woman should turn to the courts only as a last resort. The passage neither states or implies that choices G, H, and J are reasons for a woman to go to court.

21. **(D)**

Among the techniques used by the program's producers was the use of prestigious speakers, including astronomers (line 26). A, B, and C may also have been used to create realistic effects, but they are not discussed in the passage.

22. **(G)**

The first paragraph alludes to all the choices except G. There is no indication that the meteorite had been illuminated.

23. **(C)**

The third paragraph contains a list of techniques employed to convince listeners that the reported events were real. A, B, and D may have helped but they are not discussed in the passage.

24. **(G)**

One indication of spreading panic was the "flood" of calls to police and radio stations (lines 20–22). Rule out F because people were alarmed long before Cantril's study. H alludes to something that happened but not necessarily as a consequence of genuine alarm, and J not only seems to go against human nature but is not mentioned in the passage.

25. **(A)**

Taking into account the statement in lines 9–10 that the public was "relatively unfamiliar with science fiction stories at that point in history," it is reasonable to conclude that the genre was new in 1938.

26. **(G)**

Choices F and H raised doubts about the veracity of the report. J is not discussed in the passage. G is the best answer because lines 39–45 give examples of listeners who deluded themselves by giving credence to irrelevant evidence.

27. **(A)**

The lines in question describe the behavior of skeptical people who sought evidence to disprove the veracity of the program. B is not supported by the passage. C overstates the case; perhaps some, but not all, readers of *Amazing Stories* identified the program as a hoax. D is probably true but is not discussed.

28. **(H)**

The passage contains no evidence to support F and J. Choice G might appeal to those who confuse "panic" in line 48 with leaving "lasting impressions." H is supported by the implication in lines 49–50 that people with greater critical ability are likely to react differently from those who are "especially suggestible or anxious."

29. **(A)**

The author links listeners' panic to such great dangers as the rise of Hitler, the threat of a world war, and the Great Depression—crises that kept the world on edge in 1938. C and D may have played an indirect part in the panic that followed the broadcast, but they are not as important as the correct answer, A. Choice B is not stated or implied in the passage.

30. **(J)**

The last paragraph lists several causes of listeners' response to the broadcast, including the turmoil in Europe leading to World War II. None of the other choices are applicable.

31. **(C)**

By emphasizing the size of space, the author shows why solar sails hold promise as the best way to move "things around" out there. While the paragraph refers to the ideas in A, B, and D, each is meant to support the main point.

32. **(G)**

In lines 12–13, the author says that gravity controls orbiting objects. F is incorrect because the passage implies in lines 15–19 that at slow speeds orbiting objects fall into whatever it is they are orbiting. H is not discussed in the passage. J applies only when objects must be moved from one orbit to another.

33. **(A)**

The main problem with electric rockets, says the author in lines 38–39, is "the cost and mass of the solar power plant" used to generate electricity. Rule out B because by definition a solar power plant would not function outside the solar system. Eliminate C because the passage does not discuss the fragility of electric rockets. Nor is D a good answer because electric rockets are powered by electricity not by chemical fuel.

34. **(G)**

According to the passage, solar sails require no fuel at all because they are powered by the sun (H). As a result they are lighter (J) and less costly (F).

35. **(C)**

To achieve the speed required for travel into deep space rockets must carry enormous amounts of fuel—more than they can manage. Choice A may be implied in the passage but it is not stated. Choice B is an effect caused by a rocket's limited fuel supply, and D suggests nonsensically that rockets have a will of their own.

36. **(J)**

In the third paragraph (lines 19–31) the author explains that the total fuel mass needed to double the speed of the rocket increases "exponentially," which implies, in mathematical terms, far more than double the amount of fuel.

37. **(B)**

Two rockets of the same size and weight would behave identically until they reach orbit or beyond. Then, the electric rocket would be powered by the sun. Initially, therefore, it needs to carry less fuel than its chemically-energized counterpart.

38. **(H)**

By stating that a "rocket can reach the same velocity as its exhaust" (lines 19–20), the author implies that the speed of the rocket cannot exceed the velocity of the exhaust. A law of physics may imply F, but a rocket's trajectory is not discussed in the passage. Likewise, the passage largely ignores the matters raised by F and J.

39. **(B)**

The passage discusses problems of weight (lines 55–59, acceleration (47–51), and unfolding of solar sails (42–45). Although the author proposes a hexagonal shape for solar sails (line 60), determining the shape is not discussed as a problem that must be solved.

40. **(G)**

According to the passage, solar sails have "reached an advanced planning stage" (line 46). Because they don't exist yet, they are hypothetical. While solar sails might well float in the air (A), that feature is irrelevant because such sails would be constructed for use in the vacuum of space. C is a faulty choice because the reference to aluminum foil (line 56) is meant only to describe the thickness of solar sails, not the manner in which they are stored. D contradicts the the passage, which states that solar sails are *not* aluminized plastic sheets (line 55).

Answer Explanations

Test 4: Science Reasoning

1. **(C)**

This is the black part of the soybean bar in Chart I.

2. **(F)**

The gray area in the soybean bar of Chart I is larger than the gray area in any of the other three.

3. **(D)**

In Chart II, the only soybean modification is resistance to weed killers. A is wrong because Chart II shows that all four crops have weed killer tolerance but only two of them have insect protection. C is wrong because Chart I shows that about 90 percent of the corn being grown is not genetically modified. The area devoted to canola is irrelevant.

4. **(J)**

F, G, and H are wrong because soybean modification produces only weed killer tolerance, not insect protection.

5. **(B)**

This is the sum of the gray and white areas in Chart 2.

6. **(G)**

All organisms except bacterial spores can be killed at temperatures below 100°C.

7. **(D)**

This combination of temperature and time will kill bacterial spores; everything else will also be killed, since all other kinds of microorganisms will die at substantially lower temperatures.

8. **(J)**

The chart shows that at every temperature, a longer time of sterilization is needed to kill mold spores than yeast spores.

9. **(C)**

The destruction of bacterial spores is spread out, at 100°C, from 3 minutes to 3 hours, indicating that different kinds of bacterial spores will be killed at different exposure times. Killing bacterial spores also kills everything else, and yeasts are killed more quickly than bacteria.

10. **(H)**

In every case, the spore stage is more resistant to destruction by heat than the living stage. No information is presented concerning other environmental hazards. In the living form, molds are more resistant than bacteria.

11. **(B)**

The passage informs us that starch turns blue in the presence of elemental iodine, and the gist of the experiments is the determination of the liberation of iodine from the iodate.

12. **(G)**

Looking down the data columns, you can see that, as the concentration of iodate gets smaller, the time delay increases. F is wrong because this is part of the design of the experiment, not a hypothesis to be tested. H is wrong because the concentration of sulfuric acid is kept constant throughout. J is wrong because the passage says that the concentration of iodine increases gradually until it gets strong enough to turn the starch blue.

13. **(C)**

Experiment 2 shows that, as the temperature increases, the time for the reaction decreases. A and B are wrong because the iodate concentration was not changed in Experiment 2.

14. **(G)**

The iodate concentration in Experiment 2 was 5%. In Experiment 1 the time delay at 5% concentration was 29 seconds. Experiment 2 shows that this delay, with 5% iodate, occurs at a temperature between 15°C and 25°C.

15. **(D)**

The temperature given is well below the freezing point of water, and if the whole setup freezes, the whole reaction might stop. All the other answers neglect this probability.

16. **(F)**

Experiment 2 shows that the time for a 5% solution at 45°C is 22 seconds, and we would have to expect that it would be less for a 10% solution. The time would also have to be less than 18 seconds, because that was the time (Experiment 1) for 10% solution at 20°C.

17. **(A)**

The graph for fat content in males (dashed line) shows a strong dip in the years 10 through 20.

18. **(J)**

The rate of increase is represented by the steepness of the graph. The graph for fat content rises very sharply in the last 3 months before birth.

19. **(D)**

The fraction of water is larger in a man's body than in a woman's. For a woman to have as much water as a 150-pound man, she would have to weigh more than the man. B is wrong because the man's body at that age has only about 20 pounds of water more than the woman's.

20. **(J)**

On both the water and fat graphs, the lines for men and women remain parallel after age 40, showing that the differences between them do not change.

21. **(B)**

In adolescence, when sex hormone activity is beginning very strongly, the fat content of boys drops and the water content increases. A is wrong because this sex-hormone effect is not seen in girls. C is wrong because at adolescence there is a marked change in the water content of boys, but only a gradual drop in girls.

22. **(G)**

The ratings for attack against *Escherichia* are greater in four of the six trials than for any of the other microorganisms.

23. **(A)**

Ratings for alfalfa seeds against molds are 4 and 3, but only 2 and 0 against bacteria. None of the others shows this kind of difference.

24. **(H)**

The strongest attack on *Pennicillium* was made by seeds of the legumes, soybean and alfalfa.

25. **(D)**

All six seeds attacked the bread mold, at the 2 level or higher. A is wrong because the experiment does not address this question. B is wrong because all 6 of the test seeds had some effect on the bread mold. C is wrong because both the dandelion and the thistle seeds had some effect.

26. **(G)**

Neither of the legumes had any effect on *Staphylococcus*, so this family is not the place to look. F is wrong because some of the other seeds do attack *Staphylococcus*. H and J are wrong because this experiment gives no information about one microorganism attacking another.

27. **(D)**

The dandelion and the thistle seeds attacked all microorganisms, mostly at high levels. A is wrong because the experiment gives no information about microorganisms competing with each other. B is wrong because the two legumes do not show a significantly higher ability to attack than any others. C is wrong because the experiment does not deal with the question of damage to crops.

28. **(G)**

The index of refraction of each liquid is a property of the liquid used. F is wrong because the index of refraction of the liquid has nothing to do with the lens. H and J are wrong because the experimental design says nothing about temperature or color of light.

29. **(C)**

All three data tables show an increase in focal length as the index of refraction of the medium increases. This means that the rays converge further from the lens.

30. **(F)**

Comparing the results of Experiments 1 and 2 shows that the focal length of the thicker lens was always less than that of the thinner one, given the same medium.

31. **(A)**

The index of refraction of the glass is 1.720, which is less than the index for methylene iodide, the only medium in which the light does not focus. B is wrong because we have no information about what would happen if the lens is made of a different kind of glass. C is wrong because the properties of the glass surely matter, and Experiment 2 shows that the thickness of the lens is also involved. D is wrong; the thicker lens converges the light better, forming a shorter focal length.

32. (J)

Transparency is not one of the variables in these experiments. F and G are wrong because they deal with phenomena associated with the bending of light. H is wrong because it is entirely reasonable to suppose that the index of refraction of a sugar solution depends on its concentration.

33. (B)

To focus the light, a lens must have an index of refraction greater than that of the medium it is in, so the index of the lens must be at least 1.33. If it were as much as 1.50, it would form a focus in the sugar solution.

34. (G)

This is the only way to account for the accumulation of oil in porous sedimentary layers. F is wrong because Scientist 2 thinks that petroleum forms deep under the earth's crust. H is wrong because Scientist 1 does not believe this. J is wrong because Scientist 1 thinks oil has formed from marine organisms, which have not always been there.

35. (C)

One of Scientist 2's most important items of evidence is the oil found in igneous rock at great depth. A would tend to strengthen Scientist 2's case. B is wrong because one meteorite would not mean anything, in view of the fact that many of them do contain hydrocarbons. D would greatly strengthen Scientist 2's theory because Scientist 1 cannot account for oil in igneous rocks.

36. (F)

Scientist 2 believes there are vast deposits of petroleum deep in the earth's crust, left there by meteors. G is a strategy that Scientist 1 might suggest, but has nothing to do with Scientist 2's theory. H is wrong because, according to Scientist 2, the oil concentrates in sedimentary rocks. J is wrong because Scientist 2 has not suggested that the oil is still in meteorites.

37. (D)

The marine-life corpses must be covered quickly to prevent oxidative decay. A would increase decay, not prevent it. B is irrelevant. Scientist 1's theory does not involve meteorites, so C is wrong.

38. (G)

According to the theory of Scientist 1, oil forms from dead bodies, so it should form only in sedimentary rocks, which contain lots of fossils.

39. **(B)**

The fact that oil is found in association with salt seems to imply that oil has its origin in the bottom of the sea. A is wrong because this is a mere appeal to authority, not to evidence. C is wrong because both scientists agree that oil seeps upward into porous sedimentary rocks. D is wrong because Scientist 2's theory postulates that the hydrocarbons came to earth long before there were any oceans.

40. **(F)**

Scientist 2 claims that the particular combination of circumstances suggested by Scientist 1 is so rare that it could not account for all the oil there is. G is wrong because Scientist 1's theory does account for accumulation in sedimentary rocks. H is wrong because Scientist 1 used evidence, not arbitrary authority, in his arguments. J is wrong because the potential usefulness of either theory has nothing to do with its validity.

Answer Explanations

Test 5: Writing (Optional)

To evaluate your essay, complete the following checklist. Focus on both the strengths and weaknesses of your essay.

	Yes!	Mostly	Hardly	No
Does the essay address the ACT prompt?	____	____	____	____
Is the topic sufficiently narrowed?	____	____	____	____
Is the essay's main idea clear?	____	____	____	____
Have you written an introduction?	____	____	____	____
Does the essay sound natural?	____	____	____	____
Have you used plain words?	____	____	____	____
Have you used precise language?	____	____	____	____
Does your essay have a clear focus?	____	____	____	____
Do all parts fit together coherently?	____	____	____	____
Is each sentence accurately worded?	____	____	____	____
Have you trimmed needless words?	____	____	____	____
Do you show more than tell?	____	____	____	____
Have you used active verbs?	____	____	____	____
Is the language fresh?	____	____	____	____
Do you include verbal surprises?	____	____	____	____
Are the sentences varied?	____	____	____	____
Is sentence length balanced?	____	____	____	____

Does the essay have a conclusion?   ___   ___   ___   ___

Is the essay mostly error-free?   ___   ___   ___   ___

Identify the three greatest strengths of your essay:

1. _____

2. _____

3. _____

Name three specific things that you could do to improve your essay:

1. _____

2. _____

3. _____

Circle the score your essay deserves: 6   5   4   3   2   1